The Siege of
FORT WILLIAM HENRY

W. Baillie del.
W. Kulpsit 05

The Siege of

FORT WILLIAM HENRY

A Year on the Northeastern Frontier

BEN HUGHES

WESTHOLME
Yardley

Westholme Publishing, LLC
904 Edgewood Road
Yardley, Pennsylvania 19067

ISBN: 978-1-59416-146-9
Printed in the United States of America.
Book Club Edition

For Vanessa and Emily

It was a feature peculiar to the colonial wars of North America, that the toils and dangers of the wilderness were to be encountered, before the adverse hosts could meet. A wide, and, apparently, an impervious boundary of forests severed the possessions of the hostile provinces of France and England. The hardy colonist, and the trained European who fought at his side, frequently expended months in struggling against the rapids of the streams, or in effecting the rugged passes of the mountains, in quest of an opportunity to exhibit their courage in a more martial conflict. But, emulating the patience and self-denial of the practised native warriors, they learned to overcome every difficulty; and it would seem, that in time, there was no recess of the woods so dark, nor any secret place so lovely, that it might claim exemption from the inroads of those who had pledged their blood to satiate their vengeance, or to uphold the cold and selfish policy of the distant monarchs of Europe.

—James Fenimore Cooper
The Last of the Mohicans

Contents

List of Maps and Plans   xi

Prologue   xiii

Introduction   xv

PART ONE
The Players and the Stage

1
THE 35TH   1

2
NEW FRANCE   19

3
RIGAUD'S WINTER RAID   41

4
THE PROVINCIALS   56

5
FORT EDWARD   69

6
MONTRÉAL   91

7
LA PETITE GUERRE   113

8
SABBATH DAY POINT   132

9
THE CALM BEFORE THE STORM   143

10
MONTCALM'S ADVANCE   151

PART TWO
The Siege

11
THE FIRST DAY 165

12
OPENING THE TRENCHES 179

13
THE BOMBARDMENT 191

PART THREE
Dénouement

14
SURRENDER 209

15
THE MASSACRE 219

16
CAPTIVES 236

17
VICTORY 242

18
LOOSE ENDS 261

Epilogue 269

Appendix A: The Battlefield Today 273

Appendix B: Chronology 275

Appendix C: Glossary 278

Notes 287

Bibliography 315

Index 322

Acknowledgments 338

List of Maps and Plans

Indian Groups of Northeast America   *xvi*

A Plan of Albany, 1758   11

The Richelieu–Champlain Corridor   33

Plan of Fort William Henry   45

A Plan of Fort Edward and Its Environs   77

Detail from a 1758 Map of Upstate New York   85

Plan of the Town and Fortifications of Montreal   93

Lake George   137

Attaques du Fort William-Henri en Amériqué   181

The Siege of Fort William Henry   199

PROLOGUE

The Southern Shore of Lake George, August 15, 1757

Captain Israel Putnam could smell the dead long before he could see them. Advancing out of the encircling woods, the thirty-nine-year-old from Salem, Massachusetts, was lost for words. Fort William Henry was a charred ruin. The ground that ten thousand men had fought over just one week before was shrouded in silence, broken only by the occasional cry of squabbling carrion birds. After tearing down the timbers and heaping the corpses upon them, the French had set fire to the ruins, creating a giant funeral pyre. Putnam thought the "spectacle . . . too diabolical . . . to be endured." The timbers were still burning and "human . . . carcasses . . . were . . . frying and broiling in the flames." In the woods and marshes and down on the beach by the shores of Lake George, "dead bodies [lay] mangled with scalping-knives and tomahawks," and butchered "women . . . [were] still weltering in their own gore."[1]

Putnam had last been to Fort William Henry two and a half weeks before. Although raids by the Indian allies of Maj. Gen. Louis-Joseph de Montcalm had been increasing throughout July, the garrison's commander, Lt. Col. George Monro, seemed to have everything under control. Monro's confidence was understandable: Fort William Henry had been built to the latest design, had a strong garrison, formidable artillery crewed by some of the best gunners in North

America, and three thousand reinforcements under Maj. Gen. Daniel Webb were just fourteen miles away.[2] Nevertheless, six days after the French army had begun the siege, Monro found himself in an impossible position: one hundred fifty of his men had been killed by sharpshooters, round shot, and shells, his provincial allies were close to revolt, there was still no sign of Webb, and Montcalm's cannons had been dug to within one hundred yards of the palisades. His position untenable, Monro was forced to surrender. The following morning, General Montcalm's Indian allies had fallen upon the British column as it made its way unarmed and defeated to Fort Edward. A massacre had ensued. As he picked his way through the ruins, staring at the corpses of the men, women, and children he had seen alive just weeks before, Captain Putnam must have been wondering where it had all gone wrong.

INTRODUCTION

The Whole World in Flames

1550-1756

THE SIEGE OF FORT WILLIAM HENRY is a tale of violence, greed, misunderstanding, cowardice, and betrayal, but above all, it relates a clash of civilizations. Three distinct parties were involved: the Europeans, the Indians, and the American colonists. All three had representatives on both sides. The French fought alongside the Canadian militia, Algonquian-speaking tribes of the *pays d'en haut*, or high country, and "domesticated" Indians of the Saint Lawrence Valley. The British were supported by provincial militia from Massachusetts, Connecticut, New Hampshire, New York, and New Jersey, and a handful of Iroquois warriors from the Mohawk River valley. Neither alliance was without difficulties. The European elite lived by an archaic code of honor. They saw themselves as innately superior to the provincials and the "savages," and were part of a well-established hierarchy and unquestioningly followed the orders of their kings. The leading Americans, by contrast, were individualists, motivated by financial gain, political and religious freedom, and the acquisition of land. The Indians, for their part, had no understanding of private ownership at all. For them the land was its own master, a living organism ungovernable by man, and while the warriors had a well-developed sense of honor,

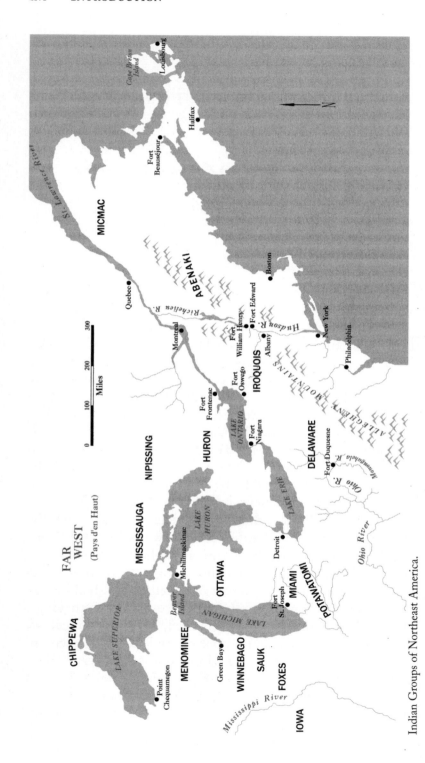

Indian Groups of Northeast America.

their code was very different from the Europeans' indeed. To understand how this web of alliances was first spun, it is necessary to look back two hundred years before the siege began—a time when North America was still largely untouched by Europeans, a time when fact merged with legend, a time when the Iroquois Confederacy began.[1]

In the mid-sixteenth century, Deganawida, a Huron brave, was born in a village on the northeast shores of Lake Ontario. In his youth, he experienced powerful visions of pan-Indian unity and began traveling through the primordial forests of northeast America, spreading a mantra of the Great Law of Peace to the scattered, warlike tribes. In the Mohawk Valley, in what would become New York State, Deganawida's preaching found fertile ground, and a loose alliance of five Iroquoian nations—the Mohawk, Oneida, Onondaga, Cayuga, and Seneca—was formed. United by a common culture and linguistic roots, the Iroquois Confederacy came to dominate northeast America. This omnipotence resulted from three factors: the tribes' central location (which gave them access to the Great Lakes via the Mohawk Valley, the Saint Lawrence basin via the Lake George–Lake Champlain corridor, and the Atlantic coast via the Hudson River), the range and impact of the Iroquois raiding parties, and their ability to present a united front—an unprecedented achievement among the anarchic tribes of the region.[2]

The first to bear the brunt of the confederacy's military might were the largely Algonquian-speaking tribes of the Great Lakes region: the Ottawa, Fox, Miami, Nipissing, Potawatomi, Sauk, Huron, and Chippewa. For the next sixty years, they suffered periodic raids by bands of Iroquoian warriors keen to take freshly cut scalps and prisoners of war. Such attacks prompted retaliatory raids, and a state of intermittent hostilities prevailed throughout the sixteenth century. Although ruthlessly waged, this warfare was more ritual than genocidal, and had little long-term impact on the tribes. At the turn of the seventeenth century, however, the balance was upset by the arrival of the first Europeans.

While explorers had previously had some contact with the Indians of North America's Atlantic coast, the tribes of the interior were largely unmolested by outsiders until Samuel de Champlain's forays up the Saint Lawrence River in 1608. After founding Québec City, Champlain pushed further into the interior and began exploring the Great Lakes, where he made contact with the Algonquian-speaking tribes. As part of a trade settlement to support the seedling colony of New France, the Indians persuaded Champlain to join a raiding party that would thrust deep into Iroquois territory. At the southern end of Lake Champlain, in the area known as Ticonderoga, the Algonquin warriors and their French allies came across a Mohawk raiding party. Champlain's firearms tipped the balance in the battle that ensued. In consequence, the tribes of the high country would remain close allies of New France until the colony's eventual destruction in 1760. The Mohawk, on the other hand, would never forget the losses they incurred that day. Thus began their centuries-long grudge against the French.[3]

Far to the southeast, a second wave of colonists had arrived. Unlike the French, who had used the Saint Lawrence to penetrate far into the interior before founding Québec, the English developed a string of independent settlements along the Atlantic coast. Jamestown was founded in 1607, Plymouth and Hampton in 1620, and Salem in 1626. The English settlements were radically different in aim and character to those of the French. While the colonists in Québec, Montréal, and Trois Riviéres integrated with the Indians, converted them to Roman Catholicism, maintained close links with the mother country, and focused on trade rather than territorial acquisition, the English settlements enjoyed considerable freedom from the edicts of Westminster, and prompted a series of wars against the native population as they expanded inland. A further difference was the size of the colonies' respective populations. While the influence, if not the dominion, of New France spread over a vast territory throughout the interior—via its trade routes along the Saint Lawrence River, across the Great Lakes and down the Mississippi River as far as Louisiana—by the mid-eighteenth century its population was just one-tenth of that of the British possessions to the southeast.

By the early 1660s, English expansion brought her colonists into conflict with a third European power. The Dutch had been present in the New World since 1614, when a series of settlements were founded along the Hudson River to profit from the fur trade. In 1664, four English frigates sailed into the harbor of Nieuw Amsterdam (New York) and demanded its surrender. Principally a mercantile operation, the Dutch colony lacked military might and reluctantly conceded. As well as taking possession of the Dutch forts and villages in the area (the most important of which was renamed Albany), the English also gained control of the region's fur trade. This lucrative business brought them into contact with the tribes of the Iroquois Confederacy, which trapped the furs in the interior, then exchanged them in Albany for the metal trade goods upon which they had come to rely. The items most prized were the knife, tomahawk, and musket. These were not only useful for hunting but also essential for fighting the confederacy's ongoing war with the Algonquin tribes of the high country and their increasingly belligerent French allies.

By the late seventeenth century, the Beaver Wars (ca. 1638–1701), as they came to be known, had escalated exponentially. What had once been a largely ritual conflict, which enabled young warriors to pass into manhood by demonstrating their martial prowess, had become a war of extermination fueled by European firearms and the merchants' greed for fur. Due to their superior organization and the low price of English trade goods, the Iroquois gained the upper hand. After decimating the fauna of their own hunting grounds, they turned their attention to those of their enemies and in the process began wiping out whole communities of Huron, Nipissing, and Potawatomi. At the same time, the Iroquois acted as middlemen, brokering trade deals between the English colonists and the tribes that resided further in the interior. Iroquoian ascendency in the Beaver Wars brought the inhabitants of New France farther into the conflict, which in turn led the English to become involved. A series of border raids ensued. Led by European colonists with considerable Indian support, these parties penetrated deep into enemy territory, burned settlements, killed those who resisted, and then returned through the wilderness with plunder, captives, and scalps.[4]

Across the Atlantic, Europe was also at war. By the end of the seventeenth century, dynastic disputes had sparked a series of conflicts, fueled by religious intolerance and mutually incompatible colonial ambition. Although each was separated by an uneasy period of peace, the bloodshed would not entirely cease until Napoleon's defeat at Waterloo, 126 years later. The American provincials renamed the first three conflicts after the reigning English monarch of the period. Hence, what was known in Europe as the War of the League of Augsburg (1688–97) was called King William's War in America, the War of Spanish Succession (1701–14) became Queen Anne's War (1702–13), and the War of Austrian Succession (1740–48) was renamed King George's War (1739–48). In the colonies each was a relatively minor affair, and any gains made were often returned as part of the peace treaty discussions that followed. The fourth conflict broke this dynamic. The French and Indian War (1754–63) would change the face of America forever.[5]

The first shots were fired on June 14, 1754. Before dawn, a young Virginian militia colonel named George Washington led a company into the backwoods of the Ohio country. The site of the confluence of two key rivers in the heart of the continent, the region had been the focus of European ambition in America since the mid-1740s. The French sought to build a string of forts across the area that would establish communications between Canada and Louisiana. The British were determined to prevent them: French success would confine King George's colonies to the eastern seaboard and deny them access to the interior. Nevertheless, as war was yet to be declared in Europe, Washington's orders were merely to warn the French off. Alongside his band of Virginians was an indigenous ally whose motivations Washington was yet to fully understand. The man in question was Tanaghrisson, a chief of the Mingos, a loosely united "tribe" made up of various refugee groups that had emigrated to the Ohio country in the mid-eighteenth century. As the Mingos were subordinate to the Six Nations, Tanaghrisson had mixed loyalties and was known as the "Half King."[6]

By the turn of the eighteenth century, the Iroquois Confederacy had developed an intricate policy toward the European nations. Unsure as to which power would eventually triumph, the Iroquois simultaneously promised alliances to the British and neutrality to the French while delivering little to either. By the 1740s the situation had changed once more. European expansion into the Ohio country was threatening to undermine the confederacy's monopoly of the fur trade. If the French or British were to attain ascendency, they would gain greater access to the tribes of the interior and therefore lessen the influence of the Iroquois. For Tanaghrisson and his Six Nations backers, it was crucial that neither side be allowed to gain a foothold in the region. If Tanaghrisson were to achieve his aims, he would need to provoke a war between the French and the British that would weaken both while strengthening his own position.[7]

The principal victim of Tanaghrisson's scheming would turn out to be a thirty-five-year-old Canadian ensign named Joseph Coulon de Villiers de Jumonville. Ordered into the Ohio country by the governor of New France to ascertain British intentions, by the morning of May 28, 1754, Jumonville and his band of thirty-five colonial regulars (*troupes de la marine*) were preparing to break camp in the bottom of a narrow wooded glen when a noise from above suddenly startled them. Fumbling with his musket, one of the Frenchmen blindly pulled the trigger. Hidden on the flank of a hill above, Washington panicked. Forgetting his orders to repel the French intrusion without bloodshed, he "gave the word for all his men to fire." Several Frenchmen were cut down by the volley. The rest "betook themselves of flight." Crashing through the undergrowth, they emerged from the glen to find themselves face to face with Tanaghrisson's war party. Fearing the Mingos more than their fellow Europeans, the French turned tail, rushed back to Washington, and begged for mercy. The Virginian granted their request, but Tanaghrisson had other ideas. Approaching the prostrate Jumonville, who had been wounded by the provincials' opening volley, he drew his tomahawk. After pronouncing "Thou are not yet dead my father," he rained a series of blows upon Jumonville's head until his skull had split open. [Tanaghrisson] then took out his brains and washed his hands with "them and . . . scalped him." When the French heard of the atrocity, there was no going back. Tanaghrisson's plan had worked. The French and Indian War had begun.[8]

When news of Jumonville's death reached Montréal, his brother, Louis Coulon de Villiers, was ordered to march to the Ohio country and establish French control. With him, aboard a flotilla of canoes, were a host of New France's Indian allies. "Domesticated" or "praying" Iroquois, who had converted to Catholicism and resettled on the Saint Lawrence River, and Huron, Nipissing, and Abenaki from the Jesuit missions to the northeast of Montréal were joined by "wild" Algonquian-speaking tribesmen from the high country. Speeded by a lust for vengeance, Villiers's advance was swift. Within twelve days of his brother's demise, he had arrived at Fort Duquesne, New France's forward base in the region. Two weeks later, marching through incessant rain, his column reached the scene of Tanaghrisson's crime. Under the dripping boughs, several bodies remained unburied. The sight urged Villiers on. The next day, he found Washington's men at a natural clearing known as the Great Meadows, two miles northwest of the area that is now Farmington. Having learned of the enemy's presence, Washington built Fort Necessity, a crude palisade ringed by a knee-deep ditch. Dominated by two wooded hills within easy musket shot, the fort became a death trap. Of the 350 Virginians and British regulars involved in the fight, 70 fell prey to Villiers's sharpshooters before a truce was called. After a brief negotiation, Washington surrendered. Thanks to his foe's unexpected clemency, the Virginian was allowed to return to his base, fifty-two miles to the southeast at Wills Creek, his pride bruised but his scalp intact. The French had won the first round.[9]

In 1755 the British raised the stakes. Two battalions of red-coated regulars, the 44th and 48th, were ordered to sail to America. Their commander, Maj. Gen. Edward Braddock, was a brave man, but arrogant and of limited vision. He "might probably have made a good figure in some European war," an observer opined, but "he had . . . too high an opinion of . . . regular troops [and] too mean a one of both Americans and Indians." Like many of his contemporaries, Braddock believed that open-plan battle tactics would suit the American conflict, but the fields of Flanders were an entirely different prospect to the dark forests of the Ohio country, as Braddock was soon to discover.[10]

After arriving at Hampton Roads in Virginia and enduring a series of exasperating conferences with self-interested colonial governors, Braddock eventually acquired the supplies he needed and set off into the unknown. With three hundred axmen at its head, his column, which included five hundred provincial troops and militia, cut its way through the wilderness, its mission to destroy Fort Duquesne. Although there was little sign of the enemy, progress was slow. To speed up his march, Braddock decided to divide his force in two. The heavy baggage would travel with the rear division, while a flying column would blaze a trail ahead. Nevertheless, it wasn't until July 9, a full month after leaving his forward base at Fort Cumberland, that Braddock came within striking distance of his target.

For Braddock, the morning of the ninth was the most nerve-racking of the entire campaign. As the troops of the advance division neared Fort Duquesne, they had to ford the meandering Monongahela River on two separate occasions. Each time, as they emerged dripping onto the far bank, they were horribly exposed, but after the second crossing had been completed without interference, Braddock began to relax. It seemed that the French had decided to wait behind their fortifications, and the Indian ambush that his redcoats and militia had feared would not materialize. Unknown to Braddock, however, at that very moment a force of nine hundred Indians, Canadian militia, and colonial regulars, led by Capt. Liénard de Beaujeu, was advancing through the woods toward them.[11]

At one o'clock the two sides met. At first the battle seemed to favor the British. Blundering out of the woods, the French were met by ordered volleys from Braddock's advance guard. On the third fire Beaujeu was killed, his Canadian militia fled, and a young Frenchman, Capt. Jean-Daniel Dumas, took command. Stripped to the waist to better enable him to fight in the forest, Dumas, aided by a Canadian métis (of mixed French and Ottawa parentage) named Charles Langlade, rallied the Indians and colonial regulars and ordered them to spread out, envelop the column, and take the high ground. The Ottawa, Delaware, Potawatomi, Abenaki, and Caughnawaga (French-allied domesticated Iroquois who had settled in a series of missions along the Saint Lawrence) did not need telling twice. This was the irregular warfare at which they excelled. Crouching behind fallen logs, bushes, and ripples in the ground, they poured a deadly fire into the British column. Schooled in the formal tactics of Europe, Braddock had no reply. Beating those who faltered with the flat of his sword, he insisted that they maintain ranks and answer the scattered marksmen with volleys fired by platoon. Their shots were wasted. Unlike the French regulars and Scottish Jacobites that the veterans among Braddock's redcoats had faced at Lauffeld and Culloden, the Indians at Monongahela were like ghosts, flitting from tree to tree through the gun smoke while yelling bloodcurdling war whoops. The British rarely saw more than five or six of them at one time.[12]

When the main body of the British column came up, it collided with the advance guard, which had been edging backward, and the troops lost all cohesion. Pushing in on one another to escape the fusillade, they began to panic. Still, Braddock would not countenance a retreat, but when he was finally blasted from the saddle late that afternoon, the British and American soldiers retreated. The Indians rose from the undergrowth to pursue them, and dozens more stragglers were butchered when they reached the Monongahela.[13] Shot through the arm and lung, Braddock lingered on for five days. "We shall better know how to deal with them another time," he said before expiring.[14] More than eight hundred of the thirteen hundred British regulars and colonial militia under his command had been killed or wounded, as were sixty-three of the eighty-nine officers involved.[15]

As the commander in chief of British forces lay dying, a second expedition was about to take place four hundred miles to the northeast. Gathering at Fort Lyman (soon to be renamed Fort Edward) on the northern frontier were thirty-five hundred provincial volunteers from Massachusetts, New Hampshire, New Jersey, Connecticut, and New York, aided by three hundred Mohawk warriors. The army was intended for a strike against Fort Saint Frédéric, a French outpost on Lake Champlain that commanded the overland route to Montréal. The commander of the provincial troops was William Johnson. A forty-year-old of Anglo-Irish origin, Johnson had risen to prominence due to his close links with the Mohawks, among whom he had lived since 1742 as an honorary sachem with the name of Warraghiyagey—the "man who undertakes great things."

By August 28, Johnson's army had reached the shores of Lake George (known to the French as Lac Saint Sacrament). While the provincials made camp on raised ground, the Mohawks were sent on scouting missions to gather intelligence. On Sunday, September 7, after a Calvinist chaplain had preached a sermon from Isaiah, one of the Indians brought news of a large body of the enemy moving from South Bay to Fort Edward. The force, consisting of 600 Indians, 684 Canadian militia, and 216 French regulars of the regiments of Languedoc and La Reine, was commanded by fifty-six-year-old Saxon-born Maj. Gen. Jean-Armand, Baron de Dieskau, the senior regular officer in New France.[16] Having learned of Johnson's plan to attack Fort Saint Frédéric, Dieskau had decided to preempt him.[17]

The next day, the French ambushed a party of 1,200 Mohawks and provincials whom Johnson had sent to reinforce Fort Lyman, halfway between Lake George and that post. King Hendrick, an aging, battle-scarred chief who had once been presented to Queen Anne, had been apprehensive about the mission from the start.[18] "If they are to be killed," he had told Johnson earlier that morning, "they are too many;

if they are to fight, they are too few." Nevertheless, Johnson ordered the scouts to proceed. Accepting his fate, Hendrick mounted a horse and went with them. One hour later, despite Dieskau's Caughnawaga allies attempting to warn their Mohawk cousins, the column fell into a trap. Fired on from high ground on three sides, the Americans and Indians fell in scores. Their leader, Col. Ephraim Williams, was killed by a musket shot through the head, while Hendrick had his horse shot out from under him and was killed with a bayonet as he lay trapped beneath it. The Mohawk chief was then scalped, the trophy "being taken off not larger than an English crown." The survivors "doubled up like a pack of cards" and fell back to Lake George. After his Indians had scalped the dead and made prisoners of the wounded, Dieskau pursued them.[19]

Having heard the firing that morning, Johnson had ordered his men to construct defenses. By the time Dieskau's Indians came boiling out of the woods at midday, the provincials were ready. Crouched behind felled trees, rolled wagons, and upturned bateaux, the men from New England held off the warriors and militia, but were powerless to prevent the advance of the regulars from Old France. Marching shoulder to shoulder six abreast down the track from Fort Edward, the white-coated grenadiers came stolidly on.[20] Shot through the buttocks early on in the fighting, Johnson had been replaced by his second, Col. Phineas Lyman, a lawyer and Yale graduate from Connecticut. Seeing the grenadiers advance, Lyman ordered one of the only British regulars with the expedition, an engineer named William Eyre, to open fire with his four guns, their muzzles thrust between the gaps in the barricades. Firing grapeshot, the guns, one of them a mighty 32-pounder, cut "lanes, streets, and alleys" through the advancing grenadiers and forced the survivors to withdraw. Although the fighting continued for four hours, with the grenadiers' dispersal, the heart had gone out of Dieskau's men. As dusk approached they melted back into the woods, leaving the American provincials masters of the field.

The Battle of Lake George had been a costly encounter. Both sides lost two hundred fifty men. Johnson's plan to advance on Fort Saint Frédéric was forgotten, and a fort was built by the lakeside to consolidate the position instead. The resulting construction, which Johnson diplomatically named Fort William Henry "after Two of the Royal Family," would mark the extent of Britain's northern ambitions on the American mainland for the next four years.[21]

Five hundred miles to the east of Lake George on the windswept peninsula of New Brunswick, a third action took place during the summer of 1755. Ordered to push the French from the island, Lt. Col. Robert Monckton had been given two hundred regulars and two thousand Massachusetts militia under Col. John Winslow. On June 6, after a weeklong voyage from Boston, Monckton's troops moved against Fort Beauséjour, a French outpost commanded by Capt. Louis Du Pont Duchambon de Vergor that dominated the isthmus connecting the peninsula to the mainland. Shortly after the siege began on June 14, the local militia that had joined Vergor lost heart, marched out of the fort, and surrendered. Two days later, after a mortar shell had killed six French officers sheltering in a so-called bomb-proof, the captain and his regulars followed suit. With Vergor's capitulation, the other French forts on the peninsula surrendered and the British conquest was complete. The population was then forcibly deported. In total, six thousand men, women, and children were herded aboard waiting transports for repatriation. Some settled in Louisiana, while a few made it to Maryland, where they lived among Roman Catholic coreligionists. Others returned to France. Many more were scattered throughout Britain's American colonies, where they were treated with contempt. Many starved to death or succumbed to disease that winter.[22]

Despite Johnson's success and Monckton's victory, 1755 had been a black year for the British. The commander in chief had been killed, his redcoats humbled on the Monongahela, and a fourth expedition, an attack against Fort Niagara on Lake Ontario, had got no farther than its forward base at Fort Oswego, where the onset of winter had frozen the advancing army in its tracks. The regulars of the 50th and 51st Regiments settled in to continue the campaign the following spring. When the winter freeze cut off their supply route up the Mohawk River, they began suffering from scurvy. Dozens died before the thaw brought some relief.

Across the Atlantic, Westminster reacted to Braddock's death by appointing a new commander. Lord John Campbell, 4th Earl of Loudoun, a feisty lowland Scot, set sail for the colonies that spring. With him, aboard a flotilla of transports, were two more regiments of red-coated regulars. One of them, the 35th, or Otway's, as it was also known, was an inexperienced unit largely composed of impressed men, pardoned criminals, and new recruits. The regiment was destined to take center stage in what would become the most notorious incident of the war.

PART ONE

The Players and The Stage

1756–1757

Uniforms of the 34th, 35th, and 36th Regiments of Foot painted in 1751. (*Royal Collection*)

The 35th

FEBRUARY–DECEMBER 1756

ieutenant Colonel George Monro was a cautious man. Just two days before the 35th Regiment of Foot was due to depart from Cork on April 15, 1756, the fifty-six-year-old had traveled to Dublin to legalize his will, stipulating that his modest estate be divided between his sons, George and Sackville, and his daughter, Jane, in the event of his death.[1] As Monro knew, traveling to North America was a risky undertaking. The British regulars sent out the previous year had suffered badly. Major General Edward Braddock and three hundred of his men had been killed at Monongahela, and Indian raids and outbreaks of smallpox were whittling away those based on the northern frontier. To add to Monro's concerns, the 35th was desperately understrength. Of the 1,000 men that regiments were theoretically meant to muster, the colonel had only 496 under his command.[2] Although a few veterans had fought at the bloodbaths of Dettingen and Fontenoy in the War of Austrian Succession, most, including the colonel himself, had never seen action before. As he stood on the deck of the transport sailing out of Cork Bay, Colonel Monro was embarking on the adventure of a lifetime.

Born in County Longford, Ireland, in 1700 to a Scottish father of sound military pedigree, Monro was respected by his contemporaries, despite his lack of combat experience. Many thought him a "brave officer" and "a man of strict honour," but his hopes of high rank had been hindered by an undistinguished career.[3] After joining the 35th as a lieutenant in 1718, he had purchased his way up through the ranks, as was common practice at the time, receiving his lieutenant colonelcy on January 4, 1750. The intervening years had been spent on garrison duty. Moving from camp to camp from Dublin to Belfast to Cork to Kinsale, the men of the 35th passed their days in interminable parades, patrols, and forced marches. Occasionally, the monotony was broken by performing policing duty at riots or minor revolts, or attending regimental and general courts-martial.[4] On one particularly memorable occasion in Dublin, one of the regulars had been shot for desertion. Infuriatingly for Monro, but no doubt much to the delight of the crowd, the prisoner, Pvt. James Brooks, who was damningly described as "a most abandoned profligate," had refused to play the part of the hand-wringing repentant. All the way from Dublin Castle to the Green, where his executioners awaited with loaded muskets, Brooks had cursed his officers and comrades alike.[5]

After a prolonged crossing in transports that stank of the vinegar used to disinfect them, the 35th landed in Plymouth in early March and was assigned barracks for what was intended to be the briefest of stays. The men and those of the 42nd Highland Regiment of Foot, which would sail with them, were urgently needed in America for an offensive planned for that summer, but William Augustus, Duke of Cumberland, King George II's second son and captain general of the British army, had not counted on the glacial sloth of naval bureaucracy. Not until mid-March did the transports required gather at Plymouth. There they were loaded with Irish butter and beef; colored beads, brass kettles, ivory combs, "iron Jewes harpes," and other gifts for Britain's Indian allies; and guns for two brigantines being built on Lake Ontario. A few days later, it was noted that the ships had not yet been fitted out to carry troops. An urgent dispatch was sent off, and on April 11, "each man rec'd a small Wooden spoon, also a bed, a blanket, rugg & pillows." The troops could then finally embark, but bad weather was to keep them in the bay for four more days.[6]

Meanwhile in London, the War Office had put two plans into action to bring the regiments bound for America up to full fighting strength. The first allowed for condemned prisoners to receive pardons should they enlist for American service; the other was the second act of impressment to be carried out in two years.[7] While Monro and the bulk of the regiment prepared to set sail from Plymouth, Maj. Henry Fletcher, the Scot's second in command, took a detachment of 10 officers and 116 men to London. There they would collect the impressed recruits assigned to the 35th who had been gathered near the Savoy Wharf on the Thames.[8]

In common with the majority of his commissioned peers, the thirty-three-year-old Fletcher was a purebred gentleman. The second son of Lord Milton, Laird of Saltoun in East Lothian and a senior high-court judge, Fletcher had been in the army for as long as he could remember. In contrast to Monro's, Fletcher's career had been one of excitement and rapid promotion fueled by his father's seemingly bottomless purse, which had seen him serve in a series of different regiments before joining the 35th two years before. As a twenty-year-old lieutenant, Fletcher had received his baptism of fire at Dettingen under George II. Remembered for being the last time a British monarch led troops in battle, it resulted in an allied victory over the French, whose youth left more than a thousand corpses to manure the field.[9]

Such a background did little to prepare Fletcher for the scenes that awaited him in London. The Savoy Wharf was seething with impressed men, four hundred seventy-one of whom were destined for the ranks of the 35th. On arrival, Fletcher inspected his regiment's haul. The major was far from pleased. Sixty-one men were immediately dismissed as unfit for service. The rest were transported down the Thames to Gravesend, where ocean-going transports awaited them.[10]

The impressment had been carried out with ruthless efficiency, as one of its victims would later attest. "For above a year before I left London," the anonymous chronicler, who would go on to fight with the 35th at Fort William Henry, wrote, "I dared not look out at night, nor walk the streets in the day, for fear of being pressed, . . . but it happened to be my turn at last all the same."[11]

On April 15 Monro's detachment finally set sail from Plymouth. Four hundred sixty-four strong, the officers and men made the Atlantic crossing in three transports—the *Essex*, the *Sydenham*, and the *Fortrose*. All were dwarfed by their escort, HMS *Grafton*, a third-rate seventy-gun ship of the line.[12] Away from the finely appointed quarters of the senior officers, where servants dished up culinary delights on silver plate and poured claret into pewter goblets, conditions onboard the transports were appalling. Chickens, dogs, cats, lice, and rats inhabited the dark, fetid spaces below decks where the sergeants and rank and file were quartered. As the ships were a breeding ground for disease, Thomas Wilkins, the 35th's forty-four-year-old surgeon, had his work cut out to keep the men and the handful of wives, mistresses, and children who accompanied them healthy. His treatments of emetics, purgings, and bleedings did little good, and by midvoyage seven hammocks were occupied by the coughing sick, and the corpse of at least one former patient had been hurled overboard. The men's propensity for sickness was not the only cause of Wilkins's discomfort. While his peers in other regiments had been provided with a complete set of surgical instruments, Wilkins had had to purchase his with funds from his own pocket before leaving Plymouth.[13]

Three months later, Major Fletcher's detachment was finally ready to leave Gravesend. In the interim, the major had had a torrid time. Theft was rife among the impressed men, there was a serious threat of mutiny, and living conditions aboard the transports were terrible. In early May an inspection had been carried out. Twenty-five more men were dismissed as unfit for service as a result. Before they eventually set sail in July, another three were claimed by writs and six others had deserted.[14]

On the morning of Wednesday, June 16, Monro's detachment arrived at New York. As the transports sailed by the Hook, the shore batteries fired a welcoming salute and the troops disembarked.[15] In the mid-eighteenth century, New York was the third largest city in British America. Although behind both Boston and Philadelphia in terms of population, it was of primary importance in international trade. More than two hundred ships a year unloaded manufactured and luxury items from Europe, such as clay pipes made by William Mamby of London, wine from Madeira, and Irish beef and butter, while animal skins and timber from the wild American interior, sugar, cotton, and tobacco from the southern colonies, and mahogany and rum from the West Indies were packed into the holds for the return leg.[16]

The officers with Monro, particularly such characters as Capt. Charles Ince of the grenadier company, a man renowned for "his fine voice, great taste, and greater judgement in music," would no doubt have made the most of New York's vibrant cultural scene.[17] Although a far cry from the debauchery and excesses of Georgian London, the city offered the men a last chance for a fine meal, a concert, or a visit to a brothel before they were shipped up the Hudson to the cultural backwaters of Albany and beyond. Those of a more pious bent were equally well catered for. New York boasted several fine churches of all denominations, including a Quaker meetinghouse and a synagogue. At night, merchants' carriages rattled down the spacious tree-lined streets, and promenading couples listened to the amorous music of native tree frogs, which, according to a visiting Swede, made such a din that it was "difficult for a person to make himself heard."[18]

For the lower ranks in the 35th, New York also held its attractions. And for at least one, they proved too much to resist. On June 21 John Clarke, a twenty-five-year-old private from Northwich, whom Monro later described as "round visage[d]" and of a "swarthy complexion," slipped out of the regiment's temporary barracks and deserted. Despite Monro's efforts to trace him, Clarke was never found. Five other privates were discharged at New York as unfit for duty, and two were sent to hospital.[19]

The day after Clarke absconded, the 35th and 42nd Regiments boarded twenty sloops for the 150-mile journey up the Hudson to Albany, the major staging post for the campaigns being fought on the northern frontier. The journey was a pleasant one. Fresh provisions of "Greens, roots & Ships Beer" were issued, and on their way upriver the sloops were accompanied by playful porpoises tumbling end over end, six-foot flat-nosed sturgeons, which were easily caught, and clouds of fireflies that would "settle on the rigging" at night. At times the tide was too strong to proceed by sail, and the captains would order the men to man the oars or lower the anchor until the worst of the current had passed. For the first twenty miles, the eastern bank was dotted with farmhouses surrounded by ploughed land, but afterward, signs of civilization became increasingly infrequent. On the fourth and final day of the journey, however, cultivated fields, littered with strange cone-shaped haystacks, and the stone and timber dwellings of the Dutch inhabitants of upper New York passed into view.[20]

The walled town of Albany, founded by the Dutch 150 years before, was "beautifully situated."[21] Built on the slope of a hill, it overlooked the river and was framed by the mountains that rose up beyond it in the west. Two stone-built churches dominated the center of town. One was English, overseen by the Reverend John Ogilvie; the other was a three-story Dutch building. Both were built on State Street, the principal avenue, which was five times as broad as the other thoroughfares and served as a marketplace on weekends. The houses on the lesser streets, where the farmers let their cattle graze in the summer evenings, were equally charming. Built in the Flemish style, they had gables "notched like steps" and idiosyncratic weather vanes adorned with "horses, lions [and] geese."[22] Outside the walls, on a second hill, steeper and higher than the first, stood a fort, "a great building of stone, surrounded with high and thick walls."[23]

Although only inhabited by 329 families, Albany was the foremost British military staging post in northern America due to its location on a vital river confluence.[24] Five miles to the north, the Mohawk flowed into the Hudson. Further upstream, it flowed by the hilltop fortresses of the Mohawk Indians, and near its source at the Finger Lakes, it passed within miles of Fort Oswego—a flash point on the ill-defined Anglo-French border and the gateway to the Great Lakes. Two days' march to the north of Albany, the Hudson led to Fort Edward, from where it was a fourteen-mile trek via a rough-cut forest road to Fort William Henry. Situated on the shores of Lake George and just one day south of the French outpost of Fort Carillon by birch bark canoe, William Henry was the northernmost point of the British frontier in mainland America.

While the Dutch inhabitants, with their outdated dress, indecipherable language, "fat mistress-[es]," and "uncouth sort of dancing," were strange enough, the most remarkable thing about Albany for the men of the 35th were the groups of Mohawk Indians who came into town to cash in beaver skins trapped in Canada or the freshly cut scalps of French officers taken from the wilds around Fort Carillon.[25] Dressed in highly decorated moccasins and buckskin breechclouts, which left their haunches bare, the Mohawks were heavily tattooed and painted. Their necks and ears were festooned with looped brass jewelry and their heads clean shaven, aside from a central tuft of hair that they dyed orange, blue, or red. Among the most feared warriors of all the Six Nations of the Iroquois Confederacy, the Mohawks bristled with muskets, tomahawks, ball-headed maple clubs, and hunting knives, which they carried in sheaths strung around their necks.[26]

"Indian dressed for war with a scalp," drawn from life, c. 1758, by British officer and caricaturist George Townshend, 1st Marquess Townshend, while he was serving on the New York frontier. (*National Portrait Gallery*)

In July, having set up a sea of tents nicknamed "Camp Mohock" at Pine Island on a hill overlooking the town, Monro began preparing his men for action.[27] The first stage was intensive training. Mr. Welch, a corporal renowned for his skills on the parade ground, drilled the men daily.[28] While the rank and file sweated their way to a mastery of battalion and company formations, the senior officers entertained themselves by hunting in the nearby forests or riding on countryside jaunts. On July 8 Maj. Gen. James Abercrombie, second in command of all British forces in North America, decided to visit the Cohoes Falls, an impressive natural phenomena and sacred site for the Mohawks, ten miles to the north of Albany. As Indian raiding parties had been known to travel through the area, Abercrombie took an escort of twenty-four men from the 42nd and 35th. That morning it was excessively hot. As the column reached the falls, Abercrombie was perspiring mildly on his horse, while his escorts, dressed in the thick red woolen coats, shirts, and breeches of the regulars, were on the point of expiring. Half-mad with the heat and his head full of nightmares of Indians torturing their captives in the woods, one of the Highlanders imagined he saw someone watching them. Unslinging his musket, he aimed at the apparition, but "before he could draw his trigger, he fell down dead." According to a local paper, "two more belonging to . . . [the 35th] fell down after the same manner, and expired immediately . . . [and] thirteen others fainted away, but were [later] brought to by being bled."[29]

When not drilling or escorting senior officers, the 35th practiced blazing off volleys of platoon fire or shooting at marks. Even this was not without incident. On July 12, while a company was loading for target practice, a soldier's gun "went off by accident, and shot two of them through the thighs." The Brown Bess musket, standard army issue of the period, fired a low-velocity .69-caliber lead ball and was often lethal at close range. Fortunately for the two privates, neither wound proved fatal. Nevertheless, life was cheap in the eighteenth century and mortal accidents were all too common. Just over two weeks later, on Tuesday, July 20, with the temperature still in the midnineties, the members of an artillery train passing through Albany decided to pause for a swim in the river. As a local newspaper nonchalantly reported, one "was taken with the cramp, and drowned."[30]

At the end of July, Lord Loudoun, the newly appointed commander in chief of British forces in America, arrived in Albany. Traveling with the fifty-two-year-old was an impressive personal entourage, which included a mistress and no less than seventeen secretaries.[31] A "rough Scotch lord, hot and irascible," Loudoun was an energetic and effective administrator, but his haughty and autocratic manner ensured he would clash with his provincial subordinates from the start.[32] His first duty was to assume command from William Shirley, the governor of Massachusetts. Next he attempted to heal a rift between the regulars and provincial troops, which had been growing since 1755. The law stipulated that provincial commissions, issued by the relevant colonial governor, would at all times be subordinate to those supplied to regulars by the king. In effect this meant that a senior provincial officer, such as Maj. Gen. John Winslow of Massachusetts, currently commanding the army defending Forts

Lord John Campbell, 4th Earl of Loudoun, commander in chief of British North America in 1757. (*National Gallery*)

Edward and William Henry, would be outranked by the most junior ensign of the 35th. The provincial officers found this unacceptable, and Winslow warned that his entire army would dissolve if the law was put into effect. Loudoun was willing to compromise. Before leaving Britain he had ensured that the law was modified, and now high-ranking provincials would be counted as "senior captains" when serving alongside their British counterparts. Loudoun thought this a most magnanimous concession. Winslow and his fellow provincials failed to agree.

The argument regarding seniority was but one of Loudoun's problems with his American troops. Essentially the disagreements stemmed from the failure of both parties to understand the starting viewpoint of the other. Loudoun saw the provincials as no different than any other British subjects and therefore felt that they must subjugate any personal whims to the will of the Crown. The provincials, by contrast, felt they deserved a measure of independence when managing what they saw as their own affairs. Although they still thought of themselves as British, the vast distance between themselves and their monarch and Westminster's policy of allowing the colonists de facto autonomy had led to the formation of some decidedly republican ideas.[33]

As well as having to put up with what he saw as Winslow's seditious demands, Loudoun was required to deal with a civilian population that insisted on negotiating his every command, and refused to comply with any request for aid or supplies without being compensated. Even by American standards, the Dutch inhabitants of Albany, whose predecessors had been forced to take the oath of allegiance in 1664 when Amsterdam's colonial pretensions had been crushed by the English, were hardly the most willing of King George's subjects. Besides maintaining their own culture, language, and religion, they charged the redcoats astronomically high prices for provisions while continuing a highly lucrative, though illegal, trade with New France.[34] Furthermore, rumors were rife that a number were spying for Montréal. According to a note written by Loudoun in August 1756, "one [Henry] Lydius . . . whom we suspect for a French spy, lives better than anybody, without any visible means and his daughters have often had presents from Mr. Vaudreuil [the governor of New France]."[35] All of this resulted in a mutual antipathy between the British and the Dutch, which occasionally boiled over into brawls.[36]

One example of this disharmony directly impacted on the 35th. Although the regiment was comfortable enough in "Camp Mohock" during the summer months, come winter its soldiers would need more permanent accommodation if they were not to be decimated by cold and disease.[37] When Loudoun announced his intention to quarter them on the civilian population, there was uproar. The mayor, a forty-eight-year-old father of seven named Sybrant G. Van Schaick whose great-grandparents had emigrated from Utrecht in 1637, was the first to voice his displeasure, dramatically declaring that he would sooner die than submit.[38] By calling Loudoun's bluff, Van Schaick was making a grave mistake. The Scot had a fiery temperament, and this latest example of colonial impertinence pushed him to the limit. Replying that he could not be expected to prevent the mayor's martyrdom, Loudoun promptly marched his troops into Van Schaick's house on Market Street. Van Schaick backed down and Loudoun responded by announcing three concessions: British

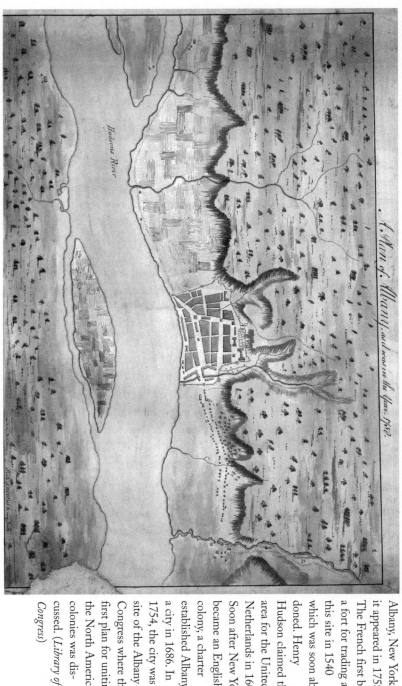

Albany, New York, as it appeared in 1758. The French first built a fort for trading at this site in 1540 which was soon abandoned. Henry Hudson claimed the area for the United Netherlands in 1609. Soon after New York became an English colony, a charter established Albany as a city in 1686. In 1754, the city was the site of the Albany Congress where the first plan for uniting the North American colonies was discussed. (*Library of Congress*)

officers, unlike the sergeants and rank and file, would have to pay for their own board and lodging; the Crown would supply the regulars' firewood and bedding; and a new barracks would be built, also at King George's expense, to prevent such difficulties in the future. Matters then appeared to improve, but the insolence of a Canadian trader resident in town later induced Loudoun to reverse the first of these proposals. When required to house a British officer, the Canadian responded by throwing his baggage into the street and barricading the door. Loudoun was determined to have the last word. "I sent a file of men and put the officer in possession [of the house]," he explained in a letter to Lord Cumberland. "If I find any more of this work, whenever I find a leading man, shut out any of the people, [I resolve] to take the whole house for a hospital, or a storehouse or let him shift for himself."[39]

In mid-August disastrous news came from the west: the French had taken Fort Oswego. Before Loudoun's arrival, Governor Shirley had planned to use the outpost as a springboard for that summer's campaign to capture an enemy fort at Niagara, but the forces of New France had preempted the move. Whereas the general assemblies of the thirteen colonies that made up British America were ruled by self-interest, New France was an autocracy, with supreme power resting in the hands of just one man: the governor, Pierre-François de Rigaud, the Marquis de Vaudreuil. While first Shirley, and then Loudoun, had been battling with the colonial councils in an attempt to secure the funds, supplies, and provincial troops needed to launch a campaign against Niagara, Vaudreuil had simply ordered an attack on Oswego, and New France had followed his command. The Marquis de Montcalm, commander in chief of all French regulars on the continent, had massed his troops before Lt. Col. James Mercer, commander of the garrison at Oswego, had even been aware of his intentions. On August 12, 1756, just a month after leaving Québec, Montcalm besieged Oswego with three thousand regulars, Canadian militia, and Indian auxiliaries. The defenders were hopelessly outnumbered, their defenses were poor, and they had been weakened by a particularly cruel winter, exacerbated by a lack of rations and frequent outbreaks of scurvy. On the fourteenth, after two days of raids on outposts and withdrawals as the French edged ever closer, Mercer had been beheaded by a French cannonball while directing the fire of a counterbattery. His decapitation proved the final straw. The surrender was signed shortly afterward by Mercer's deputy, Lt. Col. John Littlehales, and almost the entire garrison was led away as prisoners of war.[40]

As a few men who had escaped limped into Albany in the weeks that followed, further details emerged. One told of how Montcalm's Indians had fallen on the sick and wounded following the capitulation:

> They . . . behaved like infernal beings, rather than creatures in human shapes. They scalped and killed all the sick and wounded in the hospital; mangling, butchering, cutting, and chopping off their heads, arms, [and] legs with the utmost cruelty; notwithstanding the repeated intercessions of the defenceless . . . for mercy.

Another eyewitness recounted that one of those murdered that afternoon, Lieutenant de La Court, had only just had his wounds dressed before being "cut to pieces."[41]

Even disregarding the news from Oswego, September 1756 was a black month for the 35th. Things began to go wrong on the fourth with the arrival of Major Fletcher and his detachment of impressed men. Of the 376 who had sailed from London, only 351 remained when they reached Albany. Six had died at sea and nineteen had been left sick in New York.[42] Together with Monro's detachment of 400 and the 150 veterans who had been assigned to Fletcher to keep control of the impressed men, the 35th was now 900 strong.

On the morning of September 5, Monro held a regimental parade that saw his regiment united for the first time. Dressed in cocked hats crammed down over white-powdered queues, black breeches, long gaiters, and large-cuffed, red wool coats faced with yellow, the troops stood to attention as their colonel paced before them.[43] The rank and file was a motley bunch. Drawn from the lowest reaches of Georgian society, there were former laborers, farmers, weavers, cloth makers, carpenters, bleachers, and bakers. A handful of the veterans had been born into the army. The by-product of romantic liaisons between amorous redcoats and the washerwomen who became attached to individual units, they had been brought up to the sound of the fife and drum and knew no other way of life. More than half were from Britain, a third were Irish, a handful were Scots, and at least four had been born outside the British Isles.[44] Although senior officers had stipulated that only Protestants need apply, Pvt. Patrick Dunn, "a strict Papist" from Galway who had been impressed in London, and William Hughes, a twenty-eight-year-old carpenter from County Armagh, had slipped through the net.[45]

While the majority of the soldiers were in their midtwenties, there were also several older men, such as the sixty-three-year-old Hugh Neal of County Antrim. A former laborer, Neal had served in the British army for twenty-four years. Another veteran, and one of only a handful who had seen action, was Pvt. John Griffiths. "A staunch old soldier," Griffiths had volunteered for Rear Adm. Edward Boscawen's expedition to the East Indies in 1747. Most of the sergeants and below, by contrast, had never left their home shores. The majority was illiterate, a few were criminals, and many were drunks, but there was also a significant minority of educated men. William Bell was a former schoolteacher who had spent three years at Oxford University, and Warham Browne was the son of the bishop of Cork. Others were skilled craftsmen or administrators, such as the aptly named Thomas Shoe, a fifty-year-old cobbler, or Sgt. Thomas Perry from Chester, an attorney's clerk.[46]

The officers of the 35th were also relatively inexperienced. Apart from a handful of veterans like Major Fletcher, Surgeon Wilkins, and Captain Ince, who had received his first commission nearly twenty years before, the majority had been promoted shortly before they left Cork. Few had seen combat, and several were clearly not suited for the job. Within a few weeks of his arrival in America, Lt. James Belcher had had enough. "Being in a bad state of health," he wrote to Loudoun, "[I] do hearby beg leave to Resign my . . . commission." Loudoun was having none of it. Considering the state of Monro's regiment, he needed all the officers he had. Belcher's request was flatly refused.[47]

On the ninth, Privates Patrick Dunn, the Galway "papist," Edward Jeffries from Yorkshire, John Ross, Johan Lewis,

James Sheridan, and Henry Beanham deserted. From the subsequent court-martial report, it seems that Sheridan and Ross were the ringleaders. Having got the others drunk, they sneaked past the sentries and headed north toward the French frontier. The next morning, after an uncomfortable night in the woods plagued by mosquitos, black flies, and gnats, Jeffries and Dunn woke with sore heads and guilty consciences. Having heard Major Fletcher read the Articles of War on the voyage over, they knew that the punishment for desertion was death and pleaded with the others to let them return, hoping that the court might show them leniency. Rust and Lewis were furious. They "swore they would knock . . . [Jeffries's] brains out and strip him" if he persisted. Nevertheless, he remained defiant. After wandering in the woods for two to three hours, he heard gunshots. Making his way toward them, Jeffries stumbled across some pickets of the 35th. In an attempt to save himself, he swiftly gave up his fellow deserters' plans.

On hearing the news, Lord Loudoun took a personal interest in their capture. On the sixteenth he ordered Thomas Morral, the under sheriff of Albany, to post the following notice throughout the region: "All Magistrates and other Inhabitants of the counties of Albany, Ulster & Dutchess" are required to stop "any . . . persons who cannot give an account of themselves. For each person so apprehended a reward of forty shillings will be paid."[48] The next day, Loudoun sent a series of letters to the commanders of his outposts in the north, ordering them to take what measures they could to apprehend the deserters. "I wish some of your scouting parties could take them," he informed one provincial colonel, before revealing the true source of his annoyance. "There is a Poppish Priest . . . among them: I should be very glad to have him."[49]

At that moment, several dozen miles to the north, Private Dunn, the "Poppish Priest" Loudoun was so desperate to capture, was attempting to persuade his fellow deserters to turn themselves in. They remained unconvinced, and the Irishman eventually set off by himself. Soon he was hopelessly lost in the forest and had to retrace his steps and rejoin them. The next day, as the party continued north, Dunn heard cannon fire and realized they must be near Fort Edward. As it was nearly dark, he tarried for one more night, worried that he might get lost or be taken by an enemy scouting party. The next morning he set off and, as he had feared, once again lost his way. Three or four days later, a half-starved Dunn stumbled across the picket at Fort Edward.

The rest of the deserters proved more resolute. On September 19, ten days after they had left Albany, they reached a branch of the Wood Creek, halfway between Fort Edward and Lake George and only twenty miles south of the French positions at Fort Carillon. While resting before the final leg of their journey, they had the misfortune to fall in with a patrol led by Maj. Robert Rogers, the single most effective backwoods fighter that the British colonies possessed. Immediately realizing who they were, Rogers sent the deserters back to Fort Edward under escort of one of his lieutenants, a tough New Hampshire hunter named John Stark.[50]

With the prisoners under arrest, the general court-martial made short shrift of their trials. Jeffries was sentenced to death on September 20. Dunn, unfit to stand trial with his companion due to his recent exertions, received an identical sentence on the twenty-second. The others also pleaded not guilty, unconvincingly claiming at their trial in Fort Edward that they had got lost while blueberry picking on the far side of the Hudson River and had never intended to desert. They too were sentenced to hang. In Albany in late September, Jeffries and Dunn were led out from the guardroom to meet their fate. The 35th was drawn up in an open three-sided square before the scaffold to witness what happened to those who dared to defy the Articles of War.[51] After the drummers had beaten the death march, John Ogilvie, the Protestant minister of Saint Peter's church, offered the prisoners the last rites. Jeffries accepted, but Dunn remained "a strict papist" until the end.[52]

The desertions were not the only sign of disharmony in the ranks of the 35th that September. At 5 p.m. on Saturday the eighteenth, Sergeant Sprunston of Captain Ince's grenadiers had ordered his company to fall in. Most stepped into line, but Pvt. John Kelly had other ideas. The men had not yet received their sea pay, an extra allowance for those required to undertake lengthy voyages, and Kelly, having been drinking heavily all afternoon, decided to make a stand. Staggering forward, he turned to his peers and declared: "Blood and Wounds boys, don't let us fall in until we got our sea pay." On a nod from Sprunston, Corporal Leadbeater then took Kelly into custody, and the men continued with their parade. Two days later, now fearing for his life and utterly repentant, Kelly was brought before the court charged with "endeavouring to incite a mutiny." Colonel Monro and his captains, the president and board of the court, respectively, listened as Kelly claimed "drunkenness and ignorance" as his defense and promised "to behave better for the future." Deemed "young and repentant," Kelly avoided the death sentence. He was given five hundred lashes of the cat-o'-nine-tails instead.[53]

Kelly's crime was far from the worst committed by the 35th at Albany that autumn. Ensign William Skinner's servant, a private in the regiment, was responsible for a truly reprehensible act. Presumably under the influence, one night he raped a seven-year-old girl, infecting her with "the French disease," a virtual death sentence in the days before penicillin. A record of the incident survives, as Skinner begged Lord Loudoun to spare his man from the wrath of Albany's civilian court. To his credit, Loudoun refused to help, telling Skinner "that the law should take its course."[54]

After the trials of September, Loudoun grew scornful of the 35th.[55] "None of them have ever been in service," he wrote to Lord Cumberland. They "are entirely Raw . . . the most unruly [regiment] I have ever met, . . . the officers want full as much to be reclaimed as the men," and neither were to be trusted "near to the enemy."[56] It seems the only things the 35th was good for were work details and garrison duty. In September, several detachments were sent north from Albany to hold posts at the villages of Stillwater and Halfmoon and near the house of the "Widow Maginnis." Nineteen others were assigned to a "Hay Making Party," while one hundred sixty-five were detailed to three guard detachments in Albany. Several others were employed building a hospital and the new barrack block, whose construction was overseen by the most senior British engineer in America, Col. James Montressor. Despite the colonel's best efforts, the building work did not proceed well, as Brig. Gen. Daniel Webb, Loudoun's third in command, wrote on October 10: "Our works do not advance to my wish, and I am forced to things I am not inclined to, to force that accursed Regt. [the 35th] to work as it ought."[57]

Adding to the army's problems was an outbreak of small-pox, which descended on Albany that October. On the twelfth, the infection was confirmed "in three or four families" in town, and by the next day it had spread to seven houses. Sentries were posted outside the homes of those infected with strict orders "to let no one in or out." Worried that the disease would spread regardless, in a rare act of cooperation, the Dutch townspeople resolved to help Montressor build the hospital so as to have somewhere to house the sick. Soon fifty civilians were laboring alongside the privates of the 35th. While Webb still complained that Monro's men were "a dis-tressing set to have anything to do with," Montressor was delighted with the new hands and reported that the work now went on "very briskly."[58]

As October turned to November, the temperature plum-meted. Unable to stay in "Camp Mohock," the 35th was assigned billets in private houses all across town. Others were quartered with families in Ulster, Orange, and Albany coun-ties.[59] On November 3, a heavy blanket of snow covered the land, and the shipping was hauled out of the Hudson to be kept in storage for the next five months. Soon the river had frozen to a depth of four feet, and the locals began to use it as a highway for their horse-drawn sleighs.[60] For the 35th, unac-customed to such bitter cold, the official celebration of King George II's birthday on November 10 provided some distrac-tion, but by December the thermometers had plummeted to minus ten degrees Fahrenheit.[61] While the officers enter-tained themselves by holding lavish dinners and balls and by putting on the first theatrical performance Albany had ever seen, the rank and file suffered terribly. Shivering around the fireplaces in their begrudgingly surrendered accommodation, many must have wished that they had never left home.[62]

New France

Winter 1756–57

ouis-Joseph de Montcalm, the commander in chief of
His Majesty's regulars in New France, hated Canada.
For a start, the weather was appalling. Three months of swel-
teringly hot summer suddenly gave way to nine months of
bitterly cold winter, without even a hint of spring or autumn
in between.[1] The geography was equally unforgiving. Aside
from a narrow strip of cultivated farmland flanking the Saint
Lawrence River and the walled cities of Montréal and
Québec, the entire colony was blanketed with forest.
Impenetrable thickets, hidden deadfalls, and swamps made
progress nigh on impossible. A further source of discomfort
for the forty-four-year-old epicure was the astronomical
prices demanded for even the most basic commodities.[2] But it
was the inhabitants that Montcalm hated most of all. The
high country Indians who lived in the wilds and their "civi-
lized" cousins in the missions behaved like petulant children
and showed a cruelty and appetite for blood that Montcalm
had never come across in all his years of military service. The
Canadian woodsmen, or coureurs de bois, and the Indian
traders known as voyageurs, who lived alongside the "savages"
and had adopted their customs, were little better, but even so,
Montcalm thought them infinitely preferable to the worst
class of all—the governing elite.

Montcalm's problems had begun in April 1756 when he had bid his beloved wife and children farewell at the family mansion in southern France. A few days later he had boarded *La Licorne* at Brest. Montcalm hated sea voyages, and his first Atlantic crossing had been a particularly unpleasant one. "We had . . . a gale that lasted ninety hours, and put us in real danger," he later informed his wife.

> The forecastle was . . . under water, and the waves broke twice over the quarter-deck. From the twenty-seventh of April to the evening of the fourth of May we had fogs, great cold, and an amazing quantity of icebergs. On the thirtieth, when luckily the fog lifted for a time, we counted sixteen of them. The day before, one drifted under the bowsprit, grazed it, and might have crushed us if the deck-officer had not called out quickly.[3]

While Montcalm was "fortunate . . . in not being ill," his secretary, Monsieur Estève, was violently sick, and his servant Joseph "suffered cruelly," passing "seventeen days without being able to take anything but water." In fact, the entire voyage would have been a washout were it not for the company of Montcalm's newly appointed aide-de-camp, the twenty-six-year-old Louis-Antoine de Bougainville. During the seemingly endless days aboard ship, the two men formed a close friendship. Although Bougainville lacked military experience, Montcalm was charmed by his enthusiasm and thought him "a man of parts," blessed with "a military mind . . . [,] spirit and talent."[4]

In contrast to his commander, Bougainville was having the adventure of a lifetime. The young aide had only just joined the army and already it had taken him halfway around the world. What's more, he found himself in his element aboard *La Licorne*. Far from suffering from motion sickness, the sea air actually helped his asthma, and he enjoyed Montcalm's company as much as the general seemed to relish his own.[5]

That the two men got on well was unsurprising. Both had enjoyed privileged backgrounds, were well educated, and shared a love of reading. But while Montcalm had struggled to attain the exacting standards of his pedantic tutor, in the classroom Bougainville had always excelled. After achieving

fluency in Latin, he mastered math-
ematics and at the age of eighteen
had attended the University of Paris,
where he studied law. After graduating, Bougainville had worked briefly
as a notary before going to London,
where he acquired excellent English.
On his return he wrote a thesis on
calculus, which led to his election as
a member of London's prestigious
Royal Society. The journey to
England had also reawakened a
wanderlust, a yearning to see the
world that had first been sparked
during his childhood by his elder
brother's fascination with cartogra-

Louis-Joseph de Montcalm,
commander of French forces
in North America. (*Library
of Congress*)

phy. Realizing that he was not cut out for the life of a lawyer,
Bougainville had resigned from his position, joined the army
on a whim, and was delighted when he was appointed to
Montcalm's staff and ordered to sail for America.

While Bougainville was something of an intellectual,
Montcalm's real passion had always been the army. Coming
from a family with a proud tradition of service to the Crown,
at the age of fifteen he had begun his military career as an
ensign. Two years later, his father had purchased a captaincy
for the promising young officer, and he saw action at the siege
of Philipsbourg. In 1746, having risen to the rank of colonel,
Montcalm fought in the bloodiest encounter of his career.
Under the walls of Piacenza, the Austrian army smashed the
French and their Spanish allies. By the end of the day, thirteen thousand had been killed, wounded, or captured.
Montcalm was among the casualties, receiving five separate
saber cuts as he attempted to rally his troops. After being
paroled, he had returned to the battlefield and was wounded
once more, this time by a musket shot, before the peace of
Aix-la-Chapelle brought the fighting to a close.

Following the trials of the voyage, the general's first summer in New France had gone by in a blur. While Bougainville
had spent several weeks in Montréal, a low-walled town built

on an island in the Saint Lawrence, Montcalm and his second in command, François de Gaston, Chevalier de Lévis, had conducted a whirlwind tour of the colony's military outposts. On their return the governor of New France, the Marquis de Vaudreuil, had ordered a rapid deployment against the British outpost of Fort Oswego. A race down the Saint Lawrence in Indian canoes, past the rapids of Thousand Island Bay and across Lake Ontario, followed. Stunning vistas of New France's vast open waterways, encounters with exotic yet exasperating Indian allies, and breathless reports of initial clashes with the British had punctuated the journey. For Bougainville, it had been an exhausting experience, but at the same time so exciting that the days seemed to merge into one another. "I do not have an instant to myself," he wrote to his older brother, Jean-Pierre. "Scarcely do we have the time to eat and sleep. The campaign is indeed rough; the General, who was in the campaign in Bohemia, finds this one even more fatiguing."[6]

The climax of 1756 was the siege of Oswego. At first the French merely probed at the defenses, using Indian war parties that terrorized the defenders and took scalps from unwary sentries—bloody trophies that Bougainville and Montcalm later saw paraded through camp. Then, on the night of August 12, the French regulars began digging the siege trenches. As they inched their way toward the fortifications, covering parties of Canadian militia and Indian warriors under the command of François-Pierre de Rigaud de Vaudreuil, the governor's younger brother (hereafter known as Rigaud), drew the defenders' fire. Bougainville, posted with one group led by Kisensik, a Nipissing chief whom the aide would come to admire, found himself under fire for the first time. As Montcalm later recounted, Bougainville came through the test with flying colors. "You would not believe the resources I find in Bougainville," he informed a minister in Paris. "[H]e exposes himself readily to gunfire, a matter on which he needs to be restrained rather than encouraged."[7]

Over the next twenty-four hours, a frenzy of digging saw the regulars' siege lines advance to within cannon shot of the British fortifications. Then, on August 13, one of the French gunners' opening cannonades decapitated the opposing commander. With their leader gone, the British lost their stomach for the fight. "An hour later the enemy hoisted a white flag and two officers came to make proposals for surrender." Thanks to the English he had learned in London, Bougainville was sent to dictate the terms. The capitulation was signed and the celebrations began.[8] "On the ashes of Oswego we planted a cross and a post with the arms of France," Bougainville wrote to his brother. "On the cross I gave for a motto: '*IN HOC SIGNO VINCUNT*'" (With this sign they conquer); "on the post: '*MANIBUS DATE LILIA PLENIS*'" (Bring lilies with full hands).[9] In the most unlikely of settings, the young scholar's classical education had finally come into its own.

After the fall of Oswego, Montcalm and most of the French regulars returned to Montréal and Québec, but Bougainville had other plans. At his own request, he traveled past the major cities on the Saint Lawrence and continued down the Richelieu River to the Lake Champlain–Lake George corridor. As the spruce, cedar, and hemlock trees turned red, gold, amber, and brown, Bougainville took part in the autumn scouts and raiding that made up what the French termed *la petite guerre*.[10] Fighting alongside mixed bands of domesticated Abenaki from Saint Francis, Huron from Lorette, and Caughnawaga from Sault Saint Louis, as well as the "wild" Mississagua, their brethren the Chippewa (also known as Ojibwa), and Potawatomi from the high country, the young aide developed a taste for wilderness warfare. Nevertheless, the grueling lifestyle took its toll and his asthma began to plague him.[11] "I am tired out with this campaign," he wrote to his brother.

> The continual travelling, the poor food, the frequent lack of sleep, the nights spent under the open sky in the woods, [and] the expeditions with the Indians, have affected my chest a little. At the end of last month I even spat blood. . . . One needs an iron constitution not to feel the effects of such endurance.[12]

After such a dramatic summer and autumn, the winter, spent posted in Québec, came as something of an anticlimax, although Bougainville may have drawn some solace from the city's breathtaking location. Perched on a high bluff, Québec was bounded on three sides by water. To the south and east lay the mighty Saint Lawrence, while to the north was the fast-flowing Saint Charles River. The upper city, which offered splendid views over the surrounding forests, was inhabited by "people of quality" and housed the principal buildings in town. The governor's palace, numerous churches, a cathedral, a market, the College of the Jesuits, and the Hôtel-Dieu de Paris, a grand hospital, stood among wide streets made of sharp black limestone slabs that cut pedestrians' shoes to pieces. Beneath the upper terrace, reached by a torturously steep and serpentine road, stood the lower city. Although smaller in size, it was more densely populated. Along its narrow thoroughfares was another palace and grand four-story merchants' houses, which competed for space with the king's batteries protecting Québec from a river-borne invasion. Beneath the muzzles of the guns were the city's docks, from which the furs trapped by Indians and Canadian voyageurs were shipped to Old France.[13]

In October, there was some excitement as the captains of Québec's merchant fleet raced to load up and leave harbor before the river froze, but Bougainville's journal entries for the months of November and December were short by comparison to his earlier flowing prose. Daily reports on the weather are intermingled with notes on life in Québec and updates on the condition of his asthma.

> November 18: The wind . . . has been northeast . . . I took medicine today.

> November 21: Southeast wind until three, then north. Minus twelve degrees . . . As the year['s harvest] has been a very bad one . . . a police regulation has ruled . . . that bread will be distributed to the public only in the afternoon. I went to see this distribution. It presents the image of a famine. They fight to get near the wicket through which they pass the bread. Those who can not get near hold out their permits on the end of a stick.

> November 25: Strong north wind that the local people call Saint Catherine's Gale, and which they have

observed to come regularly about this time. I went in a sleigh to St. Foix, two and one-half leagues from town. The women of this country take pleasure in winter in going in a sleigh over the snow and ice in weather in which it would seem that they should not go outdoors at all.

December 15: Southwest wind, violently cold. A courier left for Montréal. Minus 21 degrees.

December 20: Snow and powdered snow. Northeast wind. The powdered snow is an extremely fine snow which, falling from the sky and combining with that which the wind raises from the roofs and roads, envelops you, blinds you, and leads astray one who knows the way very well. When one is overtaken in the open by the powdered snow, one must realize that he is really in danger. There are instances of people who in the night, a hundred paces from their houses, have perished without being able to reach them.[14]

Trapped in his quarters by the cold, Bougainville spent the festive period writing the journal, which he planned to publish on his return to France. "I passed my time in reading, meditating, and writing," he informed his brother.

This ennui which torments me has been turned to the profit of my soul. You will see a memoir I sent Madame Hérault for the Minister. It is only the germ of ideas which need to be developed. . . . My portfolio is full of observations on the customs of the Indians, their language, [and] the quality of the country.[15]

Two days after Christmas the cold lessened significantly, affording Bougainville an opportunity for a field trip to gather further notes on "Les Sauvages."

La Jeune Lorette, the young aide's destination, was a Jesuit mission for domesticated Huron Indians situated near a frozen waterfall on the Saint Charles River two leagues outside Québec. Within a ring of snow-covered fields used in the summer for sparse crops of Indian corn, wheat, rye, squash, and beans, rows of stone houses "built after the French fashion" huddled around a central fort and church presided over by the Jesuit priest. Built in 1697, the church had been modeled on the Santa Casa of Loretto in Italy and featured a steeple "covered with white tin plates." Unlike the "wild" Indians to the west, who lived communally in large wooden longhouses, the Lorette Huron, "a tall robust people, well-shaped, and of a copper color," had adopted European ways. The men, while still taking pride in adorning themselves with tattoos and boasting outlandish hairstyles, wore "waistcoats, or jackets like the French" and had largely replaced hunting with agriculture, a job that had once been an exclusively female domain.[16]

On visiting the mission church at Lorette, Bougainville was impressed by the Indians' singing. "The women's choir is quite harmonious," he recorded. "One would take them for a choir of our nuns except that almost all of our Indian women have singularly melodious voices." While Bougainville was capable of admiring certain aspects of native culture, he was still unable to entirely escape the prejudices of his age. "What struck me most was an Indian who assisted at the mass in a surplice," he remarked in the same journal entry, adding that the "savage" in question put him in mind of a "wolf in sheep's clothing."[17] After dining at the house of a local, perhaps on the Huron's winter staple of cornmeal gruel enlivened by a sprinkling of fish heads, Bougainville returned to Québec. He would remain at the capital until the end of January.[18] General Montcalm, on the other hand, was at that very moment traveling forty miles up the Saint Lawrence to Montréal to attend one of the highlights of New France's glittering social calendar. The contrast between the spartan, austere atmosphere of Lorette and the chandeliered dining rooms and dance floors of Intendant François Bigot's Montréal palace could not have been more marked.

At seven o'clock on the night of January 5, 1757, the party began. Stuffed moose heads, cod's liver, and dressed deer were washed down with the finest French wines. Afterward the guests retired to a wood-paneled dancing chamber, complete with viewing balcony for those who had overindulged at dinner. Below, forty of the colony's most alluring young ladies awaited them.[19] Playing cards were later brought out and, after the ladies had retired, the men talked and gambled into the small hours. French officers of the regulars, Canadian commanders of the militia and colonial regulars, and local merchants and officials were all present. Foremost among them, overshadowing even General Montcalm, was the governor of New France, Pierre-François de Rigaud, the Marquis of Vaudreuil.

The son of a former governor, Vaudreuil had been born in Québec in 1698. After a lengthy apprenticeship as an officer in the colonial regulars, he had been appointed governor of the vast southern territory of Louisiana, before achieving what he considered his birthright, the governorship of New France, in 1755.

Pierre-François de Rigaud, the Marquis of Vaudreuil, governor of New France. (*Archives of Canada*)

Resourceful and determined, the fifty-nine-year-old loved his country and its people unequivocally and was respected and admired by the Canadians and Indians alike. In return, Vaudreuil fiercely protected their interests from what he saw as the interfering encroachment of Old France, the latest round of which was personified by the intrusion of the Marquis de Montcalm and his regulars.

Although Vaudreuil had received Montcalm cordially at first, by the beginning of 1757 the two men were becoming increasingly bitter enemies, the most serious fallout coming as a result of Vaudreuil's myopic report concerning the French success at Oswego. The document, which the governor had sent to Versailles, stressed his own role in planning the expedition and his brother's in leading the Indians and militia, but almost entirely ignored the contribution of Montcalm and his regulars, without which the fort would never have fallen.[20] Furious when he discovered the deceit, Montcalm confronted him, and the two men had not seen eye to eye since. At the heart of Montcalm's anger was the fact that although Versailles favored his opinion over his adversary's in questions of military strategy, King Louis XV's orders gave Vaudreuil overall command. As their subordinates closed ranks behind them, New France became a colony divided between the powers of the Old World and the New. Firmly in the camp of the latter, although himself a native of Bordeaux, was the second of the colony's ruling triumvirate and the host of that evening's event, the unscrupulous Intendant François Bigot.

Since his appointment in 1748, Bigot had amassed a fortune through a variety of corrupt schemes, often aided by Joseph Cadet, the son of a Québecoise butcher whom Bigot had appointed commissary general more for his lack of morals than his financial expertise. Together they had established a network of confidants that spread across the colony. One of their regular ploys was to sell government goods at low prices to acquaintances who would then sell them on the open market at a huge profit. Other schemes were even more transparent. On one occasion, the pair bought a quantity of stores belonging to the king for 600,000 livres, which they proceeded to sell back to the royal stores for 1,400,000. Merely by moving goods and capital from one account to the other and forever skimming off the top, they became fabulously wealthy, and soon the entire colony was caught up in their crimes. From the commanders of insignificant posts deep in the wilderness, who would sell gifts provided for the Indians rather than freely distributing them, to those in charge of the transportation of military stores, who would pocket their expenses and order the citizenry to work for free in exchange for an exemption from military service—to Montcalm it seemed as if all of New France was involved.

Eventually the scale of this corruption was noted across the Atlantic. Already a diseased society, rotten with the dissatisfaction, injustice, and inequality that would lead to its bloody downfall in a little over thirty years' time, the France of Louis XV was beyond parody. From his luxurious palace at Versailles, the king had little interest in governing his empire. Instead, he spent his days planning biweekly hunting trips to his estates in Choisy, Bellevue, or Saint Hubert, or picking through his courtiers' private correspondence, obligingly provided for his diversion by Monsieur Janelle, the head of the postal service and one of several obsequious sycophants that surrounded the king. Perhaps the most damaging of Louis's myriad faults was his womanizing. He was in thrall to several ladies of the court, the foremost of whom, and the real power behind the throne, was Jeanne-Antoinette Poisson le Normont d'Étoiles, the Marquise de Pompadour. As his chief mistress and confidante, Madame de Pompadour was a manipulative figure who emasculated an already effeminate king and could make or unmake his ministers with a single piece of pillow talk.[21] Although disapproving of the goings-on in Canada, Louis was locked in a state of blissful ennui and sloth, and the vast distances between Old France and its colony, and the fact that Bigot had nearly the entire administration in his pocket, rendered it extremely difficult for the king to bring the Intendant to book for his crimes. Besides, America was insignificant in the overall scheme of the Seven Years' War, merely a sideshow compared to the slaughter taking place on the fields of Europe. Voltaire famously dismissed the colony as "a few acres of snow," and the prestigious Parisian publication the *Enyclopédie* insisted it was a place inhabited only by "bears, beaver and barbarians."[22] For a king with far more pressing concerns, the colony was hardly worth a second glance.

In February 1757, while the never-ending round of parties continued in Montréal, Governor Vaudreuil turned his attention to more serious matters. Although suspended by the winter freeze, the war was still very much uppermost in his thoughts. Oswego had been a great success, but if he was to triumph in the long term against the British, who outnumbered his troops four to one, he would need to maintain the initiative. Poring over a map of the frontier, he decided to focus his efforts on the colony of New York and ordered a winter raid on Fort William Henry. The primary aim of the attack was to burn the garrison's boats, thereby depriving the British of naval supremacy on Lakes George and Champlain, and paving the way for a much larger strike he was planning that summer.[23] A secondary intention, evidenced by the presence of siege ladders among the expedition's lengthy inventory, was to take the fort by a coup de main, an ambitious plan that would require the garrison to be taken unawares.

Although the raid was Vaudreuil's idea, as soon as Montcalm got wind of it, he was determined to get involved.

The Frenchman suggested that eight hundred of his regulars should be used, guided by a handful of Canadians and Indians, and that command of the raid should be given to either Bougainville or Lévis, his second in command. Vaudreuil, distrustful of French interference, dismissed the plan. He wanted to use fifteen hundred Canadians under the command of his younger brother, Rigaud. Because issuing rations for such a sizable force would put a major drain on the already depleted grain stores, a lengthy debate followed. Montcalm, although just as wary of using Canadian troops as Vaudreuil was of employing the French, eventually agreed to a compromise, hoping that his graciousness would give him credit for the greater arguments that were sure to follow. Rigaud would command the raid, and twelve hundred Canadians and Indians would go with him, but the honor of spearheading the assault would go to a detachment of three hundred French grenadiers.[24]

"A little man, thin and spare" who appeared nearly two decades younger than his fifty-four years, Rigaud was an experienced wilderness fighter, who had made short work of the siege of Fort Massachusetts in 1746, and had recently been appointed governor of the town of Trois Riviéres.[25] On February 14, he left Montréal for the Abenaki mission of Saint Francis to recruit Indian auxiliaries. Built on a bluff overlooking the Saint Francis River, Odanak, as it was known to its five hundred residents, had been inhabited since the mid-seventeenth century. It consisted of a series of rectangular bark-built cabins, three large storehouses holding grain, and a richly decorated chapel.[26] Inside were gold cloth draperies, copper candlesticks, a banner depicting Christ, and a solid silver statue of the Virgin Mary donated by the canons of Chartres.[27] Outside hung several British and American scalps—a grisly testament to the Abenakis' skill at raiding along the frontier.

Near the chapel was the home of the resident Jesuit priest, the thirty-three-year-old Pierre Roubaud, a Frenchman who had left his native Avignon one year before.[28] Simultaneously enamored and appalled by his charges, Roubaud was determined to make the most of his time in New France. As well as ministering to the religious needs of his flock, he was a keen writer and, by some accounts, had somewhat more than a spiritual interest in his female parishioners.[29] Regardless of the veracity of such alleged peccadillos, Roubaud and his predecessors had been remarkably successful in promoting their creed. While the Calvinist preachers of New England had made few converts among the Iroquois to the south, the Jesuits had prospered through an inclusive system that tolerated indigenous culture and beliefs. They were also well aware of the value of disparaging their enemies, as an anecdote concerning Chief Bomaseen, an Abenaki captured by the New Hampshire militia after a raid in 1694, illustrates. When the colonists asked if he was a Christian, Bomaseen readily agreed, explaining that he knew the scriptures as well as they did. When questioned further, the chief revealed that the Virgin Mary was French and that Jesus had been murdered by an Englishman.[30]

That such propaganda was so readily accepted by the Abenaki is explained by the history of the tribe. Rather than being a single people, the Indians of Saint Francis were in fact a conglomeration of linguistically related refugees forced into coexistence by the ever-expanding British colonies encroaching on their homelands to the south. Since the middle of the seventeenth century, the "people of the Dawnland," so known for their proximity to the eastern sea, had been fighting a losing battle with both the militias of New England and their Mohawk allies.[31] The struggle had begun in earnest in 1675 with the outbreak of King Philip's War, which saw the Wampanoag chief, Metacom (known as King Philip to the English colonists), soundly defeated by the colonial militias. The survivors of his tribe and their Narragansett allies relocated in an attempt to avoid further persecution. Some were taken in by the Mohegans and Mahicans of the Hudson Valley. Others moved north where they sought refuge with the Sokokis, Cowasucks, Missisquois, Winnipessaukees, Ossipees, Pennacooks, and Pigwackets.

When King William's War, the first of a series of struggles fought between Britain and France for control of North America, broke out in 1689, a second wave of refugees was pushed northward. Along with the first migrants, they fell into an alliance of convenience with New France. With the Jesuits' establishment of Saint Francis in 1700, these groups began living together for mutual security and became collectively known as the Abenaki. In 1704, in one of the opening acts of the continent's second colonial struggle (Queen Anne's War), a French and Indian force, which included several of the inhabitants of Saint Francis, raided the Massachusetts outpost of Deerfield. One hundred fifty colonists were killed or captured and the town was burned to the ground. The memory of the raid would live on for generations among the inhabitants of New England, and although Queen Anne's War was officially brought to a close in 1713, the fighting continued throughout the first half of the eighteenth century. With each successive massacre, the hatred between the Abenaki and the New Englanders grew ever deeper.[32]

With such a history of antipathy, it is unsurprising that Rigaud was successful in his quest for volunteers. When he left Saint Francis the next morning, some one hundred Abenaki warriors went with him. After donning twin Heron feathers in their scalp locks and striking the red-painted war post set up in the middle of the village with their clubs as a symbol of their intent, they set off for Fort Saint Jean on the Richelieu River.[33] Two days later Rigaud's second, Paul-Joseph Le Moyne de Longueil, a Québecoise subaltern given the brevet rank of lieutenant colonel for the duration of the raid, went west to the village of Sault Saint Louis, yet another Jesuit mission built near Montréal. Sited on the Saint Lawrence River, Saint Louis was inhabited by domesticated Indians of the Iroquois Confederacy who had left their homelands for the relative comforts of mission life at the end of the seventeenth century. Longueil was equally successful, and when he met Rigaud at Fort Saint Jean, a bastioned outpost built on the banks of the Richelieu River, one hundred warriors were with him.

Also at Saint Jean was the penultimate component of Rigaud's force: the three hundred regulars led by Capt. François Poulharies. A "gallant," industrious officer, the forty-nine-year-old from Limoux had joined the Royal Roussillon

The Richelieu–Champlain Corridor. The route between Québec along the St. Lawrence River to Lake Champlain by way of the Richelieu River provided the French and their Indian allies direct access to the heart of the British northeastern frontier. Likewise, the British would use the same route to launch attacks on Canada.

Regiment in 1734 as a second lieutenant. His rise had since been steady, though undramatic, with his latest promotion occurring on December 8, 1755, six months after his arrival in New France.[34] The men he would lead that March were a mixed unit of grenadiers from the Royal Roussillon, La Sarre, Languedoc, and Bearn Regiments.[35] The best of the French army, the grenadiers were handpicked for their height, bravery, strength, experience, and stamina. In exchange for their position of honor on the right of the line and a bonus of an extra sou a day, they were routinely assigned the most demanding and dangerous tasks.[36]

Also present at Saint Jean were 272 colonial regulars and 528 Canadian militiamen formed into sixteen mixed companies. The former was a professional force raised to protect France's colonies in 1665 that served a dual role of police force and military auxiliary. While most of the sergeants and rank and file were Frenchmen, the majority of the officers were Canadians of high birth, who were well motivated and determined to protect their homeland. The French privates, by contrast, were scraped from the dregs of society. Many viewed service in the colonial regulars as a second chance, an opportunity to atone for former sins or make up for a wasted youth. After retirement at the age of fifty-five or sixty, they were entitled to a plot of land and encouraged to settle in the colony where they had served, thereby not only boosting its population but also acting as a ready-made reserve.[37]

While the colonial regulars were not considered a match for the French regulars in open battle, in terms of both discipline and martial prowess, they were considerably more adept than the third tier of Rigaud's army: the militia. Established in 1669 by order of Louis XIV, the militiamen were civilian conscripts drawn by a system that was designed to leave enough men at home at any one time to tend the fields and maintain local trade. Each parish was required to raise a company of between 30 and 150 men led by a local hereditary landowner who would also perform a governmental function in peacetime. Aged from fifteen to sixty, the troops were unpaid, though they were issued a musket, which they were allowed to purchase at cost after their period of service had expired—a considerable inducement when living in the Canadian wilds. Like the officers who led the colonial regulars, the majority of the militia wanted to serve their country and performed well in the irregular forest warfare that defined the early colonial struggles in America. Their indiscipline, on the other hand, was in stark contrast to the regulars. While Poulharies's grenadiers had been trained to stand firm against cannon fire and were used to the draconian punishment regularly meted out by courts-martial, the militia lacked battle experience, were prone to plundering and scalping the dead, and could break under pressure in battle.[38]

Among the officers tasked to restrain their baser instincts that winter was Capt. Jean Dumas, the thirty-five-year-old Frenchman from Agenais who had orchestrated Braddock's defeat at Monongahela. Alongside him was an enigmatic German lieutenant named Wolff.[39] "A brave man," whom one contemporary observer thought "rigorous and more intelligent than he appears," Wolff was a rare example of an *officier de fortune*, a sergeant who had risen from the ranks. After serving for twenty-two years in the Bentheim Regiment, a German unit that served in the French army, Wolff had been commissioned just before sailing to New France with Baron Dieskau's expedition in 1755. Since his arrival, he had fought at the battles of Lake George and Oswego and had developed his skills as a backwoods fighter by leading numerous raiding parties against the New England frontier. Despite his "zeal" and "talents," Wolff would struggle to gain further promotion in New France. Montcalm's army was less affected by the snobbery so prevalent in the French service in Europe, but those who rose from the ranks were still derided by the cream of society that dominated the officer class.[40]

Once Rigaud had inspected his men at Fort Saint Jean, they were issued their equipment. John Victor, a militia private who was Swiss by birth but had lived in Montréal for several years, recorded everything he carried. To keep out the bitter winter cold, he and his comrades were given two pairs of moccasins, "Indian stockings . . . [,] thick mittens," two "new cotton shirts," woolen socks, one "thick red woollen cap," a "flannel waistcoat with sleeves," a "blue cloth vest and breeches," and a "greatcoat with a cap."[41] The troops were also issued with snowshoes and "Iron Creepers to walk on the ice" and were armed with three knives, a tomahawk, and a musket complete with shot and powder. In addition, each was given a small sleigh loaded with a copper kettle for cooking, a piece of canvas, a bearskin, and a blanket to sleep under, as well as rations of biscuit, bread, salt pork, and tobacco, all of which were carefully wrapped in sealskin to keep out the damp.[42] The men dragged their sleighs behind them, while the officers used horses or dogs.[43]

On February 20, the first contingent set off from Saint Jean on the three-hundred-mile journey to Fort William Henry. Major Anne-Joseph Malartic of the French regulars arrived at the fort just in time to see the men leave.[44] The next two mornings, further detachments paraded on the ice in front of the fort before setting off, but the final group—which included Rigaud and all the staff officers, the Abenaki Indians, and the grenadiers under Captain Poulharies—was delayed by "bad weather and a thaw."[45] Making camp in the woods to the right of the fort, the troops had to wait until the twenty-fifth before leaving. Guided by a Canadian named Boileau who had run a trading post in the area before the war, they followed a path leading down the west bank of the Richelieu River to its source at Lake Champlain.[46] As the ice on the lake had already begun to break up and it "was largely open water," the men had no choice but to trudge under dripping branches through the snowdrifts onshore.

On the second day, they passed Île aux Noix, an island with a French fort and barracks surrounded by frozen marshes. Twelve miles beyond was the headland of Pointe à Fer, where the lake was frozen solid once more and the men could make swifter progress across the ice. Pulling his hand sleigh behind him with "a strong rope," Private Victor found the going easy and proceeded with "very little toil or fatigue."[47] On the twenty-seventh, a snowstorm forced Rigaud to halt for the entire day. After digging away the snow in a circle, the men covered the earth with boughs cut from evergreen trees, then drew their tarpaulins over the structure to provide some protection from the storm.[48] The next morning dawned bright and clear, and good progress was made. As they marched, spectacular views of the mountain ranges that flanked Lake Champlain opened up: the Adirondacks appeared to the west and the Green Mountains to the east. Until the second of March, the troops covered between seven and ten leagues a day, but then a second thaw, a fall of powdered snow and a strong wind, delayed them once more, and it wasn't until the sixth that they reached the third of the French forts on Lake Champlain guarding the route north.

Built between 1734 and 1738, Fort Saint Frédéric, later known to the British as Crown Point, was the oldest of the forts on the Richelieu–Champlain corridor.[49] An impressive structure, the fort mounted forty cannons and boasted stout, bastioned limestone walls surrounding a four-story granite tower. Built in the shadow of neighboring mountains, Saint Frédéric overlooked Lake Champlain at a point where it narrows to a mere musket shot across, forcing all travelers to pass close under its guns.[50] Although its high tower defied the maxims of contemporary military engineering, which favored squat structures that could absorb repeated cannon fire, the fort was situated so deep in the wilderness that it was thought unlikely that any enemy would ever haul heavy siege guns so far.[51]

After two days' rest, Rigaud's men pushed on, reaching Fort Carrillon on March 9. Sited on a solid rock bluff, known to the Mohawk by the name of Ticonderoga, the fort, which was still under construction when Rigaud arrived, overlooked a vital portage or carrying place, which linked Lakes Champlain and George. Glad for a respite from the bitter weather, Rigaud remained at Carillon for six days. His men were issued axes for felling trees, collapsible scaling ladders for the coup de main, and specially designed kindling made of bundles of "resinous sticks" designed to set fire to the British canoes, whaleboats, and schooners at Fort William Henry.[52] It was also discovered that many of the militia's muskets were old, rusted, or worn, and new arms were issued to replace them.[53] As the rain had spoiled some of the food the troops carried, a further twelve days' rations were also supplied. While the men were given no "spirits, wine, nor vinegar," each officer was issued with "three pints of brandy and two pounds of chocolate," and the Indians, who had already insisted on eating more than their fair share, were given bottles of New England rum.[54]

Over the next six days, the men smoked tobacco through their clay pipes, warmed themselves around log fires in the barracks, and gambled with cards and dice, while Rigaud and his officers enjoyed the hospitality of the fort's commander, Captain Paul-Louis Dazemard de Lusignan.[55] Although popular with his officers, Lusignan was resented by his men, as he forbade them from trading with the local Indians. This was to allow his wife, Madeleine Marguerite Bouet, to build up a lucrative trade monopoly and stockpile an impressive array of goods.[56]

Also present at Carillon was a sixteen-year-old prisoner from Charlestown, Massachusetts, named Thomas Brown. Having joined Maj. Robert Rogers's Rangers, an elite scouting unit raised by the British to counter their enemies' preponderance of Indian allies, Brown had been captured along with five others after a bungled raid on a French convoy near Carillon two months before. Fourteen of his comrades had been killed in the action, including Brown's company commander, Capt. Thomas Spikeman, whom the young private had witnessed stripped and scalped alive as the British survivors fled to the south. The Indian that had perpetrated the act had not even bothered to finish Spikeman off, and the captain had later begged Brown "to give him a tomahawk, that he might put an end to his life." A strict Christian, Brown refused. "I . . . exhorted him . . . to pray for mercy," he remembered, "as he could not live many minutes in that deplorable condition, being on the frozen ground, [and] covered with snow. He desired me to let his wife know (if I lived to get home) [of] the dreadful death he [had] died." Brown was picked up by the Indians the next day, given a severe beating, and imprisoned in Carillon. Then one day in early March his routine was broken when Rigaud came to see him with an unusual proposal. "Young man," the Canadian said, "you are a likely fellow; it's [a] pity you should live with such an ignorant people as the English; you had better live with me." Not dar-

Bald Mountain, today known as Rogers Rock, is a massive shear rock face that dominates the far northwest side of Lake George. (*Author*)

ing to disagree, Brown nodded his assent, but when asked to guide the raiders across Lake George he refused, even though Rigaud offered him 7,000 livres for the service. Two other rangers captured at the same time were not so scrupulous, however. "They said they were obliged to go," Brown recalled, but "I said . . . [Rigaud] could not force them; and added, that if they went . . . they must never return among their friends; for if they did . . . [I] would endeavor . . . [to see them] hanged."[57]

On Tuesday, March 15, Rigaud's raiders set off from Carillon on the final leg of their journey. That night they camped on the west shore of Lake George and sent a scouting party forward the next morning. Fearing discovery by rangers patrolling out of Fort William Henry or Fort Edward, they laid no fires and from that point on proceeded to travel at night, advancing down the frozen lake in five columns. In the center were the regulars with Rigaud at their head, on either side were two columns of Canadian militia, and the Indian scouts patrolled the flanks.[58] The French and

Canadians spent the daylight hours of the sixteenth camped on the flanks of Bald Mountain, a massive eminence whose sheer slopes of bare rock rose up from the ice and dominated the northern section of the lake.[59] The Indians, meanwhile, set off on a scouting sortie, but returned later that afternoon having seen nothing.[60] That night, as the wolves howled in the surrounding mountains, the column advanced to Ganaouské Bay, a wide inlet just eight miles from Fort William Henry, but hidden from view by a projecting point of land. After nightfall Captain Poulharies, Dumas, and a French engineer, Capt. François-Marc-Antoine le Mercier, crept forward to reconnoiter the fort, escorted by a small band of Indians and French regulars. Climbing a hill overlooking the fortifications, they spent the night observing the garrison through their telescopes. There was considerable activity inside Fort William Henry, leading to a discussion among the officers as to whether or not they had been seen.[61] Nevertheless, upon their return, the order to attack was given. On the night of the eighteenth to nineteenth, the regulars, Indians, and Canadians were to advance across the ice in three columns, being careful to make as little noise as possible; then, with Poulharies's grenadiers leading the way, they were to use their ladders to scale the walls. Once inside, no quarter would be given. After slitting the sentries' throats, the men were to turn the fort's cannons against the garrison and put the survivors "to the sword."[62] Few of Rigaud's men slept that afternoon, as they lay shivering under their bearskins on the ice waiting for nightfall. All knew that the British garrison may have already spotted them, and without the element of surprise, many would not live to see the next day.[63]

3

Rigaud's Winter Raid

MARCH 1757

*M*ajor William Eyre felt almost entirely cut off from the outside world. Resting his telescope on the parapet of Fort William Henry, one of the northernmost points of the British Empire, the forty-nine-year-old surveyed the scene he had come to know intimately over the past two years. Blanketed in snow, the landscape was hauntingly beautiful. Lake George lay frozen between flanking mountain ranges, stretching out to the north like a finger pointing toward New France. Birch, pine, and fir trees rose from the shoreline. Climbing over the foothills in gently undulating waves, they blanketed the country for dozens of miles in every direction, only losing their grip when the bare rock of the mountain heights burst free above them. To the south, east, and west, where Colonel Whitley's Massachusetts provincials had battled with the undergrowth the previous summer, the silver-barked trees had been cut down to produce a stump-strewn killing ground stretching a clear mile from the fort's log palisade. Dark, seemingly impenetrable and fearsomely foreboding to the British regulars and provincial rangers alike, the woods beyond continued uninterrupted until Fort Edward, fourteen miles away down a rough-hewn wagon trail that disappeared down a defile toward the south.

By the winter of 1757, Major Eyre was an experienced campaigner. He had first seen action twelve years before as a practitioner engineer fighting the Highlanders at Prestonpans and Culloden during the Jacobite rebellion. In 1747, he had helped prepare the defenses of Bergen op Zoom during the Duke of Cumberland's disastrous Flanders campaign, and in 1748 he had been promoted to subengineer. Seven years later he had been commissioned as a captain in the 44th Regiment and had sailed to Virginia with Edward Braddock. Before the general left on his ill-fated campaign toward the forks of the Ohio, Eyre had been posted to New York, where he joined William Johnson's expedition to attack the French through the Lake George–Lake Champlain corridor. At first, Eyre had been responsible for supervising the construction of Fort Edward, but had later joined the main army on the shores of Lake George. When the provincials clashed with Dieskau's French regulars, Canadian militia, and Indian warriors on September 8, Eyre had employed the army's three guns with devastating effect. In no small part due to Eyre's actions, Dieskau's men had been repulsed and Eyre was promoted to major as a result. Since the battle, he had reverted to his role of engineer and had been employed in building Fort William Henry.[1]

In March 1757, one and a half years after the Battle of Lake George, the landscape around the fort seemed peaceful enough, but as Eyre knew, even in winter the woods could be a dangerous place. Much more formidable than the bears and the occasional panther, Caughnawaga, Ottawa, and Abenaki Indians allied to the French came and went as they pleased, appearing from nowhere to kill, take scalps, or snatch prisoners before making their way back to Fort Carillon, twenty miles to the north.[2] Eyre feared the Indians, and his men feared them too. The 44th had been in America for one and a half years, more than enough time to become acquainted with the indigenous inhabitants. In July 1755, while Eyre had been putting the finishing touches to Fort Edward, his men had been more than five hundred miles to the southwest. After a summer spent marching through the wilderness, elements of the regiment had been ambushed alongside a detachment of the 48th and some Virginia provincials under General Braddock. The French- and Canadian-led Indians had turned the summer glades into a hunting ground. Hundreds of redcoats and Virginian provincials had been butchered. By the time the Indians had finished, bodies lay across the field. Private Duncan Cameron, a regular of the 44th who survived by hiding himself in a hollow tree trunk, would never forget the scene. As he watched through a knot-hole, the Indians had methodically scalped the dead and wounded, oblivious to their cries for mercy and the protestations of their French "commander," Capt. Jean Dumas.[3]

Such images were not easily forgotten, but March 17 was a special day for the many Irishmen among Eyre's command. They were determined not to let the thought of being attacked by "bloodthirsty savages" ruin Saint Patrick's Day.[4] Fort William Henry was well supplied with alcohol, and soon bottles of New England rum and spruce beer were being passed round the barracks.[5] For the next two days, the fort echoed to the sound of Irish dancing tunes.[6] Eyre knew he could not afford to be complacent: the French had launched winter raids before. Nevertheless, he felt secure within the fort's sturdy ramparts. Captain John Stark, a veteran bush fighter from New Hampshire who commanded the seventy-two rangers in the garrison, had ordered the sutlers to limit his provincials' rum ration, ensuring that at least a quarter of the garrison would be fit for duty. Besides, Eyre had another reason for being so confident. He had designed the fort himself.

Rising from the lakeshore, Fort William Henry cut a stout profile. Its ramparts, thirty feet of hard-packed earth and sand, buttressed by fifteen-foot log walls capped with parapets, barely rose above the surrounding landscape. From the beginning of the build, two years previously, Eyre had followed French engineering principles, laid down by the master of early modern fortification, Sébastien Le Prestre, Marquis de Vauban. The Frenchman's key innovations were the use of low, wide walls known as ramparts, which were designed to absorb artillery fire, and the construction of diamond- or lozenge-shaped bastions built on each corner of the fort, enabling the defenders to keep up a crossfire on the enemy, no matter how close they got to the walls.

Inside Fort William Henry were twin two-story timber barracks able to house up to four hundred men with a modicum of comfort. The buildings were lined with bunks and heated by large stone fireplaces. Elsewhere were a few storehouses and a small hospital crammed with more than a hundred men. Although a few had been wounded in skirmishes, most had been laid low by one of the many ailments that constantly plagued camp life. While smallpox had slackened its grip in the winter, scurvy had become much more virulent, and "Longfever" was beginning to run riot. A well stood to one end of the parade ground, and staircases led under the walls to eight-foot-deep bunkers, or casemates, which housed the magazine and a "laboratory" where shells were loaded with powder and fuzes were fixed.[7] In times of siege, the casements could also provide shelter from bombardment.[8] Beyond the walls, Eyre had ordered his provincial laborers to dig an encircling ditch eight feet deep and thirty feet wide. Complete with a single line of stockade posts, or palisade, it covered three sides of the fort, while the fourth, which housed the main gates, was protected by the lake.

From the gate, a rough road led thirty-five yards east along the shore to a "one hundred and sixty foot long" wharf, alongside which a small fleet of boats was dragged up on the beach. Among them was a single sloop, designed to carry ten to twelve cannons, a few dozen large whaleboats, "5 Bay Boats, 4 Gondolas," and more than two hundred smaller bateaux, or whaleboats.[9] Two smaller sloops, armed with four swivel guns, had been left in the water and had since become locked fast in the ice. A fourth, named the *Lord Loudoun* and the largest of them all, boasting gun ports for sixteen cannons, was half-finished and lay resting on trellises just fifteen paces from the walls.[10] On either side of the jetty were more wooden storehouses, a pile of cut timber, an old hospital taken over by "Levie the Jew," one of the fort's resident sutlers, and a small wooden stronghold housing Captain Stark's rangers.

Despite Eyre's best attempts, William Henry had its weaknesses. While inspecting the fort earlier that winter, Lord

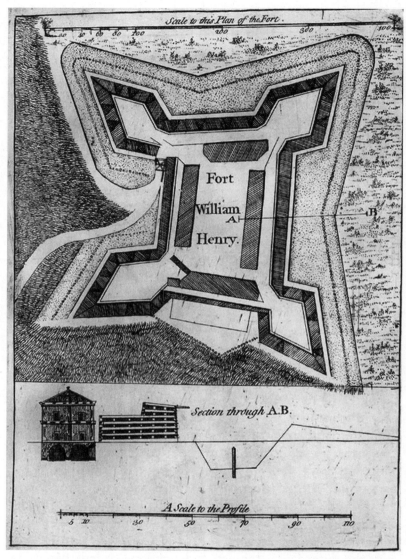

A plan of Fort William Henry published in 1765. The fort was designed by British major William Eyre and based on prevailing French principles of construction which included low, wide ramparts to absorb artillery fire and diamond-shaped bastions built on each corner to provide crossfire for the defenders. The walls were made of hard packed earth, buttressed with timber. Inside stood twin two-story barracks, several store sheds, and a hospital. Section A–B shows the profile of the fort. (*Library of Congress*)

Loudoun had noted that it had been "built on a running sand," a fault that ensured "that the ditch constantly fills up." He had also disapproved of the wood that had been used to construct the outer shell of the ramparts. "They have neither been careful to pick good timber . . . nor secured them well at the ends," the Scot reported, "and the sand [that filled the thirty-foot gap between the inner and outer walls] is so loose, that I am afraid if it were battered with cannon, it would run through between the logs."[11] The fort's proximity to the lake caused further problems. The water table was so high that some of the casemates periodically flooded, and the timbers used in their construction were beginning to rot.[12] Loudoun's final complaint concerned perhaps the most serious flaw in Eyre's design. The fort was overlooked by high ground three hundred yards to the southwest.[13] If the enemy was able to manhandle cannons up onto the rise, they could fire directly into the parade ground.

The night of Friday, March 18, was "the first day of the moon, and excessively dark."[14] Unknown to the British garrison, Rigaud's men had set off from Ganaouské Bay at eleven o'clock that night. Advancing in three columns, with Captain Poulharies's grenadiers on the right, they approached across the ice. Rigaud had ordered absolute silence, but as they neared the fort, a soldier's indiscipline betrayed them. Stamping and shivering as he paced the fort's ramparts, at 2 a.m. a sharp-eyed British sentry spotted a light out on the ice. Moments later the sound of ax blows was heard. Word was sent around the garrison, men were posted out by the shore of the lake, the rangers were ordered to come inside, and hungover Irishmen were shaken awake. Soon the walls were lined with troops, and even some of the sick roused themselves to man the defenses.[15] Rangers and regulars loaded their muskets with ball and listened intently for any sign of the enemy. Two hours later Major Eyre heard them. Then a sentry down by the lake fired. The report of his musket was echoed by a volley from the walls, and the night was shattered by the boom of one of the fort's 32-pounders.

With the element of surprise lost, Rigaud ordered the storming party to fall back. The retreat was chaotic. Fearing the cannons on the walls, several men dropped their ladders and arms as they ran. The British harassed them with a smattering of fire, but soon the night was silent once more. While his enemies stood listening on the walls, Rigaud decided to move on to his default plan: the destruction of the boats. At 4:30 a.m., a picket down by the lakeshore noticed a second group of Canadians and Indians advancing across the ice. As he opened fire, the movement was also noticed by the gunners on the walls behind him, who fired their 32-pounders. Discovered again, the French withdrew, only to repeat their efforts throughout the night. On each occasion they were frustrated. As dawn approached, they finally gave up and the whole body pulled back to Sloop Island, leaving two men dead on the ice, and dragging a wounded Indian behind them.[16]

With all seemingly peaceful once more, Major Eyre risked sending a small detachment out on a reconnaissance. He knew nothing of Rigaud's numbers and was desperate to gather what intelligence he could.[17] Strewn across the ice, his men discovered two abandoned ladders, several "Tommihawks, [and] Scalping Knives" and "several small implements for setting the vessels on fire." As the presence of the ladders indicated a numerous body of the enemy, Eyre ordered his men back to the fort. Once inside, the garrison settled in and waited for dawn.[18]

First light revealed the enemy. Gathered on the ice in front of Sloop Island, three miles distant from the fort, the fifteen hundred men made a daunting sight. Wrapped up in their winter furs and armed to the teeth, to the men on the walls they seemed "very numerous." Even Eyre was impressed.[19] There were "great numbers" of them "on the lake," the major reported, "and by degrees this grew more formidable." Later, a "large fire was seen on the east side of the lake about two miles down," and at 6 a.m. the main body of the enemy split into several small groups, each of which began making its way toward the fort along opposite sides of the lake. Eyre ordered his men to check everything was ready for action. Musket flints were replaced, extra ammunition issued, and the cannons and muskets were scoured, cleaned, and reloaded.

By 7 a.m. the French raiders were beginning to encircle the fort. Those advancing to the east crossed a hill that brought them in range of Eyre's cannons. It was the same spot on which William Johnson had built entrenchments and defeated the French and Canadian forces of Baron Dieskau eighteen months before. As each group crested the hill, Eyre "saluted them with some . . . grape[shot, fired] . . . from a 32 Pounder." The cannonade caused several casualties, and to the satisfaction of those watching from the walls "made . . . [the survivors] . . . Hoop and Yelp."[20] Later, a mortar shell tossed high into the morning air exploded among another group. Two Indians were wounded by the fizzing shell fragments, and one Canadian militiaman was blown to smithereens.[21]

Meanwhile, a party of regulars and Canadian militiamen were moving to the south to set an ambuscade across the road to Fort Edward in case any British reinforcements should appear.[22] As they moved into position, Eyre took a speculative shot with a 32-pounder. The ball crashed through the snow-blanketed woods and took off a Canadian's foot.[23] At 7 a.m., once the encirclement was complete, Indian and Canadian marksmen crawled in among the tree stumps to fire at the defenders. Their harassing fire would last until nightfall. With bullets whizzing overhead, the redcoats and rangers on the walls returned fire. At 9 a.m., Eyre ordered the signal guns to be fired to alert the garrison at Fort Edward of the French attack. Fourteen miles away, the gunners at Edward heard the cannons' report and answered them by firing signals of their own. Although he was still without direct support, at least Eyre now knew his superiors would soon be aware of his predicament.[24]

Later that afternoon, the French gathered in force behind some rocks five hundred yards to the east. Their fire swept the palisade, and Eyre returned it with his cannons. "Five or six" of the fort's garrison were lightly wounded during the day, as were a few of Rigaud's raiders who left bloody trails in the snow as their comrades dragged them clear.[25] While the firefight distracted the defenders' attention, Rigaud sent a group of Canadian militia to burn the boats on the lakeshore.[26] This time they were successful, and Eyre ordered some of his men to sally from the fort to extinguish the flames. The French turned all their fire toward them and drove them back inside.[27]

At nightfall, the marksmen among the tree trunks and behind the rocks to the east ceased fire. The British watched as the enemy withdrew into the darkness, and Fort William Henry was shrouded in silence once more. With nothing but a handful of half-burned bateaux to show for his exertions, Rigaud had no intention of retreating so soon. Once his men were out of sight, he halted and prepared for another attack against the boats. One hundred regulars of La Sarre and Béarn and two hundred militia were selected for the task.[28] Reaching their target undetected, they were able to set fire to one of the bateaux. The wind caught the flames and soon the entire line of boats was ablaze. Other raiders set the woodpile alight, but a third party was fired upon as it approached one of the sloops and was then driven off by cannon fire. By 2 a.m., the flames were leaping into the night sky and illuminated the ground for a full half mile around the fort. By the flickering light, a group of Frenchmen were seen approaching for a second attempt at a coup de main but were fired upon and swiftly dispersed. "Our Cannon Scatter'd them," one of the defenders recalled, "and killed some, which we could see by their Draggin the Dead away to the Ice [through] which they broke holes, and put them in."[29]

The next morning, seeing no sign of the enemy, Major Eyre sent out a small party to put out the fires that were still raging. The men managed to extinguish the woodpile, but several of the boats were beyond saving.[30] At 10 a.m. the enemy was seen crossing the lake in force. From Sloop Island the raiders marched across the ice to the west in an extended line, parading their ladders ostentatiously in the hope of intimidating the defenders. Watching from the ramparts, some of the British and provincials believed that the French column was about to march back to Carillon, but they were soon disappointed.[31] The French halted on the western shore two miles from the fort, where Rigaud and his senior commanders held a council of war. Having decided their next course of action, a flag party of twelve men led by Captain

Mercier approached the fort waving a red banner to indicate their intention to parley.[32]

Following the protocol of the age, Major Eyre sent a party of twelve led by Lt. Robert Drummond of the 44th to receive them. As the two parties closed, the men halted and the officers advanced alone across the ice. Watching impatiently from the fort, one of the rangers noted that "they had some Conference for a Considerable time," until "at length the [French] Officer delivered Lieut. Drummond a Letter Unsealed which he dispatched to . . . Major [Eyre]."[33] The two Europeans then chatted while awaiting the major's reply. Mercier told Drummond that he had been at the capture of Oswego, and the lieutenant also learned that the Frenchman was head of Montcalm's artillery train. Within a few minutes Lt. Adam Williamson, a young engineer who had been wounded at Monongahela, crossed the ice with an invitation from Eyre for Mercier to enter the fort. The French engineer was then blindfolded and escorted inside. Having learned of the killing of British prisoners following the surrender at Oswego, the troops watched him nervously as he entered, hoping that their commander would not put them at the mercy of the French and their "savage" allies by accepting his terms.[34]

After exchanging the expected pleasantries, Mercier informed Eyre and his fellow officers that Rigaud was "averse to the carrying on a war in these parts, [and] regretted much the miseries that attended it," but he was nevertheless obliged by his loyalty to King Louis XV, and the fact that the British had encroached on His Majesty's territory, to desire the immediate capitulation of the fort. In return, he offered the British their lives and liberty and the opportunity to carry off "their most valuable effects," stipulating only that they leave behind some trifles "to gratify the Indians." Mercier also assured them "that they need not be under any apprehension of mischief from the savages for . . . [he] had a sufficient number of regulars to protect the garrison" from any eventuality. Then came the sting: should Eyre refuse to surrender and the fort be taken by storm, "Circumstances very fatal and calamitous" could follow. The Indians, in such a situation, could not possibly be controlled.[35]

Eyre was unconcerned. He dismissed Mercier's message as a poor attempt at a ruse de guerre. With neither cannons nor the element of surprise, the French had no hope of taking the fort by storm.[36] Nevertheless, Mercier was not dismissed immediately. Begging time to consult his fellow officers in an adjacent room, Eyre decided to turn the truce to his own advantage. Stepping outside, he assured his men he had no thought of surrender. After quieting their hurrahs and yells of "Monongahela and revenge," he ordered some of them to tear down the roofs of the remaining storehouses by the lake, knowing that should they be set alight, the flames could spread to the fort.[37] Only once this was complete did Eyre give Mercier his reply: "I will defend his Majesty's fort to the last extremity." After issuing one more threat about the impossibility of controlling the Indians in the event of a successful attack, Mercier was blindfolded once more and led back to his flag party, which was still waiting on the ice.[38]

While Mercier's party returned to Rigaud, Eyre sent two of Captain Stark's rangers to Fort Edward with news of the siege and then made some final preparations for the assault he was sure would follow. "The Major came out on the Bastions," one of the defenders recalled, "[and] Order'd Sand Baggs to be fill'd and . . . laid round . . . [and] the Ramparts & Swivles to be Erected . . . [as he was] expecting to be Attack'd more fierce than ever."[39]

Disappointed with his enemy's reply, Rigaud prepared for a fresh assault. The grenadiers of Royal Roussillon and Languedoc were sent to block the road to Fort Edward, while Indian and Canadian marksmen crawled in close to the walls and began a harassing fire from the cleared ground.[40] Once again, the men on the ramparts returned fire with musketry and swivel guns while "[Eyre] went round the Bastions telling the Men, that the French would give no Quarter." His troops reacted well. According to one of the rangers, they "were not in the least Daunted nor dismay'd but laughed at the Frenchs firing, and . . . a great many of the Men who lay sick for two or three Weeks before came out on the Bastions with their Arms willing to partake the same Fate with their brethren before the Fort should be deliver'd . . . to the French."[41]

As night fell, Rigaud went after the storehouses and the remaining boats by the lake. The grenadiers of La Sarre and Béarn supported the Canadian and Indian incendiary parties with covering fire. Nevertheless, they were driven back from the sloops by heavy musketry and artillery fire from the northeast bastion. "Our Men watching their motions, sent some of them out of the land of the living," one of the rangers recalled.[42] The night was extremely dark, however, and later the French managed to cause great destruction with little loss to themselves. First, the rangers' stockade was set alight, then the storehouses and the sutler's hut belonging to Levi. As the French withdrew, the flames leapt into the sky sending showers of burning embers raining down onto the fort. For Eyre and his men, who suffered "terrible apprehensions of having our barracks set on fire," it was another exhausting night.[43]

On Monday morning the French withdrew from sight, leaving only a handful "of . . . stragglers" behind who fired a few shots in the predawn light. At 9:00 a.m. it began snowing heavily, and the fires that had been burning all night were put out. The French stragglers, unable to keep their powder dry, ceased firing, and the land fell silent once more. The snow continued all day and night, allowing Eyre's men to get a little rest and tend to their wounded. With the limited visibility, the major could not be sure if Rigaud had gone back to Carillon, or whether the temporary lull was merely another ruse to catch the garrison off guard.[44]

Meanwhile, in the French camp, just out of sight from the fort in the woods to the west of Lake George, morale was deteriorating. The weather was freezing, the snow soaked everything not covered by sealskin, the wounded were suffering terribly from the cold, and rations were running so low that in the evening they were forced to slaughter one of the packhorses for sustenance.[45] The Indians, who still insisted on extra supplies, were close to giving up, and the men's morale was sinking ever lower.[46] That night, Rigaud resolved to return home as soon as the weather offered an opportunity, but, as it continued to snow on the morning of the twenty-second, he decided to spend one more day in the vicinity of the fort.[47] That afternoon, Captain Poulharies was approached by Lieutenant Wolff, who offered to lead a final attack against the sloop lying close under the walls. Poulharies agreed, and at dusk Wolff set out with twenty volunteers.[48]

From the northeast bastion, Major Eyre watched them advance. He had hoped he had seen the last of the raiders and was determined that they should not cause more damage to the boats. Ordering his men to line the walls, he gave the signal to open fire. Time and time again, Wolff was driven back by musket volleys as he tried to approach the sloop, which was so close to the fort that its bowsprit was touching one of the bastions.[49] Two of his men, volunteers from the Languedoc Regiment, were killed and one other lightly wounded, but still Wolff persevered. At 11 p.m. the German finally achieved his aim. Moving under cover of one of the woodpiles, he made a dash for the boat and set it alight with one of Mercier's devices. With his mission complete, the German withdrew, leaving the defenders to watch impotently as the flames whipped up around *Lord Loudoun*. Although Wolff had ordered his men to remove their dead and wounded, a few were left behind. "We could here one Miserable Fellow . . . groan all Night," one of the rangers recalled.[50]

The next morning, with the sloop still burning fiercely, but no sign of the enemy, Major Eyre ordered Lt. Charles Philip Brewer to take a detachment of regulars and do a sweep around the fort.[51] They soon found John Victor, the militiaman who had thought the going easy on the way from Carillon, hiding in the swamp to the east of the walls. Victor, who had been wounded in one of the attacks on the boats, had passed a miserable night in the cold and was glad to be taken into Eyre's quarters for interrogation. Later that morning, the regulars discovered two more of the enemy had also been left behind. A badly wounded man was brought in, but died shortly afterward in the hospital, while a French grenadier named Guillaume Chasse was found behind one of the woodpiles. He later explained that "the blaze had given off so much light, that he was afraid of being seen and shot down if he [had] attempted to run off, so he [had] hid himself near it, till the garrison found him."[52]

By the time the interrogations had begun, Rigaud and his men were already on their way back to Carillon. The night

before, following Wolff's success, they had packed up camp
and set off to the north after burning the remaining siege ladders. Some of the Indians, having discovered several barrels of
alcohol in one of the outbuildings they had destroyed, had
become hopelessly intoxicated and had to be shaken awake
before the column could move out.[53] Unable to bury the dead
in the frozen ground, the French had stuffed several corpses
into a hole in the ice. Another was put into a pile of wood that
they set alight before leaving, and a dead Indian, whose scalp
had been removed by his comrades for the bounty money paid
in Montréal, was left buried under a pile of snow.

Since the start of the operation, the weather had been
against Rigaud, and on the march back across Lake George
conditions continued to deteriorate. A heavy fall of sleet and
a rise in temperature brought on a thaw, which made the
march miserable for the dozen wounded. Among them was
Captain Poulharies, the commander of the regulars, who had
burned his hand during one of the attempts to set fire to the
boats.[54] The sleighs, which could only function on solid ice,
had to be abandoned, and the men pushed on as best they
could on foot, leaving a trail of discarded equipment behind
them. When the column finally staggered into Carillon on
the twenty-fourth, "scattered and much dejected," they realized that one of the French grenadiers, "a very brave man
called Basin," was missing.[55] Blinded by the snow, Basin had
become separated from the column and would spend three
days staggering alone across the ice before reaching
Carillon.[56]

Back at Fort William Henry, Major Eyre was feeling rather
pleased with himself. Although over half of the British fleet
on Lake George was now reduced to ashes, his men had not
suffered a single fatality. Among the dozen or so who had
been lightly wounded while manning the palisade was Capt.
John Stark. The ranger had been grazed by a musket ball, the
only time he would be hit during his entire military career.[57]
With the excitement of the raid behind them, the redcoats of
the 44th were now looking forward to being relieved. They
had been garrisoning Fort William Henry throughout the
winter, and as they had been suffering badly from scurvy even

before the siege had begun, Loudoun had promised Eyre he would send fresh troops as soon as the weather allowed.

On March 29 relief arrived. Five companies of the 35th Regiment of Foot led by Lt. Col. George Monro wound their way down the track from Fort Edward, and the defenders received them with heartfelt huzzahs. The colonel, having met Eyre's messenger on his march from Albany, had abandoned all unnecessary baggage and led his men at the double, hoping to reach the fort in time to aid the defenders. En route they had slept under "Bush tents of Pine boughs" with "great fires" to warm them.[58] Loudoun later praised the 35th for the troops' endurance on the march, which he claimed they put up with "with the greatest cheerfulness." It seemed that the regiment had improved. Terrible as the men may have been just a few months before, Monro's strict leadership and insistence on drill and weapons practice had done them some good. What had once been a green regiment unworthy of frontline service had become a capable fighting machine.[59]

4

The Provincials

April–May 1757

As Monro's men were settling into the barracks at Fort William Henry, in Albany Lord Loudoun was putting the finishing touches to his plans for that summer's campaign. After the failures of 1756, the Scot intended to use the majority of his regulars to launch a decisive strike against Québec while covering the northern frontier with his remaining redcoats and the provincials. Loudoun's plan was daring and had the potential to end the war with a single stroke, but it also involved a considerable element of risk. If the army failed to capture Québec by the onset of winter, it would be caught in hostile country, surrounded by enemies, and liable to destruction. Whether or not Loudoun would have succeeded is a matter of speculation, for back in London, William Pitt, the preeminent British politician of the age, had other plans. Although not radically different to Loudoun's, Pitt's strategy, formulated in late 1756, involved a greater element of caution. Rather than going straight for New France's jugular, he planned a two-year offensive. The first stage was to strike a blow against Louisbourg, a heavily defended fortress known as the Gibraltar of the north, which controlled the entrance to the Gulf of Saint Lawrence. Once taken, the port could be used the following year as a staging post for subsequent attacks on Québec and Montréal.[1]

While the main body of the army was to be employed against Louisbourg, the secondary task of defending the New York frontier would fall to Maj. Gen. Daniel Webb, Loudoun's third in command. A "timid, melancholic" and "diffident" officer, Webb suffered from poor health and had shown a tendency toward cowardice in the aftermath of the loss of Oswego the previous summer.[2] Under this less than inspirational commander, Loudoun would leave what he considered his least capable troops. Divided between Forts Edward and William Henry and the barracks of Albany, Saratoga, and German Flats were Monro's 35th Regiment of Foot; the 3rd Battalion of the 60th, or Royal Americans, a regular regiment recently raised in the colonies as well as in Europe; two independent companies from New York; and five thousand provincial troops.[3]

Raising the provincials was not easy. Loudoun found the vacillations of their representatives exasperating. Insisting that the British Crown pay all their expenses, the colonies' general assemblies blocked the Scot's demands at every turn. Nevertheless, Loudoun was equal to the task. Using a combination of thinly veiled threats and begrudgingly conceded compromises, he persuaded the general assemblies of New England to meet his demands. Massachusetts, a colony that had supplied large numbers of recruits in 1755, contributed 1,800 men under Col. Joseph Frye; Connecticut raised 1,400 under Col. Phineas Lyman; and New Jersey, a colony that had suffered heavy losses at Oswego, mustered 531, just 50 percent of what Loudoun required. The latter were led by Col. John Parker, another veteran of King George's War.[4] New York raised a single company of 57 men under Capt. Robert McGinnis, while 500 volunteered from New Hampshire, 231 of whom, under Lieutenant Colonel Gough, would join Monro's regulars at Fort William Henry that summer. The rest were to accompany Loudoun to Louisbourg under Col. Nathaniel Meserve, an "active, sensible man" with "few scruples," and one of the few provincial officers that Loudoun considered competent.[5]

Once the assemblies had agreed to raise their quotas, the process of forming the provincial regiments began. In

February 1757, the assemblies named the colonels who would lead them. These were locally significant, respected figures and were well known in the community. Once selected, each colonel received a pack of blank commissions for ensigns, lieutenants, captains, and majors to distribute as he saw fit. Many would go to men who had previously served under the colonel in question; others were given to family members or people he knew from the local area. Unlike the regular officers, who were almost exclusively selected from the upper tier of British society, not all of those commissioned in the provincial regiments were considered "gentlemen." Indeed, it was not uncommon for laborers and farmers to attain the lower commissioned ranks.[6]

Once the officers had been selected, each was responsible for raising a specific quota of men. Captains were expected to muster fifty, lieutenants twenty-five, and ensigns fifteen. To help them raise their quotas, the junior officers often made informal deals with their subordinates. A man would be promised the rank of sergeant, for example, on the condition that he gathered five men. Such a system produced units that had little in common with their red-coated counterparts. While the regulars were starkly divided between those with commissions and those without, the provincials were much more closely knit, and the lines between the commanders and the men that they led were often blurred. Many were related or would have known each other intimately, having grown up in the same rural communities, received the same basic schooling, and attended the same church. Sons served alongside fathers, brothers with brothers, and landlords enlisted the men who would otherwise be working their fields.[7]

Provincial recruiting practices also differed from those employed by the regular units. While many of the redcoats in the 35th had been forcibly impressed, or at the least coerced into service, the provincials were nearly all volunteers.[8] Although the colonels had the right to press men from the idle elements of society if they could not fulfill their quotas, such strictures were often unnecessary, as in many ways the life of a provincial volunteer was an attractive one.[9] As well as earning a monthly wage of one pound and sixteen shillings

A 1761 print of a New York frontier settlement. The original caption was printed in both English and French. Provincial American soldiers were drawn from communities like this one for the war against France in North America. (*Library of Congress*)

(double what the redcoats received), each of the private soldiers enlisted into Colonel Frye's Massachusetts regiment, for example, stood to earn a signing-up bonus of four pounds and twelve shillings. If the recruit stayed with the army for the entire eight months of the campaign, this would result in an overall haul of eighteen pounds, ten shillings, and sevenpence, enough to buy 150 acres of land.[10]

The New England provincials were far more homogenous than the regulars. The vast majority of Frye's battalion had been born in the colonies where they were recruited. Most of the rest were from elsewhere in New England or from the colonies to the south, although there were also a few who had been born in Europe, including a Frenchman in Capt. Samuel Thaxter's company who had deserted from his own army in a previous campaign and now served among his former enemies.[11]

The majority of the provincial rank and file was in their midtwenties. Their officers averaged a decade older. Aside from a few born in the cities of Boston and New York, many came from small towns, villages, and hamlets lost in the backwoods of rural New England. As one nineteenth-century historian phrased it, "they came . . . from plain . . . Homesteads—rustic abodes, unpainted and dingy, with long well-sweeps, capacious barns, rough fields of pumpkin and corn, and vast kitchen chimneys, above which in winter hung squashes to keep them from frost."[12] Many had been farmers or laborers, a few had worked as traders, victualers, or tobacconists, and a significant minority were artisans who fashioned tools or clothing from leather, metal, or cloth.[13]

Among the mainly white recruits were a few "negroes" and a number of Indians. Some of the blacks were freedmen (such as Thomas Henry, a troublemaker from Capt. Adonijah Fitch's company), a large number of whom lived along the frontier by the mid-eighteenth century. Others were slaves accompanying their masters, such as Jock Linn of the Massachusetts regiment, who belonged to Nathaniel Whittimore, or Caesar Nero Paul, a sixteen-year-old owned by Maj. John Gilman of the New Hampshire provincials.[14]

The Indians were Mohawks or displaced Mohegans, Pequots, Nipmucks, and Mahicans. The New England homelands of the latter groups had been swallowed up in the past 150 years by the expansion of the colonies of Connecticut and Massachusetts. As a result, many were left homeless and destitute. The signing-up bonus and regular pay were significant lures, and many joined the ranks of the provincial regiments raised that spring.[15] Among those in the Connecticut provincials were Henry Shuntup, a veteran of the 1755 and 1756 campaigns, and William Mortawamock, a Mohawk from Capt. John Slapp's company who would meet a particularly grisly end.[16]

Several of the provincial troops who marched toward the frontier that spring had some military experience. A handful of the older volunteers had seen action during King George's War, and a few had served in 1755 and 1756. Many of John Parker's New Jersey Blues, so called for the color of their uniforms, had fought alongside their colonel at the fall of Oswego, and several of the Massachusetts and Connecticut volunteers had been at the Battle of Lake George the year before. Among them was a young lieutenant named David Titcomb, who had "behaved well" all day and had distinguished himself by pursuing the enemy when they fled the field late in the afternoon.[17] The majority of the provincials of 1757, however, were young and naive, and many had never even left their home counties before. In addition to the looming possibility of financial independence, a major draw for such men was the prospect of adventure and an opportunity to see the northern frontier.[18]

Adventure was no doubt a motivation for Luke Gridley, a twenty-two-year-old from Farmington, Connecticut, who served as a private under Colonel Lyman. As well as being an apprentice blacksmith, Gridley was also a keen diarist and recorded his experiences in exacting detail.[19] His journal of 1757 opens on April 8 with the volunteers for Capt. Edward Payson's company gathering at Farmington to receive their muskets and blankets and swear an oath of allegiance to George II. On the eighteenth, each man received his enlistment bonus and first month's wages, as well as an extra allowance for "Biliting" to cover the expenses he would incur on the march. With the three pounds, eighteen shillings, and ninepence in his pack and his Brown Bess musket slung over his shoulder, Gridley left Farmington four days later. He would not return home for seven months.[20]

Captain Payson's men spent the first seven days of the campaign marching. Following cut-up cart tracks, they wound their way through the Connecticut countryside. The trip was quite an education for Gridley and his fellow recruits. As they strolled through the spring sunshine, they eagerly took in the sights.[21] On the twenty-sixth, they reached the village of Cornwall and slept at widow Sedgwick's inn. The next day, they marched eight miles to dine at landlord Robbins's in Canaan, before continuing to Salisbury, where they passed the night at landlord Reeds's. On the twenty-eighth, the hundred-strong column crossed the Connecticut–New York border, no doubt a momentous occasion for those who had never left their home counties before. Later that day they passed by Livingston Forge, an iron foundry built on the banks of the Roeliff Jansen Kill River by an immigrant Scot who provided cannonballs and musket ammunition for the war.[22] In the area was a quarantine house where just a fortnight before, three men had died of smallpox.[23] On the twenty-ninth they reached the village of Claverack, a Dutch farming community built beside the King's Highway, where they had arranged to meet the other companies of Lyman's regiment.[24]

The next morning, Gridley and a few companions decided to walk the three miles to the Hudson River. At 650 yards across, it was the largest watercourse that he had ever seen. Struck by its beauty, Gridley left his fellow recruits to stroll five miles upriver. May the first was the Sabbath, always a special event for the pious New Englanders. As the regiment's chaplain had still not joined them, the men decided to hold a service of their own. It is difficult to underestimate the importance of religion in these men's lives. The influence of the church was ever present, the Sabbath was strictly observed, profanity was not tolerated, and blasphemy nigh unheard of. The men often "sought out their pastors for guidance and resorted to religious books for solace; they took notes on sermons and independently evaluated the quality of what they had heard."[25] Those who strayed from the true faith were harshly dealt with, and although the Salem witch trials that had seen twenty men and women executed in 1692 had not since been repeated, an atmosphere of religious intolerance prevailed. Many provincials saw military service as an extension of their commitment to the church. As their preachers never failed to remind them, the papist sinners of New France and their heathen allies were the instruments of Satan. If God's chosen people were to prosper, these blasphemers had to be wiped from the face of the earth.[26]

On May 2 Colonel Lyman, the commander of Gridley's regiment, arrived at Claverack. Born in Durham, Connecticut, in 1716 to a family of weavers, the forty-one-year-old was an intelligent and experienced commander, to whom even the British regular officers begrudgingly showed respect.[27] After graduating from Yale in 1738, he had worked as a tutor for three years, before studying law and starting his own practice at Suffield, then part of Massachusetts. Within eight years, Lyman had had the town annexed to his native Connecticut and was appointed to the upper chamber of the colony's legislature as a result. In March 1755, with the threat from New France increasing, Lyman gave up his lucrative position to join the army and later that year took part in the Battle of Lake George. After William Johnson had been wounded early in the fighting, Lyman had taken charge and was instrumental in repulsing the waves of attackers that pressed in on the fortified camp throughout the afternoon. Although he had performed bravely, Lyman received little credit, as Johnson insisted on keeping all the praise for himself. Nevertheless, Lyman once again answered the assembly's call the following year and led a detachment of twenty-five hundred men to Lake George. A capable and enthusiastic soldier, who liked to wear Mohawk war paint when he went into battle, Lyman was a good leader and trusted by his men, but, aside from the battle of 1755, had little experience of actual combat.[28]

With Lyman's arrival, the easygoing atmosphere in the camp at Claverack began to change. Once the colonel had installed himself and his staff at Fondie's, the best inn in town, he proceeded to dash off a series of general orders.[29] Guards were posted at all hours and the regiment was required to parade at 7 a.m. and 7 p.m. daily. The men had to turn out with "hats cocked . . . guns bright and . . . clothes clean." As Gridley noted, "this set some of us to washing quick" and on the first day prompted a dawn rush down to the river.[30] Once the troops were drawn up, the officers paced the lines "to Note every Defect" and report any man who failed to meet the required standard. From ten to twelve o'clock in the morning, and again from four to six o'clock in the afternoon, the men were exercised; and at seven o'clock in the evening a final parade was called, following which the troops were dismissed for the day.[31]

On May 4 training began. Drill did not come easily to the free-willed men of New England. The sergeants had their work cut out, and individuals who did not meet their standards were called out from the ranks for extra drill. On the fifth, Gridley was among the twenty-two men assigned guard duty. The task came as something of a relief, as it meant he was not required for drill. Still eighty miles south of the frontier, the chances of attack by an enemy raiding party were slim, and the guards spent most of the day fishing. Provisions had been scarce since they had arrived, and the sturgeon plucked from the Hudson made a welcome change from the meager quantities of bread, rice, beans, and salt pork on which they typically subsisted.[32] Having eaten their fill, the men passed the rest of the day amusing one another. To the delight and disgust of those watching, "Jonathan Beamman," a thirty-seven-year-old from Middlesex County, Massachusetts, ate three raw fish, "guts and all," as a wager. He kept down his "meal" and won "4 quarts of wine" as a result.[33]

On May 10 the routine was broken. After coming back from a fishing trip on which he had seen a six-foot sturgeon, Gridley was present at the first of many exhibitions of corporal punishment that he would witness that year. "One of Cap Gaplops [Benadam Gallup] negros [was] whipped for threting of killing a man."[34] The next day, the Connecticut provincials broke camp and set out for Schaghticoke. An Indian village populated by refugees from the New England tribes pushed north in the previous century by the British colonists' expansion, Schaghticoke was just twenty miles south of Fort Edward and was used as a staging post by the army.[35] En route they passed through Kinderhook, a Dutch town first settled over a century and a half before, famed for its meeting-house—an unusual building that seemed impossibly exotic to the little-traveled New Englanders.[36] On May 14, near the village of Troy, the men were issued with nine rounds of ammunition, the first they had been given since joining up. Later that day, they reached Schaghticoke, where the Connecticut men were joined by Colonel Frye's Massachusetts regiment.

Born in 1709 at Andover, Col. Joseph Frye was among the most experienced of all the provincial troops who would gather on the northern frontier that summer. Yet for the first thirty-six years of his life, his career had been unremarkable. While working as a farmer on the family estate, he had married Mehitable Poor sometime in the 1730s. Over the next decade the couple had eleven children, two of whom died in the great diphtheria epidemic of 1738. For the times, such a biography was far from unusual, but Frye's world radically changed in 1745. As an ensign in Col. Robert Hale Jr.'s regiment, he received his baptism of fire at the siege of Louisbourg, an eminently successful expedition that had been the main source of Massachusetts's martial pride ever since. One of the opening acts of King George's War, as the War of Austrian Succession was known in America, the siege saw thirty-five hundred volunteers from Massachusetts and New Hampshire sail to Cape Breton to attack the legendary French fortress. Largely due to the defenders' incompetence, Louisbourg fell in seven weeks. Buoyed by the glory he had gained, and enamored by the soldier's lifestyle, Frye remained in the service until the end of King George's War, when he returned to Massachusetts and was elected to serve with the general court. With the renewal of hostilities six years later, Frye was recommissioned. In 1755, he was promoted to major and served alongside Col. John Winslow at the siege of Fort Beauséjour in Acadia. Following the French surrender, Frye was charged with burning 250 Acadian homesteads and was actively involved in the inhabitants' forced deportation.[37]

By the time they reached Schaghticoke, many of Frye's men had already been marching for twenty days. Among them was Rufus Putnam, a nineteen-year-old apprentice millwright from Sutton, Massachusetts. Like his comrade Luke Gridley in the Connecticut regiment, Putnam was a keen diarist. His journal details his company's journey from Springfield, through the Green Woods to Kinderhook, and on to Schaghticoke. So far, the trip had been uneventful, the only points of note for Putnam being Capt. Ebenezer Learned's prayer meetings and the fact that the stores the company had drawn in Kinderhook "were very mean and scanty." On May 19, however, just five days after their arrival in the Mohegan village, the provincials got their first taste of action.[38]

That morning, while out hunting the New England wood pigeons that flocked in such enormous numbers prior to their spring migration that their bodies darkened the sky, a local boy had been attacked by French-allied Indians.[39] Having seen his assailants approaching, he had taken to his heels and the Indians, perhaps Abenaki from Saint Francis or marauding Ottawa from the high country, had opened fire. Five bullets passed through the boy's shirt as he ran, but none did any damage. When he stumbled into the provincial camp minutes later, the alarm gun was fired and patrols were sent out to intercept the raiders. The provincials stood little hope of catching the fleet-footed Indians in the woods, and they returned empty-handed.[40]

In response, Colonel Lyman issued orders forbidding hunting parties to leave camp without his express permission, the daily guard was raised to 109 men, and the Massachusetts regiment was issued with ammunition.[41] Many had no experience of firearms, and the results were predictable. The following morning Jedediah Winslow, a young recruit in Putnam's company, was shot through the hip when one of his comrade's guns went off accidently. Considering the low standards of eighteenth-century surgery, Winslow was remarkably lucky: the ball was cut out the same day, and although he would miss the rest of the campaign, in less than two weeks he was seen hobbling about on crutches. On the twenty-second the provincials continued their march to the north. Traveling by "an intolerably bad road," they arrived at Stillwater that afternoon and at Saratoga on the twenty-third.[42] There they set up camp in the shadow of Fort Hardy, a "bad picquetted fort" built on the east bank of the Hudson at its confluence with the Fishkill River. The spot was a pleasant one, where both "Water and air [were] good," and the men spent a couple of idle days fishing for the abundant alewife (a species of freshwater herring), giant sturgeon, or twelve-pound salmon trout, and hunting in the surrounding pine forest for deer.[43] Others spent their time writing letters home or gathered in small groups to sing, accompanied by the flute and violin. On the twenty-fifth, this idyll was shattered by the sudden implementation of British army discipline.

The night before, Daniel Boake, a serial offender from Capt. Benadam Gallup's company whose name would frequently adorn the regimental court-martial register that summer, had fallen asleep on guard duty. As Saratoga lay just twenty miles south of the frontier and had often been attacked by raiding parties over the last fifty years, the crime was treated with the utmost gravity. At 11 a.m. the next day, a regimental court-martial was convened under Colonel Lyman, Captain Slapp, Lieutenants Wells, Nicholas Nichols, and John Stoughton, and Ensign Elijah Porter.[44] After a brief hearing, Boake was sentenced to run the gauntlet. At sunset, thirty of his comrades, armed with heavy sticks, formed an aisle for him to pass down. Boake then shuffled forward, stripped to the waist. As he passed, each man rained blows down upon him while a sergeant held a halberd to his chest to prevent him from running through.[45] As Gridley observed, the punishment was "a sorrowfull sight." Boake cried out, "Lord god have mercy on me," and "the B[l]ood [went] flying [with] every stroke."[46]

The severity of Boake's punishment was a shock for the provincials. Prior to the campaign of 1757, they had employed their own code of conduct, and punishments had been comparatively lenient. Loudoun had since changed the rules and, officially, the provincials now suffered the same draconian system under which the redcoats had toiled for years. In practice, however, provincial commanders tried to wean their men away from the former code onto the latter, knowing that if their troops were suddenly exposed to the full brutality of redcoat discipline, they might rise up and rebel. Just six days before Boake ran the gauntlet, for example, Colonel Lyman had given another offender a last minute reprieve. The man in question was Teuset, an Indian recruit and one of the regiment's best hunters whose name was given as John Hatchet on the Connecticut roll. After refusing to obey an order, Teuset was put under guard, and a whipping post was set up. The whole regiment was paraded, but as Teuset was led out he begged forgiveness, and Lyman pardoned him on the understanding that the men had now all been warned.[47]

The day after Boake's punishment the Massachusetts troops marched south. Half of them headed for the mills three miles downriver, while the rest went on to Stillwater.[48] The Connecticut regiment, meanwhile, was ordered north to Fort Edward. Their tents pulled down and packed away, Lyman's men began marching out of camp at 8 a.m. They waded over the Hudson to the east bank before turning north.

Although the road was "good but narrow," the march was slow, and several stops were made. At noon, shortly after they had passed Fort Miller, or Fort Misery, as it was known to the wags of the regiment for its location "in a low unwholesome ground," the men stopped "and refresh[ed]" themselves "by a brook." Seven miles by "very bad roads" later, they reached the outskirts of Fort Edward, where they made camp for the night.[49] Jabez Fitch, a twenty-year-old sergeant and veteran of the 1756 campaign, pitched his tent, prepared some hot chocolate, and then settled back to enjoy some "good entertainment."[50] To the accompaniment of flutes, fiddles, and jew's harps, the men sang and danced while sharing bottles of New England rum. Later, the music was replaced by nervous fireside discussions, and over the course of the evening, perhaps Fitch was asked to tell the newcomers about his experiences the previous year. If so, his stories would have done little to prepare them for their fate that summer. At Lake George, 1756 had been the year of the campaign that never was. No major engagements had occurred on the northern frontier and few lives had been lost. Seventeen fifty-seven was to be a very different matter indeed.

5

Fort Edward

May–June 1757

$\mathcal{T}$wice the size of Fort William Henry, Fort Edward was
situated on the banks of the upper Hudson River,
fourteen miles to the southeast of its sister fortification.
Commanding the overland portage route to Lakes George
and Champlain, and therefore the entire New York–Montréal
corridor, the strategic value of the site had long been known.
Generations before first contact with the Europeans, the
Mohawks, whose trails crisscrossed the area, had christened it
Wahcoloosencoochaleva, or the "Great Carrying Place." In
1709, during Queen Anne's War, the British had built Fort
Nicholson, a simple wooden stockade, on the site. When the
war ended in 1713, Nicholson was abandoned, only to be
rebuilt twenty-two years later by Henry Lydius.

Known to his enemies as "the Perfidious," Lydius was a
one-eyed Dutch smuggler from Albany. Having lived in the
missions of New France for several years, he established himself as a key player in the fur trade and married a "half breed,"
Genevieve Massé, with whom he had two children. Lydius
was later banished by the authorities in Montréal, who
believed he might turn the Indians against them. After
returning to his native New York, he rebuilt Nicholson as a
trading post, renamed it Fort Lydius, and began to control the

flow of contraband between Montréal and Albany. This trade was extremely profitable for all involved. Dealing with Lydius, the Indians received "excellent cloth [sufficient] to make a dozen blankets . . . [in exchange for] 33 beaver skins." The French, by contrast, "demanded" twice the number of skins for the same amount of cloth, but of a considerably inferior quality.[1] Lydius's post prospered until its destruction by Canadian and Indian raiders in November 1745 forced the Dutchman to return to Albany.[2]

Ten years later Col. Phineas Lyman, then second in command of William Johnson's northern expeditionary force, also saw the area's potential. Weeks before his run-in with Baron Dieskau at the Battle of Lake George, Lyman ordered the construction of a fort on the site. His men named it Fort Lyman in his honor, only for Johnson to rechristen it Fort Edward in recognition of George II's grandson, the future Duke of York.[3] William Eyre, the British engineer also responsible for the design of Fort William Henry, had overseen its construction.

Following the innovations of Sébastien le Prestre de Vauban, Eyre had built a low-lying, sturdy log fort. It was surrounded by ditches, embankments, and palisades on three sides, with the fourth protected by a shallow brook that ran into the Hudson River from the east. A V-shaped outwork known as a ravelin protruded from the north wall, and bastions jutted out from three of the fort's four corners. The fourth, pressed up close to the banks of the Hudson River, was deemed unapproachable. A main gate in the north wall, and a secondary entrance to the south, led to a central parade ground of compacted earth. To the east and west stood twin two-story barracks, 18 feet wide, 16 feet high, and 110 and 160 feet long, respectively.[4] Also within the walls were a blacksmith's shop, a guardhouse, and several provision sheds. The fort's powder magazine was housed inside the east bastion, and casemates lay under its walls.[5] Fort Edward had an impressive armament. Thirty-five guns lined the ramparts, including two howitzers and four mortars, and a supply of two hundred "Handgrenades" were held in the stores.[6]

In the early summer of 1757, Fort Edward was alive with activity. Some three thousand regulars, provincials, and civilians were based in the area, making the fort and its accompanying encampment the fourth largest settlement in the American colonies. By virtue of his king's commission, Maj. Henry Fletcher of the 35th was in overall command. Along with five companies of his own regiment, which were quartered in the fort, the thirty-four-year-old had two other units of regular troops: a two-hundred-strong detachment of the 3rd Battalion of the 60th, or Royal Americans, and two companies of New York Independents under Capt. Charles Crookshanks.[7]

Raised by a parliamentary decree issued in January 1756, the 3rd Battalion of the 60th was an amalgamation of Englishmen, Irishmen, and locally recruited Americans, mixed with a significant contingent raised from the German nations allied to Britain during the Seven Years' War. Many of the latter, recruited under false pretenses by the charismatic yet unscrupulous Col. Jacques Prevost, were already disillusioned and were beginning to complain of the broken promises that had induced them to sign up. While awaiting the arrival of its regimental commander, Lt. Col. John Young from Albany, the contingent at Fort Edward was led by an intriguing character, a Swiss-born mercenary named Capt. Rudolphus Faesch. A "subaltern . . . in the French service till August 1756," Faesch had fought against the British on the European front before heading for the New World with the Royal Americans. Charming, professional, and courageous, Faesch would serve his new masters well.[8]

Major Fletcher also had two thousand provincial troops under his command. Although Colonel Frye's Massachusetts regiment would not arrive until mid-June, alongside Colonel Lyman's Connecticut volunteers were units from Rhode Island, New York, and New Jersey. The latter marched for Fort William Henry on May 29, just three days after Lyman's arrival. Sergeant Jabez Fitch watched them go. Marching out of camp with a fife player at their head, the column of five hundred men was accompanied by "10 Waggons & 36 Carts" and a number of wives, mistresses, laundresses, nurses, and prostitutes.[9] Fitch appreciated the music, but disapproved of the New Jersey Blues' consorts. The protocol of the pious New Englanders from Connecticut and Massachusetts did not allow women to travel with the troops, but the regiments raised in New York, Rhode Island, and New Jersey were a different matter.[10] Such issues had caused friction since the birth of the colonies, and in 1755 they had prompted Phineas Lyman to complain that the prostitutes "g[ave] a very great uneasiness" to his men. The colonel feared "Sacrificing all our Character" and worried that his troops would grow so outraged that they would "either mob or privately destroy" them.[11]

Also present at Fort Edward that spring were two companies of rangers. Dressed in greens and browns to blend into their environment and armed with an assortment of muskets, tomahawks, and hunting knives, the rangers were an elite unit trained in backwoods warfare in order to counter the enemy's Indian allies. The sergeants and rank and file had at first been raised exclusively from among the rugged frontier woodsmen of New Hampshire, but by 1757 their commander, Maj. Robert Rogers, was also selecting recruits from the provincial regiments of New England, and even some red-coated regulars were accepted. An effective soldier, Rogers was one of a small group of professionals who were instrumental in adjusting the way the British army conducted warfare on the frontier. While the tactics he advocated—marching in Indian file, traveling only by night, and tracking and ambushing from cover—were initially anathema to regulars who had been trained to face volley fire on the open field, by 1757 the British were beginning to adapt.[12]

In charge of one of the ranger companies based at Fort Edward was Israel Putnam, a thirty-nine-year-old captain of the Connecticut provincials. Although born in West Salem, Massachusetts, at the age of twenty-two Putnam's family had moved to Mortlake, Connecticut. While working as a shepherd on the family holding, he had gained a reputation for bravery by killing a she-wolf that had preyed on the region's lambs. Drawing on his fame, Putnam had helped raise a company for Lyman's regiment in 1755 and served as a lieutenant at the Battle of Lake George. In 1756 he was promoted to captain, and volunteered for Rogers' Rangers the following year.[13]

While the majority of the regulars were housed in the barracks in Fort Edward, the provincials and rangers set up camp on an island on the Hudson River sixty yards from the western bastions. Known as Rogers Island, since Major Rogers had trained his rangers there, it was covered with huts, tents, cabins, and lean-tos, laid out with little sense of order. A few of the dwellings were lavish constructions of two floors that exchanged hands between senior officers for considerable sums of money. Others consisted of little more than a handful of interlocking boughs torn from the nearest tree. The camp was chaotic, crowded, and unsanitary. Among the dwellings were noisome "necessary" houses, freshly dug graves, and bloodied patches of ground where animals had been slaughtered. Pigs and goats were penned up and cattle grazed by the riverside. Cats, dogs, and rats ran among the ramshackle structures, and fly-infested piles of rotting peapods, cabbage leaves, offal, skin, and bones lay festering in the sun. The stench was appalling. As one eyewitness recalled: "the imagination of man cannot [conceive of] . . . a place more . . . loathsome."[14]

At the southern end of the island were the settlement's gardens, planted with fruit and vegetables to supplement the men's rations of salt pork, beef, peas, butter, rice, and bread.[15] Also present was a smallpox hospital. Fifteen feet wide and eighty feet long, the wooden, one-story structure could accommodate more than one hundred patients. Although "camp distemper," dysentery, diphtheria, typhus, and typhoid all wrought havoc throughout the French and Indian War, smallpox was the biggest killer. Those suffering from the disease rarely recovered. Once pustules formed on the skin, death generally followed ten to fourteen days later. In the crowded conditions at Fort Edward, the disease spread rapidly throughout the spring and summer of 1757. On May 30, just five days after the Connecticut provincials had arrived, "a man in Captain Jefferies [John Jeffries] Company" fell ill and was taken to the hospital. By July 4, 101 men were sick and by October 11, 50 had died from the Connecticut regiment alone.[16] The rudimentary treatments of purging, bleeding, and emetics offered by the regimental surgeons did little to improve their patients' chances of survival. Self-inoculation, on the other hand, a crude practice disapproved of by military command, was reasonably common and occasionally effective, and opiate-based medicines could also help to ease the patients' pain. Despite the disease's highly contagious nature, visits to the hospital were occasionally allowed, as evidenced by a melancholy journal entry that Fitch made later in the campaign. "Toard night," he noted, "I went over to ye Island to Se our Sick [and] Found Corp[ora]l Andrus[. He was in] Exceeding[ly] Poor [condition and] almost without any Sense."[17]

Other hospitals had been built inside the fort, in the shadow of its walls or on Rogers Island.[18] Aside from smallpox, the health problems faced by the eighteenth-century soldier campaigning in America were legion. Arthritis ate away at his joints, and herniated disks and abscessed teeth were common. Others suffered from syphilis, palsy, tumors, or anemia.[19] The pension records of the 35th show a host of other ailments: Joshua Rawson, originally a cloth maker from Bradford, was pensioned out of the army in October 1757 for being "ruptured" and suffering from consumption; John Cameron, a fifty-five-year-old laborer from Lochaber, was "afflicted with fits"; James Murphy was "dim sighted" and suffered from "Epilepsy"; Sgt. John Crane, a veteran of twenty years, was "afflicted with madness"; and Thomas Bloom, a thirty-seven-year-old from Hopton, had "a disorder in his fundament."[20]

To the south of Fort Edward, beyond the creek, was a slight rise, all but immune to the seasonal flooding of the Hudson. Upon it stood a cluster of sutlers' houses.[21] A combination of restaurateurs, landlords, and shopkeepers, the sutlers were civilian merchants who shadowed the army and whose houses were one of the most popular destinations for the men and officers alike. Luxuries, such as sugar, chocolate, coffee, and tea, were available, and cooking kettles, nails, thread, buttons, cloth, and "sticks of mohair" for making clothes could all be bought. Unsurprisingly, alcohol and tobacco were their most sought-after commodities. Smoking was near universal in mid-eighteenth-century northeast America. Every man and boy over the age of twelve—white, black, or Indian—carried a pipe and tobacco pouch. The latter was made of treated hide, typically buckskin or leather, although a few of the wilder frontier types used cured and scraped Indian skins to carry their supplies.[22] Drinking alcohol was equally widespread. Rum from New England and Jamaica, and French brandy and wine were all popular. Although economically independent, the sutlers were still subject to military law. Each had to apply for a license before setting up shop, and besides fixing prices, Major Fletcher also forbade the selling of alcohol after nightfall. Failure to comply would result in being run out of camp.[23]

Although a camp the size of Fort Edward would have supported numerous sutlers, a certain Mr. Best appears to have been the most prominent. Judging from the size and construction of his premises and the number of servants he employed, as well as the status of clientele he attracted, he was a man of considerable means.[24] Built in June 1757 by a privately paid work party led by Jabez Fitch, the twenty-year-old sergeant of Lyman's Connecticut provincials, Best's house was 14 feet wide and 40 feet long, ringed by a wooden fence, and boasted a number of windows lined with glass as well as a cellar, a rarity in mid-eighteenth-century America. Upstairs, the premises was divided into two sections, each with its own brick fireplace. To the south were the kitchens. At the other end was a dining hall, its atmosphere thick with tobacco smoke. Inside, the customers could eat meals prepared in the kitchens or drink wine, cider, brandy, rum, or flip, a potent mixture of beer laced with rum, into which a red-hot poker was dipped to make the liquor bubble and foam.[25]

Along with the likes of Sergeant Fitch, the diners at Best's included such dignitaries as Col. James Montresor, a fifty-two-year-old engineer who arrived at Fort Edward from Albany in late June. A respected professional of thirty years' experience, Montresor came from "a very old French Huguenot family . . . [that had] fled . . . to England" to avoid the religious persecution that followed Louis XIV's revocation of the Edict of Nantes.[26] Having joined the army in 1727, Montresor had served for some time in Gibraltar and Minorca, achieving the position of second most senior engineer in the British army. After bidding farewell to his wife Mary, he had left London in 1755 with an impressive entourage of servants, aides, and helpers, and had been kept busy building garrison blocks and hospitals and improving the defenses of various fortifications in the colonies ever since. A lover of the finer things in life, Montresor dined at Best's with his fellow officers on at least two occasions that summer.[27]

When not at one of the many sutlers' houses on both sides of the river, the troops at Fort Edward were busy with work detail, guard duty, scouting, or drill. The day began at four thirty, when the morning cannon was fired from the ramparts. After dressing, shaving, and organizing their kit, the men of each regiment gathered for parade. Those with dirty clothes, missing ammunition, or damaged musket flints were put on report. Then the orders of the day, the password, and counter were announced. Typically the latter consisted of jingoistic reminders of the greatness of Britain, such as George, Lancashire, Pitt, or Kensington. On some mornings the men's quarters were also inspected. Depending on the zeal of the officer in question, the lanes between their tents or huts would be swept, rubbish tidied, and those who had failed to rise for morning parade would be rudely awakened in their beds.[28] The provincial troops would conclude their parade with a sermon given by the regimental minister. These were driven young men, such as William Crawford, a twenty-seven-year-old Princeton graduate and surgeon who also ministered to the spiritual needs of Colonel Frye's Massachusetts volunteers.[29] The Old Testament was preferred to the New, and themes such as the evil of the papist French and the wrath of God were common.[30]

After parade the men were drilled. Maneuvers, such as forming line, column, grounding arms, and coming to attention, were second nature to the redcoats. After months on the parade grounds of Dublin, Cork, Portsmouth, New York, and Albany, the men of the 35th, who drilled accompanied by the music of their drummers and fife players, moved like automatons.[31] The bungled steps of the provincials, on the other hand, were enough to make Major Fletcher weep. Unlike their full-time comrades, the provincials were summer volunteers, the majority of whom would return to their civilian lives

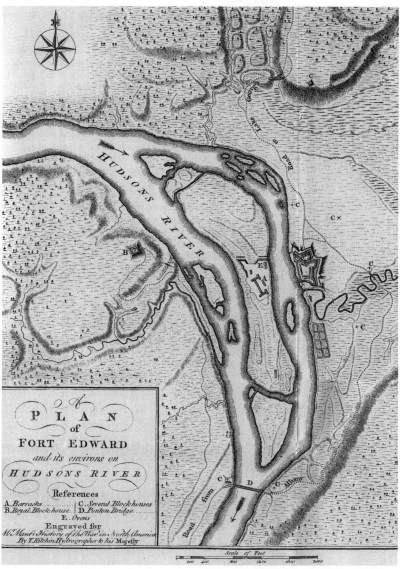

"A Plan of Fort Edward" printed in *A History of the Late War in North America* by Thomas Mante in 1772. The barracks (A) were situated at the fort next to the bread ovens (E). Blockhouses (C) guarded both the pontoon bridge (D) south of the fort as well as the eastern approach to the fort. The much larger Royal Blockhouse (B) was across the Hudson River from the fort and provided security to the west. The roads from Albany and to Lake George are shown, as well as the gardens just south of the fort established for the garrison. (*Author's collection*)

that winter. While the individual drills were in themselves superfluous in the wilderness skirmishes and siege warfare that would prove decisive in the American theater, the unthinking obedience and immediate response to barked commands that they instilled were essential. Fletcher realized this, and throughout June 1757 he tried to improve the provincials. To that end, he employed the talents of Mr. Welch, the corporal of the 35th who had been the undisputed master of the parade ground in Albany. As there were too many provincial privates to drill at one time, on May 30 Fletcher let Welch loose on their sergeants and corporals instead. That morning the following order was read out: "all ye Serjts & Corps in ye Connecticutt Regt, yt are of[f] from Duty [are required to] Turn out at 6 oClock in ye Morning To Be Exercis'd by Mr. Welch . . . till 7 oClock." Jabez Fitch and his fellow sergeants and corporals passed on what they had learned to their men later that afternoon.[32]

After morning inspections and drill, the men set about their tasks for the day. With the enemy just thirty miles away at Fort Carillon, the most important was guard duty, a job which at any given time occupied up to a quarter of all those in camp. Manuals, such as Humphrey Bland's widely read *Treatise of Military Discipline*, stipulated that "guards ordinary," meaning those permanently posted, could be divided into four categories: the quarter guard, the picquet guard, the main guard, and the provost guard. The first two were local guards raised by each battalion's colonel. The others were assigned to the camp at large. The quarter guard performed a policing function; the picquet guard was a reserve that would wait in its battalion camp until needed for emergencies; the main guard, consisting of detachments from each battalion, provided external security for the camp as a whole; and the provost guard, an amalgamation of squads from the various units in camp, functioned as a military police force. Its main duties were guarding prisoners awaiting court-martial, and supervising punishments.[33]

A second major task for those at Fort Edward was to take part in work details, which were largely assigned to the provincials. On May 30, twenty "ax men" and four "spade men" were required to build a fence around the garden on

Rogers Island. Two carpenters, civilian experts later paid by the engineer Colonel Montresor, provided instruction for the unskilled men. In June the smallpox hospital was constructed by a detachment from the Connecticut regiment, while Luke Gridley and some others built an outdoor bread oven and tar kiln. Throughout 1757, work also continued on strengthening the fort. Timber was in constant demand, and work parties were regularly sent out into the forest to fell trees. With the men working long shifts in the height of summer, accidents were common: George Graves, a sailor from Chester who had joined the 35th, suffered "a fractured leg"; the twenty-three-year-old William Blunt became "incurably lame"; and William Evans, a new American recruit for Monro's regiment, had "his thigh broke by the fall of a tree."[34]

Accidents were not the only hazard that summer. As the surrounding land was cleared, the work parties had to venture farther and farther afield, taking them beyond the protection of the sentries on the walls. As a result, guards were assigned to escort them.[35] Ever since the first thaws of spring had opened up the Lake George–Champlain corridor to enemy raiders, the troops had been involved in skirmishes in the woods. In mid-May, a party of redcoats and provincials was attacked between the forts by "a large body" of the enemy: "Four . . . [of the British] was killed, and four taken Prisoners."[36] Toward the end of the month, enemy activity increased. Near Fort William Henry two regulars, "being out for some wood," were shot and killed. Later, three rangers were captured and a private of the 35th "was knock'd on the Head with a Hatchet," just "30 Yards from Fort Edward."[37]

June had seen the escalation continue. On Friday the tenth, as Jabez Fitch was gathering fence posts to erect around Mr. Best's sutling house, a skirmish took place half a mile east of the encampment. At 11 a.m. a tree-felling party of fifteen carpenters guarded by the same number of Connecticut provincials was attacked by ninety Indians supported by a sergeant and seven privates of the French regulars. The Indians were from a variety of tribes and included at least one woman among their group. Some were domesticated Iroquois and Nipissing from the Lake of Two Mountains mission near Montréal. Others were Ottawa and Chippewa from the Great

Lakes.[38] The raiders were led by Charles Langlade, a twenty-eight-year-old métis of French-Ottawa parentage who had spent most of his life living among the Indians of Michilimackinac, a trading post situated between Lakes Huron and Michigan. "Perfectly cool and fearless . . . on the field of battle," Langlade was one of the legendary Canadian coureurs de bois, or forest runners, whose knowledge of the wilderness and ability to lead lightning raids against the frontier had already wreaked so much havoc among the British colonists of America.[39]

Against such formidable foes, the Connecticut provincials didn't stand a chance. No sooner had Lyman's men positioned themselves around their charges than Langlade gave the signal to open fire. A veteran of numerous woodland encounters, including Braddock's defeat at Monongahela, the twenty-eight-year-old had positioned his men well. Shooting from cover, the Indians and French picked their targets. Four of the guard were hit by their first discharge. A few returned fire, seriously wounding one of Langlade's Indians. The rest took to their heels. Most of those not hit by the initial fire made it back to Fort Edward, but five proved too slow. Four were overtaken and captured, including David Campbell, a one-eyed private from Killingly, while Jacob Reed of Captain Fitch's company was shot or tomahawked as he ran. Reed's body would lie undiscovered for two days. While the prisoners were disarmed and bound, the dead were stripped and mutilated. "All [were] Scalpt," Jabez Fitch recalled, and some had "their Brains Run out." For one of the victims, William Mortawomock, a Mohawk Indian who had joined the Connecticut provincials, the raiders reserved a particularly grisly fate. When his comrades discovered his body a few hours later, his heart had been cut out and a block of wood inserted in its place.[40]

Half a mile to the east, Jabez Fitch had been startled by Langlade's opening volley. Running into the fort to collect his musket, he raced to the scene of the ambush, but the enemy had already withdrawn. While Fitch and a few others were looking over the dead, Colonel Lyman led the main guard in pursuit. Split into three parties of thirty men, they found an Indian trail leading from the sight of the ambuscade.

Following it, they discovered the enemy's tracks and came across Langlade's men, busy building a litter for their wounded comrade. Opening fire, the guard quickly dispersed the French and Indians, who dragged the wounded man behind them as they withdrew. Worried about further pursuit, Langlade avoided retracing his footsteps, abandoned the canoes that he had used on the outbound leg of the journey, and decided to make for Fort Carillon on foot. Unused to hiking such long distances through the wilderness in high summer, two of the French privates and the sergeant who had volunteered for the mission became exhausted and had to be left behind. Langlade's party arrived at Carillon with their prisoners to a backdrop of celebratory gunshots on June 12. The stragglers came back by canoe two days later.[41]

Back at Fort Edward, Lyman had called off the pursuit. Worried that his force was too small and fearing a counterattack, he had to content himself with pillaging the fourteen packs—"2 Pikes 2 Dear Skins [and] several scalping knives"—that Langlade's men had left behind. In one pack was the party's muster roll, detailing the numbers involved and possible sites for future ambushes. Somewhat satisfied with the intelligence gained, Fitch and the others returned to Fort Edward. After they had buried their mutilated comrades, Lyman gave them "a dram" to calm their nerves.[42]

Such was camp life throughout the month of June: daily parades, inspection, and mundane duties, punctuated by sightings of Indians in the woods, false alarms, and sudden, sickening bouts of violence. Between the bursts of action, the men stuck to their routine. As well as guard duty, Fletcher's troops were kept busy with regular weapons training. Much time was spent "firing at marks," targets strung up in the trees that the men peppered with musket fire. The regulars also practiced volley fire in platoons, and on one occasion Jabez Fitch saw the redcoats throwing crude yet effective grenades used in siege warfare. Regular scouts also helped to relieve the boredom. Although mainly the domain of the rangers, some provincials and redcoats also joined these roving patrols, which would set off into the woods for days at a time, set up an ambush in a likely spot, and await the enemy.[43]

On June 14, it was Jabez Fitch's turn to head out into the unknown. After drawing extra ammunition and rations (three pints of peas, six ounces of butter, half a pound of rice, seven pounds of bread, and five pounds, three ounces of salt pork), he left Fort Edward early in the morning.[44] The majority of the three hundred soldiers who accompanied him were Connecticut provincials headed by an enthusiastic Colonel Lyman, who was "painted like a Mohog." Rudolph Faesch, the Swiss-born captain of the Royal Americans, and Lt. Thomas Browne of the 35th also took small detachments of their men. On the first day, the party set out to the northeast. Traveling by rough trails occasionally blocked by fallen trees or dense thickets, the men made slow progress through the wilderness, covering only five miles before halting for the night. The following morning, they came across fresh tracks. Worried that they might have been left by an enemy patrol still in the vicinity, the officers demanded silence. "We was Vary still," Fitch remembered. "Not a word [was] spoke only by Whispering." Not all of the provincials were so obedient. Some Indian recruits had smuggled spirits onto the scout, and Pvt. Solomon Chebucks became so "Disorderly" that Lyman threatened to kill him "if he Didn't Be Still."[45]

Later that afternoon, the men reached the ruins of Fort Anne. An abandoned wooden structure, the fort had been built more than forty years earlier "on a little rising ground which runs obliquely" to Wood Creek to defend the back route to Fort Edward. As it was frequently used as a rendezvous by French and Indian raiders, Major Fletcher had ordered a permanent garrison of a sergeant and twelve men, relieved every five days, to be maintained at the site.[46] Surrounded by giant white and red elms, Fitch thought it a "Pleasant Plais." Although the old soldiers' garden had long been abandoned, the area still abounded with apple and plum trees and wild strawberries, which Fitch and his comrades harvested.[47] After resting, Lyman divided his men into groups that were sent out to search for signs of the enemy.

The men of Fitch's party found themselves traveling over increasingly broken terrain, thickly forested and with spots of marshland. The provincials were plagued by mosquitos and black fly. Ever present on the frontier that summer, the pests refused to give "quarter either by day or night."[48] That after-noon, the men came across a company of rangers. Led by Capt. Israel Putnam, the latter were returning to Fort Edward with a French prisoner taken at Carillon. Putnam also brought news of the four provincials taken on June 10 from Fort Edward. The men from Connecticut were relieved to hear that David Campbell, the one-eyed private from Killingly, had reached Carillon safe and sound.[49]

On the sixteenth a flanking party of Fitch's group, having blundered into some swampy ground, saw an Indian, but the brave disappeared into the woods before the provincials could catch him. That night it rained, and the men took shelter behind some rocks in a hollow on the side of a hill. On the next day's march, Fitch heard a musket shot from the head of the column and ran forward to investigate. Private Phineas Burchard had fired at another Indian but had missed. While pursuing him, Burchard had caught his musket on a birch branch and broken the stock clean off. Later, an old enemy encampment was found and the following day, having exhausted their supplies as well as their reserves of energy, the scouts returned to Fort Edward.[50]

That afternoon a column of redcoats left the fort and headed south to Saratoga. Led by a fifty-seven-year-old ser-geant of the 35th named William Isaac, the twenty-strong detachment had orders to make a sweep of the country in search of a group of deserters who had recently fled camp. After a parade and weapons check, during which each man was ordered to load his musket with "a tin charge of Powder, one Ball, and Six Buck Shot," the column left late in the after-noon on June 18. Isaac's men marched to the brick kiln and were ferried over the Hudson in two detachments. After making a quick head count, the sergeant led them through the growing gloom. The party followed the track down the west bank of the Hudson due south, the forest thick and forebod-ing on their right flank. Three of the deserters were caught before nightfall, which forced Isaac to make camp. The col-umn was just four miles south of Fort Edward.[51]

The next morning, the men were awake long before dawn. After they had rolled up their blankets, Isaac ordered them to continue the march. The sergeant, a veteran of thirty-seven years' service, took the lead. The men followed "in Indian File," while Corporal Burns brought up the rear. Just four hundred yards down the road to Saratoga, the silence was shattered by a single musket shot whistling out of the woods. Isaac whipped around to face his attacker. "What's this? What's this?" the veteran declared as a second shot came fizzing out of the gloom. The whole tree line then erupted with flame and smoke as a volley was fired against them. One man was killed, Corporal Burns was hit, and several others wounded. Recovering his composure, Isaac yelled out, "Tree all! Tree all!" and his men took cover.[52]

After ducking behind the nearest tree trunk, Pvt. Henry Garman ventured a glance toward the enemy. One of the forty Indians hunting them spied Garman and pulled his trigger. By the light of the flash pan, Garman made out the shooter and another brave lurking in the gloom beside him and returned fire. Having given away his position, Garman then dashed toward the next tree trunk to reload. En route he stumbled over a root and went flying. His knee cut and his musket lost in the fall, Garman took cover and watched as several of his twenty-man patrol ran past him. "Come on, come on, what do you stay for?" they asked as they dashed past. Unknown to Garman, Isaac had ordered a withdrawal.[53]

Elsewhere on the road was Pvt. Jack Griffin, "a staunch old soldier" of twenty-three years' service who had fought in Admiral Boscawen's East Indies expedition ten years before. Undaunted by the bullets whipping past, Griffin was kneeling out in the open, his hammer cocked and his musket ready to fire. "He remained" in this position "for some time, intending to reserve his fire, till he should see an enemy near enough to make sure of him." Recognizing Griffin's "Green Wastecoat" in the dark, Pvt. Matthew Finlay, another straggler, called out to the veteran. "Is that you Jack?" Griffin replied, "Yes, tis I," before adding, less than reassuringly, "never fear we'll die together."[54]

Griffin's dramatics were premature. Within minutes, the firing had stopped and the Indians had melted back into the woods. Amid the choking musket smoke, Griffin, Finlay, and Garman found themselves alone. Isaac and the rest had

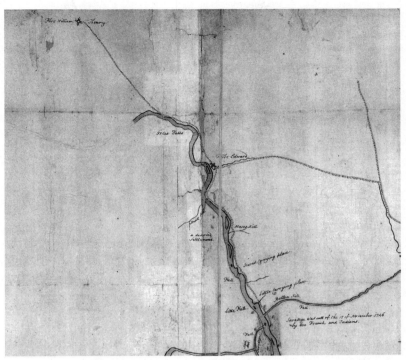

Detail from a 1758 map of upstate New York showing Saratoga (with a note referring to the French and Indian attack in November 1746 which destroyed the fort and village, killing 30 with 60 prisoners carried away) and forts Edward and William Henry. Fort William Henry was essentially the northernmost point of British control in New York at the time, and stood isolated in the wilderness, fourteen miles from Fort Edward. (*Library of Congress*)

retraced their steps to the ferry and would be back at Fort Edward by nightfall. Griffin, however, had other ideas. Leading his companions south, they reached Saratoga that afternoon after stopping to eat some bread for lunch by the side of the track. Although there was no sign of Isaac, they found five other members of the patrol at Saratoga as well as Lt. Thomas Forty. Also of the 35th, Forty was accompanied by some men he had recruited for the regiment in New York.[55] Falling in with the lieutenant, Griffin, Finlay, and Garman returned to Fort Edward later the next day.[56]

Back at Fort Edward the routine ground on. Most mornings, after the parade had been dismissed, regimental courts-martial were heard. These were relatively low-key affairs, presided over by the regiment's colonel and a handful of officers. Offenders charged with insubordination, petty theft, failure to meet the required standards on parade, drunkenness, and disobedience were hauled before them. The trials were short and predictable. Flogging was by far the most common punishment.[57] Throughout June, the whipping post was stained with the blood of several provincials and regulars alike: on the sixth, "one of Captain Galops Indeains was whipped [sixty lashes] for stealing a gun"; on the ninth, "one man was whipped 40 Laches for sitting Downe on gard"; on the sixteenth, "thare was one adris whipped 50 Lashes for sleeping on gard"; on the twentieth a clerk named Robert Niles, who went "scouting without [Colonel Lyman's] . . . Leave [was] Redueced to the Ranks: & whipped 100"; on the twenty-first "there was 2 Indeains whipd one a 100 Leches for giting Drunk scouting: the other 50 for selling Bark when he was bid to get It for a gard house"; on the twenty-second, "4 Regelars [were] whipted 40"; on the twenty-third "a Regler was whipd 100 Lashes for hollowing & scaring the Ennemy when Gennerel Limon had them partyl ambusht"; and on the twenty-sixth, "one Boston man [was] whipt 50 for pissing In a kittle of Peas."[58]

General courts-martial, held for crimes that carried a capital punishment, were far less common. At Fort Edward none were held throughout the month of June, and just one was convened in July. Although headed by Major Fletcher and dominated by the officers of the regulars, general courts-martial tried both redcoats and provincials. Crimes ranged from desertion, grand theft, and cowardice in the face of the enemy to defiance of the commissioned ranks. One of the cases heard in July concerned the theft of "two [gold] dubloons . . . some small silver . . . a pistreen cut in two and an English Shilling in a yellow silk purse." Sarah Emerson, the victim, was the wife of a redcoat in the 35th. The accused, Pvt. Peter Davis of Israel Putnam's company of rangers, was an old soldier of three years' service, who had become uncharacteristically generous with his comrades at about the same time as Mrs. Emerson's loss.

The trial ran for two days. No less than ten witnesses were called, but it was the evidence of the last to take the stand, none other than Corporal Welch, the drillmaster of the 35th, that proved decisive. On the morning in question, Mr. Welch had been "in his hut" when he had heard of the crime. Learning that the culprit "had made his escape over the Curtain [wall of Fort Edward], where the old Sally port was," Welch decided to investigate. Evidently an amateur sleuth as well as a parade ground maestro, the corporal found a fresh footprint on the floor, which he duly examined. Then, in the best traditions of courtroom drama, the boot of Peter Davis was measured, and the fact that the two were not compatible was announced to the court. Davis, who had already stated that he had received a whole year's back pay in the run-up to the crime, thus explaining his unprecedented generosity at the sutler's bar, was acquitted. Mrs. Emerson was less than pleased. She would never see her savings again.[59]

When the troops at Fort Edward weren't involved in courts-martial or busy with guard duty, work parties, or scouts, there were plenty of other diversions to keep them entertained. During the day, those with free time would rest after their exertions. On June 24, for example, after returning from his scout, Jabez Fitch found time for a nap. He was allowed to sleep right through the "fornoon" and "had some pleasing dreams."[60] Other provincials spent their free time at prayer meetings, writing letters home, or swapping, buying, or repairing kit. Another frequent task was the making of ammunition. Hunched down over a pile of glowing embers, the men would melt lead ingots in small pans, then pour the liquid into molds to make ball or bird shot or buckshot for killing small game.[61] Although it was prohibited to venture beyond the range of covering musket fire from the walls, officers occasionally went out hunting for deer or bear to supplement their rations, while the men swam or waded in the Hudson in the heat of midday, or fished for "fine trout," sturgeon, alewife, or eels.[62]

Other diversions included playing ball, a seemingly dangerous pastime, which would later cause one of the Massachusetts provincials to fall down dead in the middle of a game.[63] Jabez Fitch amused himself by going into Fort Edward to watch a tame bear "Play Som of His Tricks," or by taking walks in the gardens. On other occasions, he would go to the regulars' camp to see the changing of the guard and hear their fifers and drummers play, which he thought "Vary delightsome."[64] The young sergeant was remarkably sociable. He spent much of his time conversing with newfound friends from both the provincial regiments and, unusually, from among the regulars of "Olde England" as well. Perhaps the most interesting conversationalist that Fitch found that summer was William Bell, a globe-trotting private of the 35th. "I Got Some acquaintance with Him finding his conversation to suit me," the young sergeant recorded. "He tells Me He Spent 3 Years in ye University of Oxford. . . . But Since that He Has Bin Vary unfortunate Has Rovd abroad in ye world [and] Ben Many Years in ye Kings Servis."[65]

Fitch's predilection for befriending the regulars was not a common trait among the provincials. There was little love lost between the two camps. The majority of the redcoats thought their American comrades were the worst soldiers in the world. "Overpaid and undisciplined," they were held to be "a sickly, faint hearted rabble led by men unwilling to exercise their authority for fear of losing favour with the mob."[66] The provincials' view of the regulars was equally unflattering. Although they admired their courage under fire, sturdy constitutions, and discipline, the colonists were convinced that the redcoats were their moral inferiors. Blasphemous and ungodly, the "lobsters," as the provincials referred to them, were unthinking automatons, "who are but little better than slaves to their officers." Often lewd and almost invariably uncultured, the regulars were thought aggressive by the provincials, who remarked that they seemed to spend the majority of their free time drinking and whoring around camp.[67] This mutual antipathy occasionally broke out into competition. There were wrestling matches, shooting contests, and boat races up and down Lake George, and outright brawls between the two parties were not unheard of.[68]

During the long summer evenings at Fort Edward, while the officers drank claret and dined off fine, decorated delftware, the men lit log fires and prepared their evening meals.[69] Fresh fish from the river; redbreasted pigeon, wild turkey, rabbit, and venison trapped or shot in the woods; and cheese, fruit, and vegetables brought from the Dutch traders from Albany enlivened their rations of salt pork, beef, and mutton.[70] Later, as the sun sunk behind the Hudson, the men indulged their vices. Gambling was popular.[71] British halfpennies, Spanish silver reales, cob pieces of eight, Massachusetts shillings, and even French liards changed hands on the turn of a card.[72] Camp prostitutes, frowned upon by the New Englanders, went from table to table in the sutlers' houses and toured the men's tents plying their trade.[73] Oxford, "a negro from East Haddam [Connecticut], in Welles' Company," defied the alcohol curfew to sell rum to the Mohawk scouts and also told the regulars their fortunes for a few pennies a time.[74] As the night wore on, the camp came alive with music. Captain Jeffries's clerk was particularly talented with the fiddle, and on the evening of June 6 a large crowd gathered at Sergeant Gears's tent to hear him play. [75] Fifes, bone flutes, and jew's harps accompanied the singers, and most evenings a bottle was passed around.[76]

One of the songs popular with the regulars that summer was "Yankee Doodle," a satire on the foibles of the American provincial written by Richard Shuckburgh, a British army surgeon who had been present at the Battle of Lake George.[77] While the song would later be adopted by the Americans, and the lyrics adapted to their benefit, the original version (reproduced below) poked fun at the amateurish nature of the provincial regiments in general and Col. Ephraim Williams of Massachusetts in particular.

> *Brother Ephraim sold his Cow*
> *And bought him a Commission;*
> *And then he went to Canada*
> *To fight for the Nation;*
> *But when Ephraim he came home*
> *He proved an arrant Coward,*
> *He wou'dn't fight the Frenchmen there*
> *For fear of being devour'd.*

On the evening of June 22 there was a more unusual form of entertainment. A squad of Mohawk scouts brought in a French prisoner from Carillon, who had been taken two days before while hunting alone in the woods.[78] As was their custom, the Mohawks performed a ceremonial dance in thanks for their good fortune and made their captive "run the gauntlet" in which parallel lines of warriors, sometimes joined by their women, would rain blows onto the unfortunate captive, who was forced to run between them. Luke Gridley was among those who gathered at the "Indian camp" to watch the proceedings. Accompanied by the "rough musik" of drums covered in deerskins and "terrible and savage" chanting, the Mohawks danced circles around their quailing captive, and occasionally "horrid figures" rushed into the middle of the ring to perform a solo routine. For the Frenchman, who feared his scalp was about to be taken, it was a terrifying ordeal. For the provincials and redcoats of Fort Edward, on the other hand, the "powwow" made a fascinating spectacle.[79]

The ceremony was as nothing compared to what was going on two hundred miles to the north. While the British had no more than fifty Mohawks at Forts Edward and William Henry, at that very moment more than one thousand warriors from the Great Lakes were gathering at Montréal.[80]

6

Montréal

June 1757

By the mid-eighteenth century, two hundred years after it had first been founded, Montréal was a bustling town of more than seven thousand inhabitants, second only to Québec in terms of size and wealth in New France. Built on an island in the middle of the Saint Lawrence, the city was rectangular in shape. Its principal houses were laid out along a few paved streets that ran parallel to the riverbank. A stout stone wall, pierced by numerous gates and fronted by a flooded ditch, ringed the town. Together, these defenses had provided sufficient security from Indian raids in the early colonial period but would offer little protection from cannon fire. The stone-built churches of the Sulpicians, Franciscans, and Jesuits, the first of which was said to be the most impressive building in the whole of New France, dominated the town center. Also prominent were a convent, which took in the daughters of the finest families in town for a fee of five hundred ecus; the king's hospital, which fed and housed sick soldiers for a stipend of twelve sous per day; and the castle of the Marquis de Vaudreuil, the governor general of Canada. Beyond the walls were a few clusters of wooden houses, orchards of apple and pear trees, "excellent grain fields, charming meadows and delightful woods." To the west about a half mile from the town center was a mountain from which Montréal took its name.[1]

While the French and Canadian inhabitants were accustomed to seeing numerous Indians from the nearby missions on market day, in June 1757 the human diversity on display in front of Montréal was unprecedented. Drawn by the propaganda of French and Canadian ambassadors to the Great Lakes region who gave out gifts and held councils, the Indians were flocking to Montréal in droves. Even more persuasive had been the warriors who fought at Oswego the previous summer. Returning to their villages with the plunder they had captured, they told stories "of . . . swimming in brandy" after the fort had fallen and added that Montcalm had paid ransoms for the release of any prisoners they captured.[2] The prospect of a similarly successful campaign in 1757 was enough to attract warriors from twelve different tribes from across the Great Lakes region and beyond. It was the most successful recruiting drive in the history of New France and surpassed even Governor Vaudreuil's expectations. By mid-June 1757, one thousand warriors were encamped around Montréal.[3]

The most numerous were the Ottawa, or "cold country" Indians, as they were known in the British colonies to the south. Although drawn from seven different communities, the majority came from the cosmopolitan villages that had risen up outside the French trading posts of Detroit, Michilimackinac, Beaver Island, and Lafourche. In Montréal, each had their own temporary settlement by the river's edge. Crowded with bark or hide tepees sewn to sapling frames with spruce roots, the area was populated by the warriors, their wives and children, and packs of semi-domesticated dogs, which roamed outside.[4] Naked except for their buckskin breechclouts, the warriors wore hooped metal jewelry and adornments of stone, copper, and shell hung from their ears and noses. The men were heavily tattooed. Their torsos and faces were painted with soot, red ocher, or Chinese vermillion, a highly prized commodity that fetched a high price in beaver skins for the traders who imported it from the Orient.[5] The Ottawas' hair was cut short, pasted upright at the front, and

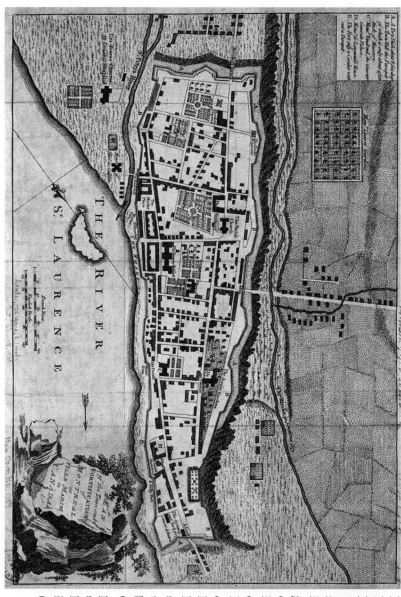

Plan of the Town and
Fortifications of
Montreal published in
1759. The wall sur-
rounding the town is
indicated by B. Several
gardens are shown
outside the town,
including the large
one owned by "Mons.r
Liners" at the top and
one below the general
hospital at the bottom
left, as well as the
seminary garden to
the left of center
below the Parish
Church. The market
place is below the
seminary garden, and
has its own gate open-
ing up along the river.
(Library of Congress)

decorated with feathers, which also hung from their ear lobes and were attached to collars that they wore around their necks. Some of the warriors carried firearms, either ancient muskets or more modern trade guns. Others had bows and arrows. The flights were made from feathers unique to each warrior so he could record his kills. Spears and heavy wooden ball-headed war clubs were also common, and each carried a large round shield made of leather stretched taut over a wooden frame. All had knives hung from sheaths suspended by a cord worn around the neck, and a few carried iron tomahawks stuffed into their belts at the small of the back.[6]

Alongside the Ottawa were their traditional allies in the fight against the Iroquois, the Potawatomi from Saint Joseph and Detroit. Bougainville, present at Montréal to see them arrive, thought the Potawatomi the "wisest and most obedient of all the Indians" he had encountered. Originally hunter-gatherers, by the 1750s they had begun to adapt to horse nomadism and had spread out from their homelands around the shores of Green Bay to hunt buffalo in the Great Plains to the southwest.[7] Nevertheless, the Potawatomi still prized the legendary fleet footedness of their warriors and celebrated their prowess with a footrace held each spring at Detroit, a native settlement that had grown up around a walled French trading post on the western shores of Lake Erie.[8] The spectacle drew Indians from across the Great Lakes. "It is the Newmarket of North America," Bougainville wrote. "Bets are made with packs of furs by the Indians and merchandise by the French. Sometimes they have as many as two thousand Indians there, some of whom come from six or seven hundred leagues."[9] Although originally of the same tribe as the Ottawa, the Potawatomi had split from their cousins at some time in the undocumented past and had since developed their own particular appearance. The men wore their hair long and straight, and were renowned for the complexity of their ear ornaments.[10]

In addition to the Potawatomi and Ottawa, there were Chippewa from Lake Superior, the third of the triumvirate of tribes known as the "Three Fires," which had joined forces against the marauding Iroquois over a century before. Close allies of the French, they had traveled from a trading post at Point Chequamegon on the south shore of Lake Superior. Having profited from the fur trade, their population had grown to one thousand, and the settlement had become the center of spiritual life for all three tribes, whose worldview was dominated by an "overwhelming fear of sorcery." Besides the supreme spirit, Manitou, whom the Iroquois also worshipped, the tribes of the Three Fires believed in a wide pantheon of malevolent spirits, including the fearsome Windigowan, giants

An 18th-century French watercolor of two Ottawa fur traders in upper Michigan. (*Peabody Museum, Harvard University*)

formed of ice who stalked the forests and practiced cannibalism.[11] Despite their shared culture and beliefs, the Chippewa dressed differently from the other tribes of the Three Fires and were physically distinct. "Much taller . . . and broader across the shoulders" and chest, the Chippewa warriors sported yarn sashes wound around their heads like turbans. Their women, who carried their babies strapped to wooden cradleboards until they were weaned at the age of three, wore buckskin dresses decorated with porcupine quills, sewn at the shoulder and held in place by a belt.[12]

Also present in Montréal was a band of troublesome Mississauga who had got drunk before leaving their homeland and had attempted to burn down the French outpost of Fort Toronto. Their designs had only been thwarted by the quick-thinking Capt. Pierre Pouchot, the commander of Fort Niagara thirty leagues to the east. As soon as he had heard of the threat, Pouchot had ordered two of his officers to row across Lake Ontario and make a show of force. On arrival, a volley from their muskets and bateaux-mounted swivel guns, ostensibly fired as a sign of respect, was enough to deter the Mississauga from their plot. They later confessed their plan, but were forgiven and would go on to perform well in the campaign that summer.[13]

Another tribe represented at Montréal was the Menominee from L'Original and Le Chat, a proud people whose children went entirely naked until the age of six. With a population of 150 warriors "always strongly attached to the French," the Menominee were known as the "wild oats people," a reference to the plant that formed the totem of their nation.[14] Among those present at Montréal were some veterans of Oswego. Bougainville, who had seen them in action at the siege, had been impressed not only by their martial prowess but also by their physique. "In general these are brawny men," the young aide had noted in his journal, "large and of good appearance; almost all are very fat."[15]

There were also western Delaware from the Ohio Valley. Regarded as the "grandfather of the Algonquin" by the other woodland tribes, the Delaware were a conglomeration of peoples united by linguistic and cultural roots who had a long and illustrious history before British expansion had forced them to abandon their homelands along the coast of what was to become New York and New Jersey. Since then, they had become one of the many migrant peoples who had found a second home in the Ohio country and its environs. Unsurprisingly, they too were eager to take up the hatchet against the British colonists who had ousted them, and some of those who traveled to Montréal may well have been present at Braddock's defeat at the Battle of Monongahela two years before. Bougainville was amazed to see the Delaware so far from home, and noted in his journal that "this nation has never before come to Montréal."[16]

There was also a handful of Miami from Saint Joseph. Sun-worshiping hunter-gatherers, unusual among the polytheistic Indian tribes, the Miami believed in the presence of a single overall deity known as the Master of Life. Their religion was highly developed and included the sacrifice of pet dogs. After the animals had been killed, their bones were burned so as to reach he who resided above. Yet another tribe with Algonquin linguistic roots that had been pushed toward an alliance with the French by Iroquoian raiding parties, the Miami were reluctant allies whose mixed loyalties would become apparent over the course of the campaign.[17]

Also present at Montréal were shaven-headed Sauk and Fox from the Mississippi. A fiercely independent people, the Fox, or Mesquaki (red earth people), had been one of the first nations to attempt to unite all the Indian tribes in the early 1700s so that they could deal with the Europeans on an equal footing. Such was not the Indian way, however. The tribes, and even individual groups within them, were anarchic in their politics and refused to conform to the wishes of a central power. When the French found out about the plan, they turned against the Fox with a vengeance. After recruiting some Chippewa allies, the French decided to make an example of the tribe and set out to exterminate them. A series of battles followed and the tribe was forced from its homeland. At first the Fox sought refuge with the Seneca, the westernmost tribe of the Iroquois Confederacy, but the move was blocked by the French. The Fox then turned to the Sauk, a culturally and linguistically related tribe that lived on the banks of the Mississippi. Despite the bribes and threats of the French, the Sauk took the Fox in and the Europeans were forced to sue for peace in 1737.[18] Twenty years later, the Fox still bore a grudge against both the French and the Chippewa, and their appearance at Montréal that summer was the first time they had been in Canada for several years.[19]

Besides the woodland Indians of the northeast, there were Winnebago from the Bay and even some Iowa from as far away as the "Western Sea." Plains Indians thousands of miles from their homelands, the Iowa were more accustomed to the wide-open vistas of the prairie than the claustrophobic primeval forests of the northeast. Unlike the vast majority of New France's Indian allies who spoke languages with Algonquin roots, the Iowa and Winnebago spoke a tongue more closely related to Lakota, or Sioux. It was unintelligible not only to the Canadian interpreters assigned to them but also to the other Indians who were to take part in the campaign.[20]

For the Canadian and French inhabitants of Montréal, the presence of so many undomesticated Indians on their doorstep was unnerving. On arrival, each group would enter town to perform ceremonial war dances in front of the houses of the principal citizens. Bougainville witnessed several performances. "In truth their dances seem like the pyrrhic and the other war dances of the Greeks," he wrote. Despite his often disdainful tone, Bougainville was extraordinarily open-minded compared to the vast majority of his peers and would later gain a reputation as an amateur anthropologist. "I found some difference in the music of the Winnebagos and the Ottawas," he noted in the same journal entry. "To the kind of little drum by which they mark the cadence join the voices of several men and women, and the whole forms a harmonious enough accord."[21]

Louis-Antoine de Bougainville, Montcalm's aide-de-camp, and future explorer of the southwest Pacific.

After announcing themselves, the Indians demanded councils with Montcalm and Vaudreuil, the great white father they knew as Onontio. While the Canadian fully appreciated his Indian allies, the Frenchman found the meetings interminable. Highly formulaic and ritualistic, they could drag on for days, as the orator of each tribe stepped up in turn to make his pronouncement. Gifts were exchanged, often in the form of wampum, mnemonic devices made from clam and conch shells or colored glass trade beads. Wampum was used to cement agreements, document treaties, councils, and speeches, and mark special occasions. The peace pipe was smoked and promises made. At other times, war parties would return from the front at Lake George with scalps or prisoners, an event that would drive the rest of the warriors into a frenzy. After receiving the prisoner with a shower of blows, dancing and ceremonies followed. The subsequent feasting put a terrible strain on the already depleted grain stocks of New France. Nevertheless, the Indians were given what they demanded—as a single refusal could see them pack up camp and return home.[22] At night, the warriors would gather at their encampments under the city walls and pass the time drinking French brandy and singing.[23]

For Montcalm, who missed his family in Candiac, the foibles and procrastination of the Indians were exasperating. "They are villains messieurs," he wrote to his mother.

> Even when fresh from their toilet, at which they pass their lives. You would not believe it but the men always carry to war, along with their tomahawk and gun, a mirror to daub their faces with various colors, and arrange feathers on their heads and rings in their ears and nose. They think it a great beauty to cut the rim of the ear and stretch it till it reaches the shoulder. . . . You would take them for so many masqueraders or devils. One needs the patience of an angel to get on with them. Ever since I have been here I have had nothing but visits, harangues, and deputations of these gentry. . . . They make war with outstanding cruelty, sparing neither men, women or children, and take off your scalp very neatly,—an operation which generally kills you. . . . Nothing but the King's service and the wish to make a career for my son could prevent me from thinking too much of my expatriation, my distance from you, and the dull existence here, which would be duller still if I did not manage to keep some little of my natural gayety.[24]

However tiresome they may have been, Montcalm knew that maintaining the Indians' goodwill was vital. The Frenchman had been pondering a major attack against Fort William Henry since the start of spring, and the warriors' ability to scout and gather intelligence was an essential part of his strategy. "In the midst of the woods of America," as Bougainville explained, "one can no more do without them than with[out] cavalry in open country."[25] With the majority of the British fleet at Fort William Henry reduced to ashes thanks to Rigaud's raid, the route that Montcalm's besieging army would take across Lake George lay wide open, and with the intelligence that Lord Loudoun had stripped his northern frontier of his best men to attack Louisbourg, the time was right to put the plan into effect. Dashing off daily orders to muster his troops, Montcalm had been far from idle that spring. His regulars had been massing at Fort Saint Jean since May. The men of La Reine Regiment were due to depart for Carillon on July 1, La Sarre on the second, Languedoc on the fourth, and Guyenne on the sixth. The French artillery, colonial regulars, and militia were still at Montréal but would soon be ready to join them. With the support of the Indians gathering outside the walls of Montréal, Montcalm would be able to inflict a crushing blow on the British, from which he hoped they would be unable to recover.[26]

The Indian councils, which had begun six months previously in the middle of winter, were still running at the rate of one or two a week by mid-July. May had seen the arrival of a deputation of Oneida. One of the five founding tribes of the Iroquois Confederacy, the Oneida were unsure whether they should raise the hatchet for the British or the French that summer or simply maintain their neutrality. On July 21, after Vaudreuil had presented them with a mighty wampum belt of six thousand red beads, they sang the war song, and all seemed settled in favor of the French. The very next day, however, they vacillated and returned home, as unsure of their allegiances as they had been when they had left several weeks before.[27] On June 14, it was the turn of the Ottawa of Michilimackinac. After complimenting Montcalm on his capture of Oswego, the tribe's orator spoke: "We wished to see this famous man who . . . destroyed the English ramparts," he began. "From his reputation and his exploits we thought that his head would be lost in the clouds. But behold," he continued, indicating the diminutive French general who stood before him, "you are a little fellow . . . [but] it is in your eyes, that we find the grandeur of the loftiest pine trees and the spirit of the eagle."[28]

On June 27 another council took place, during which a high country chief gave the French a warning of the violence they were about to unleash on the British by taking the "wild" Indians to war. "Father," he began, addressing Montcalm, do not expect that we can easily give quarter to the English. We have young men who have not yet drunk of this broth. Fresh meat has brought them here from the ends of the earth. It is most necessary that they learn to wield the knife and to plunge it into an English heart.

Bougainville, who was also present, was chilled by his words. In a letter to Madame Catherine Hérault, his sponsor back in France, he gave voice to his concerns. "Behold our comrades, dear Mama," he wrote after repeating the words of the chieftain, "what a crew, what a spectacle for a humane man."[29]

On July 1, yet another council was called. The Ottawa, Menominee, Potawatomi, Fox, and Sauk all spoke, the last representing the Winnebago as well as themselves, as the latter's language was not understood. Conspicuous by their absence were the Chippewa of Chequamegon Point. They refused to attend due to their ancient blood feud with the Fox. The Indians "presented two belts [of wampum]," Bougainville recorded,

> the first to the Marquis de Montcalm to thank him for [agreeing to lead] . . . them [in the forthcoming expedition] and praying him to take good care of them, the second to the Marquis de Vaudreuil asking him, since he did not go to war himself, that he should give of his own flesh and blood and send his brother [Rigaud].

Since it was not considered dignified to answer at once, Onontio waited until the following day before granting their request.[30]

Having secured the support of the Indians of the high country, Montcalm set about putting the final element of his plan into action. Alongside the regulars, militia, colonial regulars, and "wild" tribesmen, the marquis also wanted to recruit from among the domesticated tribes of the Saint Lawrence River. Accompanied by Rigaud and Bougainville, two Canadian officers of the colonial regulars, a detachment of grenadiers from the Guyenne Battalion, and Abbé François Picquet, a prominent Jesuit missionary, he set out for a tour of the missions.[31] On July 9 the party reached the Lake of Two

Mountains, a Sulpician settlement forty miles upriver from Montréal. When they arrived, their boat gliding between thick banks of reeds, they "were saluted by a triple discharge of two swivels and of musketry" fired by "Indians lined up on the . . . bank." Founded in 1721, the Lake of Two Mountains, or Oka, was populated by "praying" Indians who had left their homelands to live among the Sulpicians toward the end of the seventeenth century. Mohawks (a third of the tribe had joined the Jesuits fifty years before) predominated at Two Mountains, but Nipissing from Île aux Tourtes, Huron, and Algonquin, the latter a Great Lakes tribe all but wiped out by the Iroquois during the Beaver Wars, had also made the mission their home.[32]

After greeting the chiefs and the missionaries, Montcalm's party was given a tour. With a population of six hundred, Two Mountains was a sprawling settlement built in the shadow of the twin peaks from which it had gained its name. A fort manned by Canadian troops stood by the river bank. Inside was an "attractive and properly ornamented" church. Services held in the Indians' native tongues were given three times a day. Bougainville was impressed by the attendees' "exemplary devotion" and the "melodious" singing of the choir. To the west was a collection of large communal huts, or longhouses, inhabited by the Mohawk and Huron, while the Nipissing and Algonquin had constructed their own villages nearby. Bougainville thought the longhouses were "well enough built but very filthy." Dogs and children were given "free rein," and the inhabitants slept on platforms raised several feet above the floor. Grander lodges had been built for the chiefs. Each tribe had its own meeting hall, and a 300-foot-long chamber had been constructed where "the general councils of the three nations" were held.[33] Elsewhere were tribal cemeteries; fields planted with the Three Sisters of corn, beans, and squash; and a large area of cleared land where the inhabitants played lacrosse, an indigenous sport famed for its violence that the Cherokees had dubbed "the little brother of war."[34]

That afternoon, the warriors gathered at the council house "by the light of a few dim candles" to listen to Montcalm speak.[35] As one captain of the regulars attested, the general had become a master of native diplomacy. Hiding his distaste, he dealt with them "with infinite art and admirable patience."[36] With Luc de La Corne, one of the Canadian militia officers, translating, Montcalm began. After some opening platitudes, he announced his plan to capture Fort William Henry and drive on into the colony of New York. He then "ended by saying that he would give them three oxen for a feast and that he planned to sing the war song with them" later that evening. The Indians were delighted. In the last two years, the French had proved themselves more than a match for the British, and the campaign promised easy pickings. They "thanked [Montcalm and] . . . assured him that they would follow his wishes." After the meeting had broken up, Montcalm and his men went to visit the chiefs in their quarters. Among those they met were two great Nipissing warriors, Kisensik and Aoussik, both of whom had good cause to fight the British that summer.[37]

A "famous [young] warrior," hotheaded and impetuous, Aoussik had been at the siege of Oswego the year before. In the predawn light of August 12, 1756, two days before the forts were taken, he had been with a party of Indians escorting some French officers to the outskirts of the British position. Among the Europeans was an old engineer, Col. Jean-Claude-Henri de Lombard de Combles, who wandered off alone to sketch the British lines. Coming across him in the gloom, Aoussik had mistaken the engineer for an Englishman and fatally wounded him with a single shot. De Combles was "carried to his tent, but . . . died within half an hour."[38] Ever since, Aoussik had been killing the British with abandon, hoping to wipe the stain of the engineer's death from his name. According to one French memoirist, "more than thirty-three English [had fallen] . . . under his [tomahawk] stroke during the year." On one mission alone, to Fort William Henry in April, led by the Canadian officer Charles Langlade, Aoussik had taken four scalps and three prisoners from the 60th Regiment of Foot. Even so, the young warrior's bloodlust remained unquenched, and he was eager to take up the hatchet against his enemies once more.[39]

Where Aoussik was rash and instinctive, the second of the Nipissing chiefs at Two Mountains, Kisensik, was calm and considered. To understand the reason for his eagerness to return to action, it is necessary to look back at events that took place over thirty years before. In 1725 Étienne de Veniard, Sieur de Bourgmont, a famed French explorer, had taken Kisensik's father, a celebrated chieftain in his own right, to France to meet Louis XIV. Along with a handful of other Indians, Bourgmont had taken him hunting with the king, and the party later went on a tour of Versailles, Château de Marly, and Fontainebleau. Returning to his tribe with an inscribed silver gorget worn around his neck as a memento of his visit, Kisensik's father had risen greatly in his people's esteem. With the old man now in his final days, Kisensik knew he would soon inherit the gorget. He would travel to Fort William Henry with his own son that summer and desperately wanted to be able to put a few more notches on his war club so as to be worthy of the prize.[40]

While walking between the chiefs' huts that afternoon, Bougainville was struck by one resident in particular. "We saw a Nipissing Indian," he recalled,

> dishonored in the eyes of his brothers and of the Canadians because he wore breeches, covered his head, ate, dressed, and slept like a Frenchman. He goes neither to the hunt nor to war. He keeps a shop in his house filled especially with contraband goods, and he has a very lucrative business. The Indians scorn him, but do not reproach him or treat him badly. For in this place of complete liberty, Trahit sua quemque voluptas [His own liking leads each one on].[41]

It was this sense of personal liberty, universal among the tribes, that the Europeans, both French and British, found so hard to accept. Although chiefs, both of war and of peace, did exist and elders were respected, each man was free to make his own way in the world. No direct orders were given. Warriors led by example, reputation, persuasion, and suggestion. In the council chamber each man was allowed to air his point of view, and decisions were either made by consensus or not at all. There were no slaves (aside from those captured in war) and no servants. There were no policemen, courts, or jails.[42] Serious crimes, such as murder, treason, or practicing witchcraft with intent to kill, were dealt with by placing the culprit outside of the law, thereby allowing his victims (or their friends or relatives) to take whatever revenge they deemed fit without fear of reprisal.[43]

Indian parenting methods were equally idiosyncratic. While European children were beaten into conforming with the norms of society, Indian infants were largely left to their own devices. Physical punishment rarely occurred. The belief was that as they matured, children would cease to rebel, and conform to the tribes accepted standards in their own time.[44] Attitudes to women were also different. As the keepers of the village grain store, females could prevent war parties from setting out by withholding supplies. In several tribes, including the Iroquois, each clan was headed by a matriarch who decided matters of succession, had the power to remove male leaders who displeased her, and held sway over all political decisions. Attitudes to sexual practices were also difficult for the Europeans to understand. While married women were expected to remain faithful, the single, divorced, or widowed enjoyed considerable freedom and would often experiment with a number of partners before settling down, a license unknown to all but the lowest classes of contemporary European society.[45]

While these anarchic methods had their drawbacks, some Europeans came to appreciate the liberty the tribal lifestyle afforded. The Canadian coureurs de bois and voyageurs were converts as were many of those captured by war parties and adopted to replace warriors lost in battle. Some would even choose to remain with their adoptive families when presented with the chance to return to European civilization. Understanding the advantages of the Indian way of life, however, was beyond the scope of most of the Europeans who encountered them. The fact that there was no real hierarchy led the Europeans to believe that the Indians, without leaders to order them to work, lived a life of indolence. This was not the case. Each member of society gravitated toward his or her niche and filled it.[46]

Having greeted the chieftains, the French officers reconvened the council at Two Mountains later that evening. Bougainville recorded the scene:

The Indians were sitting . . . on the floor, ranged by tribes. In the middle, hung at intervals, were pots filled with meat destined for the war feast. A few candles lit up the place which seemed like a witches' cavern. Kisensik spoke first. After the ordinary compliments he asked the Marquis de Montcalm for permission to give his advice on war when the occasion offered. He then outlined his tribe's request and the number of warriors it would furnish. The chiefs of the other two nations then spoke on the same subjects.

Afterward, Montcalm thanked them, then the impetuous Aoussik took center stage.[47] An expert of the theater of council oratory, he rose, his looks, his gesture and expression denoting furious anguish. "What need," said he, "of councils, deliberations, proposals, when action is needed? I hate the Englishman. I thirst for his blood. I am going to bathe in it."[48]

He then seized a bullock's head from the cooking pot by its horns and, "stalking round with it, sang his war song. The other chiefs of the three nations followed him with the same ceremony," Bougainville recalled, "and I sang it in the name of M.de Montcalm and was much applauded. My song," Bougainville wrote, "was nothing . . . but the words 'Trample the English underfoot' cadenced to the movement of Indian cries. They then presented the Marquis de Montcalm with the first morsel [of meat], and, the war feast having started, we retired."[49]

The next morning, Montcalm's tour of the missions continued. Sailing downstream toward Montréal, the party sighted Sault Saint Louis, known to the Indians as Caughnawaga or Kahnawake. Originally founded eight miles downriver in 1676, the mission had moved twice before reaching its present location in 1716, after the soil of the first two sites had been exhausted by intensive agriculture. Although the Caughnawaga had originally attempted to remain neutral in the wars against the British colonists to the south, they had eventually been drawn into the conflicts on the side of the French. In King William's War (1689–97), they had even participated in raids on their Iroquois cousins in the colony of New York, and in Queen Anne's War (1702–13) they had taken part in several strikes against New England, including the infamous attack on Deerfield in 1704. Despite this hostility against the British, they continued to maintain business contacts at Albany and to play a key role in the fur trade with the Dutch.[50]

By 1757, Caughnawaga was the largest of all the missions on the Saint Lawrence. It had a population of twelve hundred, three hundred of whom were warriors. Like Two Mountains, the majority were Mohawks, but there were also significant minorities of Oneidas and Onondagas, both Iroquois tribes, as well as a notable Huron presence. Numerous captives also lived at Caughnawaga. According to one estimate, twenty different tribes were represented among them. Although the practice of adopting captives, both Indian and European, was universal among the woodland tribes of northeast America, it appears to have been particularly prevalent among the Abenaki and the Iroquois. As wars and raiding parties took their toll, new blood was required to make up the population. Indeed, it became so common that the British colonists' "captivity narrative" was a best-selling subgenre in the first half of the eighteenth century. These diaries provide an invaluable insight into the captives' experiences. The weakest would often not survive the journey back to Canada. Frightened that their pursuers would catch up to them, returning war parties killed and scalped the slowest while urging the strongest on. Once back at the tribes' village, the prisoners were still not safe. On arrival, many were tortured in a variety of ways. Some were used for target practice—the aim being to repeatedly wound the victim while maintaining him or her alive for as long as possible. Others were burned at the stake, a cruel fate inflicted on some of those captured at Monongahela, as a young Pennsylvanian prisoner named James Smith recorded. "About sundown," Smith wrote:

> I beheld a small party coming in with about a dozen prisoners, stripped naked, with their hands tied behind their backs and their faces and part of their bodies blacked; these prisoners they burned to death on the banks of the Alleghany river, opposite the fort. I stood on the . . . wall until I beheld them begin to burn one of

these men; they had him tied to a stake and kept touching him with firebrands, red-hot irons etc., and he screaming in a most doleful manner, the Indians in the meantime yelling like infernal spirits. As this scene appeared too shocking for me to behold, I retired to my lodging, both sore and sorry. When I came into my lodgings I saw Russel's Seven Sermons, which they [the French and Indians] had brought from the field of battle, which a Frenchman made a present of to me.[51]

As the existence of Smith's narrative testifies, many captives survived their ordeal. Some of those who were not ransomed by the French or Canadians were adopted by the tribe that had captured them. After a brief transitional period during which they were watched carefully, these new sons, brothers, daughters, and sisters were given the same freedom as any other member of the tribe. While many of the Indians, and some of the Europeans, thus adopted were accepting of their fate, others sought to escape. One who managed was Thomas Brown, the sixteen-year-old ranger from Charlestown, Massachusetts, who had been captured near Carillon in January 1757. After refusing Rigaud's request to act as a guide for the raid on Fort William Henry (see chapter 3), Brown was taken back to Oswegatchie, the mission headed by Abbé Picquet 150 miles upstream of Caughnawaga. On arrival he was forced to run the gauntlet, then was adopted by the mother of one of the braves his comrades had killed near Carillon. "The Indians appeared very sad," Brown recalled,

and my [adoptive] mother began to cry, and continued crying aloud for some time, and then dried up her tears, and received me for her son. . . . Here I saw that God could make friends of cruel enemies, as he had once turned the heart of angry Esau into love and tenderness.

Despite the kindness of his "family," Brown was intent on escape. By the time of Montcalm's tour of the missions, he was still a captive but would later abscond, and managed to get a berth in a ship sailing for Britain on July 23, 1757. Brown returned to his native New England four months later to "the great joy of" his "poor afflicted wife and family."

Looking back over the ten months of his captivity, Brown realized that the Indians were not the mindless savages he had once held them to be. "Our enemies," he wrote in the conclusion of his narrative,

> seem to make a better use of a bad religion [Roman Catholicism] than we of a good one; they rise up long before day in winter, and go through the snow in the coldest seasons, to perform their devotions in the churches; which when over, they return to be ready for their work as soon as daylight appears: The [mission] Indians are as zealous in religion. As the French, they oblige their children to pray morning and evening . . . are punctual in performing their stated acts of devotion themselves, are still and peaceable in their own families, and among each other as neighbours.[52]

Brown's epiphany was a touching moment in a brutal and terrible war. Sadly, it was a lesson that few Europeans ever learned and one that the self-assured Marquis of Montcalm would have thought ridiculous.

On July 10, 1757, while still a mile from Caughnawaga, Montcalm's party was met by "a charming sight." Their boat was approached by "two canoes," each of which held "ten naked Indians, the finest men of all the villages, painted for war in red and blue [and] adorned with bracelets of silver and of wampum." Accompanied by these escorts, the French and Canadians sailed ashore. "On the river bank," Bougainville recalled,

> we found the missionary [a Jesuit named Pére Jean-Baptiste de Neuville] who received the Marquis de Montcalm upon his stepping ashore, made a short speech and led him to the church between two rows of Indians who saluted him, the chiefs with their spears and the rest with a triple discharge from their guns. They sang the Te Deum in the Iroquois tongue, after which . . . Montcalm was led to the council chamber, where the chiefs joined him.

The subsequent meeting was similar to that held at Caughnawaga. Montcalm's proposal to attack Fort William

Henry was welcomed by the chiefs who informed the Frenchman that 258 of their warriors would accompany him. Three oxen were then slaughtered for the war feast, which, Bougainville recalled, "went off much like that of last night." There was, however, one notable exception.[53]

Over the previous year, Bougainville had come to know the Indians of Caughnawaga well. One in particular, a Shawnee woman named Cueta who had been adopted by Onoraguete, an Iroquois chieftain resident at the mission, had caught the young aide's eye. To the displeasure of Madame Hérault, his sponsor back in Paris (and no doubt of Montcalm as well), Bougainville had started a relationship with Cueta, which would result in the birth of at least one child.[54] This had brought him even closer to the Indians of the mission, and at the war feast that night he was formally adopted into the tribe. After being painted with a mixture of vermillion and bear's grease, belts of wampum were draped around Bougainville's neck. He was then led into the center of the council chamber, where the Indians welcomed him with the shrill cries they used to indicate that a living person, as opposed to the scalps of the dead, was being added to the tribe's communal spiritual strength. The young aide recorded what happened next with a mixture of amused condescension and pride. "The Iroquois . . . gave me the name of 'Garionatsigoa,'" he wrote,

> which means "Great Angry Sky." Behold me then, an Iroquois war chief! My clan is that of the Turtle, first for eloquence in council, but second for war, that of the Bear being first. They exhibited me to all the nation, gave me the first morsel of the war feast, and I sang my war song, in part with their first war chief. The others [then] dedicated theirs to me.[55]

Afterward, Bougainville was led to the river and plunged into its icy waters, thereby washing away his strangeness so he could emerge as a new man.[56]

Bougainville's journal entry throws light on another integral aspect of Indian culture of which most Europeans were only vaguely aware: the clans, a network of "relatives" that stretched beyond family boundaries denoted by the symbol of an animal, bird, or fish. The Mohawk, for example, had three clans: the Turtle, the Wolf, and the Bear. The Ottawa, on the other hand, had many more, including those of the Moose, Carp, and Black Squirrel, while the Huron had eight: the Turtle, the Wolf, the Bear, the Beaver, the Deer, the Hawk, the Porcupine, and the Snake. Even before one's tribe, an Indian's first allegiance was to his or her clan, membership of which could spread across tribal lines. Thus a Seneca brave of the Wolf clan would be bound to Mohawks of the same totem, welcomed in their houses, and barred from marrying their daughters, even though they may well have had no blood ties at all.[57]

After leaving Caughnawaga, Montcalm and his party returned to Montréal. There they found that most of the high country Indians had already left for Carillon, and the French commanders hastened to join them. As Montcalm was well aware, time was against him. His army of Indians, Canadians, and French was a fragile entity. The bonds that tied the allies together could disintegrate at any time. Another factor that worked against the Frenchman was the ever-present question of supply. After the most strenuous efforts, Governor Vaudreuil had managed to acquire a respectable quantity of provisions from the small holdings along the banks of the Saint Lawrence.[58] Nevertheless, counting Indians, both domesticated and wild, Canadian militia, French regulars, artillery, and colonial regulars, the marquis's army had swollen to some eight thousand men. His quartermasters would only be able to feed them for one month before the lack of food would force him to abandon the offensive for another year. If Montcalm was to strike a significant blow against the British that summer, he would have to act soon.

On July 12, Montcalm and Bougainville left Montréal. Among others, they were accompanied by the French general's "principal interpreter," an Irish deserter from the 50th Regiment of Foot, whose language skills would come in useful when interrogating British prisoners.[59] On July 13 they arrived at Fort Saint Jean, nicknamed Fort Mosquito by its garrison for the clouds of insects infesting the surrounding marshlands. The next day "a heavy southwest wind" forced them to beach their boats at Cape Scononton, where they caught up with a band of Ottawa and Chippewa that had left Montréal before them. While Bougainville was preoccupied with the upcoming battle, the Indians appeared to be entirely unconcerned. They "passed the time . . . bathing and amusing themselves," he observed. To Bougainville, a man influenced by the image of the noble savage, the Indians were utterly alien and physically formidable, yet as innocent as children. "They swim like fish," he remarked, "diving and remaining under water a long time. The old men make medicine at night, . . . they consult the Great Spirit to learn of the success of their expedition. They sacrificed a dog to him today." On July 16 there was a tremendous storm "all day long." The rain came down in sheets, soaking the French, Canadians, and Indians, and the wind howled and whipped up the rivers and lakes into ferocious seas. Some of the Indians thought it a portent of the slaughter that was to come.[60]

By the time Montcalm's party reached Carillon on July 18, the skirmishing around Lake George had reached fever pitch. The *petite guerre* that had been fought throughout spring had escalated into major encounters between war parties and British and provincial patrols of up to three hundred in number. The change had come suddenly, first becoming evident at the beginning of July when Capt. Israel Putnam had clashed with Charles Langlade, the partisan officer who had ambushed the carpenters outside Fort Edward nearly three weeks before. On this occasion, however, it would be Putnam who emerged triumphant, and Langlade who was left to return home to count his dead.

La Petite Guerre

JUNE 30–JULY 25, 1757

*C*aptain Israel Putnam was a difficult man to get on with. The thirty-nine-year-old from Salem, Massachusetts, had already ruffled Major Rogers's feathers, and in years to come he would fall out with George Washington too. Nevertheless, no one could accuse him of incompetence. Since his first taste of action at the Battle of Lake George in 1755, Putnam had learned quickly. By June 1757, he had been promoted to captain and had volunteered for the most dangerous service in the war: patrolling the rugged no-man's-land between Fort Edward and Fort Carillon. Despite having grown up in the relatively tame rural idyll of central Connecticut, Putnam had adapted remarkably quickly to what the Canadians termed *la petite guerre*. In early June, he and his men had captured a French prisoner outside Carillon and returned to Fort Edward without losing a single man. After a week recuperating from their ordeal, Putnam's Connecticut provincials were ready to set out again. This time their mission was to set up an ambush at East Bay on Wood Creek. Over the last few weeks enemy activity had been increasing in the area. The chances were that Putnam was going to run into something.

Setting out with sixty men on the morning of June 25, Putnam advanced northeast through the forest. That afternoon "it Raind vary steady," and at night "was Vary Wet & Cold."[1] After a few hours sheltering from the incessant downpour under their tarpaulins, Putnam's troops traversed a flat landscape of "tall and thick forests," densely packed with fir, pine, and birch. Occasionally their path was blocked by a fallen tree, and everywhere the ground was covered with the decomposing leaves of last autumn and "great quantities of moss."[2] At midday the rain stopped and the sun broke through the clouds.[3] The men were exhausted. Their clothes were heavy and sodden and they were soaked to the skin. After a second night in the open, they reached Wood Creek Falls on the morning of June 27. By now, several of the soldiers were showing the first signs of illness. To make matters worse, the creek, swollen by rainfall, proved impassable, and Putnam was forced to change his plan. Turning westward, he led his men two miles to the entrance of South Bay, where he found "a Conveanent Plais to Lay an Ambush."[4]

The spot was perfect. Putnam had chosen a "jutting precipice" that rose ten feet above the surrounding flooded land. Thirty feet wide, it overlooked a stretch of Wood Creek where it led out of South Bay, a placid lake that spread across the lowlands. Since the creek was only forty-five yards wide, if the enemy wanted to send scouts toward Fort Edward, their boats would have to pass close under Putnam's guns. Knowing that against the French, and especially their Indian and Canadian allies, he would need every advantage he could get, Putnam set about improving the position. "He erected a stone parapet thirty feet in length; and marked it with young pine-trees, cut [down] at a distance [from the ambush site], and . . . artfully placed [so] as to imitate the natural growth." The effort of felling the trees and dragging them across the flooded land proved the last straw for fifteen of Putnam's men. After the grueling march and two days and nights of exposure, they were too sick to be of any further use. Putnam ordered them back to Fort Edward, assigned several others to set up watch posts in the vicinity, then settled down to wait for the enemy.[5]

After four days, there was still no sign of the French. Running low on provisions, Putnam was "compelled . . . to deviate from a rule he had established,"—namely, "never to permit a gun to be fired but at an enemy, while on a scout." Reluctantly, he gave the men permission to open fire should any game wander within range of their guns. Later that day, a buck stumbled into the creek. Sighting his musket over the parapet, Putnam brought it down with a single shot. His men skinned the animal, butchered, and cooked it. With their bellies full for the first time in four days, soon after sunset all but the sentries had fallen asleep.[6]

It was a beautiful night. "A profound stillness reigned . . . and the full moon shone with uncommon brightness." At ten o'clock the enemy appeared. Looking to the north, one of the sentries posted "at the margin of . . . [South] bay saw a canoe glide into view, the Indians' muffled paddles barely rippling the surface of the water."[7] As he watched, fifty more appeared, "filled with men," and began "steering towards the mouth of the creek" where Putnam was posted. Sprinting southward along the shore, the sentry splashed across the flooded land and climbed up to the rise where his comrades were sleeping. Shaking them awake, he told Putnam of the enemy's approach. The men knew the plan: to let the lead canoes pass before opening fire on those in the main body. After reloading with fresh powder and a double charge of buckshot and ball, they crawled into position. Sliding their muskets forward, they drew back the hammers and waited for Putnam's signal.[8]

Charles Langlade, the commander of the French party, had warned his men to be extra vigilant that night. If living and fighting alongside the Indians of Michilimackinac had taught the young métis anything—it was caution. Nevertheless, he was brimming with confidence. So far, the British had proved unworthy of his respect. Believing themselves invincible against the French and especially their Canadian and Indian allies, the redcoats and American colonists had spent the last two years blundering through the forest beating their drums and had been soundly defeated time and time again. Only recently had some begun to adopt the subterfuge required in wilderness warfare, and even Rogers, the best they had to offer, was still amateurish by comparison to his foes.

The troops Langlade was leading that night also inspired confidence. He had known many of the two hundred Ottawa from Michilimackinac since birth. Equally deadly with the bow, tomahawk, musket, or knife, they were more than a match for the British. Guiding their high country cousins were twenty-five domesticated Iroquois from the Caughnawaga mission, an advance party of the tribe that would adopt Bougainville in ten days' time. Unlike the Ottawa, who were more than six hundred miles from their homelands, the Iroquois knew the country well—none more so than the man who led them that night, Kanectagon, who Bougainville had described as "the most famous hunter" of the tribe. Completing Langlade's party were two other Canadian officers and six cadets. Growing up in the backwoods, they had spent years hunting and raiding along the border and were just as competent as Kanectagon's men.[9]

As the Indians and Canadians paddled into Wood Creek, one of Putnam's men "accidentally struck his firelock against a stone." In the stillness of the night, the sound carried across the water. To Putnam's annoyance, "the commanding officer in the van canoe heard . . . [it] and repeated several times the savage watch word owish! Instantly the canoes huddled together," the center of the cluster directly in front of the provincials' guns. "The [Canadian] officers appeared to be in deep consultation and the fleet on the point of returning; when . . . Putnam . . . gave the signal by discharging his piece." All along the raised ground his forty-five men opened fire. With a spark, hammers cracked into frizzens, the guns barked, and a double load of musketry thundered across the water.

Although the Brown Bess muskets Putnam's men were using were hopelessly inaccurate at long range, at just twenty yards the first volley was devastating. A Canadian cadet was killed and several Indians badly wounded. A few canoes were capsized in the panic, and a handful of men fell into the water and began striking out for shore. Ascertaining that the fire was coming from the west, Langlade ordered the survivors to paddle for the far bank. Putnam's men reloaded and fired two more volleys into them before they landed their canoes. The Indians then scrambled up the rocks on the far bank and dragged their wounded into cover. Shouting to make himself heard above the din of musketry and the groans and yells of the wounded, Langlade ordered the survivors to return fire.[10]

From the paltry amount of musketry whistling around his ears, Langlade soon realized that he heavily outnumbered the British and decided to try and outflank them. Sending one party upriver and another downstream, he ordered them to cross to the far bank and try to get around behind the enemy and cut off their retreat. Putnam reacted immediately. Seeing the two enemy parties set out, he mirrored their movements, ordering Lt. Robert

Halfway Brook, a tributary of Wood Creek. Waterways were key strategic features between Forts Edward and William Henry and their control was critical to operations in the area. (*Author*)

Durkee to take twelve men to oppose the enemy moving down the creek, while Lieutenant Parsons was sent with a small squad upriver. Putnam then sent Sgt. Elias Avery and four others back to Fort Edward with a message detailing the enemy's strength and asking for reinforcements.[11] Avery set off at a run, but Putnam knew he would have to hold out for at least forty-eight hours before he could expect any support.[12] In the meantime the rest of his men, now only twenty in number, kept up "an incessant and deadly fire" on Langlade's main body on the far bank.[13] The return fire was largely ineffective, but over the course of the night three of Putnam's men were hit. Henry Shuntup, a Mahican, had his thigh smashed by a musket ball. Jabez Jones of Captain Fitch's company was "badly wounded," and John Kennedy, another of Putnam's scouts, was also hit.[14] Ordering twelve men to help them, Putnam sent them back to Fort Edward by a circuitous route that followed the course of Wood Creek before bending west toward the Hudson.[15]

As the hours passed, Langlade's flanking parties made several attempts to cross the creek, but Lieutenants Durkee and Parsons beat them back each time. Then at five o'clock, as the first light of dawn was beginning to color the eastern sky, Langlade sent out a third party "considerably" downriver. Fully occupied with the men to his front, Durkee failed to notice them until it was too late. By the time he realized his mistake, the Indians had crossed the river and were working their way back to cut off Putnam's retreat. Seeing that his position was compromised, Durkee ran back to the raised parapet to give Putnam the bad news. Putnam's men, meanwhile, were down to the last of their ammunition. Having fired their muskets all night, some had already used up the twenty-four cartridges they carried with them, while the others only had two or three balls left. Seeing his position was hopeless, Putnam ordered his men "to swing their packs" and fall back.[16]

The order came not a moment too soon. The Ottawa who had crossed downstream of Putnam's position were closing rapidly, but "by hastening the retreat, though in good order," the captain got all his men clear. So far the ambush had been an unqualified success, but on the way back to Fort Edward, Putnam's plan began to unravel. After an hour following the bank of the creek, the column ran headfirst into a volley of musketry. Knowing his men would be cut to pieces if they were caught between two bodies of the enemy, Putnam ordered them to charge. Roaring through the woods, they discovered that the "enemy" was in fact a scout of provincials from Fort Edward led by an inexperienced lieutenant named Harden. Belatedly realizing his mistake, Harden acknowledged himself to Putnam. Both sides lowered their guns, but the damage had already been done. Harden's volley had mortally wounded Elijah Sweetland, a young Connecticut provincial of Captain Wells's company. Putnam was furious, though not for the reason that might be expected. Regardless of whether they were friends or enemies, he informed the young lieutenant that his fire had been hopelessly ineffective. Having had such a clear shot, he "deserved to be hanged" for not decimating Putnam's men.

Having fashioned a stretcher for Sweetland, Putnam's column reached Fort Edward early the next morning. To the captain's surprise, the men he had assigned to escort those wounded during the ambush had still not arrived. Although ordered to take a roundabout route to throw off their pursuers, the men had decided to head directly for home. Quickly tiring of lugging their wounded comrades through the forest, they had split into two bodies. The first, of just two men, were to race back to Fort Edward for help, while the rest hid. The plan went horribly wrong. The two men became lost and did not make it back to camp for two days. The others were even less fortunate. Having hidden the wounded in a narrow valley, they were climbing a nearby slope to get their bearings when they "heard a dreadful hollowing" below them. They instantly knew what the cry signified: the Ottawa had discovered the wounded.[17]

Henry Shuntup chose to sell his life dearly. After he had loaded his gun with buckshot, the Ottawa burst upon him in strength. Shuntup fired at close range and killed three. The rest hacked him to pieces with their tomahawks.[18] Four days later, Colonel Lyman found his mutilated body. The Ottawa had pulled his nails out, cut off his lips "down to his chin and up to his nose," laying

> his jaws . . . bare; his scalp was taken off, his breast cut open, his heart pulled out and his bullet pouch put in the room of it; his left hand [was] clenched round his gall, a Tomahawk [had been] left in his bowels and a dart struck through him; [and] the little finger of his left hand . . . and the little toe of his left foot [had been] cut off.[19]

The importance of scalping in indigenous culture is well documented. Unlike colonial North America, where male status was commonly judged by wealth and material belongings, the indigenous peoples of the northeast lived in communal villages and had no sense of private property. Peers were evaluated by the deeds they performed during the hunt and on the battlefield. In an illiterate culture, scalps acted as solid evidence of enemies destroyed. They raised an individual's profile—not only making him more respected by the men of his village but also rendering him particularly eligible to single females. Scalps also had a ceremonial role and could even act as a form of currency. They could be given to a grieving family as a symbolic replacement for their dead, sacrificed to a god of war, or sent to another tribe to encourage it to join in a fight against a mutual enemy.[20]

Although originally a purely indigenous practice, during the French and Indian War, provincial Americans and Europeans also indulged. Rogers' Rangers took scalps, as did the Canadian coureurs de bois, and Maj. Gen. James Wolfe's light infantry did likewise when ravaging the countryside around Québec in the summer of 1759. There is also evidence of official British encouragement. During his ill-fated 1755 expedition, General Braddock promised his soldiers a bounty of five pounds for each Indian scalp taken; two years later Wolfe gave permission for his men to take those of enemy Indians or "Canadians dressed like Indians," and Brig. George Townshend wrote that any man who "choos'd to go out in the Woods and lay in Ambush for the Indians and bring in an Indian scalp should have 5 Guineas reward." Other officers found the practice disturbing. Lord Loudoun, for one, thought it "barbarous" and encouraged his scouts to take live prisoners instead.[21]

Pierre Pouchot, a French captain who commanded the garrison at Fort Niagara, described the mechanics in detail:

> As soon as the [victim] . . . has fallen, [the Indians] . . . run to him, put their knee between his shoulders, take a lock of hair in one hand, and with the knife in the other give a blow separating the skin from the head, and tearing off a piece.[22]

The resulting trophy could be quite small. When Chief Hendrick of the Mohawks was scalped at the Battle of Lake George in 1755, the circle of flesh was "not larger than an English crown."[23] In such cases the operation was not always fatal. While the unfortunate Captain Spikeman (see chapter 2) died shortly after his scalp was removed, a redcoat who suffered similarly not only survived but continued to serve in the army for several months before returning to Britain.[24]

After Henry Shuntup's body had been mutilated, Jabez Jones and John Kennedy were taken alive to the Indian encampment outside Carillon. On arrival, they were interrogated by the commander of the fort, Col. François-Charles de Bourlamaque, then handed back to the Ottawa. "You will not get either of these prisoners [alive]," Bourlamaque later reported to Montcalm. "The Englishman ["whom spoke little"] will die [of his wounds], and the Mahican, whose flesh is not appetizing, will be burned."[25]

After dealing with their prisoners, the Ottawa turned their attention to their dead. Twenty Indians had been wounded in Putnam's ambush, two of whom had died on the journey back to Carillon. The braves bitterly lamented their passing. As they were so few in number in comparison to the Europeans, the Indians found losses much harder to accept. With the passing of each brave, the tribe was a step closer to extinction, a fact their elaborate funeral ceremonies reflected.[26] First they approached Bourlamaque and demanded "water spirits." The brandy would help them "cry and laugh" and put them into an altered state of consciousness by which they could better commune with the dead. Bourlamaque was then required to cover their wounds with "a cap, a shirt and a pair of mittens," gifts for the afterlife, and give consolation gifts of wampum to the living. Their graves were oriented east-west and filled with an array of goods, food, tools, and weapons. Their souls then journeyed into the afterlife, "a pleasant country" reached via "a dangerous river" crossed by "a feeble bridge."[27]

Just a mile distant from the Indian camp, Fort Carillon was a hive of activity. At the beginning of May, Col. Bourlamaque had arrived with the advance party of the army: the Royal Roussillon and Béarn Regiments, three hundred colonial regulars, and "a large number of workmen of all classes" marshalled by Jean-Nicolas Desandrouins, a French engineer. On July 7 they were joined by four more regiments of regulars— La Sarre, Guyenne, La Reine, and Languedoc, all under the command of Montcalm's second, Brig. François de Lévis— and on July 18 the general and his staff arrived. Meanwhile, bands of Indians were coming and going, led by colonial officers and accompanied by interpreters and Jesuit priests. While the Indians scouted possible lines of march to Fort William Henry and sent raiding parties to capture prisoners, Desandrouins's men worked on Carillon's defenses. They dug ditches, erected earthworks and palisades, and felled trees and undergrowth to open the fort's fields of fire. Meanwhile the regulars cleared the portage, or overland carry, connecting Lakes George and Champlain; manhandled the army's cannons, boats, canoes, and bateaux across; and set up four encampments along its length. The two most advanced, commanded by Rigaud, were situated at the northern end of Lake George. Consisting of a collection of tents, huts, and lean-tos, they were occupied by Indians, colonial regulars, and units of Canadian militia who had been arriving throughout the summer. Further north were the ordered cantonments of the regulars: forests of tents flying the regimental colors. Bourlamaque commanded the first, occupied by the regiments of Royal Roussillon and Béarn, while the second, housing La Reine, La Sarre, Guyenne, and Languedoc, was under Brigadier Lévis.[28]

Twenty-five miles to the south at Forts Edward and William Henry, the atmosphere was considerably more leaden. Despite Putnam's recent success, the French raids were ever more destructive and the signs of Montcalm's military buildup were ominous. In early April, a friendly Cayuga named Otawanie had brought warnings of an attack planned on Fort William Henry for that summer; and on June 16, a French colonial regular captured by Mohawk scouts revealed that Montcalm intended to advance soon.[29] At the end of the month, two escaped British prisoners had stumbled into Fort William Henry with reports of eight thousand men massing at Carillon; and two days later, four German-speaking deserters previously sold into French service brought further news.[30] "[I] examined them all four," Colonel James Montresor of the Royal Engineers wrote, "and found that . . . Marquis Montcalm was . . . expected at Carillon with [the] . . . Battalion [of Languedoc] 500 Indians & as many Canadians as he can muster, with the Battalion of La Sarre at St Johns, and the two of Beare & Rousillon at Carillon, with the Cannon & Mortar there, to attack our Forts." As Montresor was aware, if Montcalm could get his artillery across Lake George and within range of Fort William Henry's palisades, the garrison was doomed.[31]

Further souring the atmosphere in the camps was the continuing smallpox epidemic, which was claiming victims daily, and the execution of a deserter named Dominicus Peck, which took place on July 21 at Fort Edward. A private with the 3rd Battalion of the Royal American, or 60th, Regiment, Peck had been recruited in Germany by Capt. Rudolphus Faesch on the strength of "a certain agreement," which was never "fulfilled." Although it is uncertain what this promise was, the recruiting practices of the 60th and its commander, Col. Jacques Prevost, were later the subject of an official inquiry that uncovered numerous incidents of corruption and "skulduggery."[32] The investigation came too late to save Peck, however. The British officers presiding over his court-martial were unimpressed with his pleas, found him guilty, and sentenced him to death.[33]

Sergeant Jabez Fitch was among those who witnessed the event. "[Peck] had on a white cap tied at the top with a black ribbon," the sergeant recorded.

> His countenance was very pale. As he marched very slow, he was reading in a small book. Sometimes I observed him to shut up his book & fold his hands manifesting great concern of mind. When he came to the place of execution there was about 1000 men drawn up in two lines. Then the prisoner was ordered to the spot where he was [to be] executed . . . ye guard parted [and] the grenadiers fired upon him. He immediately fell down on his face partly on one side. After sometime he made some motion with one hand. Then a number of . . . [the grenadiers] run up near him and fired upon him [until] . . . he was quite dead.[34]

Perhaps the only man at Fort Edward pleased with Peck's demise was the newly arrived commander in chief of British forces on the northwest frontier, Maj. Gen. Daniel Webb.[35] In a letter to his superior, Lord Loudoun, who was then at Halifax preparing for the attack on the French fortress of Louisbourg, Webb stated his delight at the melancholy event and wrote that he hoped it would deter further attempts at desertion. Loudoun had chosen Webb for the job of guarding the frontier for the same reason that he had given him the 35th and provincials to achieve it. The Scot thought little of the martial prowess of either, and had not suspected Montcalm would attack Webb when he had set off for Halifax that spring. The last letter Loudoun wrote to Webb before leaving New York shows how unlikely he thought an attack would be. "I could not Depart," he informed the general,

> without giving you my opinion of the situation of things on your side of the country. I am this morning informed . . . that the enemy . . . are now drawing their whole force to Quebec for the Defence of their Capital; by which means you will have nothing to oppose you at Ticonderoga & Crown Point but the Garrisons, and I imagine very few more for scouting. This intelligence only confirms me in my former opinion.[36]

Although the 35th would fight bravely that summer, Loudoun's concerns about Webb were well founded. As well as being vindictive, Webb was indecisive, lacked courage, and was plagued by hypochondria. Characterized by one influential contemporary as "the only Englishman I ever met who was a coward," his dithering would cost the troops under his command dearly. Webb's failings have been well documented. Not long after he had arrived in New York, he had made the first of a series of mistakes that were to punctuate his American career and terminate in the loss of Fort William Henry. When Loudoun had first received word of the siege of Oswego in 1756, he had ordered Webb to proceed up the Mohawk River with a "considerable" number of reinforcements. As Webb neared his destination, he received news of Oswego's fall from some neutral Indians. Rather than continuing upriver to confirm the reports or counterattack the French, Webb panicked. Ordering hundreds of trees felled to block the river, he had the recently rebuilt Fort Bull burned to the ground and retreated to German Flats, a settlement on the Mohawk halfway back to Albany, thereby effectively abandoning the entire western frontier.[37] As a result, he lost the confidence of the troops and his hypochondria worsened, as a letter written by Lord Loudoun in mid-December makes clear. "Mr. Webb . . . was about a fortnight ago attacked with a very slight fit of the palsy," Loudoun began, "which did not last a minute, and to another man, would have been of very little consequence; but all his people have died of that disease, and he is very low and down, and I cannot get his spirits up; I am very much afraid, he will not soon be able to do much business."[38] Loudoun was to be proved right.

Two days after Peck's execution, Webb witnessed a spectacle that was considerably less to his liking. Early in the morning of July 21, the largest French raiding party to date had set out from Carillon. At its head was Joseph Marin de La Malgue, one of Canada's toughest colonial regular officers. An expert on backwoods warfare, Marin came from a long and illustrious line. His ancestors had arrived in Canada with the famed Carignan-Salières Regiment, the first to be stationed in the colony, in 1665, and his father, Paul, had distinguished himself fighting against the English, dealing with the Indians, and working in the fur trade. Joseph was to follow in his footsteps. Just thirteen when he was sent into the western wilderness by his father, over the next twenty-five years he absorbed the lessons taught by the local tribes, learned Sioux and several Algonquian dialects, and became a seasoned practitioner of *la petite guerre*. As a cadet, he had spent thirteen years at the trading post of Michilimackinac; in 1739 he took part in a campaign against the Chickasaws of the Mississippi; the following year he mediated peace between the French and the Sioux of Green Bay; and in 1745 he was present at the siege of Louisbourg. The next twelve years saw Marin leading mixed bands of Indians and Canadian militia on raids all along the frontier. For his success he was promoted, reaching the rank of lieutenant in 1756. In August that year, he had orchestrated operations in the Lake George area, and on one raid on Fort William Henry alone had taken sixty-four scalps and prisoners. In December he had ventured further behind enemy lines, leading Huron and Iroquois warriors on raids around Albany.[39]

On July 18, 1757, shortly after Montcalm had arrived in camp, Marin left Carillon on what would prove his most audacious raid yet. With him were three hundred eighty men. Three hundred were Indians, mostly Ottawa, with a handful of Chippewa and Iroquois guides. The rest were colonial regulars and Canadian militia. Bougainville, having arrived at Carillon a few hours before Marin's party set out, recorded the expedition's aims in his journal. "They are to visit the head of . . . [South] Bay," he wrote, "where Indian dreams and wild terrors have fabricated an intrenched camp of four thousand men. From there, if they meet no big enemy detachments, they [will] go to lay an ambush between Fort [William Henry] . . . and Fort [Edward]." It appears that Putnam's moonlight ambush had made a lasting impression on the Ottawa, who now feared the area where they had recently lost one of their warriors. Learning of their reluctance to return to South Bay, their cousins the Chippewa "made magic and hung up a breechclout, dedicated to the Manitou," a powerful spirit who they hoped would aid them on their mission.[40]

After arriving at South Bay undetected, Marin set up camp amid the ruins of Fort Anne.[41] Although the Indians' fears of an entrenched camp in the area were clearly exaggerated, the Canadian proceeded with caution. Sending out several small parties of scouts to the south and west to gather intelligence on British movements, he kept his main body in reserve, close to the canoes in case they should need to beat a hasty retreat.[42] On July 19, one of these parties of just eight men came across a group of thirty rangers and provincials under Lieutenant Dormit of Massachusetts. Strangely, Marin's Indian scouts, who habitually moved through the forest like ghosts, were just as surprised as Dormit's provincials when the two groups ran into each other in the woods to the northeast of Fort Edward. Recovering from the shock, Dormit ordered his men to fan out and engage the enemy, "but before he could have an opportunity to fire, was shot through the Head . . . and died on the Spot."[43] Appalled, his men fled back through the woods to Fort Edward, dumping their packs behind them and leaving the Indians to their prize.[44] Dormit's body was found by Captain West ten days later. "His head and arms [had been] cut off and his body cut to pieces."[45]

Marin, meanwhile, was preparing to advance even further into enemy territory. After sending back one hundred of his men to Carillon since they lacked shoes and supplies, he searched through the discarded packs that his scouts had salvaged from the scene of the skirmish. Among Dormit's papers were detailed instructions from General Webb. "His orders," Bougainville later observed in his journal, were

> to observe the French detachments which pass in the region [of South Bay], to attack them if they are weak enough, and, if they are too strong, not to reveal themselves but to send a man to Fort Edward to warn them of the road the French took. They were cautioned that friendly Indians will come to them with a red flag in hand, that they will give them the password, which is Johnson, and will show them a passport signed William.[46]

Three days after Dormit's death, Marin advanced with his main body to Fort Edward. After pausing to "make medicine" and pray to the spirits for a fortuitous encounter, they hiked to an area to the east of the fort studded with mighty trees, several of which had recently been felled by the British for timber. It was eight in the morning by the time they arrived. Ordering half of his men on to a nearby hilltop and the rest to occupy a thickly wooded swamp nearby, Marin settled in to await the woodcutters' return. One hour later they appeared. The carpenters, mainly civilians from New York, were guarded by a "covering party" of eighty provincials led by Lt. John Titcomb, a veteran from Massachusetts who had fought at the Battle of Lake George two years before. Also present among his command were Sergeant Felton and Corporal Wiley of the 35th. With the morning light filtering through the gaps in the foliage, the carpenters set to work, while Titcomb arranged his sentries, sending off small groups of six and twelve on looping marches through the trees. Meanwhile, Marin's Ottawa warriors slid forward unseen on their bellies, notching arrows to their bows.[47]

One of the guards placed near the swamp was killed without uttering a sound. When his corpse was later discovered, six of the Ottawa's brightly plumed shafts were found lodged in his body. Another was relaxing into his duty when his attention was suddenly drawn by a blur of color that flashed by his head. Believing it to be a species of bird, the provincial watched entranced as several more flew by. "While he was ruminating on these wonderful" creatures "and endeavouring to form some idea of their colour, shape and size, an arrow buried itself into the limb of a tree just above his head." Realizing his mistake, the sentry ducked behind the trunk and hollered "Indians!"—a single word of warning that chilled his comrades to the bone.[48]

Prompted by Titcomb's order of "Tree All!" the sentries took cover. With the element of surprise gone, Marin's men took up their muskets. Yelling their war whoops, half of the Indians maneuvered to encircle the provincials, while the rest opened fire. Soon the woods were filled with smoke. Arthur Ackley recalled that it "was so thick that he could not see any of the enemy." Terrified as the Ottawa closed in, several of Titcomb's sentries cowered behind the trunks; others fled for Fort Edward, ducking from tree to tree, while a brave few clustered around Lieutenant Titcomb and the two redcoats and returned fire. As he loaded his musket for a second shot, John Cavenough had it knocked from his hands by a ball fired by the enemy. Just then Pvt. Jacob Bliss saw the Indians charging out of the woods.

Seeing his position was about to be overrun, Titcomb gave the order to withdraw. After taking a few dozen paces, Nathan Barnsham turned to look back. Thirty Indians were in pursuit, one of whom paused to hurl his tomahawk. Spinning end over end, it buried itself in Sergeant Felton's back. Richard Glub was shot and killed, and James Mingo saw another man trying to reload his musket as the Indians bore down on him. The provincial was too slow. As he was selecting his target, an Indian charged and knocked him to the ground. Before he could rise, the Ottawa pinned him to the ground with one knee planted in the center of the provincial's back, drew his knife, and scalped him.[49]

Within seconds the covering party had been overrun. Half a dozen had been killed, others wounded or taken prisoner, and the rest were hurtling back through the woods. Pausing to look for a discarded musket to replace the one he had lost moments earlier, Private Cavenough noticed Lieutenant Titcomb beside him. "Make haste my lad," the officer warned him, before dashing on. As Cavenough watched him depart, the lieutenant tripped over a log and went flying through the leaf mold. His lace hat fell from his head, his sword was lost, and his musket's stock broken off in the tumble. As he rose, Titcomb found himself face-to-face with an onrushing Indian warrior. He leveled his broken musket to defend himself and, to his surprise, the Indian pleaded for quarter. Perhaps concerned that his gun would misfire after the fall, Titcomb allowed his adversary to withdraw. "I hope I shall get another Gun and have another Brush," he called to Cavenough, then turned on his heel once more.[50]

A quarter of a mile to the west, Fort Edward was in uproar. The drummers had just rattled out the morning call when the crackling of distant musketry carrying through the woods threw the men into a panic. Captain Learned, Lieutenants Knowles and Eddy, and Ensign Gilding of the Massachusetts regiment were among the first to respond. Calling for their company to fall in, they loaded their muskets and headed toward the sound of the guns. As they neared the edge of the forest, the men began firing blindly through the woods as their retreating comrades from the covering party passed through them. A few were hit by their own men's fire, but the rest got back to Fort Edward. Meanwhile, Marin's men had moved to the edge of the forest. Taking cover behind the last line of trees in full view of Fort Edward, they engaged the provincials who had sallied out to meet them. The skirmish lasted for five minutes. Knowing that he had stirred a hornet's nest, Marin then gave the order to fall back. With a cacophony of "hideous yells," the Indians withdrew, pausing behind each tree trunk to fire and reload before moving on.[51]

Meanwhile, on Rogers Island, Capt. Israel Putnam was gathering his men. He then "plunged into" the Hudson and waded to the far bank. As the group passed the fort, Colonel

Lyman, perhaps fearing that Marin's raid was the beginning of a full-scale attack, "mounted the parapet and ordered him to proceed no farther." Stubborn as ever, Putnam "only took time to make the best short apology he could and marched on." Upon reaching Learned's company in the woods, Putnam ordered his men to charge. "The whole rushed impetuously forward with shouts and huzzas" and pushed the Indians back. As the skirmish recrossed the ground where Titcomb's men had been ambushed half an hour before, one of Marin's Indians spied Richard Glub's unscalped body. Not willing to relinquish the prize, he dashed from behind cover, decapitated the corpse with a blow from his tomahawk, and carried the head "30 yards off behind a tree in order to scalp it." Equally determined to deny the brave his grisly trophy, the provincials redoubled their efforts. Pushing forward, they forced the Indian to abandon the head with the job half done.

With the fighting fading into the woods, Colonel Lyman, at the head of numerous reinforcements, belatedly arrived on the scene. Outnumbered, Marin's men began to fall back more rapidly. After executing all but one of their prisoners, a man later said to have been saved by the attention of an Indian woman, they retreated, leaving a few of their packs and guns behind.[52] Three detachments under Captains Waldo, Learned, and West, totaling 250 men, were ordered to pursue them and kept up the chase for "ten miles."[53] Not wishing to pause long enough to reload their muskets, the Ottawa detached a rear guard that kept the provincials at bay with flights of arrows. Marin lost just one man, a colonial regular officer dressed in a "ruffled shirt" who was said to have died "of fatigue or of fear."[54] The rest, including five "lightly wounded" Indian braves who left a trail of blood across the leaf mold in their wake, got back to their canoes at South Bay and returned to Carillon. En route the braves divided the eleven scalps they had taken into thirty-eight pieces. The ruse boosted not only their bounty payments but also their prestige.[55] Meanwhile, Putnam had discovered Marin's abandoned camp at Fort Anne. The veteran ranger reckoned that it had housed as many as five hundred men.[56]

Back at Fort Edward the burials began. In total, twelve men had been killed. All except Richard Glub had been scalped and some had had their throats cut. Others had been "mangled in a most Barbarous Manner."[57] Accompanied by the patter of muffled drums, Sergeant Felton and Corporal Wiley of the 35th were buried with full military honors, while Glub's head was tied up in a handkerchief and interred with his body. Several other provincials and regulars were missing, one of whom Marin had carried back to Carillon as a prisoner. The rest, who had scattered in the woods during the fighting, returned to camp over the following days. Others had been wounded, some of them mortally. Private Pitkin of Putnam's company died at sunset on July 23, while Amos Biben, a native of Connecticut, lingered on until well after nightfall before expiring.[58]

General Webb, who had spent the morning skulking in his quarters, was horrified at the carnage inflicted so close to the walls. If the enemy could steal up to within musket shot of Fort Edward before being discovered, what chance would the defenders of Fort William Henry have, fourteen miles beyond? The next day, while Webb was still pondering this terrifying development, an express arrived from Fort William Henry bearing yet more bad news. Despite the general's orders to the contrary, the note stated that the day before Marin's attack on Fort Edward, Monro had given Col. John Parker of the Jersey Blues permission to row out into Lake George to gather intelligence on the enemy. Reading on, Webb learned that three hundred of his men had gone with him. Halfway to Carillon, the party had been ambushed at Sabbath Day Point. Although the report was unclear as to the extent of their losses, the news was far from encouraging.[59]

Sabbath Day Point

July 22–24, 1757

*B*y early summer, morale at Fort William Henry was in steady decline. Alarming reports of the French buildup at Carillon came in frequently, and Indian raids kept the men on constant alert. On July 6 Lt. Adam Williamson, the young British engineer who had parleyed with the French during Rigaud's winter raid three months before, spoke to a scouting party that had just returned from South Bay. Although they had seen no sign of the enemy, on their way back across Lake George they had picked up "a man on a point of land" who was hailing them. A survivor of a previous scout, the man "was almost starved & unable to give any account of himself." Once back at Fort William Henry his story swept around the camp, the details embellished at each retelling. On July 10, Williamson recorded that "a boat with three men returned belonging to the [thirty-strong] Scout that . . . [had gone] out on the Seventh." Two of the three men had been left to guard the boats when the party landed on the far side of Lake George, while the third had gone into the woods with the others. When the twenty-eight men were eating, they had been attacked by the enemy. The man who returned had made it back to the boats alone and "imagined the whole [of his comrades] were taken or killed." As Williamson's journal reveals, there were other survivors. "Two more [of them] came in by night," he recorded, and gave "a bad account of the affair."[1]

Despite the glut of horror stories, reliable intelligence on enemy movements was increasingly difficult to come by. Any scouting parties that dared venture to the northern end of Lake George were invariably intercepted; the woods were dominated by the enemy, who also maintained supremacy on the waters themselves. Since Rigaud had burned three of Fort William Henry's sloops, the British no longer had sufficient naval strength to ensure their crews' safety, and the only means of obtaining intelligence open to Colonel Monro was the Mohawk scouts. Although they were adept at the role, the British officers distrusted the "savages" and put little faith in their reports. Their tales of a vast army gathering in the north whose soldiers outnumbered the leaves on the trees were considered fanciful.

Driven to desperation, Monro decided to go against General Webb's wishes.[2] It was crucial that he obtain accurate reports on Montcalm's movements; and if his superior was too much of a coward to order a sortie in strength, then Monro would have to do it himself. Command of the expedition was given to Col. John Parker, a veteran who had first seen action in King George's War over a decade before. With orders to proceed to Carillon, Parker's aims were to capture prisoners and to wrest some of the initiative back from Montcalm by burning the French sawmill and boats at the northern end of Lake George.[3] Under Parker's command were three hundred New Jersey Blues, a handful of New York provincials led by Captains Jonathon Ogden and Robert McGinnis, and a single gentleman volunteer of the 35th.[4]

Volunteers were a common feature on the regimental lists of the Georgian army. Often the younger sons of upper-middle-class families who had fallen on hard times, they aspired to the officer class but lacked the funds to purchase a commission. Being afforded respect yet lacking authority, the gentlemen volunteers functioned as privates with privileges, and their only means of ascending the promotional ladder was through reckless displays of bravery on the battlefield.

Early in the morning of July 22, Parker ordered his men aboard twenty-seven whaleboats lined up on the beach before

Fort William Henry.[5] Between twenty-five and thirty-five feet long, the vessels were double-ended, flat-bottomed rowing boats built from pine planks covering an oak frame. Each cost about six pounds and six shillings to purchase and could carry up to twenty-five men and their equipment.[6] After pushing the boats into the water, the men climbed aboard and began pulling on the oars, driving the vessels across Lake George. The work was exhausting. Compared to the Indians' finely crafted birch bark canoes, many of the whaleboats were ungainly, ill-balanced vessels. The worst of them were soon lagging behind, and the party became strung out across the water.

By mid-afternoon, after rowing across the broad southern section of the lake, Parker's flotilla entered the Narrows. Just one mile across and studded with numerous wooded islets, the area made an ideal spot for an ambush. Having discarded their blue woolen coats in the heat of the day, the New Jersey provincials sweated at the oars in their shirtsleeves, while their officers scanned the shoreline for signs of imminent attack.[7] An ambush was not forthcoming, and a few hours later they left the "crooked and intricate channels" behind, and emerged into open water. Parker called a halt and decided to stop for the night. Spying a nearby island, he ordered the men to pull toward it. They drew up their dripping oars and beached the boats. The men set up camp amid the trees, rested, and ate their evening meal, while their officers organized pickets and congratulated themselves on their progress so far.

Unknown to the provincials, at that very moment they were being watched by the enemy. Lieutenant François-Xavier de Saint-Ours, a Canadian officer in charge of a reconnaissance barge, was hidden under the boughs on the shore a few miles to the north. Gauging the importance of what he saw, the thirty-nine-year-old sent a dispatch to the camps around Carillon.[8] The effect was immediate. Word of the presence of so many provincials so close to camp stirred the Indians of the high country into a frenzy. Within a matter of hours, four hundred warriors, mainly Ottawa, Chippewa, Menominee, and Potawatomi, had set out to intercept them. The braves were accompanied by Charles

Langlade, the officer whom Putnam had ambushed at South Bay on June 31, and Ensign de Corbière of the *troupes de la marine*. At their head were dozens of chiefs whose names Bougainville recorded. With the Ottawa were "La Fourche, Brisset, Pennahouel, Le Poisson Blanc, Huharnois, Le Vieux Bouchard, Makiouita, Agoda, Le Fils d'Aukameny, Ouennago, Ounenaoué [and] Oyuninenon." The Chippewa were led by "Sagné, the chief of the Saginaws of Akouoi . . . [,] Capipoeken, Aguipemosé, Nanjeoyaky, Caouchinayé [and] Chabaouia," while "Le Chat, Millouisillyny, Ouakousy, Nanaquoibis, Oybischagamé . . . [and] Nerionois" led the Menominee and Potawatomi.[9]

Accompanied by fifty French soldiers, Canadian colonial regulars, and militia, the Indians paddled across the northern stretch of Lake George, splitting into several detachments as they neared the enemy. The majority landed at Sabbath Day Point, a notable promontory on the west shore. The rest advanced to a number of small islands two miles farther south. After landing, they hid their vessels on the shoreline and concealed themselves in the forest within musket shot of the water.[10]

Before dawn the next morning, both sides sent out reconnaissance parties. Langlade ordered two canoe loads of Ottawa to head south until they caught sight of Parker's men. "At daybreak," Bougainville recorded, "the first canoe returned [without incident]," but "the second, passing in sight of the Indians on the most advanced island, was taken for the enemy. Someone [on shore] fired and . . . wounded two Ottawa chiefs, one of whom died. [This caused] great grief among the Indians [and] . . . several . . . gave up."

Packing their belongings into their canoes, they began the vast trek to their homelands at the Great Lakes six hundred miles away. The 250 men remaining, having been assured of victory by Langlade and Corbière, determined to make the British pay for their loss.[11]

Parker's scouts had also set out in two detachments before dawn. The first group of three whaleboats had been ordered to make for the northern shore of the lake, two miles from the outposts of Carillon. As they passed Sabbath Day Point,

Langlade's Indians paddled out from the shadows and surrounded them. The provincials surrendered without a fight.
The second set of whaleboats, following "at a little distance
met the same fate." Under threat of torture, the prisoners
revealed Parker's plan: after scouting the enemy defenses at
Carillon, the scouts were to have rendezvoused with the main
body at Sabbath Day Point. Langlade decided to use the
intelligence to lure Parker within range of his men's muskets.
Ordering his Ottawa warriors back to shore, where they performed the rites that would afford them good fortune in the
coming fight, Langlade and Corbière settled in to wait for
Parker to fall into their ambush.[12]

At daybreak, with a light fog still lingering over the water,
Langlade spotted the main body of provincials approaching
and sprung his trap. As Parker stared ahead through his telescope, three whaleboats crewed by Ottawa dressed in the blue
coats of the Jersey provincials moved out from the western
shore and paddled for Sabbath Day Point. Believing them to
be the ones he had agreed to meet that morning, the provincial colonel ordered his boats to follow. As they came within
gunshot of the shore, a volley erupted from the tree line. The
musketry cut through the men and thudded into the sides of
the boats. While the marksmen reloaded, fifty birch bark
canoes burst from the shore behind Parker's men, threatening
to cut off their retreat. Crewed by brightly painted Indian
braves, the canoes moved at an alarming rate. Parker ordered
his men to blast them out of the water. Already beginning to
panic, the provincials hurried their shots. The lead whipped
harmlessly overhead and the Indians came on undaunted.[13]

Following the provincials' first volley, all discipline collapsed. As the whooping braves closed in, several of Parker's
men dropped their guns and tried to surrender. Others
attempted to break through the cordon, and some even
jumped into the water and struck out for shore. Within an
instant the Indians were upon them. They caught the men
and "speared them like fish." Others attacked what remained
of the flotilla. Jumping aboard the crowded whaleboats, they
tomahawked the terrified occupants, while others dived into
the water, swam under the boats, and capsized them. In the

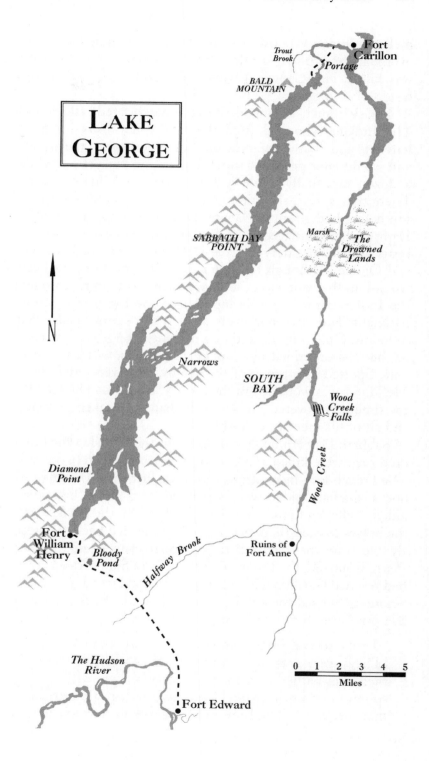

Trout Brook

• **Fort Carillon**

Portage

BALD MOUNTAIN

Marsh

The Drowned Lands

SABBATH DAY POINT

Narrows

SOUTH BAY

Wood Creek Falls

LAKE
GEORGE

N

Diamond Point

Fort William Henry

Bloody Pond

Halfway Brook

Wood Creek

Ruins of • Fort Anne

0   1   2   3   4   5
Miles

The Hudson River

• Fort Edward

melee Captain Woodward "was terribly wounded, jumped overboard and drowned"; the gentleman volunteer of the 35th was killed; and Captain Ogden was badly wounded in the head.[14]

The swimmers who made it to the beach fared little better. The Indians who had fired the first volley took up their hatchets and chased them down. Some got lost in the woods and would later perish of thirst, hunger, or exhaustion, while a dozen eventually made it back to Fort William Henry. There they spread the tale of the massacre among the garrison before being sent to Albany to recover from their ordeal. Eighty others managed to escape by water. Four of the whaleboats were led to safety by Colonel Parker and Captains Shaw and Ogden. Although the latter was bleeding from his head wound, in the confusion the crews managed to burst through the Indian cordon and disappear into the fog to the south. Moments later, two boatloads of New York provincials tried to follow. One, commanded by a provincial sergeant, succeeded, but the other, led by Captain McGinnis, was less fortunate. Spotted by a group of the enemy, they were fired upon. McGinnis was wounded in the arm by "a poisoned bullet." By the time he recovered his senses, he had been taken prisoner, and all of his men were dead.[15]

Sabbath Day Point was a disaster for the British. One hundred men were killed and one hundred sixty taken prisoner.[16] The French loss, by contrast, was light. Just three Indians and one Canadian cadet were wounded, and none had been killed.[17] Having found a few barrels of rum in the whaleboats, the braves toasted their victory as they paddled back to camp. By the time they arrived, they were roaring drunk. Father Pierre Roubaud, the Jesuit missionary from Saint Francis who had reached Carillon with a party of Abenaki warriors the day before, witnessed the cruelties that followed. "In the space of a league," the thirty-three-year-old recorded:

> I met several little companies of these captives. . . . [They] were presented to me in a very wretched state, their eyes bathed in tears, their faces covered with perspiration and even with blood, and with ropes around their necks. . . . The rum with which their new masters

were filled had excited their brains, and increased their
natural ferocity . . . [and] I was . . . soon compelled to
. . . witness . . . a spectacle much more horrible than what
I had hitherto seen. . . . In the midst of the [Ottawa]
. . . camp there was a large fire; and the stakes of wood
set in the ground betokened a feast. There was one
indeed. But, oh, Heavens! what a feast! . . . [The remains
of one of the provincial dead,] more than half stripped of
the skin and flesh, . . . [had been boiled in a cooking pot
and was now served up to the intoxicated braves.] . . . I
perceived a moment after, these inhuman creatures . . .
taking large spoonfuls of this detestable broth, without
being able to satiate themselves. . . . The saddest thing
was, that they had placed near them about ten
Englishmen, to be spectators of their infamous repast.

Sickened by the spectacle, Roubaud tried to intervene. "I
believed that by mildly expostulating with these monsters . . .
I should gain some influence over them," he explained, but his
efforts were in vain.

A Young man began to speak, and said to me in bad
French: Thou have French taste; me Savage, this meat
good for me. He accompanied his remark by offering to
me a piece of this English roast. I made no response to
his argument, which was worthy of a barbarian; as to
his offer, you may easily imagine with what horror I
rejected it.[18]

While the domesticated tribes settled along the Saint
Lawrence had been persuaded to discard cannibalism by the
missionaries, it was still practiced by the Indians of the high
country. Like many facets of tribal behavior, it was steeped in
ritual significance and tradition. Consuming the flesh of
prisoners was a way of appeasing the tribe's own dead. Also,
by eating the heart of a vanquished enemy, one could become
imbibed with his strength and spirit. As Pierre Pouchot, the
commander of Fort Niagara and a considerably more scientific observer than the overly dramatic Roubaud, recorded, the
Indians considered the "meat" thus garnered as being far from
appetizing, and the ceremony was typically performed with

the greatest of "repugnance. We have seen young people vomit more than once" on eating human flesh, the captain wrote, "and it is only by bravado, and by hardening the heart, that they sometimes get toughened to such a diet."[19]

Meanwhile, back at the Ottawa encampment, Roubaud had turned his attention to the living.

> One of the [prisoners] . . . I recognized . . . as an Officer . . . [and] immediately . . . resolved to purchase him, and assure him of liberty and life. With this in view I approached an aged [Ottawa] . . . [and] held out my hand, saluting him politely, in the hope of winning him by courteous manners. But . . . he was worse than a ferocious beast. . . . No, said he in a thundering and threatening tone,—well fitted to fill me with dread . . .—No, I do not wish thy friendship; go away! I did not think I ought to wait until he reiterated a compliment of that kind, and I obeyed him.

The next morning, a series of councils was held between the French and Indians to discuss the remaining prisoners' fate. Many braves wished to ransom the provincials to Montcalm and return to the high country. Having achieved their own personal war aims—namely, the taking of prisoners, booty, and scalps—they felt it was their duty to go home to their families before the onset of winter. To remain, as one put it, would be "tempting the Master of Life . . . after such a beautiful affair." Others, believing that they would receive better bounties for their prisoners from Vaudreuil, wished to travel to Montréal to claim their ransoms. The French, dependent upon their native allies for intelligence and their expertise at woodland warfare, were appalled at the prospect of losing so many before the campaign had even got under way, and fierce arguments ensued. "Finally everybody wanted something, everyone came at the same time, everyone shouted at once," Bougainville recorded. Although exasperated by the Indians' refusal to submit to European norms, the young aide was impressed by the kindness that some showed to their captives now that the effects of the captured rum had worn off. "They made very touching visits to their prisoners," he wrote, "caressing them, taking them white bread [and] wishing to see that they lacked nothing." Nevertheless, others continued to exhibit "monstrous cruelty," and at least one more prisoner was killed and put in the pot.[20]

Throughout the afternoon the councils continued, and it wasn't until midnight that the issue was resolved: the Indians would remain with the army, and the prisoners would travel to New France "on condition that [the French] . . . would give a receipt to each band or individual for their slaves, that the Marquis de Vaudreuil would give them white bread and blankets," and that those prisoners not sold by the time the campaign had finished would be returned to the tribes that had captured them. On July 26, the prisoners left for Montréal and the wounded were taken to Carillon, where French surgeons took care of them.[21] After being taken across the portage to the shores of Lake Champlain by their Indian masters, the prisoners were loaded onto boats "escorted by a [French] officer and some regular soldiers" and carried off to the north. Four Indian canoes loaded with their "wounded, children and sick" also departed with the column, but the vast majority of the braves remained.

As the captive provincials headed for New France, no doubt relieved to be out of the clutches of their Indian "masters," twenty-five miles to the south the British were beginning to absorb the full extent of their loss. The garrison at Fort William Henry had been reduced by a third. Whatever lingering claims Webb may have had to naval superiority had been quashed, and his troops' morale was deteriorating ever further. As the survivors of Parker's command struggled into camp, the horror stories of the fate awaiting those who fell into the hands of the enemy abounded. With each retelling, the numbers of the "savages" pitted against them grew and their cruelties intensified.[22]

On July 26, three days after the ambush at Sabbath Day Point, "a Gentleman at Fort William Henry" wrote to a friend in New York giving the details of the "melancholy affair. What could the Enemy be doing there?" he asked rhetorically in the postscript. "They certainly were going on some great Design, by being in so large a Body, as is Judged 1000 Men at least." The answer must have been as obvious to his friend as it was to himself. An attack on Fort William Henry was growing ever more imminent. If Webb failed to provide significant reinforcements, and if Montcalm was unable or unwilling to control his Indian allies, the garrison would be wiped out to a man.[23]

The Calm before the Storm

JULY 26–AUGUST 2, 1757

*T*he disaster at Sabbath Day Point finally spurred General Webb into action. On the morning of July 25, the day after he had received word of Colonel Parker's defeat, he set off for Fort William Henry. With the sudden increase in Indian attacks, Webb wasn't taking any chances. Led by Capt. Israel Putnam, his escort consisted of two companies of regular grenadiers and a detachment of 156 provincial rangers who had paraded outside the gates of Fort Edward at the firing of the morning gun.[1] Also with the column were a variety of experts in supply and siege warfare: their mission, to supervise the ongoing efforts to improve Fort William Henry's defenses. Among them were Col. James Montresor of the Royal Engineers, Lt. Col. John Young of the 3rd Battalion of the Royal Americans, Capt. Thomas Ord of the Royal Artillery, and James Furnis, a British staff officer who worked for the Board of Ordnance and was as anxious as Webb about the possibility of Indian attacks on the road from Fort Edward.[2]

Having left the fort behind them, Putnam and his rangers were ordered to scatter through the forest and scout ahead. Littered with tree stumps and tangled roots, the "road" the rest followed was rough, and progress was slow. At midday they paused at "Halfway House," a log cabin built by the

banks of a stream equidistant between the two British fortifications. After sending out a covering picket, the officers dismounted and refreshed themselves.[3] Two hours later, after
climbing for some time over rising ground, they reached
Bloody Pond, the site of a provincial ambush launched on
Dieskau's retreating troops in the aftermath of the Battle of
Lake George two years before. After the skirmish, the victorious provincials had thrown the bodies of two hundred of
their enemies into the water. When Webb and his party rode
past, it was still a melancholy spot. Some even maintained it
was haunted by the ghosts of the wounded who had been
thrown in to drown alongside their dead comrades. Such tales
and the memories evoked could have done little to improve
the general's mood.[4]

The column arrived at three thirty in the afternoon. Fort
William Henry had changed little since Rigaud's raid four
months before. The remains of the boats and outhouses
burned by the Canadians had been removed and the ground
cleared of debris. The palisade had been continued around the
fort, and the entrance to the powder magazines had been
reinforced with stone.[5] Although work had begun on two gal-
liots—large rowing boats with masts and room for several
cannons—there had been little urgency to the project: not
enough carpenters had been acquired and the boats were still
far from finished.[6] A few hundred yards to the west of the
fort, beyond the garrison's flourishing vegetable gardens, was
a steep-sided hill where a provincial camp of tents, cabins, and
lean-tos had sprung up. Erected uncomfortably close to the
surrounding forest, the camp housed the 300 who remained
of Parker's New Jersey Blues and a detachment of 231 New
Hampshire provincials under the command of Lt. Col. John
Goffe.[7] The fort itself now had twenty-six cannons, including
two 18-pounders, two 32-pounders, three 8-inch mortars,
and a single howitzer.[8] The only other change of note was the
rapidly growing graveyard to the south of the palisade, bor-
dering the road to Fort Edward.[9] Along with the victims of
Marin and Langlade's raiders, the graveyard contained dozens
of corpses whose pockmarked flesh bore witness to the smallpox epidemic that was continuing to decimate Monro's com-

mand. Thomas Wilkins, the forty-five-year-old surgeon of the 35th, had been busy attending to the needs of those afflicted since his arrival in early April, but his treatments of purging and emetics did little to aid their recovery. Among the simple wooden crosses was one marking the grave of a particularly high-profile victim. As General Webb would later admit in a letter to Lord Loudoun, the death of Capt. Richard Rogers, younger brother of the famous ranger, on June 22 had been "no small loss to us."[10]

The day after Webb's arrival, his advisors got to work. After viewing the ground and Fort William Henry's defenses, Colonel Montresor and Captain Ord made several recommendations. Foremost was the suggestion that the entrenched camp be moved. Close as it was to the surrounding forest, Montresor believed that its residents would fall easy prey to Indian ambush; and the distance it stood from the fort meant that the provincials could be cut off and would struggle to provide covering fire for the garrison. The hill to the southeast of Fort William Henry, which Johnson had fortified to resist Dieskau's attack in 1755, was far more suitable for an encampment. It was close enough to the palisade to provide easy communication and fire support; and since its slopes were comparatively shallow, failure to occupy the position would allow the enemy to place cannons upon it and fire directly into the fort's interior.[11]

On July 27, Webb convened a "Sort of Council of War" to discuss further improvements and the strategy to be adopted in case of attack. Besides the general, Colonels Montresor and Parker, Lieutenant Colonels Monro and Young, and Captains Williamson, Ord, and George Bartman (Webb's aide-de-camp) were present. The council discussed three key points:

> 1st . . . whether there was vessels sufficient to oppose the French on the water. 2nd What number of men was sufficient to defend the Fort and oppose the Ennemy in case of a Descent. Third Whether a Camp on Fort Wm Henry, Johnson's Ground and the West Ground, or one Camp alone on the retrench'd of Johnson [would be best suited for the defence].[12]

With Colonel Parker present to attest to French and Indian domination of Lake George, the first question was swiftly answered. The second received a somewhat optimistic "two thousand men," and, as for the third, "One camp alone" on the site of Johnson's 1755 stand was deemed the most sensible solution.[13]

Monro then asked Webb two questions: What was he to do should the French advance down South Bay and move on Fort Edward? And which of the two forts did Webb think the French were most likely to attack? The answer to the first was that he should march to its relief with three hundred men. The answer to the second was delivered without hesitation. "Fort W[illia]m Henry to be sure! For there was no probability & hardly a possibility of attacking Fort Edward with Cannon." Having received the reply he had anticipated, Monro developed his point. "If it is so," he told Webb, "I should think, Fort William Henry ought to have as Great a number of men as can possibly be spared. As if Fort William Henry holds, so will Fort Edward, but if Fort William Henry is taken, Fort Edward will surely fall."

Unable to refute the Scotsman's logic, Webb conceded the point, but warned him that he could only possibly spare a thousand men, whom he promised to send on Saturday, July 30. Monro then asked for one final favor. "I beg'd of the Generall," he later recalled, "if it was agreeable to him, to let me have the four companies of the 35 Regiment [then based at Fort Edward] as a part of the reinforcements he intended for me." The reply was not what the colonel had hoped. "He said he would not spare so many Regulars." Not only would Monro have to fight with limited reinforcements, but also he would have to rely on provincial troops rather than on his own men.[14]

After the council had broken up, Colonel Montresor took another look at the hill to the southeast of the fort, then retired to his quarters. That night, he wrote three letters by candlelight before turning in. The first two, addressed to Mr. Demler and Mr. Dies, were professional discourses concerning routine matters of supply. The third, penned to his wife Mary, was of a more personal nature.

Early the next morning, receiving
word of smoke sightings "some distance up the lake," Webb ordered
Captain Putnam to lead three
whaleboats full of rangers "to recon-
noitre the enemy."[15] As they disappeared around the first headland,
the morning gun fired, and the
troops encamped to the west of the
fort were ordered to pack up and
march to the hill to the east. While
they cleared the ground and rebuilt
their huts and lean-tos, Montresor
"visited the Fort with Coll Young" of
the Royal Americans. There he

Captain Israel Putnam.
(*Library of Congress*)

made several recommendations for improving the defenses,
which were immediately put into effect. Viewed as a potential
fire hazard, the storehouse outside the walls was pulled down.
Loopholes for firing muskets were cut into the sides of the
communication trench that led to the new encampment on
the hill, "the top of the Magazine [was] . . . pared off, & sand
put over it," and "the funnels or air holes stopt with sand &
[sand]bags" to prevent a stray shell from touching off the
ammunition supply. "Banquettes," earthen firing steps built
behind the parapets, were constructed, several extra loopholes
were cut into the fort's parapet, and a small earthwork
redoubt, which had been built beyond the main ring of
defenses but was now considered unsuitable, was leveled, "&
the Earth sloped down" away from the fort. This created a
glacis and provided the defenders with a clear field of fire.
Finally, "the East Bastion [was] raised [by] one Log," and
"proper Signals between . . . Fort [William Henry] and Fort
Edward" were agreed upon.[16] If Monro saw the enemy
approaching, he would fire one of his 32-pounders to alert
Webb, who would reply by sounding the two-minute guns
every quarter of an hour to show that he had understood.[17]

While Montresor and Young were discussing defensive
improvements, they were approached by Colonel Monro.
Turning to the senior engineer, Monro asked him how long

he thought the fort would hold if attacked by the enemy. "In my opinion," Montresor replied, "it could not hold out twenty four hours, if the French brought cannons against it."[18]

That evening Putnam returned. The first part of his mission had been uneventful. Having proceeded unmolested as far as the First Narrows, the lookout on the captain's lead boat had spotted three enemy canoes flying white flags. As Putnam's men rowed closer to investigate, the enemy had fled to the north. Refusing to be drawn into a blind pursuit, Putnam ordered his men to follow with caution. On approaching closer, his fears of ambush were confirmed. "Some men [were spied] on the shore [on] each side of the lake," where the islands would force his boats into a bottleneck. Loath to repeat Colonel Parker's mistake, Putnam ordered his men to return to Fort William Henry.[19]

On the morning of July 29, having left orders that reconnaissance boats should be sent up Lake George every night "to watch the Enemies motions," Webb gathered his entourage and returned to Fort Edward.[20] After they had left, Lt. Adam Williamson took charge of fortifying the provincials' new encampment. The work continued for three days. Sweating under the midsummer sun and harassed by the clouds of mosquito and black fly that rose up from the surrounding swamp, the men constructed a chest-high breastwork of logs, which followed the contours of the hill and incorporated its natural rock formations into Montresor's design. Every one hundred yards bastions jutted out, which would enable the defenders to pour a crossfire into any enemy brave enough to approach. Finally, six bronze cannons from the fort were manhandled up the slope and hauled into position.[21] Two 6-pounders were placed behind the walls of a redoubt on a hill near the center of the encampment; another was placed at the northern end, covering the entrance from the lake; one overlooked the swamp to the east; and two 12-pounders were positioned to defend the western approaches and provide covering fire for the fort.[22]

The morning of July 30 saw Monro rise early. The Scot was keen to receive the reinforcements that Webb had promised him would arrive that day. While Williamson, Collins, and the rest busied themselves with preparing the fort for attack, Monro grew increasingly impatient. Without the reinforcements, he did not have enough men to finish the defenses of the newly entrenched camp on the hill to the southeast of the fort. Monro's wait was in vain. The reinforcements would not arrive for three more days.[23]

Since his return to Fort Edward, Webb had procrastinated. Rather than immediately ordering the reinforcements to march for the lake as he had promised Monro, he delayed the decision until the morning of August 2. The reasons for his dalliance are not entirely clear. One explanation is that he had suffered yet another crisis of confidence. According to a document later written by Monro, Webb had originally intended to lead the reinforcements himself and take command at Fort William Henry on his arrival. Sometime between the morning of July 29 and August 2 he changed his mind. Perhaps Webb thought he would be better able to marshal his forces from Fort Edward, or perhaps the idea of facing Montcalm and his Indian hordes was too daunting a prospect for the general to contemplate.[24]

At dusk on August 2, the reinforcements finally arrived. At their head was Colonel Young, a wealthy American regular whose equipment included a fine "pair of silver-mounted, screw-barrelled pistols."[25] With him were 100 Royal Americans led by Captain Faesch, one of the New York Independent Companies of Foot under Capt. William Crookshanks, and 823 Massachusetts provincials led by Col. Joseph Frye. Also present was a small detachment of artillerymen led by William McCloud. A Royal Artillery captain whom Braddock had ordered confined for a short period on unspecified charges during the Monongahela campaign, McCloud was not enjoying himself that summer. His unit had been stripped of its best men and most of its supplies, both of which had been sent to Halifax as part of Loudoun's expedition.[26]

Accompanying Young's column were "nine Ox teams, & seven spar of horses," which hauled six cannons, two of iron and four of bronze, and six whaleboats behind them.[27] The journey from Fort Edward had been torturously slow. At Half

Way Brook one of the whaleboats' carriages had broken down, and the boat had to be left behind. Worried that he wouldn't arrive before nightfall, Colonel Young had then split his force into two. Leaving Capt. Joseph Ingersoll of the Massachusetts provincials to struggle on with the cannons and the remaining whaleboats, Young had led the rest of his column toward the lake. On arrival they were greeted with unbridled enthusiasm. The men at Fort William Henry had had nothing but bad news for days, and the sight of twelve hundred reinforcements came as a much-needed tonic.[28] By the time they arrived it was already dark. "It being so late," Frye wrote, "we could not encamp in any regular form; therefore [we] pitched only a few tents for the night." While the men huddled beneath their blankets, the officers set up camp beds in their tents. Neither would get much sleep that night.[29]

Shortly after Young's column arrived, the nightly patrol, consisting of fourteen men in two whaleboats, set out up Lake George. Since Putnam had nearly been lured into a trap on July 27, the patrols had caught sight of smoke on several occasions but had had no encounters with the enemy.[30] On the night of August 2, all that would change. At ten o'clock, after they had covered just four miles, they fell into an ambush. Watching from the encampment, Colonel Frye "perceived the flashes of several guns" light up the night sky. Moments later, the crackle of musketry carried across the water, causing a buzz of excitement to pass through the hilltop camp and the fort below. It wasn't until dawn, long after the initial adrenaline had been replaced by the first stirrings of fear, that the five survivors returned. As they informed the guards who received them, the horde of Indians who had killed or taken the rest was only moments behind.[31]

Montcalm's Advance

July 26–August 2, 1757

*T*wo days after the victory at Sabbath Day Point, while his Canadian militia continued hauling the boats and cannons across the portage between Lakes Champlain and George, Montcalm convened a final Indian council at the head of Wood Creek. Surrounded by hundreds of chiefs, shamans, painted braves, and curious French and Canadian onlookers, the French general presented the Indians with a wampum "belt of 6000 beads" to bind the thirty-three tribes together. Kisensik, the "famous Nipissing chief" from Oka who wore a medal given to his father by Louis XIV, was the first to reply, as Bougainville recalled:

'My brothers,' he said, [addressing] the nations of the High Country, 'we domesticated Indians thank you for having come to help us defend our lands against the English who wish to usurp them. Our cause is good and the Master of Life [Manitou] favors it. Can you doubt it, my brothers, after the fine deed you have just accomplished. We admired it, we pay you our compliments. It covers you with glory, and Lake St. Sacrement [the French name for Lake George], stained red with the blood of Englishmen, will forever attest this exploit. Let me say that it also covers us with glory, we, your brothers, and we are proud of it.'

Turning to Montcalm, the aging Nipissing continued:

'Our joy should be still greater than thine, my Father . . . thou who hast passed over the great ocean, not for thine own interest, for it is not thy cause that thou hast come to defend, it is that of the great King who said: "Go, cross the great ocean and go and defend my children."'

Kisensik then returned his attention to the warriors gathered around him.

'He [Montcalm] will reunite you, my brothers, and bind you together with the most solemn of ties. Accept this sacred bond with joy and let nothing ever break it.'

Kisensik bowed and retook his place by the fireside. His speech was translated into the various Iroquoian and Algonquian dialects by the Canadian and Indian interpreters "and received with applause." Montcalm then stepped forward. Loath to partake in such "interminable frivolities," but duty bound, the Frenchman swallowed his pride and addressed the crowd. "My children," he began in the lofty manner of the Indian council,

I am delighted to see you all reunited for the good work. So long as your union lasts the English will never be able to resist you. I cannot speak better to you than your brother, Kisensik, who has just spoken. The great King has without doubt sent me to protect and defend you, but he has above all charged me to see that you are made happy and invincible by establishing among you this friendship, this unity, this joining together to carry on the good work, which should exist among brothers, children of the same father, of the great Onontio. I give you this belt as a sacred pledge of his word, symbol of good understanding and strength through the conjunction of the different beads which compose it. I bind you all together so that nothing can separate you before the defeat of the English and the destruction of Fort George [the French name for Fort William Henry].

While the interpreters set about their work, Montcalm placed the six-thousand-bead belt into the center of the gathering and stepped back into the shadows. The belt was picked up by the orators of the various nations present who urged their warriors to accept it. When the Ottawa's turn came, Pennahouel, one of the chiefs who had taken part in the ambush at Sabbath Day Point, addressed his compatriots:

> Behold a circle is drawn around you by the great Onontio which none of us can leave. So long as we remain within its embrace the Master of Life will be our guide, will inspire us as to what we shall do and will favor all our enterprises. If some nation quits before the time, the Master of Life is not accountable for the evils that could strike them, but its misfortune will be its own and will not fall upon the nations who here promised an indissoluble union and complete obedience to their father's will.

Pennahouel then replaced the belt in the center of the gathering, and the next orator picked it up and harangued his braves to accept the challenge.

When all the other tribes had spoken, the belt was given to the Iroquois. Their 363 representatives from Oka, Caughnawaga, Presentation, and the Six Nations made them the most numerous tribe at the council, entitling them to keep it. In an act of intertribal politics, their orator offered to give the belt to the tribes of the high country, saying his people would be delighted if they were to accept it in recognition of "the help that they had . . . brought" and as "an eternal symbol of their friendship." With that the Iroquois retook his seat, and a Nipissing replied. "My brothers," he began, addressing the mass of tattooed Iroquois warriors, "we are most thankful for this mark of respect you have shown to our brothers from the West. It was also our intention, and you have only anticipated us." With the political balance thus realigned, Pennahouel took the floor once more, this time to accept the offer of the belt as a representative of the tribes of the high country. A separate council was then held among them to determine which of the "wild" tribes would be allowed to keep it.

With the ceremonial elements of the meeting addressed, Montcalm spoke of his plan of attack. Since there were insufficient boats to transport them all, the army was to be divided into two divisions. The first, a mixed band of 2,488 French soldiers, colonial regulars, Canadian militia, and Indian braves, all under the command of François de Gaston, Chevalier de Lévis, would leave from the advance camp on the morning of July 30 and march southward through the forests along the west shore of Lake George. The second party, consisting of 5,000 men under Montcalm, would leave Carillon by boat two days later and rendezvous with Lévis's men at Ganaouské Bay on August 2. From there, both bands would descend on Fort William Henry for the attack. Having heard the plan, "the nations answered that they would furnish the numbers of their warriors that they would assign to the two divisions. The report," Bougainville noted in his journal, "would be made by little sticks"—each one representing a warrior that would go with the respective parties. Before the meeting broke up, Montcalm addressed the crowd once more, begging the chiefs to exhort their young braves not to fire their guns on the advance for fear of revealing their position to the British too soon. Having received their promises, the warriors went back to their camp, and Montcalm and his officers retired to theirs.

The next day, the chiefs "turned in the sticks showing the number of men they expect[ed] to go on foot." Kisensik was reluctant to send any of his Nipissing braves with Lévis's division, "claiming that it was needlessly tiring." Fearful of a lakeside ambush on his waterborne troops, Montcalm overruled him. After the sticks had been counted, it was found that the eight Miami from Saint Joseph had deserted during the night. "A Potawatomi chief . . . offered to try to bring them back" and "was given a belt and strings [of wampum] to help him."

That night, the bloated corpse of one of Parker's men, who had been killed at Sabbath Day Point, floated past the Indian camp at the head of Lake George. According to Bougainville, "the warriors [of the high country] crowded around it with loud cries, drank its blood, and put its pieces in the kettle." By contrast, the domesticated Indians, their wilder impulses constrained by the presence of their missionaries, "spent all day in confession." By dawn the Miami had still not returned, and "about 200" Ottawa and Missisauga had also deserted. Carrying their canoes through the woods to avoid confrontations with the French, they relaunched them on Lake Champlain and began the long journey home. Bougainville was stoical about the loss. "[There was] no way to hold them," he wrote, "they had [already] made a coup [at Sabbath Day Point], and besides they lacked everything, [they had] no blankets, no deerskins, except very bad ones, no leggings [and] no vermillion."[1]

On the morning of August 29, Montcalm traveled to the advance camp at the head of Lake George to review the first division. Their commander, the Chevalier de Lévis, was an easygoing career soldier from Gascony who possessed a grace and charm befitting his lofty social status. As a member of the *noblesse de cour*, the premier elite of Bourbon France, the thirty-seven-year-old had always been destined for high command. After joining the French army in 1735, he had fought in both the Polish and Austrian wars of succession before being appointed as Montcalm's second. The two men had hit it off from the start. As well as sharing noble birth, both were professional soldiers and utterly loyal to the king. Another facet of Lévis's character that won Montcalm's respect was his ability to endure hardship alongside his men. While on campaign he would refuse to travel by horse, preferring to march at the head of his troops, and insisted on sharing their discomforts. He always volunteered for scouting missions, no matter how arduous, and frequently slept in the open at night. Equally in his element at the banqueting table, the dance floor, or the battlefield, Lévis was comfortable with the men of Old and New France alike, and his good-natured charm was appreciated by all he encountered.

In pride of place in Lévis's division, on the right-hand side of the makeshift parade ground, stood an elite shock formation of 270 grenadiers, drawn from the six line regiments that would fight at Fort William Henry. To their left were six additional companies of regular troops, all under the command of Lévis's second, Lt. Col. Étienne-Guillaume de Senezergues. Physically fit, virtuous, and brave, the forty-eight-year-old Senezergues was "an ambitious career soldier" and, like Lévis himself, something of an enigma among the pampered aristocrats who traditionally made up the upper ranks of the French army. Having joined La Sarre Regiment at the age of fourteen, Senezergues had seen action in Poland, Italy, and Germany during the wars of Polish and Austrian succession before volunteering for service in New France despite his family's disapproval. In 1756, he had distinguished himself at the siege of Oswego and won a pension of 500 livres a year. With an annual patrimony of 10,000, however, Senezergues was no mercenary, and seems to have been motivated simply by the sheer joy of his profession. When he had learned that Lévis would be leading an advance party on a perilous trek through the woods, he had volunteered to lead the accompanying regulars without hesitation. His offer had been accepted just as promptly. Lévis considered him the only man of his rank in the entire army fit for such a task.[2]

Alongside Senezergues's troops were one hundred French colonial regulars. With them, serving as Lévis's aide-de-camp, was Lieutenant Wolff, the German-born *officier de fortune* who had distinguished himself during Rigaud's winter raid on Fort William Henry. Three hundred of Wolff's countrymen would also march with Lévis. Formed into a unit of volunteers, they were led by Louis Coulon de Villiers, the Canadian officer whose brother had been killed by Tanaghrisson in 1754. Many of the Germans had been recruited in Europe under false pretenses. Several had been promised commissions, which on their arrival in New France had failed to materialize; others had signed up for the Dutch army and had later been sold to the French; and a few had joined as doctors, only to find themselves carrying a musket into battle. Realizing the duplicity shortly after arriving in Montréal in June aboard the ships *David* and *Jason*, many had already deserted to the British.[3]

Along with the French regulars, volunteers, and colonial regulars, Lévis's detachment included one thousand Canadian militia divided into three brigades. Leading the first was Luc de La Corne. An experienced fur trader, merchant, and captain of the colonial regulars, the forty-five-year-old came from a prominent Québécois family. As well as his duties with the militia, La Corne had also been appointed "general" of all the Indian troops, as he spoke "four or five" native languages "fluently" and had spent many years living among the tribes on the frontier. Considered "a great villain and as cunning as the devil" by one contemporary, La Corne was heavily involved in New France's lucrative slave trade. He himself would own twenty-four black and Indian slaves by 1760, and by exploiting his close connections with the Indians, he was able to act as a middleman when the tribes sold prisoners of war to the Québécois landowners, who were perennially short of manpower.[4] Over the years, La Corne had built up a considerable fortune. That summer, he intended to make his biggest killing thus far.[5]

The final element of Lévis's command was a detachment of five hundred Indians. Mainly Saint Lawrence Iroquois with sufficient local knowledge to guide the troops through the maze of tracks that crisscrossed the rugged western shore of Lake George, the Indians were led by Kanectagon, an Iroquois convert from Caughnawaga, renowned as a fearsome warrior and "the most famous hunter of his nation." Having fought under Langlade at Putnam's moonlit ambush at the beginning of July, Kanectagon was eager for revenge.[6]

At four o'clock in the morning, after the parade, Lévis's drummers beat the reveille, and the chevalier formed his men into order of march. Due to the pride of both the regulars and the Indians, even something so seemingly straightforward caused considerable consternation. Initially, the French officers tried to place the Indians on the right flank, but Kanectagon insisted that they take their usual position at the head of the column. Unwilling to anger his capricious allies before they had even set off, Lévis conceded the point, and the column disappeared into the enveloping woods.[7] Even for men as fit as Lévis and Senezergues, Kanectagon set a brutal pace. When not hugging the shoreline, the path was overgrown, undulating, rutted with tree roots, and crowded with low-hanging boughs. Despite having left their packs at

Carillon, the Europeans were soon exhausted. At 9 a.m. they caught sight of the first major obstacle—La Montagne Pelée, or Bald Mountain—a sheer-sided rock face devoid of vegetation that towered one thousand feet above the waters of Lake George. Forced to cut inland to avoid it, the Indians led the column through the tangled forest. Crisscrossed by streams, fallen timbers, and deadfalls, the detour was the most arduous part of the journey so far. After regaining the shore, Lévis called a halt to allow his regulars to catch their breath before pushing on once more. At 4 p.m., having covered twenty miles, the column halted for the night, making camp by the banks of a stream "in a good [defensive] position."[8]

After nightfall, as the mosquitos descended in clouds, the tension between the Europeans and their Indian allies came to a head. As Jean-Guillaume Plantavit de La Pause, a thirty-six-year-old aide major of the Guyenne Regiment, later recounted, a handful of Ottawa "were engaged in prayer and invocation" when "an officious French officer," concerned that the noise might alert a passing British boat to their presence, "attempted to restrain them." To La Pause's surprise, the confrontation was settled peacefully. "The [Ottawa] . . . replied that the Manitou would prevent their words from reaching the enemy, and" the officer "henceforth left [them] in peace." Although innocuous enough, for La Pause the incident highlighted the lack of comprehension between the allies. It also foreshadowed later misunderstandings, which would not end so amicably.[9]

The next morning the cost of the previous day's march became clear. A Canadian lieutenant and an officer of the regulars were too exhausted to continue. Placing them in the care of Lieutenant Wolff, with an escort of nineteen Canadian militiamen, Lévis ordered them back to Carillon with a note for Montcalm detailing his progress so far. The rest of his men continued south. The paths were not as rough as the first day and the column made good progress, having to cross just a single mountain before arriving at a ravine where the men made camp for the night. On August 1 the scouts led them inland. After crossing to the south bank of the stream, they followed the ravine westward and left the lake behind them.

Later that morning, they arrived at an area of open ground flanked by high mountains, where a second stream led due south to Ganaouské Bay. At 10 a.m. they reached it, halted for an hour and a half, then marched around the shore of the bay until they arrived at the rendezvous point. Lévis then ordered three vast bonfires lit to guide Montcalm's boats toward him.[10]

On the day of Lévis's departure, Montcalm's regulars had moved south to occupy the chevalier's old camp, taking as much equipment with them as they could carry. Later that night, five hundred militiamen had worked throughout the hours of darkness hauling the boats, cannons, ammunition, and supplies across the overland portage connecting Lakes George and Champlain. "One has no idea of the difficulty involved in" such an undertaking, Bougainville noted in his journal. "All this [has to be done] without horses or oxen, by men's arms alone. . . . The hardships cannot be imagined, and it is impossible to give a fair idea of it." While the militia and the regulars worked through the night, the Indians who remained around Carillon "impatiently endured their inactivity." Several complained that there was no wine or brandy to drink, and some young warriors, sick of the monotonous diet of army rations, stole and slaughtered eighteen oxen. Finally, at 3 p.m. on August 31, they could wait no longer. After leaving "a cloak, a breechclout, and a pair of leggings hung in a tree as a sacrifice to Manitou," the Indians boarded the 150 canoes they had drawn up on the beach and paddled down the lake, promising Montcalm they would wait for him three leagues to the south at Île de la Barque. A crowd of Frenchmen watched them leave. "The sight was singular, even for a soldier accustomed to seeing European armies," Bougainville wrote. "Who could imagine the spectacle of fifteen hundred naked Indians in their canoes?"[11]

Father Pierre Roubaud, the Jesuit missionary from Saint Francis, was one of the few Europeans to travel with the Indians. "We had hardly made 4 or 5 leagues on the lake," the thirty-three-year-old Frenchman recalled, "before we observed the painful signs of our late victory [at Sabbath Day Point]." The abandoned British whaleboats had run aground on the beach, and the dead, bloated, and decomposing in the midsummer heat lay all around. Those killed in the water had washed ashore and were now "stretched out on the" sands. Others, Roubaud noted, were "scattered here and there in the woods. Some were cut into pieces, and nearly all were mutilated in the most frightful manner." The Jesuit wanted to bury the dead, but the Indians insisted they push on. "About evening we landed at the place which had been assigned to us for a camp. It was a shore overspread with brambles and briers and was the haunt of an immense number of rattlesnakes. Our savages, who chased them, caught several which they brought to me."[12]

The next day at 2 p.m., with the portaging finally finished, Montcalm ordered his men to board the boats at Carillon. In total, the flotilla amounted to "250 sail." The regulars of La Reine, La Sarre, Languedoc, and Guyenne, minus their detached grenadier companies, took the lead, preceded by "a bateau carrying an 11-pounder [cannon] and two little swivels." Next came Capt. Joseph Courtemanche's Canadian militia and then the artillery consisting of thirty-six cannons and four mortars crewed by six officers and one hundred twenty men under Capt. François Le Mercier, the officer who had delivered Rigaud's ultimatum at the first siege of Fort William Henry four months before.[13] Each gun, mounted on its carriage, was strapped onto a platform that had been laid across two bateaux. Guarding the guns were the Royal Roussillon Regiment and two brigades of militia, commanded by Captains François-Xavier de Saint-Ours and Ignace-Philippe Aubert de Gaspé. Next came the boats carrying the field hospital, then those with the provisions and supplies, with a picket of the Roussillon Regiment bringing up the rear.[14]

After three hours the flotilla reached Île de la Barque, where the Indians rejoined them. Then at 6 p.m. a "severe storm" descended over Lake George, forcing Montcalm to call a halt. Hard in to shore, the boats laid anchor, while a "heavy rain" drenched the men, and the wind whipped the water into waves that broke over the sides of the bateaux. After one hour the gale subsided. The crews weighed anchor and continued down Lake George. At 10 p.m. they reached Ganaouské Bay. Spotting Lévis's signal fires "placed triangularly on the top of a mountain," Montcalm ordered the boats to sail into shore. The men disembarked and set up camp for the night, while the officers held a council of war.

At daybreak on August 2, Lévis's detachment continued its march southward, shadowed by Montcalm's flotilla, which was now headed by a swarm of canoes. Father Roubaud was with his Abenaki converts. "We paddled slowly, in order to give the boats loaded with artillery time to follow us," the Jesuit recalled, "[but] they were far from being able to manage it. By evening we were more than a full league ahead." Approaching Diamond Point, just five miles from Fort William Henry, the Indians decided to halt for the night and await further orders; since if they rounded the headland, they would reveal themselves to the British lookouts at the entrenched camp.[15] As soon as the Indians had landed at nearby Sandy Cove, scouts set out overland to spy on the enemy and find a suitable spot where the artillery could be landed the following morning. Meanwhile, the rest of the flotilla and Lévis's detachment had reached the cove, and the entire army encamped for the night.[16]

At 10 p.m., an Abenaki lookout stationed beside Father Roubaud spotted the two British whaleboats that Monro had sent out from Fort William Henry two hours before. Unaware of their presence, the provincials were heading directly toward their enemies. "The news [of their imminent arrival] was carried to all the Savages," the priest remembered, "and preparations for receiving them were concluded with admirable activity and silence." Just as the British were about to fall into the trap, "a sheep belonging to our people began to bleat," and alerted them. Realizing the danger, the British "faced about, [and] steered for the opposite shore." Within moments hundreds of Indians, "with yells as terrifying by their duration as by their number," were in pursuit. With their fear granting them new strength, the British began to pull away from their pursuers and were about to round Diamond Point when the Indians opened fire. The scattered shots fell wide, but prompted several British oarsmen in the rear boat to pick up their guns and return fire. One Nipissing chief was killed by the volley and another badly wounded, but the delay was enough for the rest of the Indians to make up the ground and board the British boats. Faced with a horde of tomahawk-wielding braves, the British threw down their guns. Three were taken prisoner, interrogated, then tortured to death by the relatives of the dead warrior. The rest were executed and scalped on the spot. Meanwhile, the second boat had reached the beach. Its occupants splashed ashore and fled into the woods. Five made it back to Fort William Henry. The others were tomahawked or shot.[17]

At dawn, Roubaud witnessed the funeral of the Nipissing chief killed in the attack. His body was

> adorned with . . . porcelain necklaces, silver bracelets, ear and nose rings, [and his skin was covered in] . . . paint and vermilion in order to make the paleness of death disappear. . . . None of the decorations of a military Savage had been forgotten: a gorget, tied with a flame-coloured ribbon, hung carelessly over his breast; the gun resting on his arm, and the war-club in his girdle; the calumet [ceremonial pipe] in the mouth, the lance in the hand; at his side the kettle, filled. In this . . . war-like attitude they had seated him on an eminence covered with grass, which served as a bed of state. The Savages, ranged in a circle around the body, maintained for a few moments a gloomy silence, which somewhat resembled grief. The Orator [then read] . . . the funeral Oration for the dead; then followed chants and dances, accompanied by the sound of tambourines set around with little bells. . . . The funeral rites were finished by interring the dead man, with whom they took good care to bury an abundant supply of provisions, fearing . . . that for want of food he might die a second time.[18]

While the Nipissing mourned their dead, the rest of the army broke camp. Boarding the boats, Montcalm's troops set sail. As they rounded Diamond Point, Lévis's troops swarmed through the forest toward Fort William Henry. The Nipissing would soon have their revenge.

PART TWO

The Siege

August 3–9, 1757

The First Day

August 3, 1757

At dawn on August 3, following a night of intermittent alarms and skirmishes between the British outposts and Lévis's Indian scouts, Montcalm's fleet rounded Diamond Point. The sentries watching from Fort William Henry and the entrenched camp were awed by the sight. The artillery bateaux were the first to appear. With their crews straining at the oars, they fired three volleys as they rounded the headland. The balls whistled over the water. Falling half a mile short of the fort, they sent up great plumes of foam as they splashed into the lake. After firing a single 32-pounder as a prearranged signal to General Webb at Fort Edward, the British gunners returned the French fire, and soon the morning air was thick with gun smoke. Next to come into view were several boats carrying the white-coated regulars, their regimental banners fluttering in the breeze. Then the militia appeared. Dressed in shirts, Indian leggings, and moccasins, they were a ragtag bunch but were armed to the teeth, each carrying a musket, tomahawk, and up to three knives. Finally, the Indians rounded the point, their canoes spreading out over the surface of the lake, blotting it from view.[1]

Watching through his telescope from the entrenched camp, Monro penned a dispatch to Webb. "The enemy are in sight upon the lake," he began. "We know that they have cannon. They cut off our [reconnaissance] boats between two and three this morning that were toward the first Island. As yet we know nothing of their numbers."

Entrusting the message to two rangers of Richard Rogers's old company, Monro ordered them to set off for Fort Edward. Leaving the log entrenchment via the main gate, the green-coated provincials disappeared into the woods to the south.[2]

So far, Montcalm's plan to distract the British with a show of force upon the lake was working to perfection. While the British gunners were wasting their powder exchanging shots with the French flotilla, Lévis's regulars were advancing through the woods along the western shore of Lake George. The Frenchmen under the chevalier's command obediently followed orders, but the Indian scouts were a law unto themselves. Keen to demonstrate their bravery, Kanectagon and his men crept as close as they dared to the British positions. Taking cover behind tree stumps in the cleared ground, they began shooting at anyone brave or foolhardy enough to peek over the walls.[3] A few of the sentries were hit, but not without reply. One of the first casualties of the siege was the son of Kisensik, the Nipissing chief who had spoken at Montcalm's council on July 27.[4]

Realizing his position would soon be invested, Monro ordered a detachment of men to reinforce the fort before it was too late. Leading the party was John Ormsby, the senior captain of the 35th. With him were two companies of Frye's Massachusetts provincials "under . . . captains Ingersoll and Arbuthnot" and a squad of red-coated regulars. Leaving the entrenched camp, Ormsby descended the hill and moved down the covered causeway by the lakeshore that connected the two positions.[5] Once installed inside the fort, Ormsby had four hundred men under his command. Sixty regulars from the 35th were supported by one hundred fifty sailors, Royal Artillerymen, and carpenters, in charge of manning the cannons and repairing the defenses. Also present were the one hundred ninety provincial troops from the entrenched camp.[6] Ormsby's first order was for a small party to sally out and round up the livestock, which had been grazing on the shores of Lake George. The operation was completed successfully and the sheep, horses, and cattle were crowded into "the Picquet Store yard."[7]

By 9 a.m. Lévis was closing on the British position. Leading his men over the thickly forested hills to the west of the fort, he gave the defenders' cannons a wide berth, before sweeping around to close off the road to Fort Edward. The sentries on the walls spotted his advance. With the grenadiers' white coats making a fine target as they passed through the trees, the British gunners opened fire. Their round shot hurtled over the garrison's gardens, before creasing the soil beyond the cleared ground and bouncing through the woods. Lieutenant Thomas Collins, the senior British artillery officer in the fort, ordered his gunners to keep firing, "but with little success, the distance being great." Ormsby then ordered Capt. William Arbuthnot "to burn and

A French grenadier like those who fought at the siege of Fort William Henry, from a 1761 German print. (*Private Collection*)

destroy some Huts and Hedges on the west of the Fort," fearing they would provide cover for enemy sharpshooters. After completing his task "with difficulty," Arbuthnot led his men back under the cover of the walls.[8]

With the French about to complete the encirclement, Monro scribbled out his second dispatch of the day: "I send this by three Rangers and shall send you three more in half an hour and will continue to do so. We have a few men wounded by their Random shott, but their [main] body has not yet appeared. I believe you will think it proper to send a reinforcement as soon as possible."

Monro's plea was reasonable, but Webb was reluctant to help. Having heard the signal gun that morning and intermittent firing ever since, the men at Fort Edward were well aware of what was going on fourteen miles to the northwest. Nevertheless, Webb merely ordered a few parties of rangers to make their way to Fort William Henry and gather intelligence on the enemy's strength.[9]

By now, Lévis's troops had completed the encirclement and were occupying the road to Fort Edward in force. With his orders completed, the chevalier sent Bougainville, who had been attached to his command that morning, to Montcalm to inform the general of the situation. "I was hard put to find him," Bougainville confessed, "seeing that he was on the move amidst hills heavy with timber, where everything is road because there is no road at all."[10] After wandering blindly through the woods for some time, the Frenchman's asthma began to plague him. "I thrice fell down fainting from exhaustion," he later admitted. Afterward he encountered Kisensik.[11] "I am going to look for my son who has been wounded," the Nipissing told him. "Except for that, I would willingly be your guide." Having passed Lévis's hospital tent earlier in his search, Bougainville was able to reassure the chieftain. "The surgeon who dressed his wound," he informed him, "assured me that the wound was light." Kisensik was satisfied with the information. "Well, I am going to guide you," he said, "the service of Onontio demands it. I shall see my son afterwards, so that there may be no mistake." The Nipissing's magnanimity impressed Bougainville. "This Indian," he later noted in his journal, "thinking and acting thus, is almost the only one of his kind."[12]

Half a mile to the north in the entrenched camp, Monro had ordered a mixed body of one hundred rangers and Massachusetts provincials, led by the twenty-five-year-old Capt. Richard Saltonstall, to dislodge Lévis's men from the road.[13] There were two reasons for Monro's decision. Besides maintaining a line of communication with Fort Edward, the sally was intended to procure a few extra logs to complete the defenses of the entrenched camp. Having only received Frye's reinforcements on the night of August 2 rather than July 30, as Webb had promised, Monro had not had enough men to finish them before the French had arrived. By the morning of August 3, however, it was already too late, as Captain Saltonstall was about to discover.[14]

Advancing out of the entrenched camp through the southern gate, Saltonstall's men soon found themselves surrounded by Kanectagon's warriors. In the ensuing skirmish, Ensign

Samuel Williams and eighteen rank and file were killed. Four others, including a Mahican volunteer, were captured, and "several [more were] wounded," before Saltonstall ordered the survivors back to camp. Sensing the possibility of an early British collapse, Lévis's Indians rushed in after them. Frye ordered his men to line the parapet, and the two sides exchanged close-range musketry for thirty minutes.[15] Captain Cunningham, a veteran of twelve years' service in the 35th, was shot in the arm, and at one stage the Indians reached the barricade and a brief hand-to-hand struggle broke out. Corporal William Hughes of the 35th, a thirty-year-old carpenter from County Armagh, was in the thick of it. As he parried the blows with his musket barrel and countered with his bayonet, an Indian brave cut off his left arm with a blow from his tomahawk. The Irishman was dragged into cover by his comrades, and his stump was bandaged by the surgeons. The Indians were then driven back to the forest by Capt. William McCloud's guns firing grapeshot with "good effect." Several were cut down as they withdrew.[16]

Seeing that a quick coup was no longer feasible, the Indians contented themselves with rounding up the horses and cattle that were milling around the low ground between the fort and the camp. Panicked by the firing, the animals had broken out of the Piquet Yard store, and the British had been too occupied to deal with the problem until it was too late. Watching from the walls, the defenders could do nothing as the Indians killed one hundred fifty head of cattle and rounded up a further twenty-five to offer to Montcalm to drag his guns in place of those which they had killed at Carillon.[17] One hundred fifty sheep and fifty horses were also taken, although two of those that had accompanied Colonel Young's reinforcements escaped and returned to Fort Edward.[18] As Father Roubaud noted, the captured livestock "were the first-fruits of this little war [for the Indian braves]."[19]

With Lévis's troops fanning out in an arc to the south, the rest of the French army arrived. Having left five hundred men under Lt. Col. Marc-Antoine Privat, the forty-seven-year-old commander of the Languedoc Regiment, to guard the boats, Montcalm had divided the rest of his command into three columns.[20] Rigaud led those on the right, Montcalm's third in command, Col. François Bourlamaque, took charge of the left, while the general himself headed those in the middle. Giving Collins's gunners a wide berth, Montcalm led the columns onto the plateau seven hundred yards to the west of the fort that had been the site of the provincial encampment just four days before. En route the Royal Roussillon Regiment, led by the fifty-two-year-old Lt. Col. Chevalier de Bernetz, was ordered to occupy the crest of a ravine on the western shore of the lake six hundred fifty yards due north of Fort William Henry.[21] Their colors flying, the men stood in line of battle, exposed to the long-range fire of the fort's gunners for an hour, before joining the rest of Montcalm's men on the hill.

With the troops in position, Colonel Bourlamaque and Capt. Jean-Nicolas Desandrouins, the Verdun-born engineer who had replaced Colonel de Combles after the accidental shooting incident at Oswego, were sent to reconnoiter the fort and the entrenched camp. Their mission was to determine whether either could be taken by a *coup de main*.[22] Keeping to the surrounding woods, the officers made a circuit of the defenses. After studying the British positions through their telescopes, they came to the conclusion that both the fort and the camp were "too strong to be attacked sword in hand."[23]

That left but a single option: a *siège en forme*. This formulaic style of combat consisted of a series of well-defined stages. The first involved cutting off the enemy from resupply. A detailed reconnaissance was then carried out to establish a weak point in the enemy fortification. A base camp was established, followed by the slow and deliberate digging of approach trenches, or saps, to bring the besiegers within cannon shot of the fort. A further trench, known as the first parallel, was then dug at right angles to the sap. This was filled with infantry whose job was to defend their gunners from enemy assaults, and position barricades, known as gabions and fascines, in front of the trench, behind which the besiegers' cannons were placed. These were known as an enfilading battery. They targeted the enemy's gunners, their mission to reduce the enemy's ability to engage in counterbattery fire. Once the first parallel was dug, the besiegers continued the sap closer to the enemy fortification. Additional parallels were then dug, in front of which further batteries were positioned until a final parallel, just one hundred yards from the enemy's fortifications, could be constructed. A final battery, known as a breaching battery, was placed beyond it.

Once this process had begun, the defenders' only hope was relief by reinforcements who could attack the besiegers' rear, thus "lifting the siege," or to sally out in force, surprise the attackers, and destroy their guns before a counterattack could be launched. Failing this, the siege would run its course. Once the attackers had set up the breaching battery, which could take anything from a few days to a matter of months, their artillery could batter a hole in the walls, known as a breach, through which their troops could attack. In the eighteenth century, siege warfare rarely reached this bloody denouement. Defending commanders typically surrendered after putting up a certain amount of resistance. This was something of a balancing act. Defend for too short a period of time, and one's honor was compromised; for too long, and the attackers' desire for revenge might overcome their wish for a swift and successful conclusion. This code was long established and well known to the Europeans on both sides at Fort William Henry. It was war as a game, and both Monro and Montcalm were astute players.[24]

With their reconnaissance complete, Desandrouins and Bourlamaque reported to Montcalm. They suggested the northwest bastion as the point of attack, and the ravine where the Royal Roussillon had stood earlier that morning as a suitable site for opening the sap. Montcalm agreed and ordered Bourlamaque, who had considerable experience of sieges during the War of Austrian Succession, to occupy the ravine with La Sarre and Royal Roussillon Brigades.[25] By midday they were in position. Bourlamaque organized a covering party and sent fifty men to wait for the arrival of the artillery barges by the lakeshore, while Desandrouins and the rest went to work making fascines and gabions, tightly packed bundles of sticks and earth-filled wicker frames, to protect the camp from British fire. Having graduated with honors from the famed engineering school at Mézières, Desandrouins was a skilled practitioner of the science of siege warfare and had chosen the position well.[26] The left flank was protected by the western shore of the lake, while the right rested on some "inaccessible ravines" a little way inland.[27] Additionally, the main ravine could act as a ready-made depot for when the ammunition, guns, and supplies arrived, keeping them out of the line of fire until the first parallel was dug. "The only disadvantage," the twenty-eight-year-old noted, was that those digging the sap would eventually have to negotiate an area of swampland between them and the fort.[28]

Montcalm, meanwhile, had made his way to Lévis's lines. Jacques Vaudry, "a . . . dealer of liquors" from Montréal who had joined the militia as a lieutenant a few weeks before, was present as the general arrived. Spotting several Canadians shooting at the entrenched camp from the tree line, the general approached. "It was in vain to throw away their powder at so great a distance," Montcalm informed them, "for [even] if they killed ten men it would be of no great significance [because] he would take the fort the next day with his cannon." Although underestimating his opponents' tenacity, Montcalm's logic was well-founded. Fort William Henry was now cut off from support. Faced with eight thousand attackers supported by thirty-six guns, Monro's twenty-five hundred stood little hope of victory. All the French had to do was dig their way closer to the walls. Sooner or later, they would be in a position to blow Fort William Henry to smithereens.[29]

At three o'clock in the afternoon, a red flag of truce was seen waving from the French lines. Calling for a cease-fire, Monro awaited the arrival of his opponent. A strange calm settled over the field. Curious, the men at the parapet risked raising their heads to scan their surroundings. The Indians also stood up from behind the tree stumps in the belt of cleared land, and both sides stared at each other, entranced. As the smoke of the guns dissipated, a deputation of French regulars was seen approaching the British lines. Not wanting the enemy to see his defenses, Monro ordered a party of his own to sally out to meet them. With a flurry of drum beats and elaborate courtesies, they stopped in no-man's-land to

parley. Leading the French delegation was Captain Fontbrune, one of Montcalm's aides-de-camp. After greeting his
opposite number, he presented a letter from his general,
which was promptly dispatched to the entrenched camp. The
enemies then made small talk while awaiting Monro's reply.[30]

Up on the hill, the Scot opened Montcalm's letter. "Sir," he
read:

> I have this morning invested your place with a numer-
> ous Army and superior Artillery, and all the savages
> from the High Country, the Cruelty of which, a
> Detachment of your Garrison have lately too much
> experienced. I am obliged, in Humanity, to desire you to
> Surrender your Fort: I have it yet in my Power to
> restrain the Savages, and oblige them to observe a
> Capitulation, as hitherto none of them have been killed,
> which will not be in my Power in other Circumstances:
> and your insisting on defending your Fort, can only
> retard the Loss of it a few days, and must, of necessity,
> expose an unlucky Garrison; who can receive no Success
> considering the Precautions I have taken. I demand a
> decisive answer immediately, for which purpose I have
> sent you Sieur Fontbrune, one of my Aids de Camp: you
> may credit what he will inform you as from me. I am,
> with Respect, Sir, your most humble, most Obedient
> Servant Montcalm.

Monro barely gave the offer a second thought. Montcalm's
thinly veiled threats were hardly likely to make the Scot forgo
his honor. Grabbing his pen, he dashed off a suitably audacious reply.[31]

Meanwhile out in no-man's-land, the Indians had taken
advantage of the cease-fire to approach the fort "in a great
crowd." An Abenaki warrior, "speaking bad French, but very
clearly," addressed the defenders watching him from the
walls. "You won't surrender," he shouted, "well, fire first; my
father will then fire his great guns; then take care to defend
yourself, for if I capture you, you will get no quarter."
Moments later, Fontbrune's party retired. The Indians sought
cover, the cease-fire came to an end, and the British cannons
opened fire once more.[32] Lieutenant McCloud, commanding

the guns in the entrenched camp, was beginning to find his range. Despite the incessant buzz of musket shot, the young artillery officer was already gaining considerable credit for his accuracy and zeal. Throughout the day, his efforts had done "great Service in beating back the Indians," and as nightfall approached, one long-range round shot "fell on an Indian Hutt [in the woods] and killed many."[33]

By late afternoon, Father Roubaud had still not found the main body of his Abenaki charges, from whom he had become separated in the confusion of the investment early that morning. While wondering how he could make himself useful, he came across the unfortunate Mahican whom the French Indians had taken prisoner during Saltonstall's sortie. "He was a man whose appearance was surely neither prepossessing nor pleasing," the Jesuit wrote. [He had] "a head enormous in its size, with small eyes, a bulky and ponderous corpulence joined to a stunted stature, [and] large and short legs . . . but, although disfigured by nature . . . he had no less right to the notice and consideration of Christian charity."

As Roubaud discovered, the Mahican was in need of his help.

> He was tied to the trunk of a tree, where his grotesque figure attracted the inquisitive attention of the passersby; yells were not spared in the beginning, but the bad treatment came afterward,—to such a degree, that by a blow, roughly dealt, one of his eyes was nearly torn from its socket. This proceeding shocked me; I went to the help of the afflicted man, from whom I drove away all the spectators . . . [and] stood guard by his side part of the day; at length I did so well that I succeeded in interesting the Savages (his masters) in his favour, so that there was no longer need of my presence to shield him from persecution.

Having saved the life of the prisoner, Roubaud continued his search through the woods for the Abenaki.[34]

Elsewhere Lt. Jacques Vaudry, the Canadian militiaman who had overheard a conversation between Montcalm and some of his comrades earlier in the day, had left his company in search of some food. Before long, he found one of the

British bullocks killed by the Indians that morning. Momentarily discarding his musket, Vaudry cut a steak for his evening meal. The Canadian would soon regret letting his guard down.[35] Watching him at that very moment were Pvt. James Collier and two other Connecticut provincials of Captain Putnam's ranger company. Hours earlier, they had been ordered to scout around Fort William Henry by General Webb and, if possible, to bring back a prisoner for interrogation. Stepping out from his hiding place with his musket leveled at Vaudry, Collier made it clear that he would kill the Canadian if he called out. After binding him securely, the scouts stole through the woods and made their way back to Fort Edward, their mission complete.[36]

At 6 p.m. Monro wrote his final dispatch of the day. "This place was so suddenly surrounded," he informed Webb,

> that there was no sending off an express. Capt. Ogden has three letters of mine to you, which he could not send off hitherto; I hope this one . . . will be sent off this night. Genl. Montcalm sent his aid de camp with a letter to me to surrender the Fort &ct. My answer was, "that we were determined to defend both the Fort and the camp to the last," they have not yet erected their batteries but the Indians have been firing upon us from the wood all day: Capt Cunningham of the 35th Regt is wounded in the arm, and a corp[oral] of the same Regt has had his arm cut off, and a few men wounded. I forgot to tell you, Genl. Montcalm says in his letter "he has a numerous army and a superior artillery to ours." I make no doubt that you will soon send us a reinforcement. The men all seem to be in good spirits.[37]

As darkness descended, the British cannons fell silent. The sun sank beneath the mountains to the west, the heat dissipated, and a distinct chill settled over the waters of the lake.[38] The French and Canadians withdrew to their camps, lit fires, and prepared their evening meals, leaving a handful of Indian sharpshooters in no-man's-land to shoot at the British sentries on the walls by the light of the moon. Other braves crept forward to take the scalps from those killed during Saltonstall's sortie. In Lévis's camp on the Fort Edward road, the Indians feasted on the slaughtered bullocks and offered prayers to Manitou, while others mourned, looked after the seven braves that had been wounded that day, set funeral pyres, or buried their dead.[39] Later that night, Kanectagon, the famed Iroquois hunter, left camp to set up an ambush deep in the woods between Forts William Henry and Edward, hoping to surprise one of the parties of provincial rangers that were keeping communications alive between the two posts. Montcalm spent the night with La Reine Regiment on the hill to the west of the fort, while in the main French camp by the lakeshore, the regulars pitched their tents and lit signal fires to serve as beacons for the artillery and supply barges, whose crews had spent the day maneuvering their boats south from Diamond Point. Throughout the night they landed, and their cargoes were unloaded and stored in the ravine.[40]

From the walls of Fort William Henry, Lt. Adam Williamson, the young engineer who had survived Rigaud's siege four months before, looked up to the entrenched camp on the hill where men were lighting large bonfires to illuminate the area and dissuade the Indian sharpshooters from crawling too close.[41] Within the palisade, the British and provincial surgeons attended to the wounded. Corporal Hughes's stump had been cauterized in the fire, and the former carpenter was now doing well. His gunshot wound bound, Captain Cunningham was soon fit for duty once more, but others had already succumbed to their injuries, and yet more would die during the night. The rest of the garrison tried to snatch a few hours sleep, but occasional gunshots, intermittent alarms, and nightmares of Indian attacks kept most awake throughout the night.

Fourteen miles to the southeast at Fort Edward, General Webb sat down to dine with Colonel Montresor.[42] Since the signal gun had been heard at five o'clock that morning, the whole camp had been on edge. Rufus Putnam, the apprentice millwright from Sutton, Massachusetts, had been out on patrol when the first gun sounded. The alarm had prompted the section to return to Fort Edward without delay. "Before we got in," the nineteen-year-old recorded, "we heard fifteen cannons fired and a great many small arms. When we [arrived] ... we found that Captain Putnam had sent off three men for spies."⁴³ Besides ordering the rangers to gather intelligence, Webb had been busy dictating letters to his aide, Capt. George Bartman. Just after dawn, the first of a series of breathless dispatches had been sent to Gabriel Christie, the assistant deputy quartermaster general stationed at Albany. "They have fir'd the Signals of the approach of the Enemy at Fort Wm. Henry," Bartman had written.

> The General therefore desires you . . . to forward the raising of the Militia; after they have reliev'd our Troops at Albany and the different Posts on Hudsons River, the remainder is to proceed to this Place.
>
> [PS] On the receipt of this you will please to send off an Express to the different Colonels of Militia . . . to hasten them up with their respective Regts. as fast as possible.⁴⁴

With all his provincials already mobilized and the bulk of the army with Lord Loudoun at Halifax, Webb had no option but to call on the militia. These part-timers—poorly trained, armed, and equipped—made even the provincials look like professional soldiers. Calling them up was the last resort.

At 1 p.m., the two rangers that Monro had sent off at dawn arrived. The note they carried prompted an agitated Webb to revise his orders to Christie.

> The Enemy is landed with a large Army to attack . . . Fort Wm. Henry, it is General Webb's orders therefore, that you do immediately send off the Garrison from Albany without waiting to be reliev'd; you are likewise to send up all the Militia that are ready to march, and send another Express to Sir Wm. [Johnson, the Indian superintendent and veteran of the Battle of Lake George] acquainting him of this, and that the General requires his immediate presence, with what Men and Indians he can collect. . . . The Troops that move up are not . . . to bring . . . Baggage but [just] their Blanketts, and make forc'd Marches.

Two and a half hours later, Webb dictated a reply to Monro:

Sir, we have just fir'd the two minute Guns repeated each quarter of an hour to shew you we knew your situation; but as for determining any further the General cannot till he has more particular intelligence from you. . . . The General doubts not but every thing will be done for the best on yours and Colonel Young's part, and is determin'd to assist you as soon as possible with the whole army if requir'd. . . . This goes by three of Putnam's Rangers with orders to destroy it if it is likely to be taken. I am Sir, with most sincere wishes for your safety till we can come to your assistance, your humble servant G. Bartman, aide de camp.[45]

After spending the better part of the summer procrastinating, Webb was finally acting with some urgency. But with the French guns beginning to arrive at Fort William Henry, and the general still reluctant to release any of his men while there remained even the vaguest possibility that his own command would be attacked, Webb's small attempts at aiding his beleaguered comrade would prove too little too late.

Opening the Trenches

August 4–5, 1757

At daybreak on August 4, Montcalm reorganized his troops. La Reine Battalion was led down the flanks of the hill to the west of Fort William Henry and joined the rest of the regulars at the main encampment by the lake. At the same time, Lévis was ordered to send the detached grenadier companies adjoined to his command back to their respective regiments; a field hospital was set up to the right of Artillery Cove where the supplies were being unloaded; and the rest of the chevalier's troops, the volunteers, and militia brigades were ordered to occupy the heights to the west of Fort William Henry, recently vacated by La Reine Brigade. In this way, Montcalm established his troops in an unbroken line stretching west from Lake George through a band of forested land, then up onto the hills occupied by the British just a few days before. Meanwhile Luc de La Corne, Montcalm's senior militia captain, positioned his Indians on the road to Fort Edward and covered the area to the south of Fort William Henry with frequent patrols.[1]

At 11 a.m., Montcalm set out on a reconnaissance patrol accompanied by Captain Desandrouins, Colonel Bourlamaque, and the rest of the engineers and artillery officers to determine where the first battery should be placed.[2] After seeing the lay of the land, they chose a spot just beyond the main ravine stretching from the lakeshore one hundred yards inland. From there, the French guns could fire directly at the exposed angle of the fort's northwest bastion. Later, a second enfilading battery would be added to the southwest of the first, which could pour a crossfire onto the defenders and also "deliver ricochet fire" onto the entrenched camp beyond.[3] Before the first parallel could be dug, however, a sap would be needed, "wide enough to hold two cannon at its opening and deep enough to shelter the gunners from enemy fire."[4] It in turn would have to be preceded by the positioning of fascines and gabions to protect the workers clearing the ground. Such was the meticulous nature of siege warfare. Nothing could be rushed, but once the machine grinded into gear, the entire enterprise took on the atmosphere of the inevitable.

With the plan established, the French and Canadians went to work. Huge wickerwork frames were filled with earth and piled together with bundles of sticks to provide cover. Then the undergrowth was cleared. Working with hoes, picks, and axes, eight hundred men cut down the trees, dug up the roots, and began work on the sap. Zigzagging toward Fort William Henry so that the British gunners could not enfilade the entire trench with a single shot, the diggers advanced foot by foot from the French encampment, then began to excavate the first parallel, behind which the first enfilading battery would be placed. According to Bougainville, "the work advanced well" in all areas, with the exception of a single patch of difficult ground, which held up progress considerably.[5] Also watching the proceedings was Father Pierre Roubaud. "On seeing the joyous manner with which . . . [the French and Canadians worked], you would have taken them for men invulnerable to the rapid and continuous fire of the enemy," the Jesuit opined. "Such conduct indicates much bravery and much love of country; but then that is characteristic of the Nation."[6]

One thousand yards to the south, on the walls of Fort William Henry, Lt. Thomas Collins was determined to interrupt the enemy's progress. A skilled artillery officer, Collins had twenty-four cannons at his disposal, crewed by a small detachment of Royal Artillerymen supported by British sailors, among the best gunners in the world. Eighteen of his

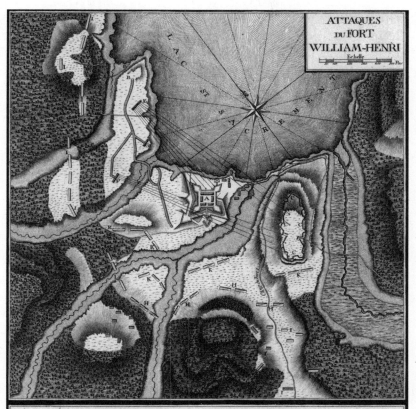

ATTAQUES DU FORT WILLIAM-HENRI
en Amérique
par les troupes françaises aux ordres du Marquis de Montcalm.
Prise de ce fort le 7 Août 1757.

Renvois:

A. Fort William-Henri B. Ouverture des tranchées la nuit du 4 au 5 Août.
C. Camp retranché, que les anglais allèrent occuper lors de l'arrivée des français.
D. Baie, où les français débarquèrent leur artillerie. E. Batterie de huit
canons & d'un mortier. F. Batterie de dix canons & d'un mortier. G. Batterie
de six pieces, dont on ne fit aucun usage. H. Position de Mr. de Levi
pendant l'investissement du fort. I. Position des troupes durant le siege.
K. Leur position après la prise pendant la demolition des retranchemens
faits par les anglais. ▰▰▰ Troupes sauvages.

A French illustration of the attack on Fort William Henry. A. Fort William Henry
B. The opening of the trenches on the night of 4 August C. The reduced camp the
English occupied in expectation of the French force D. The bay where the French
disembarked their artillery E. Battery of eight cannons and a mortar F. Battery of
ten cannons with a mortar. G. Six piece battery that was never employed in the
engagement H. Position of Monsieur de Levi during the engagement with the fort
I. Position of the troops during the siege K. Their positions after destroying and
laying claim to the English retrenchments [block] Indian troops. (*Library of
Congress*)

cannons were guns, including two giant 32-pounders, which Collins had positioned in the northwest bastion, correctly guessing that the French would direct their principal efforts against that point. The others varied in caliber, with the smallest being four bronze 6-pounders and two iron guns of four pounds. The bronze guns had one significant advantage over the iron: they were considerably less prone to metal fatigue, a factor that would play a major role in the siege. Collins also had three 8-inch mortars and a single howitzer of the same caliber, both of which would enable him to fire explosive shells on a high trajectory into the enemy's siege lines. Along with the cannons, Fort William Henry had thirteen small swivel guns, designed for use against infantry attacking the walls.[7]

Working tirelessly, the sailors and artillerymen crewing Collins's cannons fired countless shots against the French lines. The guns were loaded with round shot—solid iron balls that were fired over a low trajectory, had a maximum effective range of one thousand yards, and could punch their way through fortifications or massed ranks of troops alike. After each firing, the barrels were sponged out to extinguish any smoldering debris left behind. Then a new powder charge was put in place, followed by a piece of wadding, before a round shot was loaded. The spongeman then reversed his staff and rammed the charge home, while the ventsman blocked the touchhole with a leather thumb pad to prevent a rush of air igniting any smoldering scraps of powder that may have been left behind. The charge bag was then sliced open and a powder-filled quill inserted into the touchhole. Finally, as the crew stood well back, the charge was ignited with a linstock. The quill then burned down to the main charge, which exploded, sending the shot hurtling toward the French lines.

While most of the British round shot crashed harmlessly through the trees around the French camp or was absorbed by the fascines and gabions, some took deadly effect. Father Roubaud noticed "a Soldier—occupied in wondering at the extraordinary effect . . . [that] a cannon-ball [had had] on a [nearby] tree." Moments later, a second shot hit the white-coated regular while the priest watched aghast just "a few steps away."[8] The victim, a private of the Royal Roussillon Regiment, was killed on the spot.[9] The relentless fire also took its toll on the British guns. At some point during the second day, the 8-inch mortar on the northwest bastion burst, the metal fatigued from constant use. As the barrel ripped apart, shards of iron went scything through the air. Miraculously, no one was seriously hurt. Not wanting to leave a weakness in the fort's defenses, Lieutenant Williamson ordered his men to drag the howitzer into position to replace the burst mortar. On his rounds, the engineer also noted that the 18-pounder on the northeast bastion was showing signs of fatigue. The metal had "split at the muzzle & [was] extremely Honeycomb'd." Deciding not to risk another barrel bursting, Williamson had the gun replaced with a 9-pounder.[10]

At midday, a report reached Colonel Monro that La Corne's Indians were attempting to cut off the entrenched camp from its water supply at the base of the hill. Knowing that without water his men could not hold out for long, Monro ordered Capt. Ralph Waldo to sally out and dislodge the enemy with one hundred Massachusetts provincials. The twenty-one-year-old from Boston, who had distinguished himself following Marin's attack on Fort Edward two weeks before, set about his mission with gusto.[11] Rushing from the camp, he dislodged the Indian marksmen, but in his haste approached too closely. A body of the enemy managed to out-flank his position and shot the "brave" young captain through the body. As the provincials retreated the Indians followed them in until they reached the line of the British quarter guard. For a while it seemed as though the camp was about to be overrun, but then McCloud's artillery drove the "savages" back down the hill.[12] Captain Waldo was brought back to camp where his wound was dressed, but surgeon Miles Whitworth held out little hope for his recovery.[13] A badly wounded French Indian was also brought in by a ranger, but died shortly afterward.[14]

Meanwhile, rangers carrying Monro's dispatch written at 6 p.m. on the first day of the siege had arrived at Fort Edward. After reading of the latest developments, Webb had Bartman write a dispiriting reply. Lieutenant Jacques Vaudry, the

Canadian prisoner taken earlier that day, had misinformed the general under interrogation. Whether through ignorance or quick-witted design, Vaudry had claimed that Montcalm had eleven thousand soldiers, whereas the French army's troop strength actually amounted to a little more than eight thousand. Therefore Webb believed that even if he were able to unite all his scattered forces, he would still be outnumbered by three thousand men. As the following letter confirms, the bravado that the British general had previously displayed had now all but vanished. "[Webb] . . . has order'd me to acquaint you that he does not think it prudent . . . to attempt a Junction or to assist you till reinforc'd by the Militia of the Colonies," Bartman wrote:

> for the immediate march of which repeated Expresses have been sent. One of our Scouts brought in a Canadian Prisr. last night from the investing Party which is very large, and have possess'd all the Grounds on this side of Fort Wm. Henry. The number of the Enemy is very considerable, the Prisr. says eleven Thousand and [they] have a large Train of Artillery with Mortars and were to open their Batteries this day. The General thought proper to give you this intelligence, that in case he should be so unfortunate from the delays of the Militia not to have it in his power to give you timely Assistance, you might be able to make the best Terms [of surrender that] were left in your power. The Bearer [of this dispatch] is a Serjt. of the Connecticut Forces and if [he] is happy enough to get in [to Fort William Henry] will bring advices from you. We keep continual Scouts going to endeavor to get in, or bring intelligence from you. I am sir, with the heartiest and most anxious wishes for your Welfare, your most Obedient Humble servant, G. Bartman, aid de camp.[15]

After folding the message to the size of a postage stamp, the Connecticut ranger charged with bearing it to Monro tucked it into the lining of his jacket and set off through the woods with two companions. At some point on their journey, the provincials had the misfortune to run into Kanectagon, the Caughnawaga warrior who had set up an ambush on the road the day before. Blundering into his trap, the messengers never stood a chance. The sergeant was killed outright at the first fire. One of his companions was captured and the third man escaped "by the swiftness of his running" and got back to Fort Edward.[16] After scalping his victim and stripping him of his clothes and possessions, Kanectagon returned to the French camp in triumph. "He brought back . . . the prisoner," Bougainville recorded, "and the jacket of the dead man. In the lining we found a letter . . . which General Webb . . . wrote to Lieutenant Colonel Monro."[17] After reading the message, Montcalm was delighted. It seemed that his worst fear—that Webb would attack in strength, thus lifting the siege and placing the Frenchman between two enemy forces—would not materialize. Without reinforcements, Monro was at Montcalm's mercy: it was only a matter of time before the fort was his.

Over the next few days, the French general would formulate a cunning plan. Even though his enemies had intended that the letter should reach Monro, and normally it would aid the French cause merely to intercept it, Montcalm came to realize that it would actually suit his purposes if Webb's depressing assessment of his inability to aid the Scot were delivered. Once informed by his own superior that no reinforcements would be forthcoming, Monro would be left with an unenviable decision. Either he could stubbornly refuse to accept the inevitable and fight on until the French guns had battered a breach in the walls and his men were exposed to the Indians' mercy, or he could ask the French for terms. Believing that his opponent would opt for the latter course, Montcalm was only left with one decision: when to deliver the message that would undermine his enemy's morale. If his plan were to come to fruition, the timing would be essential. If the letter was sent too soon, Monro would not countenance surrender; too late, and Webb might just arrive after all.

Unaware of these developments, the British continued fighting. In the fort, Lieutenant Williamson ordered the roofs to be pulled off all the barracks as a precaution against the French employing heated shot once they had their batteries into operation, and McCloud and Collins's artillery had several successes, including a well-placed mortar round that fizzed through the air before falling on "an Indian hutt" and killing "Several."[18] Although the groans of the wounded continued through the night, both the men and their commanders remained in reasonable spirits. From a dispatch written to Webb at six o'clock that evening, it is clear that Monro was still expecting relief. "We are continually harass'd by the Indians all round us," the Scotsman noted, as his men once more lit bonfires around the entrenched camp.[19]

> We have had both officers and men wounded by them, we have seen off their regulars but not within shott of us; we believe they are employed in erecting their Batteries, and as we are very certain that part of the Enemy have got between you and us upon the high road, would therefore be glad (if it meets with your approbation) [if] the whole army was march'd. You may depend upon Colonel Young and me doing our part as far as [is in] his and our power.[20]

That night, spurred on by the news of Webb's reluctance to march, the French worked on their siege lines with increased vigor. Under Bourlamaque and Desandrouins's direction, four hundred workmen cut down trees, dug up roots, shoveled soil, and broke through rock with their pickaxes. The sap and first parallel grew a little with every passing hour. Nearby, at Artillery Cove, observed by the defenders on the walls of Fort William Henry, numerous boats landed throughout the night.[21] In total, twelve guns were brought ashore "as well as a few mortars and the necessary munitions."[22] Anticipating the possibility of a British attempt to sally and disrupt their preparations, Bourlamaque asked for three hundred regulars to guard his workmen. Under the command of Lt. Col. Jean-Georges Dejean de Roquemaure, the fifty-two-year-old commander of La Reine Battalion, the troops spread out over the ground ahead of the trenches, listening intently for any signs of the enemy's approach. Shortly after 8 p.m., when Desandrouins's gunners were marking out the position of the second parallel, disaster struck. Failing to answer their guard's challenge of "*Qui vive?*" the artillerymen were fired upon. Fortunately for the French, no one was hurt and the work continued shortly afterward.[23]

At 4 a.m. on August 5, Colonel Roquemaure's troops, who had been guarding the workers throughout the night, retired to the first parallel. The chance of a surprise sally was greatly reduced with the coming of daylight, and exposed on the open ground, the guard would make an easy target for Collins's cannons. The night workers then made way for a two-hundred-strong replacement, so the digging could continue that day. Observing the lines as the sun rose over the mountains beyond the lake in the east, Bougainville was impressed. "By daybreak," he recorded, "[all the positions were] under cover . . . except at the right battery, where the work progressed more slowly because it was difficult [ground]."[24] With the first parallel all but finished, and work on the second already begun, it would not be long before Montcalm deployed his heavy guns. Then the British troops' suffering would truly begin.

As soon as Collins's gunners had enough light to see by, they opened fire once more. Their shells and round shot did little damage to the trenches, but immediately began to cause casualties in the regulars' camp just beyond. Not wanting to lose any men unnecessarily, Montcalm ordered the brigades of La Sarre and Royal Roussillon to move their tents four hundred yards to the rear.[25] The commanding officers were also given orders as to how to react should the British sally out and attack them in force. The men of La Reine, La Sarre, and Royal Roussillon were to form a line to meet them, and once engaged, Lévis's militia was to charge down from the heights and hit them in the flank.[26]

Throughout the morning, more and more Indians came into Montcalm's camp. Impatient to see Onontio fire his "great muskets," they gathered in the first parallel, where they were impressed by the scientific approach the French took to warfare.[27] "A few of them," Bougainville noted, "in imitation of our trenches which they had just seen with the greatest curiosity, approached the gardens [of the fort] by moving dirt and taking cover." Used to ambushing and swiftly overrunning their enemies in the darkness of the woods, the Indians were ignorant of siege warfare. Nevertheless, as Father Roubaud observed, they proved apt pupils.

It was not possible for the enemy to take a step beyond the fort without being exposed either to captivity or to death, so alert were the Savages. You may judge of it by this single account. An English woman ventured to go to gather vegetables in a kitchen garden almost adjoining the trenches. Her boldness cost her dear, a Savage concealed in a bed of cabbages perceived her, and with his gun killed her on the spot. The enemy had no opportunity of coming to take away her body; the victor, still concealed, kept guard all day long, and [that night] took off her scalp.[28]

Bougainville, like Montcalm the day before, was less impressed by the Indians' behavior. "This shooting," he observed, "doubtless inconvenienced the enemy, bothered their workers and artillerymen and even killed a few of them, but it was not the real objective. The great usefulness of these Indians to us should be to overwhelm small parties on the . . . road [to Fort Edward] and [in the] neighbouring woods, to intercept all couriers and convoys not of great size and to warn us of major movements which might be made . . . in time for us to be prepared, and not be taken by surprise."[29]

At 4 p.m. the Frenchman's worst fears nearly materialized. Some of the Indian scouts who had remained in position in the woods to the south of Fort William Henry appeared at the French camp with news of a two-thousand-strong body of the enemy advancing from Fort Edward. Montcalm immediately ordered three grenadier companies to reinforce Lévis's detachment, and for the whole to march out and intercept them. The chevalier set off and Montcalm himself was about to follow with another body of men, when reports came back saying that it had been a false alarm.[30]

One hour later, Montcalm decided to address the issues with the Indians and convened a great council. Advancing into the center of the gathered chieftains, he ran through a long list of complaints.

[They] . . . had not remained at the camp of the Chevalier de Lévis, that the reconnaissances were not being made, that it appeared that his children had lost their spirit, that there no longer was any agreement among them, that they neglected to carry out his wishes, that instead of following his orders, they went into the cleared land around the fort and exposed themselves unnecessarily, [and] that the loss of several Indians killed in these shootings had been extremely painful to him, the least amongst them being precious.

Montcalm then explained that they could be most useful to him if they remained in La Corne's camp, restricted themselves to sending out scouting parties to the south, and kept him informed of all movements of the enemy. "Finally," Bougainville wrote, "in order to restore their spirit, to get them back again on the right path, to wipe out the past and to brighten the future . . . he would give them two belts and ten strings of wampum." Indian orators then took the floor, accepted the wampum with gratitude, and agreed to follow Onontio's commands. "They . . . added that . . . they had something on their minds . . . no one told them anything any more, . . . their chiefs were not told of the movements being made," and not only was their advice ignored but no explanation was given for so doing. "My Father," one said, gently admonishing Montcalm, "thou hast brought into these places the art of war of this world that lies beyond the great ocean. We know that in this art you are a great master, but for the science of the craft of scouting, we know more than thee. Consult us and thou will derive benefit from it."

Montcalm apologized and assured the Indians that he valued their skills highly. "He ended by telling them that tomorrow the cannon would start to fire," Bougainville remarked. "The news produced great joy in the assembly, [and it] broke up very contentedly."[31]

In the British lines, the third day of the siege had progressed much like the second. Indian sharpshooters had wounded and killed several more sentries in both the fort and the entrenched camp. More worryingly, three more guns had burst from metal fatigue on the northwest bastion of the fort.[32] The third to burst was an 18-pounder. Adam Williamson, the young engineer who had witnessed Rigaud's attack in March of that year, noted that the explosion "wounded several Men." That night there was also considerable activity down by the beach. "A boat came close to some of the Sloops with an intent to set them on fire," Williamson noted, "but was drove off by the fire from the Garrison."[33]

Following this incident, it was the turn of the French to suspect an attack on their own boats. Fearing that the British would try and burn them, Montcalm ordered his grenadiers to post a strong guard by Artillery Bay. Meanwhile the rest of the grenadiers, having returned from the false alarm on the road to Fort Edward, took over as the covering party for those working in the trenches; and at 7 p.m., a fresh shift of three hundred men moved into position to put the finishing touches to the first parallel and move the guns into place.[34]

Shortly after midnight, Lt. Ralph Waldo died of the wound he had sustained on August 4.[35] The musket ball had drilled through the Boston-born provincial's body, and there had been little that surgeon Whitworth could do. His death caused considerable consternation among his comrades: Waldo had been just nineteen days short of his twenty-second birthday.[36]

The Bombardment

August 6–8, 1757

*O*n the night of August 5, work on the French trenches progressed swiftly. By dawn, the first battery was ready and the cannons had been hauled into position. Eight were guns: three 18-pounders and five 12-pounders, their barrels alternately aligned with the fort's northwest bastion, its west and north facing walls, the boats drawn up on the beach beneath them, and the entrenched camp on the heights above.[1] The other cannon was a 9-inch mortar, which could hurl bombs directly into the fort's courtyard. Watching the French preparations was Lt. Adam Williamson. "We fired two shells & one thirty two pounder before the enemy fired," he noted in his journal.[2] Williamson's efforts did little to delay the inevitable.

With Montcalm and a crowd of Indians witnessing the event, the French cannons opened fire at 6 a.m. "They gave us two guns," Colonel Frye recalled, "and, soon after, seven more, very quick, one after the other; which hot fire they continued all day."[3] According to Father Roubaud, the French Indians greeted each shot with "cries of joy, and all the mountains resounded with the uproar."[4] The British were less impressed. "It was some time before they found their mark," one diarist noted. At 10 a.m. the French mortar opened fire. It too was inaccurate at first, with most of the shells falling short of their target, but "towards the afternoon they got their distance very well, several of their small shells falling into the parade."[5] To Colonel Frye's consternation, the French cannons also began to find their mark. "Several of our men were this day wounded in the camp," he noted, "one of whom had his thigh shot off by an 18-pounder, as he was standing sentry at [my] . . . tent door." After ripping the limb from Frye's guard, the round shot tore the canvas "to pieces" before finally coming to a halt on the far side of the hill. Examining the ball that had nearly killed him, Frye found that it bore "his majesty's mark," the impertinence of the French had plumbed new depths. Not content with merely bombarding Monro's positions, they were using British-made round shot against them, captured following the siege of Oswego the year before.[6]

The fort's defenders were also under heavy fire. On the northwest bastion, Captain Collins was in the eye of the storm. "When a shott would strike any Timbers of the Fort," he remembered, "or a shell burst within twenty or thirty yards, it would shake like an earthquake."[7] Elsewhere the French fire was even more accurate. "One of their Shott carried away the Pully of our Flag Staff," an anonymous diarist recorded. As the British colors fell to the ground, a great cheer rose from the enemy. A carpenter and his mate were assigned to rehoist it, but while they were thus employed, the French gunners fired again. To the horror of those watching, the ball decapitated the carpenter and wounded his companion. The British didn't attempt to refly the flag again.[8] Even more worrying for the defenders was the state of their guns. At one point, one of the fort's bronze 6-pounders was "ruined by a shot from the enemy," and several more barrels burst.[9] That morning, Monro wrote a dispatch to Webb detailing their predicament. "Sir," the Scotsman began, "we have had within 24 hours, two 10-pounders, one 12-pounder and one mortar burst, from which you will see the necessity of sending up a fresh supply as soon as possible. We have been obliged to give two 12-pounders from the camp, which we could very ill spare."[10]

At 2 p.m., some rangers from Fort Edward managed to sneak through the cordon of Indians and get into the entrenched camp. Monro immediately called them into his presence. Having nearly fallen into enemy hands, the men had destroyed the letter Webb had entrusted them with, but delivered a somewhat garbled verbal message instead. Exhausted and terrified after their ordeal, they spoke of the imminent arrival of the militia at Fort Edward as well as that of Sir William Johnson and his Mohawk allies. The possibility of reinforcement must have buoyed Monro, but the nature of the message left him unsure of the veracity of the rangers' report. "They delivered it in so confused a manner, I really could not rightly understand it," the Scotsman confessed.[11]

Meanwhile, the Indian sharpshooters harassing the British defenders had redoubled their efforts, inspired by their artillery's success. Standing beside the guns, Captain Desandrouins watched them advance. "Until then," the twenty-eight-year-old from Verdun noted, "they had shot at the fort and entrenched camp from out of reach, hiding behind a tree or a stump. [But, following the first fire of the French battery,] we saw them . . . slip like snakes through the undergrowth to the little marsh that was between the fort and the [main] French camp, and there, lying flat, they opened so well directed a fire into the [British] embrasures, that the enemy could barely use their artillery [to reply]."[12]

Down by the lakeshore, the Indians scored another victory. As Bougainville noted, "from the beginning of the siege the enemy unceasingly went to hide various things in the woods on the south shore, and to watch our movements from there." On August 4, the troops in the fort had thrown their excess firewood into the waters to ensure that they would not be set ablaze by French munitions, and on August 6 the Indians noted further movements in the area. Determined to put an end to their enemies' excursions, several warriors concealed themselves in the undergrowth and waited for the British to reappear.[13] Soon enough, a party of the New Jersey Blues obliged them. "Several Indians fell on . . . [them]," Bougainville recorded, "killed and wounded a few, and made two prisoners, from whom we learned nothing." The individuals in question were Thomas Cory and John Meir. While the latter was soon paroled and would be back home within three months, Cory would not see his native New Jersey again for two years.[14]

Despite such successes, the French also had some problems of their own. Having neglected to stop the vent when the barrel of one of the first battery's cannons was sponged out, a soldier of the Béarn Regiment was badly burned when the remnants of powder burst into flames.[15]

That evening, Monro wrote Webb his third letter of the day. Despite his customary formality, the Scot's desperation was all too evident. "Sir," he wrote,

> I beg pardon for saying that if the reinforcement we had reason to expect from your letter, the only one I have received from you, which bears date August 3, had arrived in time, our situation probably would have been better. . . . I have frequently as possible acquainted you with every circumstance that has passed since the enemy's appearance and therefore submit the whole to your better judgement . . . I am &c., Geo. Monro.[16]

At that very moment, Webb was dictating a reply. Since his last message, the general's morale had been boosted by the arrival of the first of the militia, a 1,500-strong detachment, which he had ordered Christie to send up from Albany on the third. Leading them into camp was Sir William Johnson and 180 of his Mohawk allies.[17] Also with the party was Col. George Augustus, 3rd Viscount Howe.[18] An inspirational thirty-two-year-old, uniquely among the gentlemen officers of the regulars, Howe shared the discomforts of the men and was loved by the redcoats and provincials alike. As a result, compared with the tone of the note captured by Kanectagon, Webb's letter of August 6 was positively optimistic. "I . . . have now got together by the March of the Militia in the highest spirits three Armies of five thousand Men . . . [I] shall set out in the night with the whole join'd together, and make no doubt of cutting the Enemy entirely off. I am, Dear Sir, till I have the pleasure of seeing you to partake of the Victory, your humble servant."[19]

The positive atmosphere at Fort Edward was not solely confined to Webb's quarters. At the morning parade the firebrand Massachusetts chaplain, Dr. William Crawford, had chosen a suitably inspiring sermon from the first book of Samuel.[20] "And Jonathan said to the young man that bore his armour," the twenty-seven-year-old roared to his congregation, "Come and let us go over unto the garrison of these uncircumcised: it may be that the Lord will work for us: for there is no restraint to the Lord to save by many or by few." Crawford's point would not have been lost on his listeners. With the militia's arrival, the papist French and their heathen allies were in for a beating. Perhaps born from the upbeat atmosphere, an unfounded rumor swept through camp that word had been received from Monro. Jabez Fitch recorded the details. "I hear that our people [at Fort William Henry] hold their ground good," he wrote in his journal, "and Col Monroe said he was as well pleased as if he was in his own country among ye potatoes."[21]

In fact, the atmosphere at Fort William Henry on the night of August 6 was decidedly gloomy. By the light of the moon, the British sentries on the palisades could make out the arrival of some supply boats from Carillon, and they could hear the French workers digging throughout the night. Five hundred men had been assigned to the task, and progress was rapid. The second enfilading battery and parallel, built to the west of the first, were soon finished and the guns—"two eighteen pounders, five twelves, one eight, two seven inch howitzers and a six inch mortar"—were dragged into place. In the predawn light the work continued. The damage done to the first battery by Lieutenant Collins's cannons was repaired, and the sap was extended toward the edge of the British gardens where the third and final battery would be dug.[22] At dawn on August 7, the British defenders were greeted by an ominous sight.[23] Desandrouins's second battery was ready for action.

At 6 a.m. Montcalm made his way to the forward trenches, and both French batteries opened fire. The first continued to pound away at the corner of the damaged northwest bastion, while the second fired "obliquely" at the western wall "and by ricochet" at the entrenched camp beyond.[24] As the sun climbed over the mountains to the east, several Indians made their way to the batteries to watch the French at work. Every two minutes a volley was fired. With each round shot that crashed into the palisades, splintering the wood and leaving gaps where the sand rushed out in cascades, the Indians let out a whoop of approval. They also applauded the mortar bombs that looped over the walls and landed in the parade ground beyond.[25] To Father Roubaud's surprise, "their admiration was neither inactive nor fruitless. They wished to try everything, so as to make themselves more useful. They aspired to become gunners, and one of the number distinguished himself; after having himself pointed his gun, he shot accurately into the reentrant angle that had been assigned to him for a mark."

The Frenchmen applauded their savage apprentice, "but he refused to repeat [his feat], notwithstanding the solicitations of the Trench [because] . . . having attained in his very first attempt that degree of perfection to which he could aspire, he ought not to hazard his fame by a second trial."[26]

As well as being in awe of the majesty of the "great muskets," Roubaud noted that the Indians were fascinated by the steady advancement of the sap toward the British lines. With the coming of dawn, two hundred day workers had replaced the five hundred who had worked through the night, and three companies of grenadiers under Lieutenant Colonel Privat, who had been assigned to guard them, also helped out with the work. "[The Indians] examined with an eager curiosity the manner in which our grenadiers proceeded to give to this sort of work the perfection which it required," Roubaud observed. "Having been taught by their eyes, they very soon tried their hands at the practical part. Armed with shovels and pickaxes they were seen making a covered way to the fortified rock . . . [and] they pushed it forward so well that they were very soon within gunshot."[27]

Before the Indians could exploit their hard work, Montcalm decided to pull the ace from his sleeve. At 9 a.m., after a final double volley fired simultaneously from both batteries to awe the British into submission, the French waved a red flag of truce from the head of the sap.[28] Spying it, Monro called a cease-fire, and for the second time since the firing had begun on the morning of August 3, the guns of Fort William Henry fell silent. As the dust settled, and the men began to raise their heads to survey their surroundings, Montcalm handed Bougainville the letter that Kanectagon had intercepted three days before and ordered the young aide to cross no-man's-land and present it to Monro. "I walked from the trenches, with a red flag carried before me," Bougainville recorded,

> accompanied by a drummer . . . and an escort of fifteen grenadiers. The English cried out to me to halt at the foot of the glacis, an officer and fifteen grenadiers [then] came out . . . to ask what I wanted, upon which I said that I had a letter from my general to deliver to the English commander. Two other officers came out from the fort, one of whom remained under guard of my grenadiers, and the other [engineer Lt. Adam Williamson], having blindfolded me, led me . . . to the fort, and then to the entrenched camp where I handed to the commandant the letter of the Marquis de Montcalm and that of General Webb.[29]

Monro's surprise can only be imagined. In front of Bougainville, no doubt the Scot hid his emotions, but he must have been gravely concerned by the unexpected developments. Previously Monro had been optimistic about the chances of relief, but Webb's letter changed everything.[30] The Scot read and reread the damning lines.

> [Webb] does not think it Prudent . . . to attempt a Junction . . . 'til reinforced by the Militia . . . in case he should be so unfortunate . . . not to have it in his Power to give you timely assistance you [should] . . . make the best Terms [of surrender] left in your Power.

Without prospect of reinforcement, the situation appeared hopeless. The scourge of metal fatigue was taking a daily toll on the fort's artillery, and Lieutenant Collins now had "but [fourteen guns] . . . One Howitz[er] and One Mortar . . . left."[31] Nevertheless, Monro was not about to give the French the pleasure of his surrender until the situation became desperate. Deciding to wait until the third battery was opened before he would consider capitulation, he thanked Bougainville for his time, ensured him that the letter made no difference to his resolution to "make a gallant defence," and sent the Frenchman back to his lines.[32]

"Then they led me back again," Bougainville recalled, "eyes blind-folded all the time, to where they had taken me from."[33] Barely had the Frenchman reached the cover of the trenches than the firing began again. To the disgust of Col. Joseph Frye, Louis Coulon de Villiers, the French commander of the volunteer battalion, had taken advantage of the cease-fire to occupy the far side of a small knoll two hundred fifty yards to the rear of the entrenched camp. With Villiers were a body of three hundred Canadians, Indian warriors, and a handful of regulars. Their position compromised by the proximity of the enemy, the defenders were determined to throw them back. First on the scene was Capt. Jonathon Taplin of the Massachusetts provincials, who had been posted on the near-side of the knoll "under cover of some logs" with a body of eighty men. Once Bougainville had got under cover, the two sides opened fire. At such close range, the musketry took deadly effect. Within minutes, scores of Taplin's men had been hit and the survivors were forced back. Seeing the danger as the enemy got ever closer to the barricades of the entrenched camp, Captains Saltonstall of the Massachusetts provincials and Crookshank of the New York Independents sallied out with two hundred men to drive them off. "A very warm dispute ensued," Colonel Frye recalled, "which continued for near three hours."[34] Finally, with the French reinforced by Indians who poured out of the surrounding woods, the defenders were forced to withdraw. They left the hillside carpeted with their dead. Fifty Massachusetts provincials and New York regulars and twenty-one Indians and Canadians had been killed or wounded. Four provincials had also been taken prisoner in what Bougainville termed "this useless affair."[35]

Meanwhile, the increasingly one-sided artillery duel between the fort and the French batteries continued. Every two minutes shells fell into the parade ground, and cannon-balls slammed into the walls. At midday the commander of the fort, Capt. John Ormsby, was badly burned by a shell that exploded inside one of the barracks. Unable to continue, Ormsby retired to his quarters where he was treated by a surgeon, while Capt. William Arbuthnot of the Massachusetts

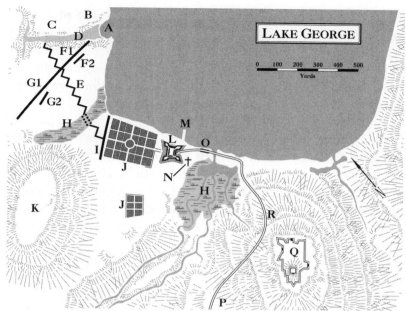

The Siege of Fort William Henry. A. Artillery cove B. Hospital tent C. French regulars camp D. Ravine E. Sap (320 yards long) F1. First parallel F2. First battery (70 yards long and 20 feet wide) G1. Second parallel (breadth of first and second parallels was 578 yards G2. Second battery (74 yards long and 26 feet wide) H. Swamp I. Third parallel J. Fort's kitchen gardens K. Levi's camp L. Fort William Henry M. Jetty N. Graveyard O. Covered way P. La Corne's camp Q. Entrenched British camp R. Road to Fort Edward.

provincials temporarily took command.[36] Unable to cope with the pressure, Arbuthnot soon asked to be relieved and was replaced by Captain Collins of the 35th.[37] Moments later, "a shell fell into the South Bastion." The spherical casing exploded, sending metal shards flying in all directions. One sliced through a man's leg, breaking the bone before flying on and imbedding itself in one of his comrades. Another shell fell into the northeast bastion and wounded "two or three" more, and a particularly lucky shot, fired from the 9-inch mortar in the first battery, landed among the ammunition supply on the already badly damaged northwest bastion.[38] The resulting explosion was devastating. Sixteen men were killed or wounded. "One of . . . [the casualties] was a

Provential Officer," Captain Collins recalled, "that never was heard of, . . . [although] part of his coat was [later] found."[39] That evening one shell even reached the entrenched camp. "[It] fell amongst the officers whilst at dinner, but did no other mischief than Spoil their . . . [food] by the dirt it tore up."[40]

On the night of August 7, a messenger arrived at the French camp from Montréal. The dispatches he carried detailed the latest developments from as far afield as "France, Louisbourg, Québec, Niagara and La Belle Riviére."[41] With his papers was a copy of the latest "list of favours granted to the French troops" by Louis XV. Among the decorations and pensions was the honor of "a red ribbon" awarded to Montcalm for his efforts in New France. "Everyone [at the French camp felt] . . . his zeal for his Majesty's service redouble in consequence," Bougainville recorded, and "even the Indians came to compliment" Montcalm "and to state . . . that they were delighted at the distinction with which the Grand Onontio had just decorated him, as they knew how highly he appreciated it." The scene moved the young aide to reflect on the success Montcalm had enjoyed in dealing with the Indians since his arrival in New France the year before, in spite of his dislike of their customs. "Tis true," he wrote in a letter to Marc-René de Voyer de Paulmy d'Argenson, the minister of war in Versailles, "that the Marquis . . . has known how to win their affections. They themselves observed that he was acquainted with their customs and manners as if he had been reared in the midst of their cabins, and what is almost unprecedented, he has succeeded in managing them, throughout this entire expedition, without recourse to either brandy or wine."[42]

Meanwhile, Bourlamaque's engineers were busy in the trenches. That evening at eight o'clock, 230 workers arrived on a boat from Carillon and were immediately set to work repairing the damage done by the British guns to the first and second batteries. Once the task was complete they continued digging the sap, which would lead to the third battery, to be excavated just one hundred yards from the fort. Realizing that the next day would bring the trenches up to the area of swampland that lay between them and the British gardens, Desandrouins ordered seventy-two of the regulars to build fascines and gabions in preparation for crossing the open ground, while the militia constructed a log bridge to carry the guns over the obstacle. In the meantime, a guard of three companies of grenadiers, seven of light troops, and a thin line of Indians and Canadians, who had crept forward to conceal themselves in the gardens, were posted to the front of the diggers in no-man's-land. Leading them was Lt. Col. Louis-Étienne-Guillaume de Senezergues, the forty-eight-year-old commander of the La Sarre Regiment who had so impressed Lévis with his stamina and professionalism on the march down the shore of Lake George.[43]

At 10 p.m., the Indians and Canadians were startled by the sudden appearance of two British deserters from the 35th. Sneaking out of one of Fort William Henry's sally ports, the redcoats crept across the gardens and were nearly upon the Indians when they opened fire. One, a foreign volunteer, was hit several times in the arm and had his shoulder broken. "At the noise of the volley . . . , the mountains round the fort resounded with the shouts of all the Indians, who were calling to and answering each other."[44] The sound unnerved the defenders and the deserters alike. After crying "out that they were . . . friends of France," both men were taken into custody and shepherded back to the trenches where they were interrogated by Bourlamaque.[45] With the interview concluded, the colonel sent the wounded man to the field hospital by Artillery Cove where he was visited by Father Roubaud. The Jesuit "enjoyed the sweet consolation of preparing the way for his speedy reconciliation to the Church."[46]

When he heard that two of the 35th had gone over to the enemy, Colonel Monro was furious. He would not have been surprised if the provincials had betrayed him, but the thought of his own men deserting to the French was too much to bear. Calling an aide to his side, the Scot dictated a new order, which was to be posted in the fort and the entrenched camp. The command was brutally succinct: "If any person proved cowardly or offered to advise giving up the fort," it stated, "he should be immediately hanged over the walls."[47]

At daybreak on August 8, Bourlamaque's night workers were replaced by a new shift of three hundred men. By midday the bridge had been laid across the marsh, fascines and gabions had been piled up on either side to provide cover for those crossing the exposed stretch, and work had begun on the third parallel. While laying the road, the workers were exposed to the fire of Collins's remaining guns. As the range diminished, the lieutenant loaded them with grapeshot, tightly packed small-caliber cannonballs, which fanned out from the barrel like the blast from a shotgun. One regular of the Béarn Battalion was killed and four others were wounded. Undaunted, their comrades carried them to the field hospital at Artillery Cove, and the work pushed on.[48]

The French gunners continued to exact a heavy toll. Shell after shell looped into the fort and the entrenched camp on the hill beyond. Every few minutes brought new casualties, and the surgeons struggled to keep up. Limbs were amputated and cast aside, shell fragments were extracted from seared flesh, and open wounds were bandaged. Among the wounded was Lt. Col. John Young of the Royal Americans. The highest-ranking casualty of the siege so far, Young had been wounded in the ankle. Several shards of bone had been driven into the flesh and he was no longer able to walk.[49]

Still there was no sign of reinforcement, and the men's morale was failing fast. Under constant fire, they were exhausted and close to the breaking point. Few had had any sleep for six days, they were unshaven, and their uniforms were stained and dirty and reeked of stale sweat. While the majority of the redcoats continued to behave "with . . . coolness and resolution," among the provincials the first signs of mutiny were beginning to appear. In the fort, some of Frye's Massachusetts regiment refused to man the ramparts. The Indian sharpshooters were becoming bolder all the time, and as they crept closer and fanned out through the gardens outside the walls, their fire became increasingly accurate. Rather than exposing themselves, the Massachusetts provincials "lay down upon their faces and fir'd straight up in the air," vainly hoping to keep the enemy at bay by the sound of their musketry alone. Driven to distraction by the interminable firing, others began to talk of sallying out to finish the fight once and for all, saying "that they would rather be knock'd in the head by the enemy as to stay and perish behind the breastwork." The men of New Jersey and New Hampshire were even more demoralized. According to Monro, unlike the men of Massachusetts, who up until then had "behav'd" well, those from New Jersey and New Hampshire "could never be brought to do their duty with regularity or precision" throughout the entire siege. Determined to maintain discipline, Monro told Frye that an example should be made of some of his men. Frye refused, saying that he "could not condescend upon any Particular man" when the decision not to fight "was the declaration of the whole body in General."[50]

By early afternoon, even the normally resolute Monro was beginning to flag. In a letter he wrote to Webb, the strain was evident:

> The fort and the camp will hold out in the hopes of the speedy relief from you which we hourly expect, and if that does not happen, we must fall into the hands of our enemies. Your letter dated 4th instant was delivered to me by an Aid de Camp of General Montcalm's. That letter falling into his hands was a very unhappy thing and has to be sure, elevated him greatly. As to the numbers of the enemy, the Canadian prisoner mentioned to you, every body here is of opinion that was greatly magnified. If they really had those numbers, they might have demolished us at once, with out loss of time. The enemy are constantly playing upon us from two batteries of nine pieces cannon. Relief is greatly wanted.[51]

Unknown to the Scot, reinforcements had actually left Fort Edward earlier that day. Although General Webb had changed his mind since the elation of the previous night and had now decided to wait for the arrival of yet more militia, Sir William Johnson had chosen to act. Exasperated by Webb's procrastination, he set out along the road to Lake George with his Mohawks and militia, only to be ordered back by Webb after covering just three miles. Disgusted, Johnson confronted Webb on his return. According to an account later related to Bougainville by an Indian allied to the French:

[Johnson had] proposed . . . to march at once on the French lines. Webb said that he would do no such thing, that he did not wish to expose himself to complete defeat in woods still red with English blood. [Dredging up memories of his 1755 victory,] Johnson replied that these same shores of Lake George would be as fatal to Montcalm as they had been to Dieskau, that French bones would cover this battlefield, and as for himself, he swore by his . . . tomahawk that he would conquer or die. [But] General Webb was not moved.

An exasperated Johnson was then said to have marched off in disgust.[52]

After leaving Webb, Johnson ordered a party of Mohawk scouts to make their way to Lake George. Their instructions were to take a French prisoner who could report on the situation at Fort William Henry. After the scouts, led by Moses, "a head man" of the tribe, had disappeared northwest into the woods, the rest of Johnson's Indians prepared to return to their castles on the Mohawk River. They had heard rumors of a possible raid on their settlements and wanted to be with their families in case they turned out to be true.[53]

Colonel James Montresor, meanwhile, had spent the day at Fort Edward drawing up plans to improve the defenses. "[I] Went with the General and Lord Howe to visit the high ground to the North of the Fort," he recorded in his journal, "& [we] marked the Trees for an Abbatis or Retrenchement to post the troops in, in Case of an attack."[54] Far from considering attacking the French, Webb was actually more preoccupied with thoughts of defense.

At 3 p.m., word of Johnson's advance reached Montcalm at Lake George. An Indian scout, using the metaphorical language typical of his nation, informed the general that the reinforcements were "more numerous than the leaves on the trees." Unaware that the Irishman had been forced to turn back after only three miles, Montcalm called his men to arms. Father Roubaud, who was passing through the main camp at the time, described the scene:

I perceived a general commotion in all the quarters of our camp. Every Corps was in motion,—French,

Canadians, and Savages; all were running to arms, all were preparing to fight. A reported arrival of the help so long expected by the enemy had produced this sudden and general activity. In this moment of alarm Monsieur de Montcalm, with a presence of mind which revealed the General, attended to the safety of our entrenchments, the service of our batteries, and the defence of our boats. He then went to take his place again at the head of the army.[55]

All around the valley, the French and their allies were in motion. Lévis was ordered to block the road to Fort Edward, where Montcalm joined him at 5:30 p.m. with La Reine Battalion and three companies of grenadiers. The Royal Roussillon, meanwhile, occupied the heights to the west of Fort William Henry, from which its troops could go to the support of either Montcalm and Lévis's men or those who remained in the trenches. At 6 p.m., his preparations complete, Montcalm advanced to meet the enemy. The regulars, formed in column, took the main road, while the Indians and Canadians spread out through the woods on either flank.[56] By dusk, however, it became clear that the rumor of Johnson's approach was a false alarm. Montcalm called off the advance, and the troops returned to their previous posts. Bougainville was stoical about the mistake. "The promptness of our movement at least served to show the Indians that . . . they could depend as much upon the vigilance as upon the valour of the French. . . . At the end of the day all the troops were back in their camp and the work did not suffer at all."[57]

At sunset, Webb dictated yet another letter to Monro in which he blamed the tardiness of others for his own inaction. "Sir," Captain Bartman wrote:

I am directed by General Webb to acquaint you, that it is entirely owing to the delay of the Militia that he has not yet mov'd up to your Assistance, but as he has now got a party of them and expects a thousand more tomorrow, you may depend, upon their arrival, that he will not fail to march to your Assistance; you will upon hearing him engag'd consult with Col. Young how you can by making a vigorous sally from the camp best support his attack. We have sent repeated Letters but are sorry only one has got in, tho we hope none have fallen into the Enemys hands, as most of the parties have returned but were all closely pursued. We shall have about an hundred and fifty Indians with Sir Wm. Johnson, but shall keep them nigh us to prevent any mistake. We wish most heartily that you may be to hold out a little longer, and hope soon to have it in our power to relieve you from your present disagreeable situation.[58]

Like all but one of Webb's previous letters, this latest missive would never reach Monro. That night, as he sat in his tent in the entrenched camp, with the sound of cannon fire ringing in his ears, the Scot began to countenance the possibility of surrender. On his orders, Lieutenants Collins and Williamson were sent out of the fort under cover of darkness to compile a detailed damage report. Their assessment was far from encouraging. Collins noted that "the timbers of the face of ye [north]East Bastion [were] knocked over two or three foot," and several of those "of ye North West Bastion" had also been severely damaged. In addition, an enemy "shell [had] knocked in the passage of the magazine under the North[west] Bastion," and another had damaged the roof "of the casement where the Laboratory was."[59] Williamson's summary was also damning. "From the state of the Artillery, Ammunition and other Stores," he wrote, the fort "was no Longer Tenable."[60]

Monro realized he had little option but to surrender. Ninety-seven of his men had been killed since the siege had begun, and perhaps twice that number had been wounded.[61] All the heaviest guns had burst, and two of the three mortars were also unserviceable.[62] That night, Monro sent word that he would hold a council of war at dawn to discuss the capitulation.[63] Although Collins's gunners kept fighting and killed or wounded a handful of Indians who approached too close through the gardens, unless Webb arrived in the next few hours, the game was up.[64]

PART THREE

Dénouement

1757–PRESENT DAY

Surrender

AUGUST 9, 1757

awn revealed the alarming proximity of Bourlamaque's third parallel. Lined with sharpshooters,
it cut across the eastern boundary of the fort's gardens just
140 yards from the walls. Later that day, or by the next morning, the French would have their cannons in position, ready to
pound the walls into oblivion. Even though they knew that
the siege was in its final throes, Collins's gunners stuck to
their task, and cannon fire was exchanged throughout the
morning. At one point, one of Collins's mortars burst.
Fortunately no men were injured, but the accident left the fort
with just fourteen small-caliber guns, one mortar, and a single
howitzer to return the fire of Bourlamaque's batteries.[1] The
situation was looking increasingly desperate for Monro. So
far, only eighty of his men had died in the siege, but if the
Scot continued to fight, he knew that his casualties would rise
rapidly.[2] Once Bourlamaque's third battery opened fire, the
bloodshed would be intense, and in the event of a breach
being forced by the French regulars, hundreds would die. By
comparison, Montcalm's men had got through the siege relatively unscathed. Just thirteen had been killed and forty
wounded, the latter including one Monsieur Le Ferve, a lieutenant of grenadiers whose hand had been wounded by the
bursting of a shell.[3] To make matters worse for Monro, morale
inside the British lines was at a low point. After yet another

sleepless night with the shells bursting around them, many of the provincials in the fort had given up even the pretense of resistance. Lying on their backs behind the palisades, they fired their muskets skyward and awaited the inevitable.[4]

At 5 a.m. Monro's council of war began. Gathered in the colonel's tent in the entrenched camp were representatives from all the units under his command. Lieutenant Colonel Young and Captain Faesch of the Royal Americans; Colonel Frye and Captain Saltonstall of the Massachusetts provincials; Colonel Gough and Major Gilman of the New Hampshire regiment; Captain Ogden of the New York provincials; Crookshanks of the Independents; Colonel Parker of the New Jersey Blues; and four officers of the 35th, including the grenadier captain, Charles Ince, were all there. The atmosphere was subdued. Although they had performed well, and to continue fighting would have meant sacrificing the majority of their men, the dishonor of capitulation was a bitter pill to swallow. Nevertheless, after some debate, they reached a unanimous decision: the fort would be surrendered to the French that morning. To guard himself from the possibility of a general court-martial, Monro had all those present sign an affidavit confirming that they agreed with his decision. Colonel Young composed the letter.

> Considering the barriers that have been erected and the near approaches the enemy has lately made, which are ready to play within one hundred yards of the Fort and likewise the excessive bad conditions of the remaining artillery . . . and that all communication between we and Fort Edward being cut off . . . [we] therefore have requested Lieu. Colonel Monro . . . to send a deputation to the French General Mons. Montcalm to obtain honourable terms for the troops in the camp and the garrison of the fort.[5]

With that the meeting broke up, and it was left to the Swiss-born captain of the Royal Americans, Rudolf Faesch, to inform the French of the decision. At 8 a.m. a white flag was hung from the palisade. As the French guns fell silent, Faesch strolled out through the main gate of Fort William Henry.[6] In the French trenches, Captain Desandrouins and a cluster of officers watched him approach. The Swiss cut an incongruous figure. Unshaven, with his hair wild and uncombed and his uniform filthy, he walked up to Desandrouins and his companions and began exchanging pleasantries in fluent French. "Some of us told him of the extreme fatigue we had suffered," the Frenchman later wrote, "and of how glad we were that the thing had finally finished." Alluding to his unkempt appearance, Faesch quipped in reply, "Not knowing to which tribe of savages I shall be allotted, I have not known which hair style to wear."[7]

Faesch was then presented to Montcalm. According to Desandrouins, the Swiss officer "charmed" the general with his amusing appearance and "merry mood."[8] Put into a good humor, and respectful of his enemies' determined resistance, Montcalm was disposed to offer good terms, and the meeting progressed amicably. After the initial discussion, Colonel Young was sent out to join them. Unable to walk due to his wounds, the Virginian mounted a horse. On his arrival at Montcalm's tent, the surrender was discussed further, and then Bougainville accompanied Young back to the entrenched camp where the details of the document were agreed to by both parties.[9] The terms, based on those "allowed to Lord [William] Blakeney at Minorca [in 1756]," were generous.[10] In deference to Monro's gallant defense, Montcalm offered him one of the highest levels of the honors of war: his men would be allowed to march to Fort Edward unmolested, carrying their arms and with their pride unsullied and their dignity intact. A further clause specified that the garrison was to leave the fort immediately, surrendering it to the command of Colonel Bourlamaque, and retiring to the entrenched camp, which the British would have to leave the following morning. Although something of a convention among European armies of the period, such generous terms were not always offered. When the defenders were deemed to have capitulated too easily, the terms of surrender were considerably harsher. Following the siege of Oswego, for example, the surrender had been unconditional. The troops had been stripped of their arms, the colors confiscated, and the men carried back to Montréal, where they were held as prisoners of war for upward of sixteen months, with many of the rank and file forced to work as laborers. At Fort William Henry, by comparison, Monro's men would be allowed to march to Fort Edward with their heads held high.

Bougainville recorded further details of the surrender in his journal. "In substance," he noted:

> the capitulation provided that the troops, both of the fort and the entrenched camp, to the number of two thousand men, should depart with the honours of war with the baggage of the officers and of the soldiers, that they should be conducted to Fort [Edward] . . . escorted by a detachment of our troops and by the principal officers and interpreters attached to the Indians, that until the return of this escort an officer should remain in our hands as a hostage, that the troops would not serve for eighteen months against His Most Catholic Majesty [Louis XV] nor against his allies, that within three months all French, Canadian, and Indian prisoners taken on land in North America since the commencement of the war should be returned to French forts, that the artillery, vessels, and all the munitions and provisions [captured at Fort William Henry] would belong to His Most Catholic Majesty, except one 6 pounder gun which the Marquis de Montcalm granted Colonel Monro and the garrison to witness his esteem for the fine defence they had made.[11]

In a letter to Monsieur Paulmy, the French minister of war, Bougainville added the following note explaining why his general had not demanded more: "[Montcalm] would have provided that the garrison would surrender prisoners of war," the aide insisted, "and this condition would probably have been agreed [by the British]; but how could the Colony [of New France] feed 2,500 additional men, so long as the inhabitants of Québec are reduced to a quarter of a pound of bread a day?"[12]

Once the terms had been agreed, but before the document had been written, Montcalm convened a council of all the Indian chiefs, "in order to appease them . . . and to render the treaty inviolable by their assent."[13] Bougainville witnessed the meeting. "[Montcalm] . . . informed them of the articles granted the besieged, the motives which determined his according them, asked their consent and their promise that their young men would not commit any disorder. The chiefs agreed to everything and promised to restrain their young men."[14]

Desandrouins, who also witnessed the council, attributed the Indians' approval to a fear of suffering more casualties should the fighting continue. The tribes had already lost a number of men during the campaign, and their fragile populations would struggle to deal with further loss. Nevertheless, the French undoubtedly realized that trouble was likely. For the Indians, victory was incomplete without the spoils of war. While the French were satisfied with their enemies' signatures on a document of surrender, the warriors required something more tangible. Without scalps, who would believe the young men's tales of bravery when they returned to their villages that autumn? And without captives, how would they be compensated for the braves that had already died?

Determined to secure the British surrender, Montcalm chose to accept the chiefs' assurances that they could control their braves, despite the precedents suggesting the contrary. The meeting then finished with the general proffering more wampum belts to the assembly, the acceptance of which, Desandrouins later wrote, was "equivalent to a solemn oath" for the Indians.[15] Satisfied that he had covered himself from future retribution, Montcalm then called an end to the meeting and went to the entrenched camp where he signed the surrender with Monro at midday. Bougainville, meanwhile, toured the fort and entrenched camp, telling the British that all barrels of "intoxicating liquor" should be stoved immediately and their contents mingled with the soil. If the Indians were to get hold of them later, he explained, there was no telling what barbarities they could descend to.[16] As a worrying prelude of things to come, even before the surrender had been officially announced, the Indians gathered around the fort and began to help themselves to any British property they could lay their hands on. One witness, watching from the entrenched camp, described their depredations. "While [the surrender negotiations were still] on the Carpet," he wrote, "the Indians came about the Fort, and with great Tranquility in their countenances; took all the Horses they could find and Led them off without taking any . . . notice of us, and without knowing, whether Colo. Young and the French General might come to an agreement about the Terms."[17]

Shortly afterward, the surrender was announced to the men, and the British garrison prepared to leave the fort. Led by Captain Collins of the 35th, they gathered as much baggage as they could carry, in accordance with the terms, and mustered in the parade ground before marching out. Meanwhile, while Bourlamaque's men were occupied with "the military ceremonial that accompanied taking possession [of the fort], crowds" of Indians clambered in "through the gun-embrasures," while others "scaled the Walls and came in, Running about, searching every Nook and Corner" for trophies to carry back to their homelands.[18] Not wanting to get caught up in a confrontation, and no doubt fearing for his own safety, Collins decided to leave them to it. Abandoning a handful of men who were too badly wounded to walk and had been left lying on stretchers in the underground casemates, the redcoats and provincials filed out through the main gates, marched along the covered causeway with muskets slung, then climbed the hill and entered the entrenched camp. At the same time, the enemy Indians crowded around them "eyeing the [troops] . . . backwards and forwards, very narrowly." Seeing the baggage the British were carrying, they "Laugh'd and made considerable Fun of us as we marched along," one of the garrison later noted, "well knowing, the property of our packs, wou'd remain [with] . . . us but a very short time." Despite making their intentions obvious, and the men exceedingly nervous, the Indians "contented themselves at first, with Howd'ye Brother and Picking his Pocket," the same witness recorded, "but it was not long before they play'd at a higher Game."[19]

Once within the walls of the entrenched camp, the men thought themselves safe, but the Indians had other ideas. Following them through the gates, for a short while they continued to plunder. James Furnis, the British staff officer in charge of ordnance supplies, was relieved when Montcalm ordered "some Companys of French Grenadiers" to fix bayonets and bodily remove them.[20] Several French officers then wandered into camp to converse with their former enemies. Among them was Captain Desandrouins of the French engineers who sought out his opposite numbers, Lieutenant Williamson and Captain Collins, to compliment them on their professionalism and gallant conduct during the defense. The British officers welcomed the Frenchmen and invited them to dine on an impressive array of delicacies, served with wine and beer.[21]

While the European officers exchanged pleasantries, just a few hundred yards to the west, the Indians in the fort had discovered the British wounded. Before the last of the four-hundred-fifty-strong garrison had even left, they began butchering them without mercy.[22] Those at the tail end of the British column heard cries of "Murder!" and "Help!" as they filed through the gates, but were too afraid to turn back.[23] In total, thirty sick and forty wounded were cowering in the sunken casemates. Captain Arbuthnot of the Massachusetts provincials witnessed what followed. "[I] saw the French Indians kill the sick and wounded," he later reported, "all [of] which was done in view of the French officers who did not attempt to hinder or prevent it."[24] At least five were killed before Bourlamaque entered with a company of grenadiers and reestablished control. The cruelties committed in the interim were legion. Some were shot in the kneecap, at least one was decapitated, and many were later found with a variety of knife and tomahawk wounds to the fronts and backs of their bodies. The corpses were mutilated, the genitals removed, and the scalps taken before the Indians were driven out of the casemate by Bourlamaque's men.[25] Captain John Orsmby, the former garrison commander who had been badly burned by an exploding shell on August 7, was among the survivors. Arriving on the scene, Father Roubaud was repelled by the stench of fear and death emanating from the subterranean shelters. "I saw one of these barbarians come out," the Jesuit remembered, "[carrying] in his hand a human head, from which trickled streams of blood, and which he displayed as the most Splendid prize that he could have secured."[26]

Although Bourlamaque stopped the killing at the fort and placed a strong guard to protect "the powder magazine and provision stores," the Indians continued looting the barracks and had also reentered the entrenched camp on the hilltop above.[27] "Despite [the] . . . guard . . . we had put on it, [they] . . . could not be prevented from entering and pillaging," Bougainville remarked. "Everything was done to stop them, [further] consultation with the chiefs, wheedling on our part, [and the use of the] authority that the officers and interpreters attached to them possessed." Nevertheless, the chaos continued. Not only were the French up against the tribes from the high country and their domesticated cousins but also many of the Canadians who fought alongside them. Militia officers, such as the forty-five-year-old veteran from Québec, Luc de La Corne, actively encouraged the Indians' depredations.

The disorder was only ended by the belated arrival of Montcalm. Rushing around the camp, he remonstrated with the Indians. Unwilling to anger the great Onontio, the warriors returned to their camp in the woods on the road to Fort Edward, and "by the evening order had been reestablished." In an effort to prevent further unrest, Montcalm "was able to arrange that . . . two chiefs from every nation should escort . . . [the British] as far as the vicinity of Fort Edward." It was also agreed that the British would now march "between Ten and Eleven O'Clock, that night" with an escort of "One hundred of the regiment of Béarn, One hundred of the Regiment of Languedoc, and a battalion of colonial regulars." Montcalm promised to be at the camp two hours before, "to see everything done, that Lay in his power, to secure our Retreat; and soon after took his Leave."[28] Any further delays would only increase the possibility of bloodshed and, as Bougainville stated, "it was known that the Indians almost never acted at night."[29] While several French officers continued to mingle with their British and American counterparts in the camp and amicably discussed the details of the siege, Montcalm and Bougainville retired to their camp by Artillery Cove.[30] As his journal attests, Bougainville was to play no further part in the campaign. "At ten in the evening I was sent . . . to carry to the Marquis de Vaudreuil the news of the surrender," and within minutes his sleek canoe had rounded Diamond Point.[31] The young aide would never see Fort William Henry again. As he later told his Parisian sponsor Madame Hérault, the "frightful spectacles" he had witnessed that summer would leave "an ineffaceable bitterness in [his] . . . soul."[32] Unknown to Bougainville, much worse was yet to come.

Amid the chaos at the entrenched camp earlier that afternoon, at least one of the Massachusetts provincials, the Frenchman who served in Capt. Samuel Thaxter's company, had fled to Fort Edward. Perhaps fearing execution as a deserter at the hands of Montcalm's regulars more than the Indians in the encircling woods, he had "jumped over the Breast-work and made his escape" as soon as he had seen "that the French flag was hoisted in Fort William Henry." Managing to sneak past the Indian pickets, he arrived at Fort Edward shortly after dusk.[33]

The Frenchman from Thaxter's company was not the only one who brought news of Fort William Henry's fall that day. The band of Mohawks that Johnson had sent out also returned with the bad tidings. While on the scout, they had lost one of their number. The "head man" Moses, who had led the party to Lake George, had been "taken in attempting to spie the situation . . . and was . . . made a sacrifice to the Enemy."[34] On the Mohawks' return, word of the defeat soon spread around Fort Edward.[35] Sergeant Jabez Fitch was devastated. "This Seems to Be the Most Unfortunate Day that Ever I Knew," he noted in his journal that evening.[36] After nightfall the men grew nervous, particularly the columns of inexperienced militia that were continually arriving at camp. They feared that Montcalm's army would be coming for them next. At 9 p.m., a single shot fired by an edgy sentry triggered a huge volley of musketry. "About a quarter of an hour later," one eyewitness reported, "Sir William [Johnson] sent Word, that their Centries had seen some Indians in the Woods, on which they fired, and that it had not been in his Power to hinder the Bulk of the Militia from doing the same."[37] In his quarters, Webb was also nervous. That night, expecting the worst, he continued to dictate letters to Gabriel Christie, the assistant deputy quartermaster general based at Albany. "The

General desires you will forward all the Militia," Bartman wrote, "and send up what Pork and bread you can possibly spare from Albany with the greatest Expedition."[38]

Back at the entrenched camp at Lake George, Monro and his men were preparing to march. Orders were given out and the men called on parade. "With great silence," one of those present recalled, "we got under arms." As the senior unit in camp, the 35th's grenadier company was chosen to lead the column. With their captain, Charles Ince, at their head, the redcoats mustered "about two or three hundred yards" beyond the camp's breastwork. They then halted for "near an Hour," but there was no sign of their escort. Eventually a French officer approached out of the gloom "and inform'd Capt. Ince . . . [that] General Montcalm had chang'd his mind." Having examined the situation at the Indian camp, Montcalm had discovered that six hundred warriors were missing. Correctly assuming that they had "Way-laid the Road," he had ordered the messenger to request the British to wait until morning.[39] Ordered to stand down, the troops settled in for another nervous night. "The Indians were in great numbers round our lines," Colonel Frye noted, "and seemed to show more than usual malice in their looks." That night Frye believed the Indians "intended us mischief."[40] With the coming of dawn, his suspicions would prove correct.

The Massacre

AUGUST 10, 1757

*B*efore the sun rose above the peaks to the east, the Indians gathered in large numbers outside the entrenched camp. They spent the predawn hours eyeing those inside as a predator views its prey. Nevertheless, Monro ordered his men to prepare to march. The longer they delayed, the worse it would be. As his men gathered their equipment, Colonel Frye watched the encircling warriors nervously. "[They were] in a worse temper, if possible, than . . . [the previous] night," the forty-eight-year-old recalled, "every one having a tomahawk, hatchet, or some other instrument of death."[1] Others were seen "examining the Priming of their Guns."[2] The British and provincials, by contrast, carried their muskets "clubbed," slung barrel down over their shoulders. Forbidden by the terms of the capitulation to load their guns and "not allowed a single round of ammunition," in the event of a fight they knew they would have to rely on their bayonets alone.[3]

At first light, the Indians forced their way into the camp. Climbing over the breastworks, they seized the horses that James Furnis had intended to use to haul the single cannon that Montcalm had granted Monro.[4] Then they looted the "heavy Baggage," before turning their attentions to the soldiers' packs. Rushing between the lines, the warriors tore them from their backs. A few of the troops resisted and some struggles broke out. Seeing that the French and Canadians, standing idly nearby, were not willing to intervene, Monro began protesting at the outrageous breach of terms. The white-coated officers offered little help. "[They] told us . . . [to] give up the baggage of the officers and men" to assuage the Indians, Colonel Frye recalled. One of the Canadian officers attached to the Indians was even more specific in his advice, telling the British officers "that if any resistance was made by which a single Indian should be killed it would not be in the power of Mr. de Montcalm to save a man from butchery." Convinced that his men were in grave danger, "at last Munroe consented" and ordered his men to throw down their packs before bloodshed ensued.[5]

With the men's packs secured, the Indians turned their attention to the sick and wounded. Lying prone in several huts and tents to one side of the camp, they made an easy target. Miles Whitworth, the surgeon of the Massachusetts regiment, had seventeen men in his care. The previous day, the French surgeon had received them into his custody and had given Whitworth a guard of French regulars to prevent them falling into the Indians' hands. During the night, however, the French surgeon and guard had disappeared, and Whitworth's charges were now dangerously exposed. As the surgeon looked on, the Indians "dragg[ed them] . . . out of their Hutts" and "Murder[ed] them with their Tomohawks and scalp[ed] them." To Whitworth's disgust, a body of three hundred troops under the Canadian officer Luc de La Corne, which was "posted round the lines . . . not further than forty feet from the Hutts," did nothing to intervene.[6] Seeing that no one would aid them, some of the wounded crawled into the ranks of the nearby provincial units where their comrades were able to provide some protection. Others "endeavoured to avert the fury of their enemies by their shrieks and groans." Their efforts were to no avail and they "were soon dispatched."[7]

"Terrified" by "the horrid Cruelties," the British and provincial units lost cohesion. Emboldened, the Indians dashed forward and "began to take the officers' hats, swords, guns, and clothes, stripping them all to their shirts, and on some left no shirt at all."[8] Colonel John Young of the Royal Americans had his pair of "silver mounted" pistols stolen, James Furnis was stripped of his boots, and surgeon Thomas Wilkins of the 35th lost two large chests of medicine and all the surgical instruments he had purchased in Portsmouth, until "[not] so much as a lancet [was left]."[9] Near the rear of the column, Maj. John Gilman of the New Hampshire regiment lost all his baggage, including a greatcoat, several silk jackets, a half-dozen teacups, a punch bowl, and a sword with a silver hilt. Nearby, Lt. Selah Barnard was having considerable problems of his own.[10] Determined not to lose "a small trunk containing his effects" that he had carried all the way from Foster, Massachusetts, the thirty-two-year-old began a desperate tug-of-war with two Indian braves. "Threatening the warriors "with instant death if they persisted in their design," Barnard "for some time held the trunk from their grasp" before finally being forced to release it when several of the warriors' comrades joined the struggle.[11] Meanwhile, the men were also being robbed of everything they had. Sergeant William McCrakan of the New Jersey Blues lost twenty-four pounds and his personal papers, drums were snatched from the musicians, halberds wrested from the hands of the sergeants, and muskets wrenched from their owners' grasp.[12]

While most of the Indians targeted their enemies' possessions, others began securing prisoners of war. Initially, as they could be disposed of easily on the Montréal slave market, "the Indians and Negroes belonging to the Provincial Regiments" were taken. Hauled from the lines, they were bound and carried into the woods. Among them were Caesar Nero Paul, Maj. John Gilman's sixteen-year-old slave, and Jock Linn, property of Nathaniel Whittemore of Massachusetts.[13] Several others, having "inraged the Indians" by their resistance, were cut to pieces. According to Colonel Frye, at least one was "burnt alive."[14] Witnessing the horrendous spectacle proved too much for one company of redcoats. Deciding they would rather take their chances in the woods than meekly waiting their turn to be slaughtered, they rushed through the gates and headed off down the track to Fort Edward. As soon as one company had moved, the rest began to follow. Soon the entire column of twenty-five hundred men, women, and children, with the regulars at their head and the New Hampshire provincials bringing up the rear, was making its way out of camp.[15] Sergeant Jonathan Carver of the Massachusetts regiment thought that the worst was now behind them. "We expected every moment that the [French] guard . . . would have arrived, and put an end to our apprehensions," he recalled. The forty-seven-year-old could not have been further from the mark. With their enemies flying before them, the Indians only grew bolder. While the initial attacks had been committed by just a handful of individuals, hundreds now joined in.[16]

According to Bougainville, who later heard of the details of the massacre, the killing was begun by a group of Abenaki from Panaouské, a village in what is now Maine, whose inhabitants had a history of mutual antipathy with the British. Swarming around the tail of the column, they gave the "war whoop" and fell on the men, killing and scalping them as they ran.[17] Sergeant Carver recalled that the women and children with the British and provincial units were among the first to be targeted. Dragged from the line and into the woods, they "were dispatched in the most wanton and cruel manner."[18] Some of the women had "their Bellies ript open, [and] their Bowels torn out," while the younger children were grabbed by their "ankles" and swung against the trees until "their Brains [were] beat out."[19] Carver did not have long to pity them. The sergeant soon had more pressing concerns of his own. "Three or four of the savages laid hold of me," Carver remembered, "and whilst some held their weapons over my head, the others . . . disrobed me of my coat, waistcoat, hat, and buckles, omitting not to take . . . what money I had in my pocket. As this was transacted close by the passage that led from the lines on to the plain, near which a French centinel was posted, I ran to him and claimed his protection; but he only called me an English dog, and thrust me with violence back again into the midst of the Indians."[20]

Elsewhere Carver's colonel, Joseph Frye, was also in trouble. "I was strip'd . . . of all my Arms and Cloathing," he later told a friend, "[until] I had nothing left but Briches Stockings

A 1760 woodcut—one of the earliest illustrations of the massacre at Fort William Henry—showing Indians using clubs, spears, and swords to slaughter the British who had surrendered. While inaccurate in the weapons used, it captures the ferocity of the attack and the outrage felt by the British public. (*John Carter Brown Libary*)

Shoes & Shirt, the Indians [were] round me with their Tomehawks Spears &c threatening Death [so] I flew to the Officers of the French Guards for Protection but they would afford me none, therefore [I] was Oblig'd to fly in[to] the woods."[21]

By now, the redcoats at the head of the column were aware of the slaughter happening at the rear. This "occasioned an order for a halt, which at last was done in great confusion."[22] By the time they had formed up and were ready to march to the aid of their comrades, the men at the rear had fled in all directions. "Some [ran] toward the woods, [and] some toward the French tents," Father Roubaud recalled, "[a few headed] toward the fort, [and] others [fled] to every place that seemed to promise an asylum."[23] The provincials who sought the protection of the redcoats at the head of the column only succeeded in throwing the latter into confusion, and as the Indians followed the fugitives into the ranks, the panic became complete. Many of the British officers couldn't believe how quickly the situation had deteriorated. "It was strange to see," one explained. "The Men; who but the morning before, [had] pursued these Savages into the . . . Woods . . . were [now] Scared to such a degree, that they threw away . . . everything, and each . . . endeavored to shift for himself."[24]

Meanwhile, Sergeant Carver was still attempting to throw off his pursuers. Spotting a knot of his comrades who "were crowded together at some distance," he tried to force his way through the melee to join them. "Innumerable were the blows that were made at me with different weapons as I passed on," he recalled. "One of [the Indians] . . . thrust at me with a spear, which grazed my side, and from another I received a wound . . . in my ankle." With the adrenaline coursing through his veins, Carver pushed on and "at length . . . gained the spot where [his] . . . countrymen stood, and forced . . . [himself] into the midst of them." The sergeant was bruised and bleeding from innumerable small scratches, and his shirt hung in tatters about his body, but for the moment at least, he was safe.[25]

By now, Monro and a small cluster of officers had also gained asylum. Moments earlier, seeing the situation rapidly deteriorating, the Scot had sought out Montcalm to implore the Frenchman to intervene. Since the Indians had fallen on the rear of the column, he and "those nearest about him" had been harbored by a party of the French and taken into their camp for protection.[26] Although Monro lost at least one of his black slaves in the ensuing struggle, he got into the camp safely and there confronted Montcalm, who had only just learned of the Indian attack.[27] Appalled, the Frenchman rushed to the road and tried to halt the slaughter. Father Roubaud later provided the following account: "[Montcalm] seemed to be in several places at once," the priest recalled, "he would reappear, he was everywhere; he used prayers, menaces, promises; he tried everything [to get the Indians to cease the bloodshed], and at last resorted to force."[28]

Bodily hauling the Indians away from their victims, Montcalm tore his shirt from his body to expose his bare chest and "bade them kill their father" instead of his enemies.[29] Seeing the example of their general, other French officers and soldiers began to intervene. The Chevalier de Lévis exposed himself to danger "a thousand times," heading "wherever the tumult appeared the most violent." Bourlamaque pleaded with the Indians to put down their weapons, and a few French grenadiers were wounded while trying to help their former foes.[30] Some of the French efforts were counterproductive. On finding Colonel Young's nephew at the mercy of a number of Indians, Montcalm thrust his way among them and rescued the lad. His efforts were successful, but also resulted in the deaths of several others, whose captors preferred to take their prisoners' scalps than risk having to turn them over alive to the French.[31]

Further up the road to Fort Edward, the killing was still going on. Sergeant Carver, who moments before had thought himself safe in the midst of a huddle of his comrades, now found his group "much thinned." The Indians had grabbed those from the outer ring, killed a few, and taken the rest prisoner. Since "death seemed to be approaching with hasty strides," Carver and twenty others decided to make a break for it. Things did not go according to plan. "In a moment we were all separated," the sergeant recalled. Barely giving a second glance to the fate of his comrades, Carver ran through the encircling Indians. "Some I overturned, being at that time young and athletic," he recalled, "others I passed by, dextrously avoiding their weapons; till at last two very stout chiefs, of the most savage tribes . . . whose strength I could not resist, laid hold of me by each arm, and began to force me through the crowd."[32]

Meanwhile, Colonel Frye was also in considerable difficulties. Having succeeding in making it into the woods with Captain Hitchcock, a fellow member of the Massachusetts provincials, the colonel concealed himself behind a tree. No sooner had he done this than he noticed a group of Indians approaching. "Then the case was ticklish," admitted a later narrator of the tale, "but [the] Colonel stepped aside and they both dropped [to the ground], the Colonel expecting a tomahawk in his skull every moment, but the enemy not seeing them passed them by. Then [the] Colonel and his fellow traveller rubbed dirt on his white shirt that it might look like ground." Having thus effected a makeshift camouflage, the two men pushed on deeper into the woods and began the fourteen-mile journey to Fort Edward.[33]

By a stroke of good fortune, Sergeant Carver also managed to escape. Having resigned himself to his fate, the sergeant was being herded toward a swamp by his two captors, when "an English gentleman of some distinction" dashed across their path. Considering the gentleman a better catch, "one of the Indians instantly relinquished his hold" on Carver, and dashed after him. The gentleman proved more than a match for his adversary, however, and hurled the warrior to the ground, at which point the other brave who had been holding Carver released him to aid his companion. Seizing his chance, the sergeant dashed toward yet another knot of holdouts—redcoats who had maintained their discipline and were managing to keep the Indians at bay. "Before I had taken many steps," Carver recalled, "I hastily cast my eye towards the gentleman, and saw the Indian's tomahawk gash into his back, and heard him utter his last groan." Not willing to wait for further invitation, Carver dashed on, briefly taking "a fine boy [of] about twelve years of age" under his wing, before he too was "torn from [the sergeant's] . . . side, and . . . was soon demolished." After tarrying briefly with the redcoats, Carver hid himself in a thicket for several minutes, caught his breath, then pushed on.[34]

Others from the Massachusetts regiment who managed to escape included Capt. John Burk and a private by the name of Nathaniel Loomis from Southampton.[35] Stripped to his underwear in the initial confusion, Loomis was taken by the wrists by two Indians and led into the woods. Thinking himself doomed, he summoned all his strength and managed to swing his assailants into two trees, thus stunning them long enough to make his escape.[36] Selah Barnard, the lieutenant from Foster, Massachusetts, who had been determined to keep hold of his trunk, also managed to get clear of his assailants. Led into the woods as a captive, Barnard waited for an opportune moment before making his move. "Being athletic, and remarkably nervous in his arms," the lieutenant roused "his whole strength" and hurled his captors down in opposite directions. Not willing to tangle twice with the mighty provincial, the Indians then allowed Barnard to escape, contenting themselves with the contents of his trunk.[37]

James Furnis, the British officer who worked for the Bureau of Ordnance, was not so fortunate. Having been stripped of his boots as he left the entrenched camp, he had run for three miles through the woods before two Indians had caught up with him and forced him back toward the fort.[38] By the time Furnis reached William Henry, the massacre was over. Of the 2,308 men who had surrendered on the ninth, some 200 had been killed. Fifty corpses lay along the road to Fort Edward. The rest had been butchered in the woods nearby. Of the survivors, 900 had been captured by the Indians and 100 had found refuge with the French. The rest, some 1,100 men, were scattered throughout the woods. Disoriented following the confusion that morning, they would spend the next few days making their way back through the wilderness to Fort Edward individually or in small groups.[39] Of all the regiments involved, the New Hampshire provincials under Lt. Col. John Gough had suffered the heaviest casualties. Finding themselves at the rear of the column with the camp followers, 80 out of 231 had been killed or taken prisoner during the massacre.[40] By comparison, Frye's Massachusetts provincials had come through relatively unscathed. Of the 45 officers who had survived the siege, only 5, or one in nine, were listed as missing in early September.[41] The regulars, for their part, had lost just one in eight. Roughly 100 members of the 35th, the Royal Americans, and rangers were listed as killed or wounded or remained unaccounted for when a return was made on August 25.[42]

As James Furnis was approaching Fort William Henry, his captors were stopped by a French guard who forced them to hand over their prisoner. Delighted to be out of the clutches of the "savages," Furnis was escorted into the fort and reunited with Colonels Young and Monro and "several [other British] Officers." Some had surrendered to the French a mile up the road to Fort Edward, following the British column's collapse. Others, like Furnis himself, had been taken back from the Indians.[43] The French spent the rest of the morning coaxing the tribesmen to give up their prisoners. Some were taken by force and others by bribery. Many more, hidden from the French in the woods, would not be recovered until reaching Montréal.[44]

Captain Desandrouins of the French engineers was among those who spent the morning liberating the captives. Exhausted following his demanding role during the siege, the twenty-eight-year-old had awakened late that morning. Learning of the massacre, he dressed in a blue infantry mantle so as not to be confused for a British soldier, then made his way toward the fort to see what he could do to aid his former enemies. After just four hundred yards, he came across an Indian attempting to hide his prisoner. Desandrouins grabbed the warrior by the wrists, but the prisoner was so frightened and disoriented that he didn't even attempt to run. After another French officer passed by and completed the rescue, escorting the prisoner to the safety of the French camp, Desandrouins determined to seek out the British engineers he had befriended the previous day. Speaking with several Canadian officers attached to the Indians, he managed to track down one Dutch, one Swiss, and one British officer he had met over lunch. Later, after enlisting the aid of Abbé Picquet, the Jesuit missionary from Presentation, he discovered where Lieutenant Williamson had been hidden. The young engineer was in a deplorable state. Naked and terrified, he was delighted to see the Frenchman, who not only brought him into the safety of the fort but also managed to retrieve his dress uniform from the Indians.[45]

Father Roubaud was also busy that morning. Appalled by the suffering of his fellow Europeans, the Jesuit made his way into the fort to see what could be done. "A crowd of women came [up to me]," he recalled, "[and] with tears and groans surrounded me, [and] threw themselves at my feet." The women were British and provincial camp followers who had been separated from their families during the massacre. At first, Roubaud was unsure of what he could do, but then a French officer arrived with some news. "[He] informed me," the Jesuit recalled,

> that a Huron, at that very time in his camp, was in possession of an infant six months old, whose death was certain if I did not immediately go to its rescue. I did not hesitate. I ran in haste to the tent of the Savage, in whose arms I perceived the innocent victim, who was tenderly kissing the hands of its captor and playing with some porcelain necklaces that adorned him. This sight gave a new ardour to my zeal. I began by flattering the Huron, with all the eulogies that truth could permit me to bestow on the bravery of his Tribe. He understood me at once: 'Here,' said he to me very civilly, 'dost thou see this infant? I have not stolen it; I found it deserted in a hedge; thou wishest it, but thou shalt not have it.'

Determined to wrest some good from the terrible events of that morning, Roubaud tried to bribe the Huron into giving up his prize. At first, the warrior was not interested, but after a brief consultation with his fellow tribesmen, he made an alternate offer: he would give the baby to Roubaud in exchange for an enemy scalp. "It will soon be seen," Roubaud replied, "if thou art a man of honour." With that he "set out in haste for the camp of the Abnakis." Flushed with victory, his charges were all too happy to oblige.

> I asked the first one I met if he were the possessor of any scalp, and if he would do me the favour of giving it to me. . . . He untied his bag, and gave me my choice. Supplied with one of those barbarous trophies, I carried it in triumph. . . . Joy lent me wings; [and] in a moment I was with my Huron. 'Here,' said I on meeting him, 'here is thy payment.' [After examining the bloody trophy the Huron seemed satisfied.] 'Well then!' he replied, 'here is the infant, take it away; it belongs to thee.'[46]

Three hours later, after a morning spent touring the camps, Roubaud finally located the child's mother.

By the afternoon of the tenth, the French had managed to rescue four hundred of the Indians' captives. Stripped, beaten, and bloody, they were reclothed and held in the fort or the camp by Artillery Cove. A group of the Massachusetts provincials who were taken back to William Henry made a gruesome discovery. On going down to the casemate, they found the mangled corpses of the sick and wounded who had been slaughtered by the Indians the day before.[47]

Monro, meanwhile, had made an official complaint to Montcalm and warned the Frenchman that he could no longer look upon the terms of the surrender as binding. Montcalm replied that "he was heartily sorry for what had happened but protested that it was not in his power to prevent it." Lieutenant William Hamilton of the 35th, another officer who had found sanctuary with the French in the fort, reiterated Monro's point about the validity of the surrender. Exasperated, Montcalm lost his composure, warning the young lieutenant that "he would certainly hang up any officer or soldier included in the capitulation that should be taken in arms before the time of not serving was expired."[48]

While Monro, Hamilton, and the others were safe within the fort, five hundred more British and American troops were not so fortunate. After being hidden in the woods by their Indian captors until the French had called off their search, they were taken to Montréal and sold into slavery. Among them was a drummer boy of the 35th and an eighteen-year-old ensign from Massachusetts named John Maylem.[49] Captured by three Indians about a mile and a half from Fort William Henry, Maylem was disguised as a warrior to deter the interest of the French, then taken to Lake George, where a flotilla of twenty canoes was waiting on shore. Along with fifty other prisoners, who were also disguised with Indian war paint, Maylem was bundled aboard and carried away to the north.[50]

The vast majority of the eighteen hundred Indians with Montcalm's army left for their homelands on the afternoon of August 10. While those who had taken Maylem and the fifty others the ensign had seen aboard the boats had done well for themselves from the campaign, many others left angry and empty-handed. Having been forced to give up their prisoners to Montcalm's men, and feeling themselves cheated by the terms of the British surrender, several vowed never to take up the hatchet in support of the French again. Before departing, several braves committed one final atrocity. Unsatisfied with their plunder, they dug up the graves of the redcoats and provincials buried outside Fort William Henry and scalped them.[51] Among the bodies mutilated was that of Richard Rogers, the brother of the famous ranger.[52] By the end of August 10, just five hundred warriors remained. Most of them were domesticated Abenaki or Nipissing, a tribe that had grown close to Montcalm's regulars due to the influence of its Francophile chief, Kisensik.[53]

The first of the British and provincial troops who had escaped the massacre began arriving at Fort Edward just three hours after it had begun. At 10 a.m., a group of thirty redcoats carrying the colors of the 35th was seen "running down the Hill, out of the woods, [and] along the Road . . . from Fort William Henry." They were in a deplorable state. Breathless, "Extreamly confused" and "mostly stripped," they blurted out garbled accounts of the events of that morning to the sentries that received them. As the rumors of the "frightful massacre" flew around camp, exaggerated with each retelling, Ensign Portis and Captain Cunningham of the 35th and Lieutenant Collins of the Royal Artillery arrived with the second group of survivors.[54] The troops and camp followers at Fort Edward pressed them for information on comrades and family members who were still missing.[55] General Webb reacted by posting a guard of three hundred men under Maj. Augustine Prévost, a Swiss-born officer of the Royal Americans, a mile up the track to meet any more men coming in and to provide advance warning should the French attack.[56] He also ordered a signal gun to be fired once every two hours to guide any survivors lost in the woods toward them.[57] That evening Edward White, James Furnis's servant, arrived at the fort. Colonel James Montresor, Furnis's friend and colleague, pressed him for news of what had become of his master. The little that he knew left the engineer deeply worried. "[White] said that he had left his Master in the rear," Montresor wrote in his journal that evening, "but did not see him afterwards."[58]

Back at Fort William Henry, Montcalm was busying him-self redeploying his troops. At midday, La Sarre and Royal Roussillon Brigades occupied the hill to the west of the fort; Saint-Ours, one of the Canadian officers, moved his militia brigade to the lakeshore; and Captain Gaspé's brigade occu-pied the gardens.[59] While these movements were carried out, the French surgeons attended the British wounded who remained under their protection, and a list was compiled of all the matériel captured as a result of the siege. In total 25 guns, 3 mortars and a howitzer (some of which had burst), 36,000 pounds of gunpowder, 2,522 cannonballs, 545 shells, 1,400 pounds of musket balls, 1 case of grenades, and "a vast quan-tity of flour and lard" were recovered. Some of the ammuni-tion was buried at Artillery Cove for later retrieval.[60] The rest, together with the functioning guns and food, was loaded onto boats by a detachment of one thousand men and sent back to Carillon, along with a letter destined for Governor Vaudreuil in Montréal detailing the appalling behavior "of the sav-ages."[61]

On August 11, fifteen hundred French and Canadian workers began demolishing the fort and the entrenched camp. Stripped of the vast majority of his Indian scouts and with his supplies rapidly dwindling, Montcalm had little option but to return to Carillon. The Canadians with the army would also need to return to their fields as soon as possible if that years' harvest stood any chance of success.[62] Keen to rejoin their families, the workers proceeded with "prodigious activity."[63] The casemates were filled with earth, the barracks and remain-ing outbuildings were burned to the ground, the palisades torn down and put to the torch, and the earthworks leveled. "It was only during the burning that we comprehended the greatness of the enemy's loss," Father Roubaud recalled. "Casemates and secret underground passages were found filled with dead bodies, which for several days furnished fresh fuel for the activity of the flames."[64]

At noon on August 11, from a vantage point on the battle-ments of Fort Edward, Col. James Montresor saw a column of smoke rising above the forest. The engineer immediately realized its significance. His suspicions were later confirmed by the reports of several French deserters who stated that

Montcalm had "put fire to the fort & that the Indians were going off displeased."[65] Webb was greatly relieved that his enemies were returning to the north. That afternoon he wrote to his superior, Lord Loudoun, who at that time was still at Halifax with the bulk of the British troops in North America, hoping that the fog would lift long enough for his invasion fleet to attack Louisbourg before the onset of winter made the operation impossible.[66] Apart from informing Loudoun of some of the details of the siege, the main purpose of Webb's letter appears to have been to excuse his own inaction. "The enemy are 11–12,000 strong," he wrote. "[This] has [recently] been confirmed by two Lieuts. and two soldiers who deserted from them . . . [and] put it out of my power to be of any service to the besieged . . . [as] I had not above . . . 4500 men fit for duty"

The general also found time to attack the provincials. "I should be guilty of a great piece of injustice," he informed Loudoun, "did I not give the Praises to the behaviour of the Regular Troops during the siege that they really deserve, for none could behave better, [by contrast] the provincials . . . were rather backward, I suppose owing to their being so little accustomed to that kind of war."[67]

That evening, Col. Joseph Frye and Captains Hitchcock and McCloud staggered into camp.[68] Having got hopelessly lost in the woods, Frye had sustained himself by eating wild whortleberries. By the time he reached Fort Edward, guided by the signal gun, which continued to fire every two hours, he was exhausted and close to collapse.[69] Another who had had a miraculous escape was Maj. John Gilman of the New Hampshire provincials. After losing his property and his sixteen-year-old slave in the struggle on the morning of August 10, he had been chased through the woods and "obliged to swim [across] the Hudson River three times" before finally eluding his pursuers.[70] On August 13 Sgt. Jonathan Carver arrived, "after passing three days without subsistence, and enduring the severity of the cold dews for three nights." A few other survivors would continue to come in to camp as late as August 19, nine days after the massacre had scattered them through the woods.[71]

During the late afternoon of August 14, as if the siege and massacre had not been bad omen enough, there was a solar eclipse. According to Sgt. Jabez Fitch, it was raining heavily and the sky "was So Clouded that we could Scaircely Perseve it."[72] At 5:55 p.m., the silhouette of the sun appeared "like a Gold-Ring" peeking from behind the edge of the moon.[73]

Earlier that morning, Montcalm had sent Lieutenant Savournin of La Sarre Regiment and Joseph Marin, the Canadian coureur de bois, with a thirty-strong escort to Fort Edward to discuss the transfer of the British prisoners remaining in French hands. Since the vast majority of the Indians had already departed, it was deemed safe for them to return. Only two British officers were to remain: Captain Faesch, who would stay with Montcalm as a hostage until certain French prisoners were returned to Montréal as specified in the surrender terms, and Captain Ormsby, who was still too badly wounded to travel. Savournin was also entrusted with two letters from Montcalm. The first was addressed to Webb; the second to Lord Loudoun. Both explained the French version of events, which claimed that the British were to blame for the massacre for not defending themselves with more rigor and for giving their executioners liquor, a charge that Monro would later refute. Under a flag of truce, the French were allowed to approach Fort Edward unmolested, then Savournin was blindfolded and taken inside to meet Webb. After exchanging the usual courtesies, the officers worked out the arrangements for the following day, and Savournin and his escort returned to Lake George.[74]

On August 15, Webb sent two companies of British grenadiers and two hundred volunteers to Half Way Brook. There they would meet Monro and the last of the British prisoners, who were escorted by a French and Canadian guard led by Luc de La Corne. It was a bitterly cold morning and pouring with rain.[75] When the prisoners proceeded down the road to Fort Edward, there was a grim reminder of the defeat and the massacre that had followed. "Near Thirty Carcasses . . . were . . . seen [on the road and in the woods nearby]," one of the British recalled, "and from the frequent Stench . . . [we] had reason to imagine, many more Lay scattered about." After a brief ceremony at Half Way Brook, the prisoners were handed over to the British grenadiers, then escorted back to Fort Edward, which they reached at 3 p.m. Sergeant Jabez Fitch watched them arrive. At the head of the column was the bronze 6-pounder that Montcalm had granted the defeated in the terms of the surrender. Behind it, "Monroe [was] Rid in on a Hors" with James Furnis and Lt. Adam Williamson walking beside him, while the wounded Col. John Young was carried in on a stretcher. Also present was twenty-seven-year-old Ezekiel Stevens of Derryfield, New Hampshire. Despite having been "tomahawked" and scalped on the day of the massacre, Stevens was fit enough to march.[76]

Back at Lake George, with the demolition of Fort William Henry complete, Montcalm's troops were growing restless. Even though the majority of the British and provincial dead had been burned along with the palisades and outbuildings, many more corpses remained undiscovered in the woods, and the stench of death hung in the air. On August 14, a soldier of La Sarre's Regiment had been executed for showing disrespect to the Canadian coureur de bois Charles Langlade, and a private of Royal Roussillon had been made to run the gauntlet for selling brandy to the handful of Indians who remained at the camp. On August 17, discipline deteriorated even further. Canadian officers and men began to board their boats, intending to leave for home, even though Montcalm had not granted them permission. A squad of regulars was ordered to fire a warning volley over their heads to stop them. Realizing that his army was on the verge of disintegration, Montcalm then gave the order to leave. The French and Canadians broke camp, boarded the boats, and rowed across Lake George to the north, leaving the ruins of Fort William Henry smoldering behind them.[77]

Captives

AUGUST 14, 1757–DECEMBER 1763

On August 14, the first of the Indians to leave Fort William Henry arrived at Montréal. Bougainville, who had been sent to the capital with dispatches five days earlier, saw them paddling up the Saint Lawrence "in a crowd with about two hundred English [prisoners]." Once they had established themselves on the green outside the city walls, Vaudreuil "scolded them for having violated the capitulation." The Indians, Bougainville recalled, "were told that they must give up [their prisoners], who were captured unfairly, and that they would be paid for them, two kegs of brandy a piece."[1] Vaudreuil's demand was met with contempt. As one warrior told Abbé Picquet, the Jesuit priest, the taking and killing of captives in warfare was their right. "You are satisfied with a fort," he explained, "and you let your enemy and mine live. I do not want to keep such bad meat for tomorrow. When I kill it, it can no longer attack me."[2] Besides, Vaudreuil's opening offer was considerably under the going rate. In Montréal, the center of New France's burgeoning slave trade, a prisoner could fetch at least ten times as much.[3] After selling some of the plunder they had captured to the French and Canadian residents—including Colonel Young's fine "silver mounted" pistols, which fetched two and a half gold coins apiece—the Indians settled in for a lengthy period of negotiation.[4]

Their prisoners suffered terribly. "[The Indians] get drunk," Bougainville noted, "and the English die a hundred deaths from fear every day." On August 15, "in the presence of the entire town," one of the prisoners was killed. His body was chopped into pieces and cooked in a bubbling kettle strung over an open fire. "His unfortunate compatriots" were forced to eat his remains. The killing sent a clear message to Vaudreuil. The Indians knew that the British authorities would hold the governor accountable for the captives' welfare, and by the public and barbaric manner of the prisoner's death, they were strengthening their bargaining position. Vaudreuil was now desperate to secure their release, and presents were proffered to ease the negotiations. "Each [warrior] received [a] complete outfit," Bougainville remarked, "varying according to the rank which each holds in his village." Gifts of "tobacco, vermillion, lace" and more "brandy" followed.[5]

After two weeks of haggling, the Indians settled for 130 livres in goods and thirty bottles of brandy for each captive redeemed. In total, three hundred were ransomed. In his journal, Bougainville hints that several Canadians who had been present at the siege profited from the transaction and refers to one in particular whom he thought "unworthy of the name of an officer." During the course of the negotiations, the man in question was seen "leading . . . a Negro kidnapped from the English commander under the pretext of appeasing the shades of a dead Indian, giving his family flesh for flesh." It seems likely that this was Luc de La Corne—the Canadian slave owner who had looked on impassively as eighteen of surgeon Miles Whitworth's charges were butchered in the entrenched camp, and was described by a future acquaintance as "a great villain and as cunning as the devil."[6] Having completed their business, the Indians gathered ten miles downriver at the village of Lachine, where a final alcohol-fueled party was held before they departed for their homelands in the high country. "They were swimming in . . . liquor," Bougainville recalled, "drinking it by kegfulls and not leaving the keg until they fell down dead drunk."[7]

After being ransomed, the captives were transferred to a French prison in Montréal, while the sick and wounded were taken to hospital. A list signed by Montcalm on September 2 names forty-nine of the latter. Among them were two women, Jean Foutenir and Marie Brusle, who were accompanied by their children. Two of the sick died in hospital on August 27. The rest would remain in Montréal for several weeks.[8]

One hundred fifty miles to the south, Maj. Gen. Daniel Webb was busy dismantling the army he had gathered at Fort Edward. With no sign of a French advance, the men who had come in from Fort William Henry and the militia that had been gathering in the neighboring encampment were allowed to return home. On August 13, Colonel Frye and the survivors of the Massachusetts regiment headed for Albany. The next day, the first of the militia also broke camp and marched south.[9] On August 16, Colonel Monro and those of the 35th who had escaped the massacre joined them. The men who had remained at Fort Edward throughout the siege were not allowed to go, a fact that caused considerable resentment. The night after Frye had departed, Lt. Samuel Knowles of the Massachusetts regiment—a veteran of three campaigns, including the 1745 victory at Louisbourg—voiced his dissatisfaction. He felt that since the French had already returned north, his men should all be allowed to go home. The next day, the discontent bubbled over into mutiny when the New York provincials attempted to desert, threatening to kill their officers if they tried to stop them. Order was forcibly restored and a series of courts-martial followed. A mutinous sergeant was shot and several others arrested, among them Captain Knowles. On August 16, Knowles was found guilty and the next day had his sword ceremonially broken over his head and was dismissed from the service.[10]

When Frye arrived in Albany on August 15, news of the fall of Fort William Henry and the subsequent massacre spread throughout the colonies. The reaction of the press was one of unbridled outrage. After Monongahela and Oswego, the massacre at Fort William Henry was the final straw. As the "savages" could not possibly be held to account for their baser instincts, the French were roundly blamed, and the event was used as a rallying cry to unite the British and provincials. "'Tis certain that the Growth of the English Colonies has long been the grand Object of the French Envy," explained one widely circulated report, which first appeared in print on August 22:

> and tis said that their Officers have orders from their superiors . . . to make the present War as bloody and destructive as can be possible! Tis evident, that all their Measures tend this Way. . . . To what a Pitch of Perfidy and Cruelty is the French Nation arrived? Would not an ancient Heathen shudder with Horror, on hearing so hideous a Tale![11]

On August 16, while returning from his abortive attempt against Louisbourg, Lord Loudoun first heard of Montcalm's attack. Two days later, with his fleet still tacking its way southward down the coast of Nova Scotia toward New York, he learned of Monro's surrender and the massacre that had followed. In response, he penned a dispatch to Webb. "I am on the way," Loudoun reassured his subordinate, "with a force sufficient to turn the scale, with God's assistance; and then I hope we shall teach the French to comply with the laws of nature and humanity. For although I abhor barbarity, the knowledge I have of Mr. Vaudreuil's behavior . . . and the murders committed at Oswego and now at Fort William Henry, will oblige me to make those gentlemen sick of such inhuman villany whenever it is in my power."

When Loudoun landed at New York on August 31, he learned of Montcalm's withdrawal. Nevertheless he immediately marched north, and encamped his army astride the Hudson, disingenuously claiming that he might yet turn the campaign on its head by seizing Carillon.[12]

Meanwhile in Montréal, Montcalm and Vaudreuil were doing their best to stem the wave of moral outrage emanating from the British colonies to the south. Following the siege, both sent letters to Lord Loudoun denying their culpability. These were later printed in the American press. Vaudreuil blamed the redcoats and provincials, claiming they had given the Indians liquor in the buildup to the massacre. The Canadian governor also implied that it was the passivity of the troops that had inspired the Indians to such violence. Such claims were not well received by the British. In an official report released in early November, Monro strenuously denied Vaudreuil's charges and insisted that he had personally overseen the destruction of "every drop of liquor" in the entrenched camp "immediately After the Capitulation was sign'd."[13] The report also accused the French and Canadians of standing idly by while the worst outrages were committed. While Montcalm's defense was aided by the fact that he had given 2,000 livres from his own pocket to buy back some of the hostages taken in the aftermath of the massacre, the contemporary press had already decided who was to blame: the French and Canadians were guilty and would be made to pay for their crimes.

A month after they had been captured, the first of the British and provincial prisoners ransomed in Montréal began to make their way home. The first stage of their journey took them downriver to Québec, where they were held in cells until ships could be made ready for their departure. Captain Thomas Shaw of the New Jersey Blues, who had been taken prisoner at Sabbath Day Point, described the conditions. "The Small Pox raged in the Prisons," he recalled. The allowance of "9 oz. of bread and the same weight of Fish" was hardly sufficient to support the men, who were required to toil throughout the day in the city's magazine. Several died in captivity, before the survivors were bundled aboard three ships waiting in the harbor on September 27. Captain Shaw found himself on a French schooner, along with Lieutenant Day of Frye's regiment and ninety-three of his men. Captain Faesch, two other officers, and 135 men, five women, and three children were taken onboard the *Saint Dominique*, and the *Saint Charles* sloop carried fifty-eight others, including six women and a single child named Alexander Innis.[14] The flotilla called in at Louisbourg between October 11 and 14 before sailing on to Halifax. On the voyage, smallpox continued to plague the prisoners, and some others were afflicted with "purple fever." At least four died and twenty others were sick by the time the ships arrived between October 16 and 20. In total, three hundred four prisoners were returned that month. At Halifax they were unloaded, transferred to British ships, and sent farther south. The schooner *Success* took forty-eight men to Boston on November 4. Three days later, Captain Nickols's schooner took twenty-six more to the same destination. Governor Thomas Pownall of Massachusetts noted that they were "all naked" when they arrived.[15]

Many of those taken at Sabbath Day Point and Fort William Henry would remain in captivity considerably longer.[16] Even while Shaw was sailing for Halifax, several other prisoners were en route to France. Some of them died in prison on arrival. One was Dennis Jennings, a private who had been taken at Sabbath Day Point. Jennings passed away on December 26, 1757, in La Rochelle.[17] After ten months the rest were exchanged for French prisoners held in Britain. Following their release, some, such as Pvt. James Kearny, formerly of the New Jersey Blues, joined the British redcoats.[18] Others—like the New Hampshire soldiers Josiah Bean, William Rackliff, and surgeon John Lamson—secured passage back to the American colonies onboard Royal Navy transports. Even so, Rackliff would spend four more months walking and working his way across country before he eventually returned home.[19]

Those taken directly back to the Indians' villages would endure similarly lengthy odysseys. Francis Finney, who was taken prisoner by the Caughnawaga, was held in one of the Saint Lawrence River missions for two years before making his escape. After joining the British army, then at Carillon, he eventually made his way back to his hometown of Plymouth, Massachusetts, in 1759.[20] William Warren, another provincial private, remained in captivity for one year longer. Captured by the Abenaki, Warren was hauled off to Saint Francis and was not released until September 1760, following the fall of Montréal. Even Warren's adventure pales by comparison beside that of Joshua Rand of Charlestown, Massachusetts. Taken by Ottawa braves in the aftermath of the massacre, Rand was smuggled through Montréal and carried upriver to the Great Lakes, where he lived in a village to the north of Michilimackinac for four and a half years. When finally allowed to leave, he spent twenty months making his way home, eventually reaching Charlestown in December 1763.[21]

Victory

AUTUMN 1757–SUMMER 1760

*F*or those who had managed to return to Fort Edward in the week following the massacre, the war went on. While General Webb and the garrison of Fort Edward reluctantly remained at their posts, the survivors of Fort William Henry, exhausted after the six-day siege, were allowed to return south to recover. The men and officers of the 35th that had taken part returned to Albany. Although in no way held accountable for the defeat, Lt. Col. George Monro was devastated by the loss of Fort William Henry. What had been the fifty-seven-year-old's first combat command had ended in disaster. Monro spent the autumn penning several documents intended for the attention of Lord Loudoun that pinned the blame firmly on General Webb. Webb's culpability was never publicly announced, however. Haunted by the defeat, Monro's health went into decline. On November 3, while walking the frozen streets of Albany, he suffered an attack of apoplexy and died. Monro was buried the next day in Saint Peter's church. Ironically, several months later, confirmation of his superiors' continuing faith in him arrived in the form of a letter containing a promotion to colonel.[1]

While Monro's reputation survived the debacle of Fort William Henry, those of Maj. Gen. Daniel Webb and his immediate superior, Lord Loudoun, would suffer temporary setbacks. Within six months of the massacre, both men had been recalled to Britain. Although "heavily criticized" for his role during the siege, Webb was protected from official censure and public humiliation through his connections with men of influence. On his return to London, he was reassigned and would receive two promotions in the coming years. In June 1759, he was made major general of cavalry and two years later achieved the rank of lieutenant general. In an army obsessed with personal honor, however, his reputation would never fully recover. Writing to Gen. Jeffery Amherst from a British camp near Giessen, Germany, in July 1759, he complained of his treatment at the hands of his fellow officers: "I have been treated like a dog," he protested, "and . . . have room for complaint against some of your friends."[2]

Loudoun's post–William Henry career followed a similar trajectory. After his recall he was promoted to lieutenant general, but was not favored with an active role until the Spanish invasion of Portugal in 1762 prompted Britain to dispatch an expeditionary force. Initially employed as second in command, Loudoun was later promoted. The war pitted the heavily outnumbered British forces against a sluggish Spanish foe. It was a conflict of defense and maneuver that featured no major battles and was brought to an end with a negotiated peace in November 1763. Upon his return to Britain, Loudoun was made governor of Edinburgh Castle and in 1770 was promoted to full general. His twilight years were dedicated to botanical experimentation on the grounds of his family seat in Ayrshire. Loudoun died on April 27, 1782, eight days shy of his seventy-seventh birthday.

Following Loudoun's recall from America, Britain's policy for the Seven Years' War underwent a radical transformation. This was a result of a shift in the balance of power in Westminster, which saw the Great Commoner, William Pitt, rise to prominence. By using the Royal Navy to deliver expeditionary forces to the far-flung outposts of empire, Pitt ensured the army could achieve local superiority and destroy French trade. The next five years would see successful attacks on Havana, Guadeloupe, Manila, Pondicherry, and Senegal. In America, Pitt managed to sidestep the biggest stumbling block to victory: the colonial assemblies' reluctance to pay for the war. By covering all their expenses—from quartering the redcoats to the annual bills for raising the provincial troops— Pitt ensured the colonists' full support. Loudoun's replacement as commander in chief was Gen. James Abercrombie. While developing a reputation for being overly cautious, which would result in his men nicknaming him "Nanny Crombie," he was fortunate to be supported by a number of vigorous senior officers. Where Loudoun had had to endure the vacillation of Webb, Abercrombie had the undoubted talents and energy of Colonels James Wolfe and Lord George Howe to counter his own timidity.[3]

Another significant development in the American theater during the winter of 1757–58 was the smallpox epidemic that ravaged the Indian settlements of the Great Lakes. Following the massacre at Fort William Henry, the warriors of the high country had unwittingly carried infected scalps, clothing, and prisoners back to their villages. With little previous exposure to European disease, the tribes were decimated. The Menominee alone were said to have lost three hundred warriors, and the mixed Ottawa, Chippewa, and Ojibwa settlement of Michilimackinac was devastated. The register of Saint Anne's Church was filled with the names of the victims, and the tribes' oral tradition has left a vivid account of their suffering: "Lodge after lodge was totally vacated—nothing [was to be seen] but the dead bodies lying here and there . . . entire families were . . . swept off by this terrible disease." What was once a continuous strip of habitation running for sixteen miles along the shore between Lakes Huron and Michigan "was entirely depopulated and laid waste." According to Jonathan Carver, the Massachusetts sergeant who had had a lucky escape at Fort William Henry, the Indians' attempts to relieve their suffering only hastened their demise. "Whilst their blood was in a state of fermentation," he wrote, "and nature was striving to throw out the peccant matter, they checked her operations by plunging into the water [of the lake]: the consequence was that they died in their hundreds. The few that survived were transformed by it into hideous objects, and bore with them to the grave deep indented marks of this much dreaded disease."[4]

The year 1758 was to be one of mixed fortunes for the British in America. Committing his country to huge debt in his desire for victory, Pitt ordered three campaigns launched against the French. Brigadier John Forbes, a fifty-year-old Scottish veteran of the War of Austrian Succession and a master of logistics, was to repeat General Braddock's ill-fated attack against Fort Duquesne at the forks of the Ohio; Gen. Jeffery Amherst was to besiege Louisbourg; and Abercrombie was to lead an attack against Fort Carillon.

Abandoning Braddock's route from Virginia, Forbes forged a new path across Pennsylvania, building a road as he advanced that would link Fort Duquesne directly to Philadelphia—a strategy bitterly opposed by Lt. Col. George Washington and his Virginians, who accompanied the expedition. Despite a bruising encounter on September 15—which saw the advance guard, under Maj. James Grant, decimated by French and Indians in a small-scale repeat of Braddock's disaster—Forbes's ponderous yet methodical progress was ultimately rewarded with victory. Knowing they were outnumbered, the French burned Fort Duquesne and retreated inland at the end of November 1758, leaving the British in control of the forks of the Ohio. For Forbes it proved a bittersweet victory. His health ruined by the pressures of command, the Scot died in his quarters in March 1759.

Abercrombie's fate was equally grim. At the start of his campaign against Carillon, during an insignificant skirmish at Trout Brook on July 6, his inspiring second, Brigadier Howe, was killed.[5] With "the idol of the army" dead, the troops' morale went into free-fall, and Abercrombie's disastrous decision making was allowed to proceed unchecked. Contrary to accepted military logic, which demanded he soften up the enemy with an artillery cannonade from some nearby heights, Abercrombie ordered his 6,000 regulars to make a frontal assault against Montcalm's position. Meanwhile, the 12,000 provincial troops he had raised for the campaign looked on idly from the edge of the forest. Among them were Pvt. Rufus Putnam and Colonels Phineas Lyman and Joseph Frye.

Due to Abercrombie's vacillation following Howe's death, Montcalm had had time to prepare his position well. On a hill to the west of the fort, his men constructed a defensive abatis, a barrier of felled tree trunks whose interlocking branches were sharpened to a razor point. Lining this formidable obstacle were 3,600 regulars, colonial regulars, militia, and a handful of Indian braves. The attack on July 8, 1758, was a bloodbath. Wave after wave of redcoats was thrown against the French position. Unable to penetrate the defenses in the face of a withering fire, each attack was repulsed with heavy casualties. By the time Abercrombie called off the attack at 7:30 p.m., 1,944 of his men had been killed or wounded. There was no doubt as to who was to blame, and Abercrombie was recalled to London in consequence. Among the French losses of 377 men were several veterans of the siege of Fort William Henry, including Bourlamaque, who was shot through the shoulder, and Bougainville, whose forehead was grazed by a musket ball.[6]

As the summer wore on, the fighting around Lake George broke up into a series of skirmishes, patrols, and raids reminiscent of the first half of the 1757 campaign. On July 27, La Corne executed a perfect ambush on a British supply train at Half Way Brook. His Canadians and Indians fell on the column, butchering 116 men and thirty-five teams of oxen.[7] The next day, Maj. Robert Rogers was sent out from Fort Edward to exact revenge. At the head of 700 rangers, regulars, and provincials, he led a sweeping patrol, which took in South and East Bay and Fort Anne. Leading the advance guard was Maj. Israel Putnam. On August 8, having found no sign of the enemy, Rogers led his men back to Fort Edward. "Early in the morning . . . we decamped from the place where Fort Anne stood, and began our march," Rogers recalled. "Major Putnam with a party of Provincials marching in the front, my Rangers in the rear, [and] Capt. [James] Dalyell with the regulars in the centre. . . . After marching about three-quarters of a mile," Putnam ran straight into a trap.

Four hundred fifty French, Canadians, and Indians led by Joseph Marin, the Canadian coureur de bois who had attacked Fort Edward two years before, were concealed in a horseshoe formation around the head of the track that the provincials were following. Putnam, another officer, and two of his men were wrestled to the ground by Abenaki braves before the bulk of the provincials even realized they were under attack. A sharp skirmish ensued. After an hour, the numerical superiority of the British began to tell. Outflanked and outnumbered, Marin had no choice but to withdraw. A leather thong was tied around Putnam's neck, and he was pulled through the forest by his captors until they had outdistanced their pursuers sufficiently for Marin to call a halt. Putnam was then tied to an elm tree, and firewood was placed around his feet. As the flames licked up about him and the braves tormented him by hurling their tomahawks into the tree trunk, Putnam thought his end had come. When he learned of his old adversary's fate, Marin came to his aid and ordered his release. A relieved Putnam was taken to Carillon, where he was later ransomed and returned to Fort Edward in time for the 1759 campaign.[8]

The 35th and the 3rd Battalion of the Royal Americans were employed in the third of Pitt's attacks of 1758: the siege of Louisbourg. After gathering at Halifax, the invasion fleet, consisting of forty ships carrying almost fourteen thousand men, sailed north. They arrived at Gabarus Bay, seven miles from the walled city, on June 2. Buoyed by the news that the French fleet had been blockaded on the other side of the Atlantic, that afternoon Gen. Jeffery Amherst and newly promoted Brigadiers James Wolfe and Charles Lawrence scoured the shore for a possible landing site. The task was not easy. The coastline was treacherous and every accessible point was strongly guarded by the French. Eventually three sites were decided upon. While Brigadiers Lawrence and Edward Whitmore would make feints against Flat Point and White Point, Wolfe was to head the main attack against Freshwater Cove, a crescent-shaped beach a quarter of a mile long, covered by one thousand Frenchmen and eight cannons dug in on a nearby bluff. Led by Lt. Col. Henry Fletcher, Monro's former second in command, the 35th were among the troops spearheading the attack.

Due to high water and heavy fog, it wasn't until June 8 that the assault began. Boarding the ships' boats, the redcoats were rowed ashore. The French gunners allowed them to close before opening fire. The round shot and grape were devastating. Sergeant James Thompson of the 78th Highlanders recalled the scene:

> The French were peppering us with canister shot, whilst musket balls fired from 24-pounders came whistling about our ears. . . . One 24-pound shot . . . passed under my hams and killed Sergeant McKenzie, who was sitting as close to my left as he could squeeze . . . it carried away the basket of his broadsword which, along with the shot, passed through Lieutenant Cuthbert . . . tore his body into slivers, and cut off both legs of one of the two fellows that held the tiller of the boat. . . . After doing all this mischief, the shot stuck in the stern post.[9]

Seeing the terrible effect of the French guns, Wolfe feared his command would be wiped out and called off the attack. On the far right of the line, Lt. Thomas Browne of the 35th mistook the signal for a command to push on. Finding himself covered from the fire of the guns by a rocky outcrop, Browne and his men were able to land. They rushed ashore and a sharp fight ensued. Lieutenant James Cockburn was wounded, but the defenders were pushed back.[10] Seeing their success, Wolfe ordered the rest of his men to support them. The boats landed, the French withdrew, and the beachhead was won. The next day, the siege of Louisbourg began. By July 26, six weeks after the landing, all the French guns facing the British lines had been dismounted by accurate cannon fire, and a breach had been battered in the walls. Seeing his position was untenable, the French commander, Augustin de Boschenry, Chevalier de Drucour, surrendered. Although harsh, Amherst's terms were accepted and British troops occupied the city.[11] News of Louisbourg's fall was greeted with wild enthusiasm on both sides of the Atlantic. After three years of defeats, massacres, and bitter disappointment, the victory raised flagging public spirits in Britain and the American colonies alike, and boosted support for the war. With the will to win firmly established, and further bolstered by the battle cry "Remember Fort William Henry!" the British forces would make the following year's campaign decisive.

Despondent at the losses of Louisbourg and Fort Duquesne, the French faced a bitter winter. "Murmurs, even discontent, are extreme throughout the army," Bougainville observed, and Montcalm was increasingly infuriated at François Bigot's corruption and what he saw as the incompetence and unreliability of his Canadian and indigenous allies.[12] Following the victory at Fort Carillon on July 8, the French commander had attempted to resign, only to see his offer rebuffed by Versailles. In a last attempt to save the colony, Montcalm sent Bougainville to France to plead for more troops, supplies, and funds. With ice floes floating down the Saint Lawrence, the young aide set sail on the *Victoire* on November 11. Bougainville had high hopes for his mission and remained undaunted even after an atrocious voyage of fifty-two days of raging seas and "detestable" weather.[13] After three years of total war in central Europe, however, France could offer the beleaguered defenders of its colony little practical support. In the words of the colonial minister, Nicolas René Berryer, "when the house is on fire one cannot occupy one's self with the stable." When Bougainville returned, he brought no more than four hundred recruits "and a few munitions." The writing was on the wall. New France's days were numbered.[14]

The French were not the only ones suffering that winter. In Canada, the harvest had proved as disastrous as the two that had preceded it. The grain stores were empty, almost all of the colony's cattle and many of the horses had already been slaughtered for food, and the price of a barrel of flour had risen to 200 francs. Furthermore, with Louisbourg in British hands, it was a simple matter for the Royal Navy to blockade the Saint Lawrence. While Bigot and his ilk continued to throw extravagant parties and indulge in decadent feasts, the people starved. New France's Indian allies were also losing their stomach for the fight. Ever since Montcalm's terms to Monro at Fort William Henry had robbed them of the plunder, scalps, and prisoners that they considered their right, the Indians had been less than spirited in their support, and the smallpox epidemic of late 1757 had severely weakened their military might. Fewer and fewer warriors had been campaigning with Montcalm's armies, and the chieftains were beginning to doubt the wisdom of their alliance with New France. Rather than pledging full support to Onontio, many were now sending delegates to take part in Sir William Johnson's conferences in the Mohawk Valley. The tide was beginning to turn against the French, and the Indians knew it. As Pierre Pouchot, the captain of the Béarn Battalion in command at Fort Niagara, observed: "They understand very well the advantage of adhering to the stronger side, for, although some of them are genuinely fond of us, they only like Europeans in relation to their own self interests."[15]

The British launched three more attacks in 1759: General Amherst, Abercrombie's replacement as commander in chief, led another assault against Carillon; Brig. John Prideaux moved on Fort Niagara; and Brigadier Wolfe advanced on Québec. Sailing up the Saint Lawrence, on June 28 Wolfe landed his troops on the Île d'Orléans and prepared to besiege the city. His army consisted of eight thousand troops, among them were two units that had been at Fort William Henry: the 3rd Battalion of the 60th, or Royal Americans, and Major Fletcher's 35th. Built on a high bluff perched above the Saint Lawrence and surrounded on three sides by water, the walled city of Québec was in a strong position. While his rangers conducted raids up and down the Saint Lawrence, and his artillery pounded away at the city from the heights of Point Lévis, Wolfe spent the first two months of the operation probing the defenses for weaknesses. Although none were apparent, with the summer already waning, and under increasing pressure from his senior officers, Wolfe was forced to attack.

On July 31, he moved against an entrenched position on the heights of Beauport overlooking the Saint Lawrence, five miles upriver from Québec. From the first, the attack was a disaster. After sailing up and down the river for several hours in an attempt to deceive the enemy, the boats were launched at 5:30 p.m. as summer storm clouds gathered overhead. Landing in deep mud, four thousand regulars waded ashore under heavy fire from the heights. The first to reach the French position were thirteen companies of grenadiers (including that of the 35th led by Capt. Charles Ince), and a detachment of two hundred Royal Americans. Seeing the bayonet-tipped line surging toward them, the French retreated to a second position, from which they were able to pour fire down upon the enemy. As the British charged once more, the thunderclouds broke overhead, soaking both sides and rendering their firearms useless. Unable to climb the slippery slopes or fire upon the enemy, the British slid back to their first position. A stalemate ensued and Wolfe called the attack off. The British waded out to their boats, leaving numbers of wounded behind them. As they were rowed out to the transports in midriver, a handful of Indian braves stole down the slopes to finish off the wounded and scalp the dead. British losses were heavy: four hundred thirty-three—including one colonel, eight captains, twenty-one lieutenants, and three ensigns—were killed, wounded, or captured. The Royal Americans and grenadiers bore the brunt of the loss. The 35th's grenadier company alone had twenty-five killed, and Lt. Charles Gore, Ensign Theophilus Blakeney, and Captain Ince were reported missing.[16] On learning of the British defeat, Vaudreuil was delighted. "I have no more anxiety about Québec," he wrote to Bourlamaque, then in charge at Fort Carillon. "Wolfe, I can assure you, will make no progress. Luckily for him, his prudence saved him . . . and he contented himself with losing about 500 of his best soldiers. Deserters say that he will try again in a few days. That is what we want; he'll find somebody to talk to."[17]

At Fort Niagara, four hundred miles to the southwest, the second British campaign of the summer was under way. After traveling up the Mohawk River, Brigadier Prideaux had sailed across Lake Oswego and besieged the fort with two thousand regulars and one thousand provincial troops. Also with the expedition were one thousand Iroquois, mustered by Sir William Johnson. Seeing that the British were in the ascendency, the Iroquois had finally agreed to support them in force. A week after opening the trenches on July 10, the British guns opened fire. Although Prideaux was killed on the first night by a shell fragment fired by one of his own howitzers, the siege progressed well. Within three weeks, more than one hundred of the six-hundred-strong garrison had been killed, and a breach had been blasted through the fort's log walls. Nevertheless, the French commander, Capt. Pierre Pouchot, did not give up hope. Relief was close at hand. With the British trenches within musket shot of the fort, a column of eleven hundred French, Canadians, and Indians, led by Captains François-Marie Le Marchand de Lignery and Charles Philippe Aubry, arrived on July 23. After attending a council called by an Iroquois emissary, the Indians with the French refused to advance. The British used the delay to their advantage. Throwing a breastwork across the track leading to Fort Niagara, the redcoats of the 46th Regiment of Foot loaded their muskets and took up position. The French duly advanced and were shattered by a single close-range volley. The survivors were hunted down by Johnson's Iroquois. Three hundred forty-four were killed or captured. Among the latter was Joseph Marin. Witnessing the slaughter through his telescope from the walls of Fort Niagara, Pouchot realized the end was near. On July 25 he surrendered. While his men would spend the rest of the war in prison in New York, Pouchot would be exchanged in December and would be back in New France for the end of the war.[18]

In Québec, Wolfe was on the verge of a breakthrough. On the night of September 12, while a three-thousand-strong detachment under Bougainville shadowed a British naval decoy fifty miles upriver, Wolfe's redcoats landed unopposed at the L'Anse au Foulon, a narrow bay at the foot of a cliff, just three miles from Québec. Although Vaudreuil had previously shown concern at the bay's vulnerability, Montcalm had deemed the cliffs unassailable after posting a token force of one hundred militia to guard them. Montcalm's overconfidence would prove his undoing and the detachment's commander, Capt. Louis Du Pont Duchambon de Vergor, could not have been more poorly chosen. Two years previously, he had surrendered Fort Beauséjour on Acadia, after the most pitiful of defenses. Furthermore, on the night of September 12, Vergor's command had been reduced to just forty men. The rest had been granted permission to return to their homes for the night, so they could help with the harvest scheduled for the following morning. While the remnant slept in their tents, Wolfe's redcoats stole ashore beneath them. Led by Col. William Howe, whose brother George had been killed at Trout Brook in 1758, an advance guard of twenty-four men climbed the cliffs and fell upon the Canadians with fixed bayonets. After dispatching a messenger to warn Montcalm, Captain Vergor was shot and captured and his men fled. Unwilling to believe the messenger, Montcalm's aides dismissed the news without passing it on.

By dawn, forty-five hundred British regulars had formed up on the Plains of Abraham, an open expanse to the southwest of Québec within sight of the city walls. Just two men deep, the line was anchored on a forest to the north and the cliffs overlooking the Saint Lawrence in the south. In the position of honor on the far right of the line was the 35th, while the 3rd Battalion of the Royal Americans was held in reserve. At 10 a.m., after being alerted to the presence of the enemy, Montcalm ordered a general advance. Although the armies were numerically equal, Wolfe held a distinct advantage. All of his troops were regulars, whose training had prepared them to fight in close formation on an open field. More than half of the army that opposed them were militia, colonial regulars, or Indians, to whom such tactics were anathema. For one of the few times in the entire war, the redcoats' training would tip the balance in their favor.

The French line grew ragged as it advanced. While the white-coated regulars of the Béarn, La Sarre, Guyenne, Languedoc, and Roussillon Regiments held their fire and maintained discipline, numbers of the militia and colonial regulars dropped to one knee to shoot at the thin red line that opposed them. By the time they got within effective range, many had already discharged their muskets. As a result, the volley they fired was ineffective. The British waited silently until the enemy was just forty yards away. On Wolfe's command they fired, reloaded, and fired again. To the French, it sounded like a double cannon shot. Before the smoke had cleared, the British charged. The French fled before the bayonets bit home. To their delight, the 35th found that they were facing the Royal Roussillon Regiment, one of the units that had fought against them at Fort William Henry. Reveling in their revenge, the men picked up the Frenchmen's discarded plumes and put them in their own hats as they pursued them across the plain. Wolfe would not live to relish his success. Shot through the wrist, chest, and stomach, he collapsed on the right of the line and died just after learning of his victory. Surgeon Thomas Wilkins of the 35th was with him at the time.[19] Moments later, on the other side of the field, Montcalm was mortally wounded. As he was being borne toward the walls of Québec by the tide of his fleeing troops, grapeshot fired from the British army's only gun ripped open his stomach. Bleeding profusely, he was led through the gates and laid down in the cathedral, where he died at four o'clock the next morning. Having received word of the British landing, Bougainville's 3,000 were rushing back to the scene. By the time they arrived, it was too late. The battle was already lost.[20]

For such a brief clash, casualties had been heavy. Of Wolfe's men, 1,412 had been hit, the vast majority lightly wounded by long-range fire during or prior to the French advance. The 35th reported 111 losses, while the 3rd Battalion of the 60th registered 215. Among the former was Lt. Charles Gore of Ince's grenadier company. Having made his way back to his regiment alongside his captain following the battle of Beauport, he was wounded on the Plains of Abraham, but would soon recover. As many of their men deserted in the aftermath of the defeat, French casualties would never be comprehensively established: roughly 200 died and 1,200 were wounded. Many were veterans of Fort William Henry. Lieutenant Colonel Senezergues, Lévis's second in command at Lake George, was among those found dead on the field. Québec surrendered on September 17 and was occupied by British troops the next day.

The final campaign of 1759 saw the fall of Fort Carillon. After building a new fort on the site of the old entrenched camp above Fort William Henry, General Amherst's army sailed up Lake George and besieged Carillon on July 21. Colonel Bourlamaque, despite having received orders to withdraw to the north of Lake Champlain, held off the British and provincials for four days before igniting the magazine and blowing up the fortifications. Bourlamaque then fell back to Fort Saint Frédéric, which he also destroyed before retreating further to a stronghold at Île aux Noix. Cautious as ever, Amherst refused to follow his enemy and spent the remainder of the summer rebuilding Forts Carillon and Saint Frédéric, renaming the former Ticonderoga and the latter Crown Point.

As a single concession to adventurism, Amherst ordered Maj. Robert Rogers to attack the Abenaki mission of Saint Francis on the upper Saint Lawrence River. The raid had dual objectives: besides drawing attention away from Wolfe's siege of Québec, it also served as a warning to New France's vacillating Indian allies of the consequences of siding against the British army. Long a thorn in the side of the colonies and widely blamed for initiating the massacre at Fort William Henry, Saint Francis's Abenaki community was the perfect target. Amherst's instructions were clear: "Remember the barbarities that have been committed by the enemy's Indian scoundrels," he advised. "Take your revenge, but don't forget that, tho' those villains have dastardly and promiscuously murdered . . . women and children of all ages, it is my orders that no women or children be killed or hurt."[21]

Rogers set out from Crown Point on the evening of September 13. Boarding a flotilla of whaleboats, his men paddled north, keeping close to the shore to avoid detection. In total, Rogers commanded two hundred men, a mixture of veteran rangers, redcoats of the 44th Foot under Lt. James Dunbar, and a number of provincials drawn from the Jersey Blues, Massachusetts, Rhode Island, and Connecticut regiments. Among the latter was Lt. Nathan Brigham, a Massachusetts man who volunteered for the mission to avenge comrades killed at Fort William Henry.

After ten days Rogers reached Missisquoi Bay at the north end of Lake Champlain. After hiding his boats in the undergrowth and leaving two Indian scouts to watch over them, the major led the rest of his men overland to the northeast. On the second day of the march the scouts caught up with terrible news: the boats had been discovered by a party of four hundred French, Canadians, and Indians. Realizing the enemy would soon be in pursuit, Rogers pushed his men to their limits to outpace them. As they forced their way across endless swamps, Rogers determined to carry out the raid regardless, and formulated an audacious plan of escape. No longer able to return to Missisquoi Bay, where an ambush would surely be awaiting him, he decided to head for British territory by way of Lake Memphremagog and the Connecticut River to Fort No. 4 in New Hampshire, an extraordinary march that would see his men traverse some 250 miles of wilderness.

Twenty-two days after leaving Crown Point, the raiders reached their objective. Many of the warriors of Saint Francis were absent, either helping defend Québec or out in the wilds searching for Rogers's party. Father Roubaud was also away, having traveled to the town of Trois Riviéres. Those who remained were celebrating a wedding feast. After the last of the revelers had turned in, Rogers launched his attack. The villagers were taken by surprise and the fighting was one-sided. By dawn, forty Indians had been killed, many shot in their beds or burned alive in their huts. Just one of the raiders had died. Despite Amherst's instructions, two-thirds of those killed were women and children. Twenty others were captured.

Rogers's return journey through the wilderness was an epic of survival. Weighed down with plunder captured at Saint Francis and carrying little to eat, his men suffered terribly. Many died of exhaustion as they traversed the mountains, forests, and swamps that lay between them and salvation. Others were captured or killed by bands of pursuing French, Canadians, and Indians. With little game in the woods, a few resorted to cannibalism. According to one survivor, Pvt. Robert Kirkwood of Montgomery's Highlanders, Rogers himself murdered one of the captives, a plump Indian woman whose body he cut into portions and shared with his men. "We then broiled and eat the most of her," Kirkwood recalled, "and received great strength thereby." By the time Rogers staggered into Fort No. 4 on October 31, just three men remained. Of the rest, fifty-eight had returned to Crown

Point within a few days of starting the expedition, one had been shot dead at Saint Francis, and forty-nine had been killed or captured following the raid. In the weeks that followed, roughly fifty more survivors reached Crown Point or Fort No. 4. The rest perished in the woods.[22]

By the winter of 1759–60, New France was close to collapse: the grain stores were empty, British blockades had cut off the colony from resupply, her Indian allies were deserting in droves, and her territory was rapidly decreasing. Nevertheless, the following spring, the remnants of the French army came close to recapturing Québec. Following their mauling at the Plains of Abraham, the white-coated regulars and Canadian militia had regrouped at Montréal under the Chevalier de Lévis. Buoyed by news of low morale, poor supplies, and an outbreak of scurvy among the British garrison at Québec, Lévis marshaled his troops. On April 20, 1760, with the last of the winter ice still clinging to the banks of the Saint Lawrence, he sailed upriver with seven thousand men. Lévis landed at Saint Augustin on April 26, and pushed back a British advance post at Old Lorette with ease. The next day, Brig. James Murray marched out from Québec to meet him. At the village of Saint Foye, he deployed his men on a ridgeline. The 3rd Battalion of the 60th and the 35th were held in reserve. Despite commanding just thirty-eight hundred men, Murray attacked as the French advanced up a road cut through the forest to the southwest of the village. He initially pushed Lévis back, but when the Frenchman realized his numerical advantage, he redoubled his efforts, and a fierce battle ensued. After two hours the British were forced to withdraw. There were heavy casualties on both sides. Colonel Bourlamaque was badly wounded in the leg by a British cannonball, which killed the horse he was riding. Called into action in the latter stages of the battle, Captain Ince, commander of the 35th's grenadiers, was hit during a skirmish for a windmill north of the road to Québec.[23] He managed to retreat with the rest of the army, but later died of his wounds. Lévis followed up his victory and began to besiege the city, but abandoned the attempt when the British were resupplied by two frigates, which sailed up the Saint Lawrence in May.[24]

With Lévis forced back, the summer of 1760 saw three British armies converging on Montréal, the colony's only remaining possession of significance. The first—ten thousand men under Amherst—gathered at Oswego. After crossing the lake, they would proceed up the Saint Lawrence from the east. The second, which was thirty-four hundred strong, began at Crown Point. Under Brig. William de Haviland of the 27th Regiment of Foot, it would push up Lake Champlain and the Richelieu River, before turning west for the final descent against the capital. Brigadier Murray was to lead the third. Under his command were twenty-four hundred men, including both the 35th and the 3rd Battalion of the 60th. Murray's orders were to advance against Montréal from Québec. The French did what they could to counter these attacks, but were now hopelessly outmatched. The recently released Captain Pouchot was ordered to hold the upper Saint Lawrence against Amherst with three hundred men. Hurriedly constructing a fort on an island in midstream, he settled in to await the onslaught. Bougainville, meanwhile, was preparing to block de Haviland's troops at Île aux Noix, a fortified island at the southern end of the Richelieu River.[25]

Murray's army, though the smallest of the three, made the best progress. Embarking in thirty-two vessels from Québec on July 15, it sailed past a force of two thousand French and Canadians at Trois Riviéres, then landed at the town of Sorel, forty miles upstream of Montréal. En route, his men had paused at various villages to skirmish with small enemy detachments, barter with locals, and extract oaths of neutrality from the population. At Sorel, they were met by twenty-five hundred French regulars and Canadian militia under the overall command of Colonel Bourlamaque. Wishing to avoid unnecessary bloodshed, Murray issued a proclamation urging the inhabitants to remain in their homes, and promising to respect the lives and property of any who surrendered. After witnessing the destruction of one of their detachments at Sorel, the Canadian militia was only too happy to oblige. By the end of August, half of Bourlamaque's troops had deserted. Murray, meanwhile, encamped on an island in midriver, dispatched rangers to get word of Amherst and de Haviland's progress before proceeding further. While the army waited, several British prisoners captured earlier in the war were returned. Among them was a drummer boy of the 35th. Taken prisoner at Fort William Henry, he had been held for three years in an Indian village. According to the regiment's official history, "the poor boy had quite forgotten how to speak English, but was very glad to escape, as may be imagined."[26]

One hundred miles to the south, de Haviland had outmaneuvered Bougainville's troops. While occupying the French with cannon fire from their front, the brigadier had dispatched a small body of rangers and light infantry with three guns to sweep around the fort and cut off its supply lines to the north. The move forced Bougainville to abandon his defenses, and on August 27 he conducted a treacherous night march through the marshes. After considerable hardships, he joined Bourlamaque on the banks of the Saint Lawrence. De Haviland, who had been pursuing the French relentlessly, then united with Murray near Sorel. Meanwhile, General Amherst was having more difficulty. Although Pouchot's three hundred men had been unable to detain him for long, the seven great rapids at the head of the Saint Lawrence proved a formidable obstacle. Forty-six boats were wrecked by the rushing waters and treacherous rocks, and eighteen more were badly damaged. In total, eighty-four men were drowned.

Despite those losses, Amherst's army proceeded up the Saint Lawrence, and by September 6 his troops were encamped before the walls of Montréal. The next day, Murray's troops disembarked to the northeast and de Haviland's men landing to the south of the city completed the encirclement. Seeing his situation was hopeless, Vaudreuil called a council of war to discuss the possibility of surrender. Lévis was appalled. He demanded permission to continue the fight to the death, but Vaudreuil overruled him. Disgusted, the chevalier stormed out of the meeting, returned to his regulars, and burned the colors, so he wouldn't have to suffer the indignity of surrendering them to the enemy. Vaudreuil then sought a parley with Amherst, and New France capitulated on September 8, 1760. The French were denied the honors of war. Despite the valiant defense they had conducted over the last six years, Amherst considered them unworthy opponents. Just as Montcalm's allies had failed to respect their prisoners at Fort William Henry, Amherst would not give the French the satisfaction of an honorable surrender at Montréal.[27]

Although the British allowed the inhabitants to continue practicing Catholicism, and there was little outward change in the culture and society of Canada, several of the leading citizens were expelled. Governor Vaudreuil and Intendant Bigot were ordered to sail to Paris, where they were imprisoned in the Bastille while an inquiry looked into their role in the loss of the colony. Vaudreuil was acquitted of all responsibility and released after just three months. Bigot, on the other hand, had all his property confiscated and was banished from France for life. The former intendant settled into a comfortable exile in Switzerland, where he died in 1778.[28] After a brief period of imprisonment in Britain, Joseph Marin, the Canadian coureur de bois who had attacked the outposts at Fort Edward in the summer of 1757, was sent to France, where he lived on a meager pension provided by the Crown. In 1773, he was appointed lieutenant colonel and with his son took part in an attempt to establish a French colony in Madagascar. Shortly after their arrival in 1774, both developed fever and died.[29]

Loose Ends

1760–1814

While Vaudreuil's surrender was the final act of the French and Indian War in North America, elsewhere the Seven Years' War continued until 1763. In mainland Europe, Austrian, Russian, French, British, Hanoverian, and Prussian armies endured horrendous bloodshed with little territorial gain, while in the wider colonial conflict, the British scored several notable victories. The redcoats, provincials, and Royal Navy combined to defeat French and Spanish garrisons at Havana, Manila, Sierra Leone, Martinique, and Guadeloupe; and in India, French influence was effectively shattered with the fall of Pondicherry. Each operation involved an amphibious "descent," or raid—a hazardous maneuver, of which the British would become the undisputed masters and would go on to use with great success in the Revolutionary and Napoleonic Wars. The veterans of Fort William Henry continued to play their part. Under the newly promoted Lt. Col. Henry Fletcher, the 35th won praise at Martinique and Havana, where tropical disease proved far deadlier than the enemy. Also at Havana was Col. Phineas Lyman of Connecticut, in command of the provincial division of twenty -three hundred men.

In February 1763 the Treaty of Paris brought an end to the fighting. At the negotiation table, Britain gained control of all of France's lands in the Americas, with the exception of the lucrative sugar islands of Guadeloupe and Martinique, and Saint Pierre and Miquelon, two rocky atolls in the mouth of the Saint Lawrence, which would serve as a base for France's cod fishing industry. Havana and Manila were returned to the Spanish, but the British received the colony of Florida and all Spanish lands to the east of the Mississippi in return. The result was what Pitt had long dreamed of: undisputed control of the entire Atlantic seaboard of North America. Within twenty years, however, most of the territory would be lost.

Three months after the Treaty of Paris, Britain's new American possessions were threatened when a major Indian uprising broke out in the high country. The tribes resented Governor Amherst's heavy-handed approach. Whereas the French had treated them as allies and respected their beliefs and culture, the new British governor looked on the Indians as inferior subject peoples. The uprising was led by an Ottawa chief named Pontiac, whose diplomatic skills fostered the largest Indian alliance ever seen. Ottawa, Chippewa, Potawatomi, Huron, Miami, Wea, Kickapoo, Delaware, Shawnee, and Mingo all took part. The majority of the Iroquois, still tightly bound to the British, were notable by their absence, although some Seneca were involved. From mid-May to mid-June, the Indians scored several successes in the Great Lakes region, the Ohio country, and western Pennsylvania. Forts Sandusky, Saint Joseph, Miami, Oui-atenon, Michilimackinac, Venango, Le Boeuf, and Presque Isle were all burned to the ground and their garrisons slaughtered. Fort Detroit, besieged since May 7, and Fort Pitt, under attack since June 22, managed to hold out.

Britain's response was threefold. First, Amherst was recalled to London in August 1763 and replaced by Maj. Gen. Thomas Gage. Second, a diplomatic mission led by Sir William Johnson headed for Fort Niagara. Although few representatives of the tribes attended, Johnson managed to persuade the Iroquois to actively back the British, and one group even sent a war party against the tribes of the Ohio country that had sided with Pontiac. Third, two expeditions were sent west to crush the uprising. The first, led by Col. John Bradstreet, traveled across Lake Erie to relieve Fort Detroit. Negotiating with the Indians en route, Bradstreet reached his destination on August 26. Outnumbered, the Indians lifted the siege and agreed to a treaty. Although Bradstreet had achieved his primary goal, his negotiations proved inept. He had little understanding of native culture and through his ignorance offended many of those he dealt with.

The second expedition, of five hundred troops under Col. Henry Bouquet, set out to relieve Fort Pitt. Hearing of their approach, the Indians broke off the siege and marched to meet them. The Battle of Bushy Run saw the British and provincial militia construct a crude redoubt from sacks of flour and hold off the Indians' attacks from 1 p.m. on August 6 until early the following morning. Then a vigorous counter-attack broke the enemy, who fled into the wilderness and failed to reform. After relieving Fort Pitt, Bouquet marched to the Muskingum River in the Ohio country, from where he could threaten several Indian villages. As Bouquet had intended, the warriors preferred to negotiate. By 1764, more through diplomatic than military means, Pontiac's grand alliance was beginning to fall apart. The following year, he traveled to Fort Ontario to meet with William Johnson, and a peace treaty was negotiated. On one point, both sides concurred: whites and Indians were unable to live with one another. As a result, a demarcation line, known as the Royal Proclamation, was drawn across America to limit European settlement to the territories east of the Appalachians.[1]

With the continent finally at peace, veterans of the French and Indian War looked forward to receiving land grants in the territories won from the French. One of the applicants was Phineas Lyman. On behalf of a consortium of veterans, the former colonel spent eight years in Britain lobbying the authorities, until he finally succeeded in 1773. After returning to his native Connecticut, Lyman, his eldest son, and eight slaves set off to establish a new home 380 miles up the Mississippi River. The site was a small settlement called Natchez, which had been surveyed and chartered the previous year by Israel and Rufus Putnam, two of Lyman's former comrades in arms. The new territory proved to be a malarial zone, and mortality rates were high. Lyman died in 1774, just one year after his arrival.[2]

The following year saw the outbreak of the American War of Independence. Unwilling to respect the demarcation line and increasingly angered by British interference, excessive legislation, and arbitrary and unrepresentative taxation, the American colonists rebelled against the Crown. The war reunited many of the veterans of Fort William Henry. After twenty years of garrison duty in Britain, the 35th returned to America. Although the majority of the survivors of the French and Indian War had been pensioned off the year before, a handful made the journey across the Atlantic. Among them was the former ensign William Brown. Landing at Boston, the battalion's grenadier and light companies were thrown into action at the Battle of Bunker Hill. Major General Israel Putnam, who had fought alongside the 35th at Fort Edward eighteen years before, led the American defense. The Battle of Bunker Hill was a pyrrhic victory for the British. While forcing the Americans to withdraw, the redcoats' casualties were devastating. Only five of the 35th's grenadier company and three of its light company were unscathed. William Brown was among the dead. Conversely, the battle was Putnam's finest hour. As a result, he was promoted to fourth in command of what the rebellious colonists dubbed the "Continental army." Major General George Washington later replaced Putnam, however, and his reputation took a further blow at the Battle of Long Island in 1776 when he was forced to order a hasty retreat.[3]

Other veterans of the Lake George campaign of 1757 who took part in the War of American Independence included Jabez Fitch, the former sergeant and diarist, who served in the Connecticut forces until 1783; Rufus Putnam, who commanded two regiments at the Battle of Saratoga; and Joseph Frye, who reached the rank of brigadier general in the Continental army before retiring from frontline service at the age of sixty-four.[4] Other Americans fought for the Crown. Robert Rogers briefly served as Brig. Gen. Guy Carleton's right-hand man in the Canadian campaign of 1776; Charles Langlade, the coureur de bois who had fought at Sabbath Day Point, led a war party of Ottawa in Lt. Gen. John Burgoyne's campaign of 1777; and Sir William Johnson's descendants led

Loyalist and Mohawk resistance against the rebels in northern New York.[5]

When the French joined forces with Washington in 1778, another veteran of Fort William Henry entered the fray. Since the end of the French and Indian War, Louis-Antoine de Bougainville had led an interesting life. In 1760, after separating from Cueta, the Shawnee woman who later gave birth to his child, he had returned to Paris. In an attempt to blot out the scenes of butchery and betrayal that he had witnessed in the wilderness, for three years Bougainville had dedicated his life to the pursuit of pleasure and was frequently seen patronizing the capital's brothels and gambling dens. By 1763, he tired of this aimless existence and conceived an outlandish plan to place a colony of displaced Acadians on the Falkland Islands. His two-ship flotilla, loaded with 130 crew, colonial regulars, and colonists, all of whom had Canadian or Acadian origins, set out from Saint-Malo on September 15, 1763. Founded the following February, the colony, known as Fort Saint Louis, was a success. The hardy Acadians prospered on the barren isles, but political pressure from Spain, which viewed the southern Atlantic as the back door to South America and therefore its exclusive domain, forced Louis XV to cede control of the project to Madrid. Bougainville was disappointed, but a new opportunity was about to present itself. Awakening to the importance of establishing a presence in the south Pacific, the French foreign minister, Étienne-François, Comte de Stainville, Duc de Choiseul, offered Bougainville command of an expedition to circumnavigate the globe. If he succeeded, he would be the first man of his nation to achieve it.[6]

Leaving Nantes in the frigate *La Boudeuse* on November 15, 1766, Bougainville stopped at Montevideo, before proceeding to Fort Louis in the Falklands to pick up any Acadians who preferred not to live under Spanish rule. Fifteen took up the offer. After a lengthy delay, while he awaited the arrival of the second ship, Bougainville left the Falklands on June 1. The expedition put into Rio de Janeiro and Montevideo, then turned south. After a series of delays, accidents, and repairs, his ships entered the Strait of Magellan on December 6, 1767. Violent storms and encounters with Patagonian Indians followed. On January 26, 1768, the ships emerged into the vastness of the Pacific Ocean. Two months later they called in at Tahiti, then passed close by the Great Barrier Reef before visiting Papua New Guinea and the Moluccas. On March 16, 1769, Bougainville returned to Saint-Malo, completing the circumnavigation in two years, four months, and one day.[7]

In 1777, after publishing two journals relating his adventures, Bougainville was given command of the *Bien Aime*, a seventy-four-gun ship of the line. Across the Atlantic, the American War of Independence was in its second year. When the British were defeated at the Battle of Saratoga, twenty miles south of the ruins of Fort William Henry, King Louis XVI sensed an opportunity to take revenge on his old enemies and declared war. Bougainville was transferred to *Le Guerrier* and ordered to join a fleet being formed in Toulon. On April 13, he set sail for America. After four months at sea, the fleet arrived in Boston Harbor. Relations between the former enemies were tense: brawls were common and several deaths ensued. One day, while the French were still busy making routine repairs to their ships, a small delegation of Iroquois arrived. Among them was the grandson of Onoraguete, the chief who had adopted Bougainville into the Turtle clan two decades before. Bougainville greeted his nephew with warmth, but was ridiculed by his fellow officers for socializing with the "savages."[8]

On September 5, 1781, Bougainville took part in the Battle of the Chesapeake. In command of *L'Auguste*, he traded broadsides with British warships until darkness forced both fleets to break off the action. The battle was tactically inconclusive: more than three hundred casualties were caused, but the only ship sunk was the British *Bristol*, which foundered after the battle. Strategically, however, it was decisive, with the French under Adm. François-Joseph Paul, Comte de Grasse, driving off Rear Adm. Thomas Graves's British fleet and sealing off the sea as an escape route for Lt. Gen. Charles Cornwallis's army, cut off and besieged by American and French forces at Yorktown.

Bougainville's next meeting with the British, at the Battle of the Saintes half a year after Cornwallis's surrender, resulted in a shattering defeat. On April 12, 1782, the fleets clashed off Guadeloupe, the British led by Adm. Sir George Brydges Rodney. Two thousand Frenchmen were killed or wounded in the fighting, five of their ships of the line were captured and one destroyed. Midway through the action, *L'Auguste*'s rigging was damaged by raking broadsides, and she drifted helplessly while the rest of the French fleet was badly mauled. De Grasse, who had contributed to the victory at Yorktown, made history as the first French admiral to surrender to the enemy. After his parole, he requested a court-martial. While de Grasse was absolved of blame, Bougainville was made the scapegoat for the defeat and court-martialed upon his return to France. A public reprimand and official ban from the court at Versailles followed. It was an ignominious end to a successful and varied military career.[9]

In 1789 the French Revolution broke out. Surprisingly, the nobles who had fought at Fort William Henry escaped the period largely unscathed. Although Bougainville was arrested in 1794 and his execution appeared inevitable, he was saved when Maximilien de Robespierre's fall prompted a degree of sanity to return to Paris. The Chevalier de Lévis died of natural causes two years before the revolution broke out, but even then was not entirely spared the retribution of the masses. During the chaos, his remains were desecrated, and his widow and three daughters sent to the guillotine.

By the end of the eighteenth century, nearly all of the veterans of the campaigns around Lake George had died. William Eyre, the officer who had designed Forts Edward and William Henry, was one of the first to pass away. Having remained in America until the autumn of 1764, he obtained permission to return home after eight years of foreign service. When his ship was within sight of the British coast, a storm blew up. Eyre was swept overboard and drowned.[10] Daniel Webb died in 1771; the engineer, Col. James Montresor, having outlived two of his three wives, passed away in Kent on January 6, 1776; Joseph Frye, after founding the town of Fryeburg in Maine, died at the age of eighty-four; and Israel

Putnam passed away in Brooklyn, Connecticut, in 1790, where he was buried in an impressive tomb in the city's South Cemetery.[11]

A few veterans lived to see the turn of the nineteenth century. After fighting alongside the British in the American War of Independence, Charles Langlade served in the British Indian Department until his death in 1801. In his twilight years, spent at the frontier trading post of Green Bay, he was said to enjoy spinning tales of the ninety-nine battles he had fought during his career.[12] Thoroughly rehabilitated following his disgrace at the Battle of the Saintes, Louis-Antoine de Bougainville passed away in Paris in 1811. In recognition of his services to France, Emperor Napoleon ordered his body interred in the Pantheon, while his heart was buried alongside the grave of his wife, Flore-Josèphe, in the small cemetery of Saint-Pierre in Montmartre.[13] Jabez Fitch died in Hyde Park, Vermont, at the age of seventy-five, and Thomas Wilkins, the surgeon of the 35th who had been robbed of all of his instruments during the massacre, passed away in 1814 at his home in Galway, Ireland. Wilkins, perhaps the last survivor of all protagonists in the siege of Fort William Henry, had reached the extraordinary age of a hundred and two.[14]

EPILOGUE

Echoes

THE STORY OF THE SIEGE AND MASSACRE of Fort William Henry has been told in many ways. In the late 1750s it was used by British propagandists to damn the French. The casualties were exaggerated, and the cruelties of the Indians were pored over in titillating detail. The "savages" were painted as being barely more conscious of their atrocities than beasts, and the French were held accountable for not preventing their allies from sinking to such depths of depravity. This was used to rouse the American colonists to expel the French from the continent. Considered reporting played little part. The numbers cited as victims of the massacre rose each time the story appeared in print. Initial reports of just ten killed, quoted in the *New York Mercury* on August 22, 1757, ballooned to thirteen hundred by the time John Entick's *General History of the Late War* was published in 1763.[1]

Pontiac's uprising saw a shift in the way the story was told. The Indians, previously portrayed as pawns of their European masters, were recast as the chief villains of the piece. Their culpability was used to justify British retaliation and the redcoats' ongoing expansion into the west. In France, Desandrouins, Malartic, and Bourlamaque all published memoirs aiming to redress what they perceived as imbalanced reporting. In their versions, the British and their provincial allies were blamed for their own demise: they should have defended themselves more stoutly and were responsible for enraging the warriors by offering them liquor in an ill-advised attempt at conciliation. French protestations barely registered across the Atlantic. They were already swimming against a growing tide and in 1778, when a new publication was released, the American version of the story was cemented in the consciousness of the public.

In *Travels through the Interior Parts of North America*, Jonathan Carver, a veteran of the Lake George campaign of 1757, alleged that the French had "tacitly permitted" the massacre to unfold, but it was for the Indians that he reserved his most vehement ire. "It was computed," Carver claimed, "that fifteen hundred persons were killed or made prisoners by these savages during the fatal day." Carver also claimed that the smallpox epidemic that raged through the high country in the autumn following the massacre represented "the immediate judgment of heaven." The disease, he implied, was "intended as an atonement for this slaughter." Although Carver couched his words carefully, the message was clear: the Indians had been forsaken by God. This legitimized the seizure of their lands and excused the continuing genocide of their people.[2]

This pattern of Indian demonization continued during the American War of Independence. The majority of the Woodland tribes rejected the overtures of the American republicans and either stayed neutral in the fighting or remained loyal to the British Crown. When King George III conceded defeat in 1783, the tribes found themselves facing the consequences. The Royal Proclamation was abandoned and settlers, following earlier illegal pioneers, pushed over the old demarcation line in ever-increasing numbers. As the indigenous inhabitants tried to defend their homelands, a series of conflicts ensued. The first (such as the Chickamauga Wars of 1776–94) were punitive missions designed to exact revenge for the pro-Loyalist stance that many tribes had adopted during the revolution. Soon, however, the wars became little more than barely sanctioned landgrabs, and the Indians were pushed ever farther into the west.

In 1826, the publication of James Fenimore Cooper's *The Last of the Mohicans* added yet another nail to the Indians' coffin. Cooper's tale, though sympathetic in its portrayal of

Uncas and Chingachgook, depicts the majority of the Indians as godless savages, fit for extermination. Throughout the nineteenth century the Indian wars went on. The power of the Creeks was broken in 1814, the Black Hawk War saw the Sauk and Fox thrown out of their homelands in Wisconsin and Illinois, the Seminoles were crushed in Florida in the mid-nineteenth century, and the Red River War of 1874–75 saw the surrender of the Arapaho, Comanche, Cheyenne, and Kiowa. What had begun on the eastern seaboard in the early seventeenth century, and was "justified" by the storms of publicity that followed events such as the massacres at Deerfield and Fort William Henry and Custer's last stand, came to a conclusion with the death of Indian self-determination at Wounded Knee on December 28, 1890.

APPENDIX A

THE BATTLEFIELD TODAY

In the decades following the siege of Fort William Henry, the southern shore of Lake George was in constant use by the British and American military. Fort George, built on the site of Monro's entrenched camp in 1759, was occupied throughout the French and Indian War and retained a garrison during the American War of Independence. On the ruins of Fort William Henry itself, smallpox hospitals were built, and Fort George was converted to house thousands of patients from New England and northern New York.[1] Following the defeat of the British in 1783, the site was abandoned until 1854, when a palatial summer resort, named the Fort William Henry Hotel, was built by the Delaware and Hudson Rail Company. The hotel thrived until it was destroyed by fire in 1908, but was rebuilt three years later. While smaller and less grand than its predecessor, the New Fort William Henry Hotel was also a success, and business continued to prosper.

A few hundred yards away, the ruins of Fort William Henry remained undisturbed. Buried by several feet of earth in thick woodland, only the uppermost bastions were visible. In 1917 James Austin Holden, a guest at the hotel, wrote the following description:

> At Lake George the ruins of Fort William Henry and Fort George, their trenches and walls overgrown with turf and evergreens, their slopes grassed and concealed by underbrush, remain mute reminders of a day long since gone by. . . . So peaceful and serene the scene, we who visit . . . can scarce visualize the scenes of blood and carnage, of disaster and death, which once marred these sylvan camps.[2]

In 1952 a consortium of businessmen headed by Harold Veeder purchased the ruins, intending to reconstruct the fort and turn it into a tourist attraction. Archaeologist Stanley Gifford was hired to dig the site before construction began.

His excavations started in the spring of 1953 and continued through 1954. The discovery of human remains aroused considerable interest, but when the money ran out, the dig was terminated and the reconstruction of Fort William Henry began. Using Major Eyre's 1755 plans and Gifford's more recent discoveries, Veeder's company, the Fort William Henry Corporation, soon completed the rebuild, and the fort was opened to the public in 1955. Today it is visited by seventy to eighty thousand tourists a year. During the two-hour tour, they are given a crash course in the French and Indian War by a guide dressed in colonial garb. Before being channeled through the gift shop, visitors witness "redcoats" firing muskets and cannons and learn of the horrors that happened over two and a half centuries before.[3]

APPENDIX B

CHRONOLOGY

1524: Giovanni de Verrazano, an Italian-born explorer in the service of the French Crown, explores the eastern coast of North America.

ca. 1550: The Iroquois Confederacy is formed.

1607: Jamestown, the first colony in English America, is founded.

1608: Québec is founded by Samuel de Champlain.

1609: Battle of Ticonderoga (Huron victory over the Mohawk).

1614: Albany is founded by the Dutch.

ca. 1638–1701: The Beaver Wars (Iroquois vs. Huron and their Algonquin allies).

1664: The Dutch are forced to cede New Amsterdam (New York), Albany, and all their other American possessions to England.

1676: Mission of Caughnawaga founded near Montréal.

1688–97: King William's War (the War of the League of Augsburg, 1688–97).

1700: Abenaki mission of Saint Francis founded on the upper Saint Lawrence River.

1702–13: Queen Anne's War (the War of Spanish Succession, 1701–14).

1722: The Tuscarora join the Iroquois Confederacy, which now becomes the Six Nations.

1744–48: King George's War (the War of Austrian Succession, 1740–48).

1754–60: The French and Indian War (the Seven Years' War, 1756–63).

1754 June 14: Washington defeats the French at Jumonville's Glen.

1754 July 3: French defeat Washington at Fort Necessity.

1755 June 8: British capture Fort Beauséjour.

1755 June 17: British seize Acadia.

1755 July 9: Braddock defeated at Monongahela.

1755 September 9: The Battle of Lake George.

1756 April 3: Montcalm and Bougainville sail from Brest for New France on *La Licorne*.

1756 April 15: Elements of the 35th and 42nd Regiments sail from Plymouth for America.

1756 June 14: Maj. Gen. Daniel Webb arrives at New York from Britain.

1756 June 16: Elements of the 35th and 42nd Regiments arrive at New York.

1756 June 26: Elements of the 35th and 42nd Regiments arrive at Albany.

1756 July 26: Lord Loudoun arrives at New York.

1756 August 14: The French capture Fort Oswego on Lake Ontario.

1757 March 17–21: Rigaud's winter raid on Fort William Henry.

1757 March 29: Lt. Col. Monro and five companies of the 35th arrive at Fort William Henry.

1757 March–April: The provincial troops of Massachusetts, Connecticut, New Jersey, New Hampshire, and New York muster.

1757 May–June: The provincials encamp at Forts Edward and William Henry.

1757 June: France's Indian allies from the high country gather at Montréal.

1757 July 1: Capt. Israel Putnam's moonlight ambush at South Bay.

1757 July 9: Montcalm holds a council of war at the Lake of Two Mountains (Oka).

1757 July 10: Montcalm holds a council of war at Sault Saint Louis (Caughnawaga).

1757 July 18: Montcalm arrives at Fort Carillon.

1757 July 23: Joseph Marin de La Malgue attacks carpenters outside Fort Edward. Simultaneously, several miles to the north, the Battle of Sabbath Day Point takes place.

1757 July 25: General Webb arrives at Fort William Henry.

1757 July 27: Webb convenes a council of war at Fort William Henry.

1757 July 29: Webb returns to Fort Edward.

1757 July 30: Lévis's division leaves Fort Carillon.

1757 August 1: Montcalm's division leaves Fort Carillon.

1757 August 2: Reinforcements led by Colonels Young and Frye arrive at Fort William Henry.

1757 August 3: The siege of Fort William Henry begins.

1757 August 9: Lt. Col. Monro surrenders Fort William Henry.

1757 August 10: The massacre at Fort William Henry.

1757 November 3: Colonel Monro dies of apoplexy in Albany.

1758 July 8: British repulsed with heavy loss at Fort Carillon.

1758 July 26: The British seize Louisbourg after a successful siege.

1758 August 27: American provincials under Lt. Col. John Bradstreet capture Fort Frontenac.

1758 November 26: Brig. John Forbes captures the remains of Fort Duquesne.

1759 June 26: The British capture remains of Fort Carillon and rename it Ticonderoga.

1759 July 25: The British take Fort Niagara.

1759 September 13: A mortally wounded Maj. Gen. James Wolfe is victorious at the Battle of the Plains of Abraham.

1760 September 8: Vaudreuil surrenders Montréal to the British, effectively bringing the French and Indian War to a close.

1763 February 10: The Treaty of Paris formally concludes the Seven Years' War.

1763 April 27: Pontiac's uprising begins.

1763 October 7: King George III signs the Royal Proclamation, prohibiting settlement west of the Appalachian Mountains.

1763 October 31: Pontiac agrees to peace terms.

1826 January: *The Last of the Mohicans* is published.

1854: The Fort William Henry Hotel is built to the north of the ruins.

1908: The Fort William Henry Hotel is destroyed by fire.

1911: The New Fort William Henry Hotel is built.

1920: *The Last of the Mohicans* is released as a film, starring Wallace Beery.

1936: *The Last of the Mohicans* film starring Randolph Scott is released.

1952: The Fort William Henry Corporation purchases the ruins, and archaeological digs begin.

1954–1955: Fort William Henry is reconstructed and opened to the public.

1992: *The Last of the Mohicans* film starring Daniel Day-Lewis is released.

APPENDIX C

GLOSSARY

ABENAKI. A collective term for several Indian tribes originally from northern New England and southeastern Canada. Pushed out of their homelands in the south by British colonization, at the turn of the eighteenth century the Abenaki allied themselves with the French and resettled in the Jesuit missions of Saint Francis and Bécancour on the Saint Lawrence River, from which they launched a series of raids on their enemies in New England.

ALGONQUIN. Either a French-allied Indian tribe from the north of Lake Ontario, which was nearly wiped out by Iroquois raiding parties during the Beaver Wars (ca. 1638–1701), or a collective term for the Great Lakes tribes (such as the Ottawa, Chippewa, Potawatomi, Mississauga, Menominee, and Nipissing) who share common linguistic and cultural roots and were traditionally allied in a centuries-long conflict against the Iroquoian tribes to their south.

BASTION. Lozenge-shaped towers jutting out from the four corners of a fortification that enabled the defenders to fire on any enemies who reached the foot of their walls.

BATEAUX. Flat-bottom boats used to carry people and cargo on rivers and lakes.

BEAVER WARS (ca. 1638–1701). An Indian conflict, the Beaver Wars were an attempt by the Iroquois Confederacy to seize control of the hunting grounds of the Huron and their Algonquian-speaking allies of the Great Lakes to satisfy a growing demand for furs from European traders. The Indians swapped the furs for firearms, leading to further escalation of the conflict.

BREACHING BATTERY. A battery of guns that the attackers positioned in front of the final parallel in siege warfare. The breaching battery fired at a weak point in the walls of an enemy fortification until a hole, or breach, was made, through which the infantry could advance.

BRITAIN/BRITISH. The correct term for British forces after May 1, 1707, when the Acts of Union officially merged the Crowns and parliaments of England and Scotland into the United Kingdom of Great Britain. The term "British army" sparked less resentment among the large percentage of Welsh, Scottish, and Irish soldiers who filled its ranks than the previous "English" reference, but such details were lost abroad, where allies and adversaries alike continued to either call British soldiers "English" or used the two terms interchangeably.

CANISTER. A type of artillery round widely used throughout the horse-and-musket era, canister shot consisted of a tin can tightly packed with musket balls, which would burst open shortly after leaving the gun's muzzle. Although only effective at ranges of less than four hundred yards, canister was lethal against infantry.

CANNON. Artillery employed in the horse-and-musket era, cannons included guns (artillery that fired round shot, grape, or canister over a flat trajectory), mortars, and howitzers.

CASEMATES. Reinforced bunkers dug under the walls of a fort where the garrison could take cover when under bombardment.

CAUGHNAWAGA. Either the Indian name for the mission of the Lake of Two Mountains or a collective term for the French-allied "domesticated" Iroquois who had settled in a series of Jesuit missions along the Saint Lawrence River in the late seventeenth century.

CHIPPEWA (OJIBWA). A French-allied Indian tribe of Algonquian linguistic and cultural roots from the northern shores of Lake Superior. Although the tribe is also known as the Ojibwa, the term *Chippewa* is preferred, as it was in more common usage at the time.

CLANS. Networks of "relatives" in Indian culture represented by specific animals (such as the turtle, bear, or wolf) to which each individual of a tribe was assigned. An individual's clan could supersede family allegiances and was thought to dictate one's personality and skills.

COLONIAL REGULARS (*troupes de la marine*). An arm of the French military formed in the early seventeenth century by Armand Jean du Plessis, Cardinal Richelieu, to garrison the country's overseas colonies, the colonial regulars played a vital role in the French and Indian War. Although the rank and file was largely recruited in France, the officers were almost exclusively Canadian. Well armed and disciplined, the colonial regulars were masters of backwoods fighting, but were also capable of performing a more traditional battlefield role.

COUREURS DE BOIS. Canadian backwoodsmen who bridged the cultural divide between their countrymen resident in the towns and cities of the Saint Lawrence and the Indians of the high country, the coureurs de bois acted as middlemen in the fur trade and led raiding parties of Indian auxiliaries across the British frontier.

DELAWARE. A blanket term for a conglomeration of Indian tribes that had once dominated the area that is now Pennsylvania. By the mid-eighteenth century, the Delaware had been driven into the geopolitically decisive region of the Ohio country by British expansion. In the French and Indian War they remained largely neutral, hoping that the Europeans would expend their energies fighting one another, but occasionally favored the French.

"DOMESTICATED" INDIANS. A contemporary term for French-allied Indians who had converted to Catholicism and lived in the missions along the Saint Lawrence River. Also known as "praying" Indians.

ENFILADING BATTERY. Batteries of guns positioned in front of the first parallels in siege warfare, the enfilading batteries were designed to destroy the enemy's artillery capacity by killing the gunners or dismounting the guns. Once this was achieved, the engineers could advance closer to the walls and set up a breaching battery beyond the final parallel. See also Breaching battery.

ENGLAND/ENGLISH. A blanket term used by the French to denote the British forces (regulars) and their allies (provincials, militia, and Indian auxiliaries and scouts).

FASCINES. Bundles of brushwood positioned in front of artillery batteries to provide cover for the attacking gunners during siege warfare.

FIRE-STEP (banquette). A raised platform built on the rampart of a fortification, from which the defenders could fire over the parapet and down upon their enemies.

Fox. An Indian tribe of the Algonquian linguistic family, the Fox, or Meskwaki (red earth people), originally inhabited Chequamegon Point on the southern shore of Lake Superior. In the late seventeenth century they moved to the outpost at Green Bay, but by 1712 had come into conflict with the French, whom they resented for meddling in intertribal politics. In the fighting that followed, the Fox were pushed ever farther south by the French and their Chippewa allies, but after forging a strong alliance with the Sauk, they were granted a general pardon in 1737. Relations remained strained, and in the French and Indian War the Fox were among the most unwilling of Montcalm's allies.

GABIONS. Large wickerwork baskets tightly packed with soil, gabions were positioned in front of enfilading and breaching batteries in siege warfare and served to absorb enemy fire.

GLACIS. A manmade earthen bank that sloped gently away from a fort's palisade, the glacis enabled the defenders to sweep the approaches with fire without having to constantly change the angle of their guns.

GORGET. A decorative metal collar worn by Europeans, Americans, and Indians alike, a gorget could denote rank, status, or power.

GRAPESHOT. An artillery round consisting of a cluster of small cannonballs (often nine) fired simultaneously. Grapeshot was at its most effective against infantry or cavalry at close range.

GUN. A cannon designed to fire round shot, canister, or grapeshot at a relatively flat trajectory.

HIGH COUNTRY (*pays d'en haut*). A contemporary term denoting the Great Lakes region. In the mid-eighteenth century, the area was dominated by Algonquian-speaking woodland tribes. Although largely independent, they came under considerable French influence through trading with the colony's network of isolated outposts in the region.

HOWITZER. A short-barreled cannon, the howitzer was designed to fire shells over short distances on an arced trajectory and with a steep angle of descent, making it ideally suited for siege warfare.

HURON. A high country Indian tribe of the Iroquoian linguistic family, the Huron's homelands spread to the northwest of Lake Ontario. Despite their common heritage, the tribe was a traditional enemy of the Iroquois Confederacy and was nearly wiped out in the latter years of the Beaver Wars. Facing annihilation, in the seventeenth century many of the survivors moved to Lorette, a Jesuit mission close to Québec.

IOWA. A prairie Indian tribe of Siouan roots, the Iowa were a seminomadic horse-rearing people. By the mid-eighteenth century they inhabited the area that is now Missouri, and were the most distant tribe to send warriors to participate in the siege of Fort William Henry.

IROQUOIS CONFEDERACY (or Six Nations). An alliance of six linguistically and culturally related Indian tribes (the Oneida, Seneca, Cayuga, Onondaga, Mohawk, and Tuscarora) founded in the mid-sixteenth century, the Iroquois were the most dominant force in northeast America in the precontact period. Prior to the European arrival, the confederacy had dominated intertribal politics in the woodland region of northeast America. From their homeland along the Mohawk River and the southern shores of Lake Ontario, they sent raiding parties into the high country to plunder the

Algonquian-speaking tribes of the Great Lakes region. Increasingly involved in the fur trade, the Iroquois initially favored the British in the Anglo-French wars, but by the mid-eighteenth century were treading a diplomatic tightrope between the two European giants. By the outbreak of the French and Indian War, only the Mohawk remained committed to King George.

LIVRES. French currency based on the value of a pound of silver, equivalent to the English pound sterling, replaced by the franc in 1795.

MAHICAN. Of Algonquian roots, the Mahican were originally from the Hudson River valley but were forced eastward due to pressure from the Mohawk and British and Dutch colonists. By the mid-eighteenth century, many had been converted to Christianity and were living in settled communities among the British colonists of central Massachusetts.

MENOMINEE. A high country tribe of Algonquian linguistic roots, the Menominee, or "wild rice people," were native to the Green Bay and Fox River regions of Lake Michigan. Heavily involved in the fur trade, they became close allies of the French in the mid-seventeenth century and by 1736 were one of the dominant tribes in the area.

MÉTIS. A term of French origin that denotes people of mixed race and is etymologically linked to the Spanish word "mestizo."

MISSISSAUGA. An Algonquin tribe closely related to the Ottawa, Potawatomi, and Chippewa, by the mid-eighteenth century the Mississauga were loosely allied to the French and inhabited the northwest shore of Lake Huron.

MIAMI. Linguistically of Algonquian roots, in the mid-seventeenth century the Miami were driven from their homelands along the southeast shore of Lake Michigan by Iroquois raiding parties, as European demand for furs ignited the Beaver Wars. By the 1750s they were based in the center of the area that is now Indiana, had adopted certain aspects of the Great Plains culture, and were loosely allied with the French.

MOHAWK. Founding members of the Iroquois Confederacy, the Mohawk lived in communities known as "castles" built along the Mohawk River in the colony of New York. The tribe was the closest indigenous ally of the British during the French and Indian War, largely due to the influence of Sir William Johnson, New York's Indian commissioner.

MOHEGAN. An Algonquian-speaking tribe from southern Connecticut, by the mid-seventeenth century the Mohegan's homelands had been appropriated by the British colonists, and many of its warriors fought with the provincial militia.

MORTAR. A squat-barreled artillery piece designed to fire explosive shells in a high arc into the heart of an enemy fortification, the mortar had limited range but was deadly in siege warfare.

NIPISSING. Of Algonquian linguistic roots, the Nipissing was an Indian tribe whose homelands lay to the northeast of Lake Huron. After being repeatedly raided by the Iroquois during the Beaver Wars, they developed close links with the French, and in the late seventeenth and early eighteenth centuries, the majority relocated to the Jesuit mission of the Lake of Two Mountains near Montréal.

NIPMUCK. An Indian tribe of Algonquian linguistic roots, the Nipmuck were native to Massachusetts. By the mid-eighteenth century they had been absorbed into the Bay Colony: many were practicing Christians and several fought in the provincial militia.

ONONTIO. An Indian term of respect, commonly translated as "great white father," which was used by both the Algonquian and Iroquoian linguistic groups to refer to the governor of New France. Latterly, it was also used to address General Montcalm and even the kings of France.

OTTAWA. A high country Indian tribe of Algonquian cultural and linguistic roots, the Ottawa, or "cold country" Indians, as the British colonists referred to them, were among the founding members of the "council of the Three Fires." This pact bound them to aid the Potawatomi and Chippewa in their fight against Iroquois raiders during the Beaver Wars. The Ottawa were also closely tied to the French and provided a large contingent of warriors for the 1757 siege of Fort William Henry.

PALISADE. A series of wooden stakes or fence posts encircling a defensive structure.

PARALLEL. A trench used in siege warfare that was dug at right angles to the sap, or approach trench, and parallel to the line of the enemy fortification under attack. The parallel protected the attackers' infantry, who in turn provided cover for their artillerymen working in the battery built ahead of the parallel trench. Often, a series of parallels were constructed over a period of days, weeks, or months, each closer to the defenders' fortifications than the last.

PAYS D'EN HAUT. See High country.

PEQUOTS. An Indian tribe of Algonquian linguistic and cultural roots native to central Connecticut. Like their cousins—the Mahican and the Nipmuck—many had converted to Christianity by the mid-eighteenth century, and several warriors served in the provincial militia.

PETITE GUERRE. French for "little war," *la petite guerre* was low-level combat involving skirmishing and raiding, whose proponents fought as individuals from cover and melted back into the wilderness before the enemy could react. Although the Indians were the masters of *la petite guerre*, the Canadian militia and colonial regulars were also well versed in this form of warfare, which proved anathema to the European regulars in the early years of the French and Indian War. In modern parlance, the Spanish word "guerrilla" is preferred.

POTAWATOMI. A high country Indian tribe of Algonquian linguistic roots whose homelands spread to the south of Lake Michigan, the Potawatomi were founding members of the "council of Three Fires," an alliance formed with the Ottawa and Chippewa to counter Iroquoian aggression during the Beaver Wars.

PROVINCIALS. Semiprofessional American troops recruited from the British colonies. The provincials' contracts stipulated that they were to serve for a single campaign. The units normally mustered in April and were disbanded in September to November of the same year. Each was led by a prominent local figure, and many of the officers and rank and file would have known one another from civilian life.

RAVELIN. A detached triangular fortification built in front of the main walls of a fort or castle that was designed to break up the attackers' assault. The walls of a ravelin were low and the defenders' firing angles carefully calculated so that the ravelin could not provide cover for attacking forces.

ROUND SHOT. Solid iron cannonballs used to batter a breach into enemy fortifications or fired at infantry or cavalry targets at long range.

SALLY PORT. A small, reinforced gate in the walls of a fortification, which enabled the defenders to charge out and make surprise attacks on the enemy, or "sally." Often, the aim of such an attack was to overwhelm the enemy gunners in their trenches and "spike" (or sabotage) their cannons before retiring once more inside the walls.

SAP. An "approach trench" dug by the attacking force in siege warfare, the sap advanced from the base camp toward the enemy fortification. Parallels were then dug at right angles to the sap, and batteries positioned in front of them.

SAUK. An Indian tribe of Algonquian linguistic and cultural roots whose homelands were situated on the western shores of Lake Michigan. The Sauk were close allies of the Fox and often joined the French on raiding parties.

SIX NATIONS. See Iroquois Confederacy.

SOU. A French copper coin one-twentieth the value of a livre.

SUTLERS. Traveling merchants who followed an army on campaign. Sutlers sold food, drink, tobacco, clothing, and military equipment. Permanent fortifications, such as Forts Edward and William Henry, typically had one or more sutlers on site.

SWIVEL GUN. A small gun mounted on a swiveling bracket positioned on the walls of a fortification or the side of a boat, which could be aimed and fired by a single man.

VOYAGEURS. Nomadic entrepreneurs who traveled the forests and waterways of New France's interior trading weapons and iron goods with the Indians for furs, which they sold on returning to the colony. In wartime, the voyageurs' knowledge of the wilderness and Indian languages made them especially suited to play a leading role in *la petite guerre*.

WAMPUM. Colored glass beads and shells combined into patterns on a "belt," which had great symbolic value for the woodland Indians. Strings of wampum were given to seal an alliance, encourage a friendly tribe to go to war against a mutual enemy, or as blood money to placate a dead warrior's grieving relatives.

"WILD" INDIANS. European term used to denote any Indians who continued to live in their traditional manner and practiced native religions. Also see "Domesticated" Indians.

WINNEBAGO. An Indian tribe of the Siouan linguistic family whose homelands covered the southern half of the area that is now Wisconsin.

NOTES

PROLOGUE

1. Memoirs of Israel Putnam, in *Great Warpath*, Starbuck, p. 87.
2. Lt. Col. George Monro to Maj. Gen. Daniel Webb, memorandum regarding strength of garrison at Fort William Henry, 1 November 1757, in *Relief is Greatly Wanted*, Dodge, p. 54, LO 4367.

INTRODUCTION

1. When exactly the confederacy was first formed is open to debate. The current consensus puts its foundation at some point between 1450 and 1600.
2. Peckham, *Colonial Wars*, p. 17.
3. Bearor, *Leading by Example*, p. 99; Trigger, *Handbook*, pp. 78–89. It is important to note that while the Mohawk were enemies of the French throughout the period, other elements of the Six Nations, particularly the Seneca, were their allies.
4. Trigger, *Handbook*, pp. 89–101.
5. Pocock, *Battle for Empire*, p. 13; Debo, *History of the Indians*, pp. 70–71.
6. Anderson, *Crucible of War*, p. 56.
7. Ibid., pp. 11–32; Trigger, *Handbook*, p. 421.
8. Anderson, *Crucible of War*, pp. 55–58.
9. Parkman, *Montcalm and Wolfe*, pp. 76–79.
10. Crocker, *Braddock's March*, pp. 202–9.
11. Ibid.
12. Crocker, *Braddock's March*, pp. 207–224; Anderson, *Crucible of War*, pp. 100–102.
13. Crocker, *Braddock's March*, pp. 207–224; Anderson, *Crucible of War*, pp. 100–102.
14. Crocker, *Braddock's March*, pp. 222, 234.
15. Ibid., p. 227.
16. French regiments commonly had two battalions. In all cases, only one battalion of each regiment was sent to New France.
17. O'Toole, *White Savage*, p. 31.
18. Ibid., p. 10.
19. Parkman, *Montcalm and Wolfe*, pp. 151–55.
20. O'Toole, *White Savage*, pp. 139–40.
21. Ibid., p. 151.
22. Peckham, *Colonial Wars*, pp. 142–43; Parkman, *Montcalm and Wolfe*, pp. 120–44.

Chapter One: The 35th

1. James Austin Holden, "Last of the Mohicans, Cooper's Historical Inventions, and his Cave," *Proceedings of the New York State Historical Association* 16 (1917): 212–55, http://external.oneonta.edu/cooper/articles/nyhistory/1917nyhistory-holden.html. Monro left his children £200.

2. LO 4749.

3. George Christie (quartermaster at Albany) to Col. George Monro, 11 August 1757, CO 5/888, ff.56.

4. "Lieutenant-Colonel George Munro," The 35th Foot Project, http://www.btinternet.com/~the35thfootproject/georgemunroe.html and Martineau, *History of the Royal Sussex Regiment.*

5. *Saint James Evening Post*, September 19–22, 1730, in *History of the Royal Sussex Regiment*, Martineau, p. 37.

6. LO 1166, 4254; Pargellis, *Lord Loudoun*, pp. 47–50, 69.

7. Pargellis, *Lord Loudoun*, p. 67.

8. LO 2774.

9. *Roussillon Gazette*, no. 32 (Autumn 2009): 23. At Dettingen, French casualties, including killed, wounded, and captured, were four thousand.

10. LO 2774.

11. *Drewry's Derby Mercury*, November 30–December 7, 1759.

12. "HMS *Grafton*," *Wikipedia*, last modified May 2, 2010, http://en.wikipedia.org/wiki/HMS_Grafton_(1750); Lucier, *French and Indian War Notices*, p. 83; Pargellis, *Lord Loudoun*, p. 49.

13. WO 1/973, ff.1, 191–92; LO 4749.

14. LO 2774, 1131.

15. Lucier, *French and Indian War Notices*, p. 83.

16. Benson, *Kalm's Travels in North America*, p. 134; Starbuck, *Excavating the Sutlers' House*, p. 103.

17. Trimen, *Historical Memoir of the 35th*, p. 208.

18. Benson, *Kalm's Travels in North America*, pp. 130–33.

19. LO 1388, 4749.

20. Benson, *Kalm's Travels in North America*, pp. 340–45; LO 1237, 1356.

21. John Cleaveland to Mary Cleaveland, 16 June 1758, in *A People's Army*, Anderson, p. 73.

22. Quoted in Anderson, *A People's Army*, p. 72.

23. Benson, *Kalm's Travels in North America*, pp. 340–45.

24. Pargellis, *Lord Loudoun*, p. 195.

25. Journal of John Grant, in Brumwell, *Redcoats*, pp. 164–65.

26. Trigger, *Handbook*, pp. 296–322.

27. LO 2774.

28. There are several references to Mr. Welch in the sources. See Ford, *General Orders of 1757*, p. 15; Mason, *Diary of Jabez Fitch*, pp. 3, 28.

29. "Diary of Ogilvie," p. 374; Lucier, *French and Indian War Notices*, p. 102.

30. "Diary of Ogilvie," p. 375.

31. Peckham, *Colonial Wars*, pp. 157–58.

32. Parkman, *Montcalm and Wolfe*, p. 412.

33. Anderson, *Crucible of War*, pp. 142–49.

34. Anderson, *A People's Army*, p. 86.

35. Quoted in Parkman, *Montcalm and Wolfe*, p. 217.

36. O'Toole, *White Savage*, p. 43.

37. LO 2774.

38. "History of Albany, New York," *Waepedia*, http://wapedia.mobi/en/History_of_Albany,_New_York.

39. Pargellis, *Lord Loudoun*, p. 196.

40. Anderson, *Crucible of War*, pp. 150–57; Parkman, *Montcalm and Wolfe*, pp. 192–208.

41. Casterline, *Colonial Tribulations*, p. 46.

42. LO 2774.

43. Martineau, *History of the Royal Sussex Regiment*, p. 17.

44. Brumwell, *Redcoats*, p. 318.

45. "Diary of Ogilvie," p. 375; WO 116/5, fol. 43.

46. WO 71/65, pp. 318–26; WO 116/5, ff.37, 119; Mason, *Diary of Jabez Fitch*, pp. 12–14; WO 116/5, ff.34, 37, 43.

47. LO 1419, 2227, 4608; Trimen, *Historical Memoir of the 35th*, p. 181.

48. LO 1817.

49. LO 1829.

50. Rogers, *Journals*, p. 38; LO 1886.

51. Pargellis, *Lord Loudoun*, p. 334.

52. WO 71/44, ff.139–51; "Diary of Ogilvie," p. 375.

53. WO 71/44, ff.139–40.

54. Pargellis, *Lord Loudoun*, p. 335.

55. Parkman, *Montcalm and Wolfe*, p. 412.

56. Pargellis, *Military Affairs in North America*, p. 235.

57. LO 2774, 1997.

58. LO 1991, 1997, 2004, 2014, 2020, 2024.

59. LO 2158, 3515.

60. Benson, *Kalm's Travels in North America*, p. 339; LO 2143.

61. Anderson, *A People's Army*, p. 115.

62. "History of Albany, New York," *Wapedia*, http://wapedia.mobi/en/History_of_Albany,_New_York.

CHAPTER TWO: NEW FRANCE

1. Hamilton, *Adventure in the Wilderness: The American Journals of Louis Antoine de Bougainville, 1756–1760*, p. 99 (hereafter cited as *Bougainville Journals*).

2. Parkman, *Montcalm and Wolfe*, p. 188.

3. Quoted in Parkman, *Montcalm and Wolfe*, pp. 183–84.

4. Ibid., p. 182.

5. Louis-Antoine de Bougainville to Jean-Pierre de Bougainville, 29 March 1756, in *Sea Has No End*, Suthren, p. 38.

6. Louis-Antoine de Bougainville to Jean-Pierre de Bougainville, 28 August 1756, in *Bougainville Journals*, p. 330.

7. Montcalm to minister, late 1756, in *Sea Has No End*, Suthren, p. 46.

8. *Bougainville Journals*, p. 26.

9. Ibid., p. 330.

10. For tree species found around Lakes Champlain and George in the eighteenth century, see Trigger, *Handbook*, p. 149.

11. O'Toole, *White Savage*, p. 182.

12. Louis-Antoine de Bougainville to Jean-Pierre de Bougainville, Autumn 1756, in *Sea Has No End*, Suthren, p. 52.

13. Benson, *Kalm's Travels in North America*, pp. 426–31.

14. *Bougainville Journals*, pp. 71–75.

15. Louis-Antoine de Bougainville to Jean-Pierre de Bougainville, 3 July 1757, in *Bougainville Journals*, pp. 330–31.

16. Trigger, *Handbook*, pp. 368–93; Benson, *Kalm's Travels in North America*, pp. 462–63, 471.

17. *Bougainville Journals*, p. 76; Benson, *Kalm's Travels in North America*, pp. 462–63.

18. *Bougainville Journals*, p. 76.

19. Louis-Joseph de Montcalm to his wife, 16 April 1757, in *Montcalm and Wolfe*, Parkman, p. 471.

20. Suthren, *Sea Has No End*, p. 52.

21. Kennett, *French Armies in the Seven Years' War*, p. 3.

22. Quoted in Kennett, *French Armies in the Seven Years' War*, p. x; quoted in Carroll, *Wolfe and Montcalm*, p. 50.

23. CO 5/48, ff.187–88.

24. Parkman, *Montcalm and Wolfe*, p. 228.

25. CO 5/48, ff.187–88.

26. Trigger, *Handbook*, p. 153.

27. Brumwell, *White Devil*, pp. 198–201.

28. Ibid., pp. 91–92.

29. Ibid., p. 257.

30. Peckham, *Colonial Wars*, p. 48.

31. Bearor, *Leading by Example*, p. 49.

32. Brumwell, *White Devil*, pp. 35–37.

33. Bearor, *Leading by Example*, pp. 47, 53.

34. Fournier, *Combattre pour la France en Amérique*, p. 518.

35. Malartic, *Journal*, p. 95.

36. O'Callaghan and Fernow, *Documents*, p. 549; Casgrain, *Collection des manuscrits du maréchal de Lévis*, 3:28–29.

37. For an exhaustive discussion of the colonial regulars, see Gallup and Shaffer, *La Marine.*

38. Mary McD. Maude, ed., *Dictionary of Canadian Biography*, vol. 3, pp. xvii–xviii; Windrow, *Montcalm's Army*, pp. 13–14.

39. O'Callaghan and Fernow, *Documents*, p. 571; Stoetzel, *Encyclopedia of the French & Indian War*, p. 128.

40. Bearor, *Leading by Example*, pp. 119–32; Kennett, *French Armies in the Seven Years' War*, pp. 58–59.

41. CO 5/48, ff.187–88.

42. Malartic, *Journal*, p. 96.

43. CO 5/48, ff.187–88. *Bougainville Journals*, pp. 87–88.

44. Malartic, *Journal*, p. 95.

45. Ibid., p. 97.

46. Malartic, *Journal*, p. 96; *Bougainville Journals*, p. 125.

47. CO 5/48, ff.187–88. *Bougainville Journals*, p. 88.

48. Bearor, *Leading by Example*, p. 4.

49. Anderson, *Crucible of War*, p. 117.

50. *Bougainville Journals*, p. 92.

51. Brumwell, *White Devil*, pp. 26–27.

52. *Bougainville Journals*, pp. 92, 94, 96; Parkman, *Montcalm and Wolfe*, p. 224.

53. *Bougainville Journals*, p. 94.

54. CO 5/48, ff.184–86.

55. Brumwell, *White Devil*, pp. 28–29.

56. Information obtained at the Crown Point Museum.

57. Ranger Brown's Narrative, in *Narratives of the French and Indian War*, Eastburn, Putnam, and Hawks, pp. 13–17 (hereafter cited as *Narratives of the French and Indian War*); Malartic, *Journal*, p. 98.

58. *Bougainville Journals*, p. 95; CO 5/48, ff.187–88.

59. Now known as Rogers Rock in memory of the ranger officer.

60. O'Callaghan and Fernow, *Documents*, p. 571.

61. Ibid.

62. CO 5/48, ff.184–86.

63. *Bougainville Journals*, p. 95.

Chapter Three: Rigaud's Winter Raid

1. Stoetzel, *Encyclopedia of the French & Indian War*, p. 140.

2. O'Toole, *White Savage*, p. 39.

3. Crocker, *Braddock's March*, p. 226.

4. Stark, *Memoir and Official Correspondence*, pp. 20–21 is the source of the Saint Patrick's Day story, and Brumwell, *Redcoats*, pp. 12, 60, 105, and 108 provides ample evidence of the 44th's Irish bent and predilection for debauchery.

5. Spruce beer was an antiscorbutic often doled out to troops serving in the American wilderness. It was made from the outer sprigs of the spruce tree, water, hops, molasses, and a little ginger.

6. Griffis, *Sir William Johnson and the Six Nations*, p. 160.

7. LO 4395; LO 6686.

8. Engineer Gordon's report, in *Military Affairs in North America*, Pargellis, pp. 177–80.

9. LO 2069, 2242; Pouchot, *Memoir Upon the Late War*, p. 62.

10. *Bougainville Journals*, p. 97.

11. CO 5/48, ff.4.

12. Ibid.

13. Pargellis, *Military Affairs in North America*, p. 178.

14. CO 5/48, ff.184–86, 187–88.

15. CO 5/48, ff.137–54.

16. O'Callaghan and Fernow, *Documents*, p. 571.

17. CO 5/48, ff.175–76.

18. WO 34/101, ff.88–90.

19. Ibid.

20. Ibid.

21. *Bougainville Journals*, p. 96.

22. CO 5/48, ff.184–86.

23. *Bougainville Journals*, p. 96.

24. Scull, *Montresor Journals*. Quoted in Hill, *Old Fort Edward Before 1800*, p. 113.

25. CO 5/48, ff.175–76.

26. O'Callaghan and Fernow, *Documents*, p. 571.

27. *Bougainville Journals*, p. 96.

28. Ibid.

29. WO 34/101, ff.88–90.

30. CO 5/48, ff.175–76.

31. Lucier, *French and Indian War Notices*, p. 218.

32. *Bougainville Journals*, p. 96; WO 34/101, ff.88–90. As the French used a white banner in battle, they used a red one to indicate a temporary truce during this period.

33. WO 34/101, ff.88–90.

34. CO 5/48, ff.175–76; Stark, *Memoir and Official Correspondence*, p. 22.

35. CO 5/48, ff.173–74.

36. *Bougainville Journals*, p. 97.

37. Ibid., p. 97. Stark, *Memoir and Official Correspondence*, p. 22.

38. CO 5/48, ff.175–76.

39. WO 34/101, ff.88–90.

40. *Bougainville Journals*, p. 97, CO 5/48, ff.175–76.

41. WO 34/101, ff.88–90.

42. Ibid.

43. CO 5/48, ff.177–78.

44. Ibid.

45. WO 34/101, ff.88–90.

46. CO 5/48, ff.184–86.

47. *Bougainville Journals*, p. 97.

48. *Bougainville Journals*, p. 97; Bearor, *Leading by Example*, pp. 123–24.

49. O'Callaghan and Fernow, *Documents*, p. 572.

50. WO 34/101, ff.88–90.

51. WO 34/101, ff.88–90; CO 5/48, ff.179–80.

52. Lucier, *French and Indian War Notices*, p. 229.

53. O'Callaghan and Fernow, *Documents*, p. 572.

54. Malartic, *Journal*, pp. 101–2.

55. Lucier, *French and Indian War Notices*, p. 260.

56. Malartic, *Journal*, pp. 101–2; Fournier, *Combattre pour la France en Amérique*, p. 220.

57. Stark, *Memoir and Official Correspondence*, p. 23.

58. LO 4642b.

59. CO 5/48, ff.137–54.

Chapter Four: The Provincials

1. Anderson, *Crucible of War*, pp. 172–73, 179.

2. Ibid., p. 185.

3. Peckham, *Colonial Wars*, p. 160.

4. Anderson, *A People's Army*, p. 13; Putnam's Journal for 1757, in *Narratives of the French and Indian War*, p. 75; Stoetzel, *Encyclopedia of the French & Indian War*, p. 302; Casterline, *Colonial Tribulations*, pp. 6, 31.

5. Steele, *Betrayals*, p. 96; Frye's Journal, in *Port Folio*, Dennie and Hall, p. 357; CO 5/48, ff.5.

6. Anderson, *A People's Army*, p. 55.

7. Ibid., pp. 39–43.

8. Ibid., p. 52.

9. Ibid., pp. 39–41.

10. Ibid., pp. 38–39, 225. Prior to decimalization in 1971, there were twelve pennies in a shilling and twenty shillings in a pound.

11. Rufus Putnam's Journal for 1757, in *Narratives of the French and Indian War*, p. 91.

12. Parkman, *Montcalm and Wolfe*, p. 149.

13. Anderson, *A People's Army*, pp. 53–54.

14. Gridley, *Diary*, p. 27; O'Toole, *White Savage*, pp. 290–98; Brown, *Pauline Elizabeth Hopkins*, pp. 20–25.

15. Mason, *Diary of Jabez Fitch*, p. ii.

16. Gridley, *Diary*, pp. 56, 39; Thomas L. Doughton, "Nedson, Dorus and Dixon Families: Nineteenth-Century Native Indian Community at the Massachusetts and Connecticut Border," http://freepages.genealogy.rootsweb.ancestry.com/~massasoit/nedson.htm.

17. WO 41/66, ff.39–48.

18. Anderson, *A People's Army*, pp. 70–72.

19. Charles Rufus Harte, "Connecticut's Iron and Copper, Part 1," *Sixtieth Annual Report of the Connecticut Society of Civil Engineers, 1944*, http://www.peabody.yale.edu/collections/min/CT_Minerals_Pt1.pdf; Harris Family Tree website, http://www.gurganus.org/ourfamily/ browse.cfm?pid=96104.

20. Gridley, *Diary*, p. 23.

21. Anderson, *A People's Army*, p. 72.

22. Town of Ancram, NY, website, http://www.townofancram.org/history.

23. Gridley, *Diary*, p. 24.

24. Captain Franklin Ellis, "The Settlement of Claverack, 1878," http:// www.usgennet.org/usa/ny/county/columbia/clav/settlemt_clav.htm.

25. Anderson, *A People's Army*, p. 217.

26. Ibid., pp. 118, 156, 196–211.

27. LO 1929.

28. Mason, *Diary of Jabez Fitch*, p. 4; Stoetzel, *Encyclopedia of the French & Indian War*, p. 302.

29. Ford, *General Orders of 1757*, p. 3.

30. Gridley, *Diary*, p. 25.

31. Lyman, *General Orders of 1757*, pp. 2–3.

32. Gridley, *Diary*, p. 24; Anderson, *A People's Army*, p. 85.

33. Gridley, *Diary*, p. 25; Randall and Farnsworth Lines, Eleventh Generation website, http://www.pcez.com/~bigshoe/du/ Farr/randall.html.

34. Gridley, *Diary*, p. 27.

35. Bearor, *Leading by Example*, p. 116, 7n.

36. Gridley, *Diary*, p. 27; Anderson, *A People's Army*, p. 72.

37. Stoetzel, *Encyclopedia of the French & Indian War*, p. 165.

38. Putnam's Journal for 1757, in *Narratives of the French and Indian War*, pp. 75–77.

39. Benson, *Kalm's Travels in North America*, p. 369.

40. Gridley, *Diary*, pp. 28–29.

41. Ford, *General Orders of 1757*, p. 4.

42. Hervey, *Journals*, p. 26.

43. Bearor, *Leading by Example*, p. 110; LO 1342.

44. Ford, *General Orders of 1757*, p. 12.

45. Holmes, *Redcoat*, p. 313.

46. Gridley, *Diary*, p. 31.

47. Anderson, *A People's Army*, p. 131; Gridley, *Diary*, pp. 28–29.

48. Putnam, *Journal*, p. 78.

49. Hervey, *Journals*, p. 27; LO 1342.

50. Mason, *Diary of Jabez Fitch*, p. 2.

CHAPTER FIVE: FORT EDWARD

1. Hamilton, "John Henry Lydius, Fur Trader at Fort William Henry," pp. 270–80.

2. Anderson, *Crucible of War*, p. 78; Hamilton, "John Henry Lydius, Fur Trader at Fort William Henry," p. 279.

3. Starbuck, *Rangers and Redcoats*, pp. 1–14.

4. Ibid., p. 62.

5. Starbuck, *Great Warpath*, pp. 76–77.

6. LO 6686.

7. Lord Loudoun to William Augustus, Duke of Cumberland, 25 April 1757, New York, in *Military Affairs in North America*, Pargellis, p. 347.

8. Brumwell, *Redcoats*, pp. 19, 74; WO 1/1, ff.129–32.

9. Mason, *Diary of Jabez Fitch*, p. 2.

10. Steele, *Betrayals*, pp. 38–39.

11. Quoted in O'Toole, *White Savage*, p. 131.

12. Starbuck, *Rangers and Redcoats*, pp. 16–18; see also Brumwell, *White Devil*, and Rogers, *Journals*.

13. Stoetzel, *Encyclopedia of the French & Indian War*, p. 419.

14. Anderson, *A People's Army*, pp. 95–97; Starbuck, *Great Warpath*, pp. 54–81; Starbuck, *Rangers and Redcoats*, p. 93; Mason, *Diary of Jabez Fitch*, pp. 3–4.

15. LO 3375.

16. Gridley, *Diary*, pp. 32, 40; Mason, *Diary of Jabez Fitch*, p. 3; Anderson, *A People's Army*, p. 100.

17. Starbuck, *Rangers and Redcoats*, pp. 68–77; Mason, *Diary of Jabez Fitch*, p. 17.

18. Starbuck, *Great Warpath*, p. 57.

19. Starbuck, *Massacre at Fort William Henry*, pp. 66–67.

20. Chelsea Pension records, WO 116/5, ff.43, 114.

21. Starbuck, *Excavating the Sutlers' House*, p. 23.

22. O'Toole, *White Savage*, p. 268.

23. Starbuck, *Excavating the Sutlers' House*, pp. 18–19.

24. Bearor, *Leading by Example*, p. 185; LO 2195.

25. Starbuck, *Excavating the Sutlers' House*, pp. 17–36; Brumwell, *White Devil*, p. 23; Mason, *Diary of Jabez Fitch*, pp. 34–35.

26. Scull, *Montresor Journals*, p. 3.

27. Scull, *Montresor Journals*, pp. 3–4.

28. Ford, *General Orders of 1757*, pp. 13, 25.

29. Putnam's Journal for 1757, in *Narratives of the French and Indian War*, p. 40.

30. Anderson, *A People's Army*, pp. 196–223.

31. Mason, *Diary of Jabez Fitch*, p. 16.

32. Anderson, *A People's Army*, pp. 77–78; Ford, *General Orders of 1757*, p. 15; Mason, *Diary of Jabez Fitch*, p. 3.

33. Anderson, *A People's Army*, p. 81.

34. Chelsea Pension records, WO 116/5, ff.46.

35. Ford, *General Orders of 1757*, p. 14; Gridley, *Diary*, pp. 31–32, 36; Anderson, *A People's Army*, pp. 79–80.

36. Lucier, *French and Indian War Notices*, p. 244.

37. Ibid., p. 249.

38. O'Callaghan and Fernow, *Documents*, p. 569.

39. Gridley, *Diary*, p. 34; Mason, *Diary of Jabez Fitch*, pp. 4–5; Malartic, *Journal*, pp. 96, 112–13; Lucier, *French and Indian War Notices*, p. 259; Stoetzel, *Encyclopedia of the French & Indian War*, pp. 265–66; O'Callaghan and Fernow, *Documents*, p. 579; *Bougainville Journals*, p. 116.

40. Gridley, *Diary*, p. 34; Mason, *Diary of Jabez Fitch*, pp. 4–5; Lucier, *French and Indian War Notices*, p. 259; Hill, *Old Fort Edward Before 1800*, pp. 116–17.

41. O'Callaghan and Fernow, *Documents*, pp. 569, 579; Malartic, *Journal*, pp. 112–14.

42. Gridley, *Diary*, p. 34; Mason, *Diary of Jabez Fitch*, pp. 4–5; Lucier, *French and Indian War Notices*, p. 259.

43. Gridley, *Diary*, p. 33; Mason, *Diary of Jabez Fitch*, pp. 2–4; Ford, *General Orders of 1757*, pp. 13, 19, 24.

44. Ford, *General Orders of 1757*, p. 24.

45. Mason, *Diary of Jabez Fitch*, p. 6.

46. Ford, *General Orders of 1757*, pp. 17–18.

47. Mason, *Diary of Jabez Fitch*, p. 6; *Kalm's Travels in North America*, pp. 362–63.

48. Knox's Journal, in *Redcoats*, Brumwell, p. 150.

49. Hill, *Old Fort Edward Before 1800*, pp. 116–17.

50. Mason, *Diary of Jabez Fitch*, pp. 6–7.

51. Lucier, *French and Indian War Notices*, p. 262; WO 71/66, fols. 332–346; WO 116/5, ff.43.

52. Ibid.

53. WO 71/66, fols. 332–46.

54. Ibid.

55. LO 6076.

56. WO 71/66, fols. 332–46.

57. Anderson, *A People's Army*, pp. 122–23.

58. Gridley, *Diary*, pp. 33–38.

59. GCM records, WO 71/65, ff.369–81.

60. Mason, *Diary of Jabez Fitch*, p. 7.

61. Starbuck, *Rangers and Redcoats*, pp. 80, 90.

62. A reference to eel fishing is made in the General Court-Martial of Peter Davis, WO 71/65, ff.369–78; Ford, *General Orders of 1757*, p. 18; LO 2069.

63. Putnam's Journal for 1757, in *Narratives of the French and Indian War*, p. 85; Mason, *Diary of Jabez Fitch*, p. 24.

64. Mason, *Diary of Jabez Fitch*, pp. 26–27, 36.

65. Ibid., pp. 12–13.

66. Anderson, *A People's Army*, p. 167.

67. Ibid., pp. 116–20.

68. Ibid., p. 116; *Bougainville Journals*, p. 90.

69. Starbuck, *Excavating the Sutlers' House*, pp. 60–61.

70. Ibid., p. 49.

71. Starbuck, *Excavating the Sutlers' House*, p. 49; Mason, *Diary of Jabez Fitch*, p. 35.

72. Starbuck, *Excavating the Sutlers' House*, pp. 93–98.

73. Anderson, *A People's Army*, pp. 118–19.

74. Mason, *Diary of Jabez Fitch*, p. 14; Gridley, *Diary*, p. 43.

75. Mason, *Diary of Jabez Fitch*, p. 4.

76. Starbuck, *Excavating the Sutlers' House*, pp. 99–106; Mason, *Diary of Jabez Fitch*, p. 37.

77. O'Toole, *White Savage*, p. 304.

78. Malartic, *Journal*, p. 116.

79. Gridley, *Diary*, p. 37; Brumwell, *Redcoats*, p. 166.

80. *Bougainville Journals*, p. 117.

CHAPTER SIX: MONTRÉAL

1. Benson, *Kalm's Travels in North America*, pp. 411–14.

2. *Bougainville Journals*, p. 116.

3. *Bougainville Journals*, p. 117; Anderson, *Crucible of War*, p. 187; Parkman, *Montcalm and Wolfe*, p. 236.

4. Johnson, *American Woodland Indians*, p. 41.

5. O'Toole, *White Savage*, p. 54.

6. Trigger, *Handbook*, pp. 772–77.

7. *Bougainville Journals*, p. 132; Trigger, *Handbook*, pp. 725–42.

8. O'Toole, *White Savage*, p. 221.

9. *Bougainville Journals*, p. 45.

10. Trigger, *Handbook*, pp. 725–42.

11. Johnson, *American Woodland Indians*, p. 36.

12. Trigger, *Handbook*, pp. 747, 777; Blackbird, *History of the Ottawa and Chippewa*, p. 79; Johnson, *American Woodland Indians*, p. 42.

13. Pouchot, *Memoir Upon the Late War*, 1:82–83.

14. Trigger, *Handbook*, p. 708; *Bougainville Journals*, p. 8.

15. *Bougainville Journals*, p. 9.

16. *Bougainville Journals*, p. 120; Debo, *History of the Indians*, p. 13; Trigger, *Handbook*, pp. 213–39.

17. Trigger, *Handbook*, pp. 686–87.

18. Ibid., p. 636; Bearor, *Leading by Example*, pp. 78–79.

19. Pouchot, *Memoir Upon the Late War*, 1:79; Trigger, *Handbook*, p. 644.

20. *Bougainville Journals*, pp. 117, 151; Debo, *History of the Indians*, pp. 10–11.

21. *Bougainville Journals*, pp. 112–22.

22. Ibid., pp. 108, 115.

23. Ibid., pp. 112–22.

24. Louis-Joseph de Montcalm to his mother, in *Montcalm and Wolfe*, Parkman, pp. 187–88.

25. *Bougainville Journals*, p. 149.

26. Ibid., p. 120.

27. Ibid., pp. 111–12.

28. Ibid., p. 115.

29. Louis-Joseph de Montcalm to Madame Catherine Hérault, 30 June 1757, in *Bougainville Journals*, p. 331.

30. *Bougainville Journals*, pp. 120–21.

31. Louis-Joseph de Montcalm to François-Charles de Bourlamaque, Montréal, 28 June 1757, in *Collection des manuscrits du maréchal de Lévis*, Casgrain, 5:178.

32. *Bougainville Journals*, pp. 122–23; Trigger, *Handbook*, pp. 472–79; Johnson, *American Woodland Indians*, p. 12.

33. *Bougainville Journals*, pp. 122–23; Trigger, *Handbook*, pp. 376–77.

34. Brumwell, *White Devil*, p. 127.

35. Casgrain, *Collection des manuscrits du maréchal de Lévis*, 3:232.

36. Malartic, *Journal*, p. 109, 1n; O'Callaghan and Fernow, *Documents*, pp. 574–75.

37. *Bougainville Journals*, pp. 122–23.

38. Halpenny, *Dictionary of Canadian Biography*, p. 406.

39. Pouchot, *Memoir Upon the Late War*, pp. 63–64, 76; Parkman, *Montcalm and Wolfe*, p. 205.

40. Stoetzel, *Encyclopedia of the French & Indian War*, p. 257; Norall, *Bourgmont*, p. 86.

41. *Bougainville Journals*, p. 123. This is a quotation from Virgil.

42. Lewis, *For King and Country*, pp. 80–81.

43. Trigger, *Handbook*, p. 372.

44. Lewis, *For King and Country*, p. 80.

45. O'Toole, *White Savage*, p. 105; Lewis, *For King and Country*, pp. 79–80.

46. Lewis, *For King and Country*, p. 81.

47. *Bougainville Journals*, p. 123.

48. O'Callaghan and Fernow, *Documents*, p. 560.

49. *Bougainville Journals*, pp. 123–24.

50. Trigger, *Handbook*, pp. 470–71.

51. From *Account of Remarkable Occurrences in the Life of Col. James Smith*, written by himself, in *Montcalm and Wolfe*, Parkman, p. 114.

52. From Ranger Brown's Narrative, in *Narratives of the French and Indian War*, 1:50–65.

53. *Bougainville Journals*, pp. 124, 150.

54. Suthren, *Sea Has No End*, pp. 54–55, 184.

55. *Bougainville Journals*, p. 124.

56. Elements of this paragraph are taken from a description of William Johnson's adoption into the Mohawk tribe. As the Caughnawaga were also Mohawks, both ceremonies would have shared much in common. See O'Toole, *White Savage*, p. 68.

57. Lewis, *For King and Country*, pp. 77–78; Trigger, *Handbook*, pp. 370–71, 426–27, 776–77.

58. O'Callaghan and Fernow, *Documents*, p. 574.

59. LO 4471.

60. *Bougainville Journals*, pp. 125–30.

Chapter Seven: La Petite Guerre

1. Mason, *Diary of Jabez Fitch*, p. 7.

2. Benson, *Kalm's Travels in North America*, pp. 361–62.

3. Mason, *Diary of Jabez Fitch*, p. 7.

4. Ibid., p. 8.

5. Humphreys, *Essay on Life of Israel Putnam*, p. 48; *Bougainville Journals*, p. 136.

6. Humphreys, *Essay on Life of Israel Putnam*, p. 49; Mason, *Diary of Jabez Fitch*, p. 9.

7. The Official Diary of Lieutenant–General Adam Williamson, NAM MSS 7311, p. 1 (hereafter cited as *Williamson Diary*).

8. Humphreys, *Essay on Life of Israel Putnam*, p. 49; Lucier, *French and Indian War Notices*, pp. 278–79; Putnam's Journal for 1757, in *Narratives of the French and Indian War*, p. 82.

9. *Bougainville Journals*, pp. 121, 156.

10. Putnam's Journal for 1757, in *Narratives of the French and Indian War*, p. 82.

11. Mason, *Diary of Jabez Fitch*, p. 8; *Williamson Diary*, NAM MSS 7311, p. 1.

12. Scull, *Montresor Journals*, p. 18.

13. Humphreys, *Essay on Life of Israel Putnam*, p. 50.

14. *Bougainville Journals*, pp. 121–22.

15. Humphreys, *Essay on Life of Israel Putnam*, p. 51; Mason, *Diary of Jabez Fitch*, p. 9.

16. Humphreys, *Essay on Life of Israel Putnam*, p. 51.

17. Benson, *Kalm's Travels in North America*, p. 9.

18. Humphreys, *Essay on Life of Israel Putnam*, pp. 51–52; *Bougainville Journals*, pp. 121–22.

19. Putnam's Journal for 1757, in *Narratives of the French and Indian War*, p. 83.

20. O'Toole, *White Savage*, p. 80.

21. LO 2196.

22. Pouchot, *Memoir Upon the Late War*, 2:246–47.

23. O'Toole, *White Savage*, p. 139.

24. Brumwell, *Redcoats*, p. 301.

25. *Bougainville Journals*, p. 122.

26. Gallup and Shaffer, *La Marine*, p. 233.

27. Malartic, *Journal*, p. 120; Trigger, *Handbook*, pp. 729, 777.

28. Malartic, *Journal*, pp. 104–25; *Bougainville Journals*, pp. 130–31; Gabriel, *Desandrouins*, pp. 82–83; Lévis, *Journal*, pp. 82–85.

29. O'Toole, *White Savage*, p. 186.

30. Steele, *Betrayals*, p. 96; *Williamson Diary*, NAM MSS 7311, p. 1.

31. Scull, *Montresor Journals*, pp. 18–19.

32. Brumwell, *Redcoats*, p. 74.

33. WO 71/65, ff.365

34. Mason, *Diary of Jabez Fitch*, p. 13.

35. CO 5/48, ff.298–301.

36. LO 3864.

37. O'Toole, *White Savage*, p. 180.

38. Pargellis, *Military Affairs in North America*, p. 345.

39. Bearor, *Leading by Example*, pp. 161–62.

40. *Bougainville Journals*, p. 130.

41. Lucier, *French and Indian War Notices*, p. 279.

42. *Bougainville Journals*, p. 135.

43. Lucier, *French and Indian War Notices*, p. 279.

44. Gridley, *Diary*, p. 43.

45. Putnam's Journal for 1757, in *Narratives of the French and Indian War*, p. 86.

46. *Bougainville Journals*, p. 136.

47. Mason, *Diary of Jabez Fitch*, p. 14.

48. Humphreys, *Essay on Life of Israel Putnam*, pp. 43–44.

49. WO 71/66, fols. 39–52.

50. Ibid.

51. Lucier, *French and Indian War Notices*, p. 280; Scull, *Montresor Journals*, p. 22.

52. Putnam's Journal for 1757, in *Narratives of the French and Indian War*, p. 85; Hill, *Old Fort Edward Before 1800*, p. 126.

53. Putnam's Journal for 1757, in *Narratives of the French and Indian War*, p. 86.

54. *Bougainville Journals*, p. 141.

55. Lévis, *Journal*, p. 84; NY Col. MSS, vol. 10, *Paris Documents*, p. 599.

56. Lucier, *French and Indian War Notices*, pp. 280–81.

57. Ibid.

58. Ibid.; Mason, *Diary of Jabez Fitch*, p. 14; Gridley, *Diary*, pp. 43–44.

59. Scull, *Montresor Journals*, p. 22; Ewing, "Eyewitness Account of Surrender of Fort William Henry," p. 310.

Chapter Eight: Sabbath Day Point

1. *Williamson Diary*, NAM MSS 7311, pp. 1–2.
2. Daniel Webb to Lord Loudoun, 1 August 1757, Fort Edward, CO 5/48, fols. 298–301.
3. Lévis, *Journal*, p. 87.
4. Casterline, *Colonial Tribulations*, pp. 6, 121.
5. LO 4245.
6. Bellico, *Sails and Steam in the Mountains*, p. 23; LO 4408.
7. Cooper, *Last of the Mohicans*, p. 189.
8. Stoetzel, *Encyclopedia of the French & Indian War*, pp. 450–51.
9. *Bougainville Journals*, p. 143.
10. Ibid., pp. 140–41; Lévis, *Journal*, pp. 86–87.
11. *Bougainville Journals*, pp. 140–41.
12. *Bougainville Journals*, p. 142; *Lloyd's Evening Post and English Chronicle*, September 2, 1757.
13. *Lloyd's Evening Post and English Chronicle*, September 2, 1757.
14. *Lloyd's Evening Post and English Chronicle*, September 2, 1757; *Bougainville Journals*, pp. 142–43; WO 116/5, fol. 234; CO 5/48, fols. 298–301; Pierre Roubaud's letter, in *Jesuit Relations and Allied Documents: Travels and Explorations of the Jesuit Missionaries in New France, 1610–1791*, Thwaites, http://www.archive.org/stream/jesuitrelations36jesug-oog/jesuitrelations36jesugoog_djvu.txt (hereafter cited as *Roubaud's Letter*).
15. *Lloyd's Evening Post and English Chronicle*, September 2, 1757; *Bougainville Journals*, pp. 142–43; WO 116/5, fol. 234; CO 5/48, fols. 298–301; *Roubaud's Letter*.
16. Casterline, *Colonial Tribulations*, p. 68.
17. Lévis, *Journal*, p. 87.
18. *Roubaud's Letter*.
19. Pouchot, *Memoir Upon the Late War*, 2:257–58; Brumwell, *White Savage*, p. 93.
20. *Bougainville Journals*, p. 144.
21. LO 4471.
22. *Bougainville Journals*, p. 141; *Williamson Diary*, NAM MSS 7311, p. 2.
23. *Lloyd's Evening Post and English Chronicle*, September 2, 1757.

Chapter Nine: The Calm before the Storm

1. Lyman, *General Orders of 1757*, p. 54.
2. CO 5/48, fols. 298–301.
3. Scull, *Montresor Journals*, p. 22.
4. Cooper, *Last of the Mohicans*, pp. 123–24.
5. LO 3728.
6. CO 5/48, ff. 298–301.

7. Steele, *Betrayals*, p. 96; Ewing, "Eyewitness Account of Surrender of Fort William Henry," pp. 310–11; Casterline, *Colonial Tribulations*, p. 72.

8. LO 4395.

9. Starbuck, *Massacre at Fort William Henry*, p. 59.

10. CO 5/48, ff.298–301.

11. Ibid.; Scull, *Montresor Journals*, p. 24.

12. Scull, *Montresor Journals*, p. 24.

13. Scull, *Montresor Journals*, p. 24.

14. HL, LO 4479.

15. Steele, "Suppressed Official Report of Siege at Fort William Henry," p. 346; CO 5/48, ff.298–301.

16. Scull, *Montresor Journals*, p. 24.

17. "Letters of George Bartman," p. 419.

18. LO 4479.

19. CO 5/48, ff.298–301.

20. Steele, "Suppressed Official Report of Siege at Fort William Henry," p. 346.

21. Although contemporary sources referred to such cannons as "brass," they were in fact made of bronze.

22. Scull, *Montresor Journals*, p. 24; Ewing, "Eyewitness Account of Surrender of Fort William Henry," p. 311; *Williamson Diary*, NAM MSS 7311, p. 3; Dennie and Hall, *Port Folio*, p. 358.

23. LO 5309.

24. LO 4479.

25. Knox, *Siege of Québec*, p. 222.

26. Crocker, *Braddock's March*, p. 149; LO 3590.

27. LO 4048, 4081.

28. Steele, "Suppressed Official Report of Siege at Fort William Henry," p. 346.

29. Dennie and Hall, *Port Folio*, pp. 356–57.

30. Steele, "Suppressed Official Report of Siege at Fort William Henry," p. 346.

31. Dennie and Hall, *Port Folio*, p. 357; *Williamson Diary*, NAM MSS 7311, p. 3; Ewing, "Eyewitness Account of Surrender of Fort William Henry," p. 311; Hays, *Journal*, p. 146.

CHAPTER TEN: MONTCALM'S ADVANCE

1. *Bougainville Journals*, pp. 146–52.

2. Stoetzel, *Encyclopedia of the French & Indian War*, pp. 462–63; Lévis, *Journal*, p. 88; Fournier, *Combattre pour la France en Amérique*, p. 557.

3. *Williamson Diary*, NAM MSS 7311, p. 1; *Bougainville Journals*, p. 116.

4. Steele, *Betrayals*, p. 229.

5. Stoetzel, *Encyclopedia of the French & Indian War*, pp. 260–62; Dodge, *Relief is Greatly Wanted*, p. 126.

6. *Bougainville Journals*, p. 154.

7. Macleod, *Canadian Iroquois and the Seven Years' War*, p. 100.

8. Lévis, *Journal*, pp. 92–93.

9. Lapause, *Journal en partant de Montréal*, p. 346; Fournier, *Combattre pour la France en Amérique*, p. 513.

10. Lévis, *Journal*, pp. 93–94.

11. *Bougainville Journals*, pp. 154–57.

12. *Roubaud's Letter.*

13. CO 5/48, ff.308.

14. *Bougainville Journals*, p. 156.

15. *Roubaud's Letter;* NY Col. MSS, vol. 8, pp. 600–601; *Bougainville Journals*, p. 157.

16. *Bougainville Journals*, p. 158.

17. Ibid., 158; *Roubaud's Letter.*

18. *Roubaud's Letter.*

Chapter Eleven: The First Day

1. *Roubaud's Letter;* Hays, *Journal.*

2. CO 5/48, ff.306–7.

3. *Bougainville Journals*, p. 160.

4. Ibid., p. 160.

5. Dennie and Hall, *Port Folio*, p. 357.

6. Steele, "Suppressed Official Report of Siege at Fort William Henry," p. 344. The sources are contradictory as to the exact composition of the fort's garrison during the siege. On November 1, 1757, Monro wrote that there were one hundred regulars, two hundred provincials, two officers of the 35th, one officer of the Royal Americans, and thirty sailors.

7. Hays, *Journal*, p. 146.

8. Ibid.; Steele, "Suppressed Official Report of Siege at Fort William Henry," p. 343.

9. CO 5/48, ff.306–7; Mason, *Diary of Jabez Fitch*, p. 17.

10. *Bougainville Journals*, p. 160.

11. Louis-Antoine de Bougainville to Jean-Pierre de Bougainville, 19 August 1757, in *Bougainville Journals*, pp. 331–32.

12. *Bougainville Journals*, p. 160.

13. Putnam's Journal for 1757, in *Narratives of the French and Indian War*, 3n, p. 75.

14. LO 5309.

15. CO 5/48, ff.308.

16. CO 5/48, ff.306–7; Dennie and Hall, *Port Folio*, p. 358; Hays, *Journal*, p. 146.

17. *Bougainville Journals*, p. 159.

18. NY Col. MSS, vol. 13, *Paris Documents*, p. 601; LO 4105.

19. *Roubaud's Letter.*

20. *Relation de la prise du Fort Georges*, p. 7; Fournier, *Combattre pour la France en Amérique*, p. 521.

21. Fournier, *Combattre pour la France en Amérique*, p. 227.

22. Stoetzel, *Encyclopedia of the French & Indian War*, pp. 115–16.

23. NY Col. MSS, vol. 13, *Paris Documents*, p. 601.

24. See Muller's *Attack and Defense of Fortified Places* for further details on siege warfare of the period.

25. NY Col. MSS, vol. 13, *Paris Documents*, p. 601; Stoetzel, *Encyclopedia of the French & Indian War*, pp. 46–47.

26. Stoetzel, *Encyclopedia of the French & Indian War*, pp. 115–16.

27. *Bougainville Journals*, p. 159.

28. Stoetzel, *Encyclopedia of the French & Indian War*, pp. 115–16; Gabriel, *Desandrouins*, pp. 87–88; Hays, *Journal*, p. 146.

29. CO 5/48, ff.308.

30. Steele, "Suppressed Official Report of Siege at Fort William Henry," p. 343; Dennie and Hall, *Port Folio*, p. 358.

31. Steele, "Suppressed Official Report of Siege at Fort William Henry," p. 344.

32. *Bougainville Journals*, pp. 159–60.

33. Hays, *Journal*, p. 147.

34. *Roubaud's Letter*.

35. *Bougainville Journals*, p. 160.

36. CO 5/48, ff.308; *Fitch Diary*, p. 17; Gridley, *Diary*, p. 46; LO 4081

37. CO 5/48, ff.306–7.

38. *Bougainville Journals*, p. 168.

39. Ibid., p. 159.

40. Lévis, *Journal*, pp. 98–99; NY Col. MSS, vol. 13, *Paris Documents*, pp. 601–2.

41. *Williamson Diary*, NAM MSS 7311, p. 3.

42. Scull, *Montresor Journals*, p. 26.

43. Putnam's Journal for 1757, in *Narratives of the French and Indian War*, p. 87.

44. "Letters of George Bartman," p. 419.

45. Ibid.

Chapter Twelve: Opening the Trenches

1. Malartic, *Journal*, pp. 137–39.

2. *Bougainville Journals*, p. 160.

3. Ibid., p. 161.

4. "Account of Attack and Taking of Fort William Henry," p. 95.

5. *Bougainville Journals*, p. 162.

6. *Roubaud's Letter*.

7. LO 4395, 4923; Steele, *Betrayals*, pp. 97–99; Steele, "Suppressed Official Report of Siege at Fort William Henry," p. 344.

8. *Roubaud's Letter*.

9. NY Col. MSS, vol. 13, *Paris Documents*, p. 602.

10. Steele, *Betrayals*, p. 100; LO 4061.

11. Sisler Locy Davis Bloomberg Genealogy website, http://www.diane-sisler.com/sisler–p/p435.htm#i22428.

12. Hays, *Journal*, p. 147.

13. Dennie and Hall, *Port Folio*, p. 359.

14. Hays, *Journal*, p. 147.

15. "Letters of George Bartman," p. 421.

16. *Roubaud's Letter*.

17. *Bougainville Journals*, p. 162.

18. *Williamson Diary*, NAM MSS 7311, p. 3; Hays, *Journal*, p. 147.

19. NY Col. MSS, vol. 13, *Paris Documents*, p. 602.

20. CO 5/48, ff.306–7.

21. *Williamson Diary*, NAM MSS 7311, p. 3.

22. *Bougainville Journals*, p. 162.

23. NY Col. MSS, vol. 13, *Paris Documents*, p. 602.

24. *Bougainville Journals*, p. 162.

25. *Bougainville Journals*, p. 162; Malartic, *Journal*, pp. 138–39.

26. Malartic, *Journal*, p. 139.

27. *Roubaud's Letter*.

28. Ibid.

29. *Bougainville Journals*, p. 163.

30. NY Col. MSS, vol. 13, *Paris Documents*, pp. 602–3.

31. *Bougainville Journals*, pp. 164–65.

32. Dennie and Hall, *Port Folio*, p. 359.

33. *Williamson Diary*, NAM MSS 7311, p. 3.

34. NY Col. MSS, vol. 13, *Paris Documents*, p. 603.

35. Dennie and Hall, *Port Folio*, p. 359.

36. Sisler Locy Davis Bloomberg Genealogy website, http://www.diane-sisler.com/sisler–p/p435.htm#i22428.

CHAPTER THIRTEEN: THE BOMBARDMENT

1. *Bougainville Journals*, p. 166.

2. *Williamson Diary*, NAM MSS 7311, p. 3.

3. Dennie and Hall, *Port Folio*, p. 359.

4. *Roubaud's Letter*.

5. Hays, *Journal*, p. 147.

6. Dennie and Hall, *Port Folio*, pp. 359–60.

7. LO 4395.

8. *Williamson Diary*, NAM MSS 7311, p. 3; Hays, *Journal*, p. 147.

9. Dennie and Hall, *Port Folio*, p. 360.

10. Dodge, *Relief is Greatly Wanted*, pp. 69–70. From a later document, a return of guns in the fort at the time of the capitulation written by Captain Collins of the Royal Artillery on August 20, it would appear that Monro was mistaken. The two 10-pounders he refers to as having burst were actually 18-pounders.

11. Dodge, *Relief is Greatly Wanted*, p. 70.

12. Gabriel, *Desandrouins*, p. 90; Stoetzel, *Encyclopedia of the French &*
Indian War, p. 115.
13. *Bougainville Journals*, pp. 161–62, 166.
14. Casterline, *Colonial Tribulations*, p. 76.
15. NY Col. MSS, vol. 13, *Paris Documents*, p. 603.
16. Dodge, *Relief is Greatly Wanted*, p. 70.
17. O'Toole, *White Savage*, p. 188; Scull, *Montresor Journals*, pp. 26–27.
18. Scull, *Montresor Journals*, p. 27.
19. "Letters of George Bartman," p. 422.
20. Putnam's Journal for 1757, in *Narratives of the French and Indian*
War, p. 89.
21. Mason, *Diary of Jabez Fitch*, p. 18.
22. *Bougainville Journals*, p. 166.
23. Dennie and Hall, *Port Folio*, p. 360.
24. *Bougainville Journals*, p. 166.
25. Malartic, *Journal*, p. 140.
26. *Roubaud's Letter.*
27. Ibid.
28. *Bougainville Journals*, p. 166.
29. Ibid., pp. 166–67; *Williamson Diary*, NAM MSS 7311, p. 4.
30. Steele, "Suppressed Official Report of Siege at Fort William Henry,"
p. 346.
31. Ibid.
32. NY Col. MSS, vol. 13, *Paris Documents*, p. 603.
33. *Bougainville Journals*, p. 167.
34. Dennie and Hall, *Port Folio*, p. 361.
35. *Bougainville Journals*, p. 167; NY Col. MSS, vol. 13, *Paris Documents*,
p. 603.
36. Dennie and Hall, *Port Folio*, p. 361.
37. Ibid.
38. Hays, *Journal*, pp. 148–49.
39. LO 4395.
40. Hays, *Journal*, p. 149.
41. *Bougainville Journals*, p. 167.
42. NY Col. MSS, vol. 13, *Paris Documents*, p. 613.
43. François Gaston de Lévis to Marc-Rene de Voyer de Paulmy
d'Argenson, 1 September 1757, in *Collection des manuscrits du maréchal de*
Lévis, Casgrain, 10:127–32.
44. "Account of Attack and Taking of Fort William Henry," p. 94;
Ewing, "Eyewitness Account of Surrender of Fort William Henry," p.
312.
45. NY Col. MSS, vol. 13, *Paris Documents*, p. 604.
46. *Roubaud's Letter.*
47. Hays, *Journal*, p. 148.

48. NY Col. MSS, vol. 13, *Paris Documents*, p. 604; *Bougainville Journals*, p. 168.

49. CO 5/48, fols. 312–13; LO 4507.

50. LO 4479, 5309.

51. Dodge, *Relief is Greatly Wanted*, pp. 71–72.

52. Louis-Antoine de Bougainville to Madame Catherine Hérault, 21 April 1768, in *Bougainville Journals*, p. 333; O'Toole, *White Savage*, pp. 189–90.

53. LO 4482.

54. Scull, *Montresor Journals*, p. 27.

55. *Roubaud's Letter*.

56. "Account of Attack and Taking of Fort William Henry," p. 94.

57. NY Col. MSS, vol. 13, *Paris Documents*, p. 604; *Bougainville Journals*, pp. 168–69.

58. "Letters of George Bartman," p. 423.

59. LO 4395.

60. Steele, "Suppressed Official Report of Siege at Fort William Henry," p. 347.

61. Dodge, *Relief is Greatly Wanted*, p. 97.

62. LO 4395.

63. Ewing, "Eyewitness Account of Surrender of Fort William Henry," p. 312.

64. Hays, *Journal*, p. 149.

Chapter Fourteen: Surrender

1. LO 4395.

2. Steele, "Suppressed Official Report of Siege at Fort William Henry," p. 351.

3. NY Col. MSS, vol. 13, *Paris Documents*, p. 625.

4. Dodge, *Relief is Greatly Wanted*, p. 78; Dennie and Hall, *Port Folio*, p. 362.

5. Dodge, *Relief is Greatly Wanted*, p. 103.

6. Dennie and Hall, *Port Folio*, p. 363; "Account of Attack and Taking of Fort William Henry," p. 95.

7. Gabriel, *Desandrouins*, pp. 94–95; Connell, *Plains of Abraham*, pp. 100–101.

8. Gabriel, *Desandrouins*, p. 95.

9. Dennie and Hall, *Port Folio*, p. 363.

10. Ewing, "Eyewitness Account of Surrender of Fort William Henry," p. 313. At Fort Saint Philip in Port Mahon, Minorca, Lt. Gen. William Blakeney held out against a French force of fifteen thousand for two months, losing four hundred of his twenty-eight-hundred-strong garrison in the process. Marshal Armand de Vignerot du Plessis, Duc de Richelieu, granted Blakeney honorable terms of surrender in respect of his gallant defense. Far from being censured for the defeat, Blakeney was awarded an Irish peerage on his return to London.

11. *Bougainville Journals*, pp. 169–70.

12. NY Col. MSS, vol. 13, *Paris Documents*, p. 615.

13. *Roubaud's Letter*.

14. *Bougainville Journals*, p. 170.

15. Gabriel, *Desandrouins*, p. 96.

16. NY Col. MSS, vol. 13, *Paris Documents*, p. 615.

17. Steele, "Suppressed Official Report of Siege at Fort William Henry," p. 347.

18. *Roubaud's Letter*; Steele, "Suppressed Official Report of Siege at Fort William Henry," pp. 348–49.

19. Steele, "Suppressed Official Report of Siege at Fort William Henry," pp. 348–49.

20. Ewing, "Eyewitness Account of Surrender of Fort William Henry," p. 313.

21. Steele, *Betrayals*, p. 112.

22. Steele, "Suppressed Official Report of Siege at Fort William Henry," p. 349.

23. Steele, *Betrayals*, p. 111.

24. LO 4660, 4654.

25. Starbuck, *Massacre at Fort William Henry*, p. 64.

26. *Roubaud's Letter*.

27. NY Col. MSS, vol. 13, *Paris Documents*, p. 615.

28. Steele, "Suppressed Official Report of Siege at Fort William Henry," p. 349.

29. *Bougainville Journals*, pp. 170–72.

30. Dennie and Hall, *Port Folio*, p. 365.

31. *Bougainville Journals*, p. 171.

32. Ibid., p. 332.

33. Rufus Putnam's Journal for 1757, in *Narratives of the French and Indian War*, p. 91.

34. LO 4482.

35. Rufus Putnam's Journal for 1757, in *Narratives of the French and Indian War*, p. 91.

36. Mason, *Diary of Jabez Fitch*, p. 18.

37. Lucier, *French and Indian War Notices*, p. 292.

38. "Letters of George Bartman," p. 423.

39. Steele, "Suppressed Official Report of Siege at Fort William Henry," p. 349.

40. Dennie and Hall, *Port Folio*, p. 365.

CHAPTER FIFTEEN: THE MASSACRE

1. Dennie and Hall, *Port Folio*, pp. 365–66.

2. Steele, "Suppressed Official Report of Siege at Fort William Henry," p. 350.

3. Carver, *Travels Through North-America*, p. 316.

4. Ewing, "Eyewitness Account of Surrender of Fort William Henry," p. 313.

5. Steele, "Suppressed Official Report of Siege at Fort William Henry," pp. 350–51; Dennie and Hall, *Port Folio*, pp. 365–66; LO 4332.

6. *Affidavit of Miles Whitworth, Surgeon of the Massachusetts Regiment, Taken before Governor Pownall, October 17, 1757*, in *Montcalm and Wolfe*, Parkman, p. 473; CO 5/48, fols. 312–13.

7. Carver, *Travels Through North-America*, pp. 316–17.

8. Dennie and Hall, *Port Folio*, p. 366.

9. Knox, *Siege of Québec*, p. 222; Scull, *Montresor Journals*, p. 28; WO 1/973, fols. 1191–92; LO 6792.

10. Brown, *Pauline Elizabeth Hopkins*, p. 17.

11. Trumbull, *History of the Indian Wars*, p. 143.

12. Ewing, "Eyewitness Account of Surrender of Fort William Henry," p. 313; Casterline, *Colonial Tribulations*, p. 182; LO 6664.

13. Brown, *Pauline Elizabeth Hopkins*, pp. 20–25.

14. Dennie and Hall, *Port Folio*, p. 366; Steele, "Suppressed Official Report of Siege at Fort William Henry," p. 351.

15. Steele, "Suppressed Official Report of Siege at Fort William Henry," p. 350.

16. *Roubaud's Letter*.

17. *Bougainville Journals*, p. 172.

18. Carver, *Travels Through North-America*, p. 317.

19. Lucier, *French and Indian War Notices*, p. 295.

20. Carver, *Travels Through North-America*, p. 318.

21. Col. Joseph Frye to Thomas Hubbard, Speaker of the House of Representatives of Massachusetts, 16 August 1757, Albany, NY, in *Montcalm and Wolfe*, Parkman, p. 472.

22. Dennie and Hall, *Port Folio*, p. 366.

23. *Roubaud's Letter*.

24. Steele, "Suppressed Official Report of Siege at Fort William Henry," p. 351.

25. Carver, *Travels Through North-America*, pp. 318–19.

26. CO 5/48, fols. 312–13.

27. *Bougainville Journals*, p. 175.

28. *Roubaud's Letter*.

29. Mante, *History of the Late War in North America*, p. 95.

30. *Bougainville Journals*, pp. 172–73; *Roubaud's Letter*.

31. *Roubaud's Letter*.

32. Carver, *Travels Through North-America*, pp. 320–21.

33. Coffin, "Ride to Piggwacket," p. 285.

34. Carver, *Travels Through North-America*, pp. 321–24.

35. Trumbull, *History of the Indian Wars*, p. 143.

36. "Prisoners at Fort William Henry, 1757," http://genforum.genealogy.com/7yearswar/messages/24.html.

37. Trumbull, *History of the Indian Wars*, pp. 143–44.

38. Ewing, "Eyewitness Account of Surrender of Fort William Henry," p. 313.

39. Steele, *Betrayals*, pp. 129–48; Dodge, *Relief is Greatly Wanted*, pp. 95–98.

40. Belknap, *History of New Hampshire*, p. 231.

41. Dennie and Hall, *Port Folio*, pp. 366–68.

42. Dodge, *Relief is Greatly Wanted*, p. 96.

43. Ewing, "Eyewitness Account of Surrender of Fort William Henry," p. 314.

44. *Bougainville Journals*, p. 173

45. Steele, *Betrayals*, pp. 119–20.

46. *Roubaud's Letter*.

47. LO 4654.

48. LO 4332.

49. Martineau, *History of the Royal Sussex Regiment*, p. 40.

50. Steele, *Betrayals*, p. 121.

51. Pouchot, *Memoir Upon the Late War*, 1: p. 91.

52. Rogers, *Journals*, p. 56.

53. *Roubaud's Letter*.

54. Scull, *Montresor Journals*, p. 28; "Letters of George Bartman," p. 424.

55. Lucier, *French and Indian War Notices*, p. 294.

56. Mason, *Diary of Jabez Fitch*, p. 19.

57. Gridley, *Diary*, p. 49.

58. Scull, *Montresor Journals*, p. 28.

59. Malartic, *Journal*, pp. 146–47.

60. Rogers, *Journals*, p. 66.

61. Gabriel, *Desandrouins*, p. 97; *Roubaud's Letter*.

62. Anderson, *Crucible of War*, p. 200.

63. Gabriel, *Desandrouins*, pp. 97–98.

64. *Roubaud's Letter*.

65. Scull, *Montresor Journals*, p. 28.

66. Anderson, *Crucible of War*, p. 207.

67. CO 5/48, fols. 312–13.

68. Scull, *Montresor Journals*, p. 28; Mason, *Diary of Jabez Fitch*, p. 19.

69. Trumbull, *History of the Indian Wars*, p. 143.

70. Brown, *Pauline Elizabeth Hopkins*, p. 25.

71. Putnam's Journal for 1757, in *Narratives of the French and Indian War*, p. 75.

72. Mason, *Diary of Jabez Fitch*, p. 20.

73. Gridley, *Diary*, p. 49.

74. *Bougainville Journals*, p. 173; Mason, *Diary of Jabez Fitch*, p. 20; Scull, *Montresor Journals*, p. 29.

75. Gabriel, *Desandrouins*, pp. 97–98; *Roubaud's Letter*.

76. *Bougainville Journals*, p. 173; Mason, *Diary of Jabez Fitch*, p. 20; Scull, *Montresor Journals*, p. 29; Steele, "Suppressed Official Report of Siege at Fort William Henry," p. 351; Steele, *Betrayals*, p. 129; "Ancestors of William Scott McGonigle," http://familytreemaker.genealogy.com/users/m/c/g/Eleanor-J-Mcgonigle/PDFGENE2.pdf.
77. *Bougainville Journals*, p. 174.

CHAPTER SIXTEEN: CAPTIVES

1. *Bougainville Journals*, p. 174.
2. Quoted in Steele, *Betrayals*, p. 131.
3. "Slavery in New France," Wikipedia, last modified January 31, 2011, http://en.wikipedia.org/wiki/Slavery_in_New_France; Ed Crews, "Rattle-Skull, Stonewall, Bogus, Blackstrap, Bombo, Mimbo, Whistle Belly, Syllabub, Sling, Toddy, and Flip: Drinking in Colonial America," Colonial Williamsburg's website, http://www.history.org/foundation/journal/holiday07/drink.cfm; Peter C. Mancall and Joshua L. Rosenbloom, "Slave Prices and The Economy of the Lower South, 1722-1809," http://eh.net/Clio/Conferences/ASSA/Jan_00/rosenbloom.shtml; Benson, *Kalm's Travels in North America*, pp. 207–8.
4. Knox, *Siege of Québec*, p. 222.
5. *Bougainville Journals*, pp. 174–78.
6. *Bougainville Journals*, p. 175; Stoetzel, *Encyclopedia of the French & Indian War*, pp. 260–62.
7. *Bougainville Journals*, p. 179.
8. LO 3893.
9. Scull, *Montresor Journals*, p. 29.
10. WO 71/66, ff.52–56; Scull, *Montresor Journals*, p. 29; Parkman, *Montcalm and Wolfe*, p. 258.
11. Lucier, *French and Indian War Notices*, p. 296.
12. Parkman, *Montcalm and Wolfe*, p. 257.
13. LO 4345.
14. LO 6678.
15. Captain Shaw's Report, in *Colonial Tribulations*, Casterline, appendix 3; LO 4661, 4758, 4778, 6795.
16. Casterline, *Colonial Tribulations*, p. 84.
17. Ibid., p. 116.
18. Ibid., p. 112.
19. Steele, *Betrayals*, p. 142.
20. A list of additional manuscripts of the French and Indian War, prepared from the originals under direction of the library committee, by Charles Henry Lincoln, Worcester, Massachusetts, http://www.archive.org/stream/listofadditional00amer/listofadditional00amer_djvu.txt.
21. Steele, *Betrayals*, pp. 139–40.

CHAPTER SEVENTEEN: VICTORY

1. Inglis, "Colonel George Monro and the Defence of Fort William Henry," pp. 389–403.

2. "Daniel Webb . . . A General Webb of Deceit? Or . . . How Blundering Hypochondriacs and Pompous Lords Lose Battles," On the Trail of the Last of the Mohicans, last modified June 25, 2011, http://www.mohicanpress.com/mo08008.html.

3. Peckham, *Colonial Wars*, pp. 165–66.

4. "A Brief History of Michilimackinac," Mackinac State Historic Parks, http://www.mackinacparks.com/history/index.aspx?l=0,1,4,32,41,46; Kessing, *Menominee Indians of Wisconsin*, p. 74; Blackbird, *History of the Ottawa and Chippewa*, p. 10; Carver, *Travels Through North-America*, p. 326.

5. Putnam, *Journal*, p. 66.

6. *Bougainville Journals*, p. 236; Dictionary of Canadian Biography Online, s.v. "Bourlamaque, François-Charles De," accessed September 20, 2011, http://www.biographi.ca.

7. Putnam, *Journal for 1778*, p. 73; Rogers, *Journals*, p. 97.

8. Bearor, *Leading by Example*, pp. 165–70.

9. Account of Sergeant James Thompson, 78th Highlanders, in *There Was a Soldier*, Konstam, pp. 43–44.

10. Trimen, *Historical Memoir of the 35th*, p. 30.

11. Parkman, *Montcalm and Wolfe*, pp. 286–98.

12. *Bougainville Journals*, p. 286.

13. Ibid., p. 322.

14. Ibid.

15. Pouchot, *Memoir Upon the Late War*, p. 105.

16. Parkman, *Montcalm and Wolfe*, pp. 372–74; Trimen, *Historical Memoir of the 35th*, p. 33; "With Wolfe To Québec," The 35th Foot Project, http://www.btinternet.com/~the35thfootproject/quebec.html.

17. Parkman, *Montcalm and Wolfe*, p. 374.

18. Pouchot, *Memoir Upon the Late War*, pp. 177–95; Anderson, *Crucible of War*, pp. 330–39.

19. *Limerick General Advertiser*, February 18, 1814.

20. Anderson, *Crucible of War*, pp. 344–68; Parkman, *Montcalm and Wolfe*, pp. 387–407.

21. Rogers, *Journals*, p. 116.

22. Brumwell, *White Devil*, pp. 183–237; Rogers, *Journals*, pp. 115–25.

23. Pouchot, *Memoir Upon the Late War*, p. 231.

24. Parkman, *Montcalm and Wolfe*, pp. 422–37; WO/71/68; Trimen, Historical Memoir of the 35th, p. 39.

25. Parkman, *Montcalm and Wolfe*, pp. 438-39; Sheppard, *Empires Collide*, pp. 240–42.

26. Trimen, *Historical Memoir of the 35th*, p. 40; Parkman, *Montcalm and Wolfe*, pp. 439–41; Sheppard, *Empires Collide*, pp. 240–42.

27. Sheppard, *Empires Collide*, pp. 234–45; Parkman, *Montcalm and Wolfe*, pp. 438–45.

28. Dictionary of Canadian Biography Online, s.v. "Bigot, François," accessed September 20, 2011, http://www.biographi.ca.

29. Dictionary of Canadian Biography Online, s.v. "Marin de La Malgue, Joseph," accessed September 20, 2011, http://www.biographi.ca.

Chapter Eighteen: Loose Ends

1. Sheppard, *Empires Collide*, pp. 249-54; Anderson, *Crucible of War*, pp. 535–46, 617–40. This treaty was altered in 1768 after negotiations carried out between William Johnson and the Six Nations. The new boundary followed the south bank of the Ohio River.

2. "Phineas Lyman (1716–1774)," Historical and Genealogical Resources, last modified February 1998, http://www.suffield-library.org/localhistory/lyman.htm.

3. Trimen, *Historical Memoir of the 35th*, p. 184.

4. Mason, *Diary of Jabez Fitch*, introduction.

5. O'Toole, *White Savage*, pp. 326–36; Brumwell, *White Devil*, pp. 279–80.

6. Suthren, *Sea Has No End*, pp. 105–26.

7. Ibid., pp. 163–74.

8. Ibid., pp. 180–84.

9. Ibid., pp. 188–94.

10. Stoetzel, *Encyclopedia of the French & Indian War*, p. 140.

11. Ibid., p. 348.

12. Ibid., p. 266.

13. Suthren, *Sea Has No End*, p. 200.

14. *Limerick General Advertiser*, Feb. 18, 1814.

Epilogue

1. Entick, *General History of the Late War, New York Mercury*, August 22, 1757.

2. Carver, *Travels Through North-America*, pp. 324–26.

Appendix A

1. Starbuck, *Great Warpath*, p. 15.

2. Quoted in Starbuck, *Massacre at Fort William Henry*, p. 16.

3. Starbuck, *Massacre at Fort William Henry*, pp. 18–24; The Fort William Henry Museum & Restoration, http://www.fwhmuseum.com/visitors.html.

BIBLIOGRAPHY

ABBREVIATIONS FOR MANUSCRIPTS

Huntington Library, San Marino, California
LO   Loudoun Papers, Boxes 15–106 inclusive
(1755–1758)
National Archives, Kew, London
CO 5   Colonial Office, America and West Indies
WO 1   War Office, In-Letters
WO 34   Amherst Papers
WO 71   General Courts-Martial, Proceedings
WO 116   Out-Pension Records, Royal Hospital, Chelsea
Admission Books
National Army Museum, Chelsea, London
NAM MSS 7311   The Official Diary of Lieutenant-General Adam
Williamson
New York State Library, Albany
NY Col. MSS   New York Colonial Manuscripts, 1638–1800.

PUBLISHED PRIMARY SOURCES

"An Account of the Attack and Taking of Fort William Henry." In
Dominion of Canada: Report of the Public Archives for the Year 1929,
edited by Arthur G. Doughty. Ottawa: F. A. Acland, 1930.

American Almanac and Repository of Useful Knowledge for the Year 1838.
Vols. 9–10. Boston: Gray and Bowen, 1838.

Bartman, George. "The Siege of Fort William Henry: Letters of George
Bartman." *Huntington Library Quarterly 12*, no.4 (1948–49).

Benson, Adolph B. *Peter Kalm's Travels in North America: The English
Version of 1770.* New York, Dover Publications, 1987.

Blanchet, Jean, ed. *Collection de manuscrits contenant lettres, mémoires, et
autres documents historiques relatifs á la Nouvelle-France.* Vol. 4. Québec:
A. Coté et Cie, 1885.

Carver, Jonathan. *Travels Through the Interior Parts of North-America.*
Walpole, NH: Isaiah Thomas, 1813.

Casgrain, H. R., ed. *Collection des manuscrits du maréchal de Lévis.* Vol. 3,
Lettres de la cour de Versailles au baron de Dieskau, au marquis de
Montcalm et au chevalier de Lévis. Québec: L. J. Demers and Frére,
1890.

———. *Collection des manuscrits du maréchal de Lévis.* Vol. 5, Lettres de
M. de Bourlamaque au chevalier de Lévis. Québec: L. J. Demers and
Frére, 1891.

———. *Collection des manuscrits du maréchal de Lévis*. Vol. 6, Lettres du marquis de Montcalm au chevalier de Lévis. Québec: L. J. Demers and Frére, 1894.

———. *Collection des manuscrits du maréchal de Lévis*. Vol. 10, Lettres de divers particuliers au chevalier de Lévis. Québec: L. J. Demers and Frére, 1895.

Catlin, George, *North American Indians*. New York: Penguin Classics, 2004.

Coffin, Paul. "Ride to Piggwacket." In *The Memoirs and Journals of Rev. Paul Coffin, D. D.* Portland, ME: B. Thurston, 1855.

Dennie, Joseph, and John Elihu Hall. *The Port Folio*. Vols. 40–42; Vols. 220–227 of American Periodical Series, 1800–1850. Philadelphia: Editor and Asbury Dickens, 1819.

Eastburn, Robert, Rufus Putnam, and John Hawks. *Narratives of the French and Indian War*. 2 vols. Cheshire, UK: Leonaur, 2008.

Entick, John. *The General History of the Late War*. London: E. and C. Dilly, 1763.

Ewing, William S., ed. "An Eyewitness Account by James Furnis of the Surrender of Fort William Henry, August 1757." *New York History 42* (July 1961): 307–16.

Ford, C. Worthington, ed. *General Orders of 1757, Issued by the Earl of Loudoun and Phineas Lyman in the Campaign Against the French*. New York: Gilliss Press, 1899.

Gabriel, Charles-Nicolas. *Le maréchal de camp Desandrouins, 1729–1792: Guerre du Canada, 1756–1760; Guerre de l'indépendance américaine, 1780–1782*. Verdun: Renvé-Lallemant, 1887.

Gridley, Luke. *Luke Gridley's Diary of 1757 While in Service in French and Indian War*. Hartford, CT: Case, Lockwood and Brainard, 1906.

Hamilton, Edward P., ed. *Adventure in the Wilderness: The American Journals of Louis Antoine de Bougainville, 1756–1760*. Norman: University of Oklahoma Press, 1990.

Hays, Isaac Minis. *A Journal Kept During the Siege of Fort William Henry, August 1757*. BiblioLife, 2009.

Hervey, William. *Journals of the Hon. William Hervey in North America and Europe, From 1755 to 1814*. Bury St. Edmund's: Paul & Mathew, 1906.

Humphreys, David. *An Essay on the Life of the Honorable Major-General Israel Putnam*. New York and London: Garland Publishing, 1977.

Knox, John. *The Siege of Québec and the Campaigns in North America, 1757–1760*. Mississauga, ON: Pendragon House, 1980.

Lapause, *Journal en partant de Montréal*.

Lévis, François-Gaston. *Journal des campagnes du chevalier de Lévis: En Canada de 1756 à 1760*. Montréal: Beauchemin, 1889.

Lucier, Armand Francis. *French and Indian War Notices Abstracted from Colonial Newspapers, 1756–1757*. Vol. 2. Westminster, MD: Heritage Books, 2007.

Malartic, Anne-Joseph-Hippolyte de Maures, comte de. *Journal des Campagnes au Canada de 1755 à 1760.* Dijon, France, 1890.

Mason, Richard A., ed. *The Diary of Jabez Fitch, Jr. in the French and Indian War, 1757.* Rogers Island Historical Association, 1966.

Muller, John. *The Attack and Defense of Fortified Places.* J. Millan, 1757.

O'Callaghan, E. B., and Berthold Fernow, eds. *Documents Relative to the Colonial History of the State of New York.* Vol. 10, Paris Documents. Albany, NY: Weed, Parsons, 1853–87.

Ogilvie, John. "The Diary of Reverend John Ogilvie, 1750–1759." *Bulletin of the Fort Ticonderoga Museum 10,* no. 5 (February 1961).

Pargellis, S., ed. *Military Affairs in North America, 1748–65: Selected Documents from the Cumberland Papers in Windsor Castle.* New York: D. Appleton-Century, 1936.

Pouchot, Pierre. *Memoir Upon the Late War in North America, Between France and England.* 2 vols. Roxbury, MA: W. Elliot Woodward, 1866.

Putnam, Rufus. *Journal of Gen. Rufus Putnam Kept in Northern New York During Four Campaigns of the Old French and Indian War, 1757–1760.* Albany, NY: Joel Munsell's Sons, 1886.

Relation de la Prise du Fort Georges, ou Guillaume-Henry, situé sur le Lac Saint-Sacrement, & de ce-qui s'est passé cette année en Canada. Paris: Du Bureau d'Adresse, aux Galeries du Louvre, 1757.

Rogers, Robert. *Journals of Robert Rogers of the Rangers: The Exploits of Rogers and the Rangers in His Own Words During 1755–1761 in the French and Indian War.* Cheshire, UK: Leonaur, 2005.

Scull, G. D., John Montresor, and James Gabriel Montresor. *The Montresor Journals.* In Collections of the New-York Historical Society 14. New York: Printed for the Society, 1882.

Stark, Caleb. *Memoir and Official Correspondence of Gen. John Stark.* Concord: G. Parker Lyon, 1860.

Steele, Ian K. "Suppressed Official Report of the Siege and 'Massacre' at Fort William Henry, 1757." *Huntington Library Quarterly 55,* no. 2 (Spring 1992): 339–52.

Thwaites, Reuben Gold, ed. *The Jesuit Relations and Allied Documents: Travels and Explorations of the Jesuit Missionaries in New France, 1610–1791.* Cleveland: Burrows Bros., 1896–1901.

Trimen, Richard, ed. *An Historical Memoir of the 35th Royal Sussex Regiment of Foot.* Whitefish, MT: Kessinger, 2007.

Secondary Sources

Anderson, Fred. *Crucible of War: The Seven Years' War and the Fate of Empire in British North America, 1754–1766.* London: Faber and Faber, 2001.

———. *A People's Army: Massachusetts Soldiers and Society in the Seven Years' War.* New York: Norton, 1984.

Bearor, Bob. *Leading by Example: Partisan Fighters and Leaders of New France, 1660–1760*. Vol. 3. Westminster, MD: Heritage Books, 2007.

Belknap, Jeremy. *The History of New Hampshire*. Vol. 2. Boston: Bradford and Read, 1813.

Bellico, Russell P. *Sails and Steam in the Mountains: A Maritime and Military History of Lake George and Lake Champlain*. Fleischmanns, NY: Purple Mountain Press, 2001.

Blackbird, Andrew J. *History of the Ottawa and Chippewa Indians of Michigan*. Ypsilanti, MI: Ypsilanti Job Printing House, 1887.

Brown, Lois. *Pauline Elizabeth Hopkins: Black Daughter of the Revolution Gender and American Culture*. Chapel Hill, NC: University of North Carolina Press, 2008.

Brumwell, Stephen. *Redcoats: The British Soldier and War in the Americas, 1755–1763*. New York: Cambridge University Press, 2007.

———. *White Devil: A True Story of War, Savagery, and Vengeance in Colonial America*. Cambridge, MA: Da Capo Press, 2006.

Carroll, Joy. *Wolfe and Montcalm: Their Lives, Their Times and the Fate of a Continent*. Richmond Hill, ON: Firefly, 2004.

Casterline, Greg. *Colonial Tribulations: The Survival Story of William Casterline and His Comrades of the New Jersey Blues Regiment French and Indian War, 1755–1757*. Lulu Online Publishing, 2007.

Coffer, William E. *Phoenix: The Decline and Rebirth of the Indian People*. New York: Van Nostrand Reinhold, 1979.

Connell, Brian. *The Plains of Abraham*. London: Readers Union Hodder and Stoughton, 1960.

Cooper, James Fenimore. *The Last of the Mohicans*. London: Wordsworth Editions, 2002.

Crocker, Thomas E. *Braddock's March: How the Man Sent to Seize a Continent Changed American History*. Yardley, PA: Westholme, 2009.

Debo, Angie. *A History of the Indians of the United States*. London: Pimlico, 1995.

Dodge, Edward J. *Relief is Greatly Wanted: The Battle of Fort William Henry*. Westminster, MD: Heritage Books, 2009.

Fournier, Marcel, ed. *Combattre pour la France en Amérique: Les Soldats de la guerre de Sept Ans en Nouvelle–France, 1755–1760*. Montréal: Société Généalogique Canadienne–Française, 2009.

Gallup, Andrew, and Donald F. Shaffer. *La Marine: The French Colonial Soldier in Canada, 1745–1761*. Westminster, MD: Heritage Books, 2008.

Griffis, William Elliot. *Sir William Johnson and the Six Nations*. New York: Dodd, Mead, 1891.

Halpenny, Frances G. *Dictionary of Canadian Biography, 1741–1770*. Vol. 3. Toronto: University of Toronto Press, 1974.

Hamilton, Edward P. "John Henry Lydius, Fur Trader at Fort William Henry." *Bulletin of the Fort Ticonderoga Museum 11*, no. 5 (1964).

Hill, William Henry. *Old Fort Edward Before 1800*. Fort Edward, NY: Honeywood Press, 1956.

Holmes, Richard. *Redcoat: The British Soldier in the Age of Horse and Musket*. New York: Norton, 2002.

Inglis, John. "Colonel George Monro and the Defence of Fort William Henry." *Proceedings of the New York State Historical Association 13* (1914): 389–403.

Johnson, Michael G. *American Woodland Indians*. Oxford: Osprey Publishing, 1990.

———. *Indian Tribes of the New England Frontier*. Oxford: Osprey Publishing, 2006.

Kennett, Lee. *The French Armies in the Seven Years' War*. Durham, NC: Duke University Press, 1967.

Kessing, Felix M. *The Menominee Indians of Wisconsin*. Philadelphia: American Philosophical Society, 1939.

Konstam, Angus. *There Was a Soldier: First-Hand Accounts of the Scottish Soldier from 1707 to the Present Day*. London: Hachette Scotland, 2009.

Lewis, Thomas A. *For King and Country: The Maturing of George Washington, 1748–1760*. New York: John Wiley, 1993.

Macleod, Peter D. *The Canadian Iroquois and the Seven Years' War*. Toronto, ON: Dundurn Press, 1996.

Mante, Thomas. *The History of the Late War in North America and the Islands of the West Indies*. Whitefish, MT: Kessinger, 2005.

Marston, Daniel. *The Seven Years' War*. Oxford: Osprey Publishing, 2001.

Martineau, Gerard Durani. *A History of the Royal Sussex Regiment*. Chichester: Moore and Tillyer, 1953.

McLynn, Frank. *1759: The Year Britain Became Master of the World*. London: Pimlico, 2005.

Norall, Frank. *Bourgmont: Explorer of the Missouri, 1698–1725*. Lincoln, NB: University of Nebraska Press, 1988.

O'Toole, Fintan. *White Savage: William Johnson and the Invention of America*. London: Faber and Faber, 2005.

Page, Thomas. *The Civilization of the American Indians*. Outlet, 1980.

Pargellis, Stanley. *Lord Loudoun in North America*. New Haven, CT: Yale University Press, 1993.

Parkman, Francis. *Montcalm and Wolfe*. New York: Modern Library, 1999.

Peckham, Howard H. *The Colonial Wars, 1689–1762*. Chicago: University of Chicago Press, 1964.

Pocock, Tom. *Battle for Empire: The Very First World War, 1756–63*. London: Michael O'Mara Books, 1999.

Sheppard, Ruth, ed. *Empires Collide: The French and Indian War, 1754–63*. Oxford: Osprey Publishing, 2006.

Starbuck, David R. *Excavating the Sutlers' House: Artifacts of the British Armies in Fort Edward and Lake George.* Hanover, NH: University Press of New England, 2010.

———. *The Great Warpath: British Military Sites from Albany to Crown Point.* Hanover, NH, University Press of New England, 1999.

———. *Massacre at Fort William Henry.* Hanover, NH: University Press of New England, 2002.

———. *Rangers and Redcoats on the Hudson: Exploring the Past on Rogers Island, the Birthplace of the U.S. Army Rangers.* Hanover, NH: University Press of New England, 2004.

Steele, Ian K. *Betrayals: Fort William Henry & the "Massacre."* New York: Oxford University Press, 1990.

Stoetzel, Donald I. *Encyclopedia of the French & Indian War in North America, 1754–1763.* Westminster, MD: Heritage Books, 2008.

Suthren, Victor. *The Sea Has No End: The Life of Louis Antoine de Bougainville.* Toronto: Dundurn Press, 2004.

Trask, Kerry A. *Black Hawk: The Battle for the Heart of America.* New York: Owl Books, 2007.

Trigger, Bruce G., ed. *Handbook of North American Indians. Northeast Vol. 15.* Washington: Smithsonian Institute, 1978.

Trumbull, Henry. *History of the Indian Wars.* Boston: Phillips and Sampson, 1846.

Windrow, Martin. *Montcalm's Army.* Oxford: Osprey Publishing, 1973.

CONTEMPORARY NEWSPAPERS AND MAGAZINES

Drewry's Derby Mercury, Derby, England 1759
Lloyd's Evening Post and British Chronicle, London, England 1757
London Chronicle, London, England 1757
Public Advertiser, London, England 1757
Read's Weekly Journal or British Gazetteer, London, England 1756

ONLINE RESOURCES

The 35th Foot Project
http://www.btinternet.com/~the35thfootproject/georgemunroe.html.
Ancestors of William Scott McGonigle
http://familytreemaker.genealogy.com/users/m/c/g/Eleanor-J-Mcgonigle/PDFGENE2.pdf.
Colonial Williamsburg
http://www.history.org/foundation/journal/holiday07/drink.cfm.
Dictionary of Canadian Biography Online
http://www.biographi.ca.
The Fort William Henry Museum
http://www.fwhmuseum.com/visitors.html.
History of Albany, New York
http://wapedia.mobi/en/History_of_Albany,_New_York.

History of Town of Ancram, New York
http://www.townofancram.org/history.
James Fenimore Cooper Society Website
http://external.oneonta.edu/cooper/articles/nyhistory/1917nyhistory-
holden.html.
Mackinac Website
http://www.mackinacparks.com/history/index.aspx?l=0,1,4,32,41,46.
Mohican Press: Daniel Webb—A General Webb of Deceit?
http://www.mohicanpress.com/mo08008.html.
Our Family History
http://www.dianesisler.com/sisler-p/p435.htm#i22428.
Our Family Tree
http://www.gurganus.org/ourfamily/browse.cfm?pid=96104.
RootsWeb
http://freepages.genealogy.rootsweb.ancestry.com/~massasoit/nedson.htm.
The Settlement of Claverack
http://www.usgennet.org/usa/ny/county/columbia/clav/settlemt_clav.htm.
Slave Prices and the Economy of the Lower South
http://eh.net/Clio/Conferences/ASSA/Jan_00/rosenbloom.shtml.
Suffield Library Local History: Phineas Lyman
http://www.suffield-library.org/localhistory/lyman.htm.
Wikipedia: Slavery in New France
http://en.wikipedia.org/wiki/Slavery_in_New_France.
Wikipedia Web site on HMS *Grafton*
ttp://en.wikipedia.org/wiki/HMS_Grafton_1750.
Yale Peabody Museum of Natural History
http://www.peabody.yale.edu/collections/min/CT_Minerals_Pt1.pdf.

INDEX

Abenaki, xxii, xxiv, 23, 30-32, 36, 42, 65, 107, 138, 161, 173-174, 222, 231, 241, 247, 255, 275, 278
Abercrombie, James, 8, 244-246, 250
Adirondacks, 37
Aix-la-Chapelle, 21
Algonquin, xviii-xix, 96-97, 102, 275, 278, 282
American War of Independence, 264, 266-268, 270, 273
Amherst, Jeffery, 243, 245, 247-248, 250, 254-256, 258-260, 262
Aoussik, 103, 106
Appalachian Mountains, 263, 277
Arapaho, 271
Arbuthnot, William, 166-167, 198-199, 215
Artillery Cove, 179, 186, 199, 201-202, 216, 230, 232
Aubry, Charles Philippe, 252
Augustus, George, 194
Augustus, William (Duke of Cumberland), 2, 42
Avery, Elias, 117

Bald Mountain, 39-40, 158
Barnard, Selah, 221, 226-227
Barnsham, Nathan, 128
Baron Dieskau, xxv-xxvi, 35, 42, 48, 70, 144-145, 204
Bartman, George, 145, 177-178, 183-184, 205, 218
Battle of Bunker Hill, 264
Battle of Bushy Run, 263
Battle of Lake George, 42, 60, 63, 70, 72, 89, 113, 120, 127, 144, 177
Battle of Long Island, 264
Battle of Monongahela, 96
Battle of Saratoga, 264, 266
Battle of the Chesapeake, 266
Battle of the Plains of Abraham, 277
Battle of the Saintes, 268
Battle of Ticonderoga, 275

Beamman, Jonathan, 64
Beanham, Henry, 15
Bean, Josiah, 241
Béarn Regiment, 34, 49, 52, 121-122, 194, 202, 216, 250, 253
Beaver Island, 92
Beaver Wars, 102, 275, 278, 281-284
Beery, Wallace, 277
Belcher, James, 14
Bell, William, 14, 88
Bentheim Regiment, 35
Berryer, Nicolas René, 249
Biben, Amos, 131
Bigot, François, 26, 28, 249
Black Hawk War, 271
Blakeney, Theophilus, 251
Blakeney, William, 211
Bland, Humphrey, 78
Bliss, Jacob, 128
Bloody Pond, 144
Bloom, Thomas, 74
Blunt, William, 79
Boake, Daniel, 66
Board of Ordnance, 143
Boscawen, Edward, 14, 84
Boston Harbor, 266
Bouet, Madeleine Marguerite, 38
Bouquet, Henry, 263
Bourlamaque, François
    bombardment of Fort William Henry and, 200-202, 209
    de Haviland outmaneuvering his troops and, 259
    desertions and, 258
    digging trenches and, 186
    final campaign of 1759 and, 254-255
    interrogation of prisoners and, 121
    massacre and, 225
    memoirs and, 269
    reconnaissance patrol and, 179
    Royal Roussillon and, 122
    siege of Fort William Henry and, 246
    surrender of fort and, 211, 214-216

taking position on left and, 170
Vaudreuil's letter and, 251
war as a game and, 171
wounding of, 257
Bradstreet, John, 262-263, 276
Brewer, Charles Philip, 53
Brigham, Nathan, 256
Bristol, 266
British Indian Department, 268
Brooks, James, 2
Brown Bess muskets, 8, 61, 116
Browne, Thomas, 82, 248
Browne, Warham, 14
Brown, Thomas, 38, 108-109
Brown, William, 264
Brusle, Marie, 238
Burchard, Phineas, 83
Bureau of Ordnance, 227
Burgoyne, John, 264
Burk, John, 226

Cadet, Joseph, 28
Cameron, Duncan, 43
Cameron, John, 74
Campbell, David, 80, 83
Campbell, John, see Lord Loudon
Cape Breton, 65
Cape Scononton, 112
Cardinal Richelieu, 279
Carignan-Salières Regiment, 125
Carleton, Guy, 264
Carver, Jonathon, 222, 224-226, 233,
    244, 270
Caughnawaga, xxiv, xxvi, 23, 42, 106-
    111, 116, 153, 157, 185, 241,
    275-276, 279
Cavenough, John, 128-129
Cayuga, xvii, 122, 281
Chasse, Guillaume, 53
Château de Marly, 104
Chebucks, Solomon, 82
Cherokee, 102
Cheyenne, 271
Chickamauga Wars of 1776–94, 270
Chickasaws, 125
Chief Bomaseen, 31
Chief Hendrick, 120
Chingachgook, 271
Chippewa, xvii, 23, 79, 94-95, 97,

101, 112, 126, 134-135, 244,
    262, 278-279, 281-284
Christie, Gabriel, 177, 194, 217-218
Clarke, John, 5
Cockburn, James, 248
College of the Jesuits, 24
Collier, James, 175
Collins, Thomas
    bursting of mortars and, 209
    causing casualties in the regulars'
        camp and, 187
    damage done to first battery and,
        195
    damage report and, 206
    interrupting the enemy's progress
        and, 180
    position of cannons and, 182
    preparing fort for attack and, 148-
        149
    scourge of metal fatigue and, 197
    second group of survivors and, 231
    senior British artillery officer at
        fort, 167, 170
    under heavy fire and, 192
    well-placed mortar round and, 186
    workers coming under fire and,
        202
Comanche, 271
Connecticut River, 256
Cooper, James Fenimore, 270-271
Cornwallis, Charles, 266
Cory, Thomas, 193
Courtemanche, Joseph, 160
Cowasucks, 31
Crane, John, 74
Crawford, William, 76, 194-195
Crookshanks, Charles, 71
Crookshanks, William, 149, 210
Cueta, 110, 265

Dalyell, James, 246
d'Argenson, Marc-René de Voyer de
        Paulmy, 200
Davis, Peter, 86-87
de Bernetz, Chevalier, 170
de Boschenry, Augustin, 248
de Bougainville, Louis-Antoine
    arguement between Webb and
        Johnson, 203-204

audacious raid of de La Malgue
    and, 126-127
Battle of the Chesapeake and, 266
Battle of the Saintes and, 268
bloated corpse and, 154
blocking de Haviland's troops and,
    258
British landing and, 255
casualties and, 198
cease-fire and, 196-198
ceremonial war dances and, 98
church services of Indians and, 102
command of raid and, 30
command of the *Bien Aime* and,
    266
council at Two Mountains and,
    105-106
death of, 267
de Haviland outmaneuvered troops
    and, 259
dictating terms of surrender and,
    23
digging trenches and, 180
discontent in the army and, 249
early years of, 21
encirclement of fort and, 168
enemy positions and, 193
expedition to circumnavigate the
    globe and, 265-266
gathering intelligence and, 99
Indian council and, 151
Indian culture and, 26, 110-111
Indian desertions and, 155
Indians' behavior and, 188
Indians observing trench digging
    and, 187
Indians' refusal to submit to
    European norms and, 140
Iroquois and, 116
La Licorne and, 275
leaving Montréal and, 111-112
letter to brother and, 22
letter to Madame Catherine
    Hérault and, 101
massacre and, 222
Maximilien de Robespierre and,
    267
Menominee and, 96
Montcalm's advance and, 159

Montcalm's opinion of, 20
Montcalm's zeal for his Majesty's
    service and, 200
Nipissing's magnanimity and, 104,
    168
Onontio's commands and, 189
Pére Jean-Baptiste de Neuville and,
    109
plan of attack and, 154
Potawatomi and, 94
prisoners and, 236-241
Québec and, 24
shadowing a British naval decoy
    and, 252
stoical about mistake and, 205
surrender of Fort William Henry
    and, 211-213, 216-217
Webb's letter and, 185
word of the British landing and,
    254
wounding of, 246
wounding of Ottawa chiefs and,
    135
de Bourgmont, Sieur, 104
de Bourlamaque, François-Charles
    at Sorel and, 258
    batteries of, 209
    de Haviland outmaneuvering
        Bougainville's troops and, 259
    digging trenches and, 186, 200-
        202
    final campaign of 1759 and, 254-
        255
    interrogation of prisoners and, 121
    letter from Vaudreuil and, 251
    massacre and, 225
    memoirs and, 269
    reconnaissance patrol and, 179
    reconnoitering the fort and, 170-
        171
    Royal Roussillon and, 122
    surrender and, 211, 214-216
    wounding of, 246, 257
de Champlain, Samuel, 275
de Combles, Jean-Claude-Henri de
    Lombard, 103, 170
Deerfield, massacre and, 271
de Gaspé, Ignace-Philippe Aubert,
    160, 232

de Gaston, François (Chevalier de
Lévis)
advance to western shore of Lake
George and, 166
advancing on Fort William Henry
and, 162
attempt to dislodge his men from
road and, 168
blocking road to Fort Edward and,
205
bonfires and, 159
British armies converging on
Montréal and, 258
closing on British position and,
167
Col. de Senezergues and, 156
death of, 267
de Montcalm's arrival at lines at,
172
encirclement of fort and, 168
feast on slaughtered bullocks and,
175-176
French illustration of the attack on
Fort William Henry, 181
Indian scouts and, 165
Kanectagon and, 157
massacre and, 225
mauling at the Plains of Abraham
and, 257
military experience and, 155
militia and, 187
Montcalm's issues with Indians
and, 188
Montcalm's plan of attack and, 154
Montcalm's reorganization of
troops and, 179
Montcalm's review and, 155
possibility of an early British collapse and, 169
premier elite of Bourbon France
and, 155
progress report to Montcalm and,
158
reinforcements and, 188
signal fires of, 161
tour of the colony's military outposts and, 22
de Haviland, William, 258-259
de La Corne, Luc

ambush on a British supply train
and, 246
appointed "general" of all the
Indian troops and, 157, 189
Canadian militia and, 156-157
cutting off the entrenched camp
from its water supply and, 183
encouraged the Indians' depredations and, 216, 237
massacre and, 220
Montcalm's plan to capture Fort
William Henry and, 103
Montcalm's reorganization of
troops and, 179
prisoners and, 234
siege of Fort William Henry and,
199
de La Malgue, Joseph Marin
attack on Fort Edward and, 128-
130, 183, 246, 260, 276
audacious raid of, 126
capture of, 252
coming to Putnam's aid and, 247
death of, 260
Dormit's death and, 127
expert on backwoods warfare and,
125
prisoners and, 131, 234
smallpox epidemic and, 144
de La Pause, Jean-Guillaume
Plantavit, 158
de Lignery, François-Marie Le
Marchand, 252
de Longueil, Paul-Joseph Le Moyne,
32
de Lusignan, Paul-Louis Dazemard,
38
de Montcalm, Louis-Joseph
Abercrombie's attack and, 245
arriving at Lévis's lines and, 172
artillery and, 123
at forward trenches and, 195-196
audacious raid of de La Malgue
and, 126
blocking road to Fort Edward and,
205
boarding the boats at Carillon and,
160
bombardment and, 191

bonfires and, 159
bronze 6-pounder and, 235
Bourlamaque's report to, 121
buying back hostages and, 240
cannons and, xiv
Captain Vergor's death and, 253
captives and, 237-238
cease-fire and, 173, 196-197
Cherokee meeting and, 102-103
Chevalier de Lévis and, 155
corruption and, 28
council at Two Mountains and, 106
council of war and, 276
Daniel Webb and, 149
Diamond Point and, 165
digging trenches and, 187
first Atlantic crossing and, 20
Fort Saint Jean and, 100
Fort William Henry's palisades
    and, 123
Fox and, 281
François Bigot's corruption and,
    249
François-Charles de Bourlamaque
    and, 121
friendship with de Bougainville
    and, 20-21
governor of New France and, 27
hatred of Canada and, 19
high country chief's advice and,
    100-101
honor of "a red ribbon" and, 200
Indian allies and, 142, 149
Indian council at Wood Creek and,
    151
Indians' behavior and, 188
Indians killing of cattle and, 169
issues with Indians and, 188-189
Johnson's advance and, 204
Kisensik and, 151-152
leaving Montréal and, 111-112
letter to Lord Loudoun and, 234
Lord Loudoun and, 124, 239
low casualties of siege and, 209
massacre and, 224-225
military buildup of, 122
Monro's complaint to, 230
New France's glittering social cal-
    endar and, 26

Oswego attack and, 12-13, 23, 50
overconfidence of, 252
plan of attack and, 154
plans to distract the British and,
    166
prisoners captured by Mohawk
    scouts and, 122
procrastination of the Indians and,
    99
proposal to attack Fort William
    Henry and, 109-110
raids by Indian allies and, xiii
ransoms for release of prisoners
    and, 92, 140
redeploying his troops and, 232
reorganization of troops and, 179
reports on Montcalm's movements
    and, 133
setting up army for battle and, 170
snobbery in the French service and,
    35
soldiers under command and, 184
surrender of Fort William Henry
    and, 210-218
ten naked Indians and, 109
tour of colony's military outposts
    and, 22
tour of missions and, 108
transfer of British prisoners and,
    234
Two Mountains and, 102
Vaudreuil's raid and, 29-30
victory at Sabbath Day Point and,
    151
war as a game and, 171
Webb's letter to Colonel Monro
    and, 185
wounding of, 21
de Neuville, Pére Jean-Baptiste, 109
de Rigaud, Pierre-François (Marquis
    de Vaudreuil)
Adam Williamson and, 190
bounties for prisoners and, 140-141
British fleet reduced to ashes and,
    99-100
castle of, 91
early years of, 27
final act of French and Indian War,
    261, 277

Fort Saint Jean and, 35
François Le Mercier and, 160
imprisoned in the Bastille and, 260
Indian councils and, 98
journey to Fort William Henry
    and, 36-40
L'Anse au Foulon and, 252
Lake of Two Mountains and, 101-
    102
massacre and, 232, 236-237, 239-
    240
militia and, 34
New France and, 12, 92
parley with Amherst and, 259
quest for volunteers and, 32
raid on Fort William Henry and,
    108, 144, 156, 276
siege of Oswego and, 22
supplies for the army and, 111
surrender and, 216, 251, 261, 277
taking position on right and, 170
wilderness fighter and, 30
de Robespierre, Maximilien, 267
de Roquemaure, Jean-Georges
    Dejean, 186-187
de Saint-Ours, François-Xavier, 134,
    160, 232
Desandrouins, Jean-Nicolas
bombardment of fort and, 193, 201
Fort Carillon and, 121-122
Indian sharpshooters and, 193
liberating the captives and, 228
memoirs and, 269
reconnaissance patrol and, 179
reconnoitering the fort and, 170
siege warfare and, 172, 186
surrender and, 210-211, 213, 215
war as a game and, 171
de Senezergues, Étienne-Guillaume,
    156-157, 201, 254
d'Étoiles, Jeanne-Antoinette Poisson
    le Normont, 29
de Vauban, Sébastien le Prestre, 70
de Veniard, Étienne, 104
de Vergor, Louis Du Pont
    Duchambon, xxvii, 252-253
de Verrazano, Giovanni, 275
de Villiers, Louis Coulon, xxii, 156,
    198

Diamond Point, 161-162, 165, 176,
    217
Dieskau, Jean-Armand, xxv-xxvi, 35,
    42, 48, 70, 144-145, 204
Drummond, Robert, 50
Dumas, Jean, xxiv, 35, 40, 43
Dunbar, James, 256
Dunn, Patrick, 14-16
du Plessis, Armand Jean, 279
Durkee, Robert, 117-118

Edict of Nantes, 75
Edinburgh Castle, 243
Emerson, Sarah, 86
Entick, John, 269
Enyclopédie, on America and, 29
Essex, 4
Evans, William, 79
Eyre, William
    attack on fort and, 46-55
    cut off from the outside world and,
        41
    death of, 267
    design of Fort William Henry and,
        45, 70
    firing on grenadiers and, xxvi
    Jacobite rebellion and, 42
    rebuilding Fort William Henry
        and, 274
    Saint Patrick's Day celebration and,
        43
    weaknesses of Fort William Henry
        and, 44-45

Faesch, Rudolf, 71, 82, 123, 149,
    210-211, 234, 240, 149, 210
Falkland Islands, 265
50th Regiment of Foot, 111
Finger Lakes, 6
Finlay, Matthew, 84-85
Finney, Francis, 241
Fishkill River, 66
Fitch, Adonijah, 60
Fitch, Jabez
    building house for Mr. Best and,
        75
    court-martial of Peck and, 123
    death of, 268
    flanking party of, 83

massacre and, 234
mutilation of soldiers and, 80-81
New Jersey Blues' consorts and, 71
prisoners and, 235
resting and, 87
ruins of Fort Anne and, 82
rumor swept through camp and,
    195
sharing information with men and,
    78
skirmish and, 79
smallpox and, 74
soldier's celebration and, 68
surrender of fort and, 217
War of American Independence
    and, 264
watching a tame bear and, 88
Fletcher, Henry
    Articles of War and, 15
    attack against Freshwater Cove
        and, 247
    bungled steps of the provincials
        and, 76
    courts-martial and, 86
    detachment to London and, 3
    drilling of provincials and, 78
    French and Indian raiders, 82
    landing in Albany and, 13
    men under his command and, 71
    officers of the 35th and, 14
    praise at Martinique and Havana,
        261
    Québec and, 250
    selling of alcohol and, 75
    threat of mutiny and, 4
    weapons training and, 81
Fondie's, 63
Forbes, John, 245, 276
Fort Anne, 82, 126, 130, 246
Fort Beauséjour, xxvii, 65, 252, 275
Fort Bull, 124
Fort Carillon, 7, 16, 37-39, 42, 49,
    52-54, 78, 81, 83, 90, 100,
    108, 111-113, 121-123, 125-
    127, 130-136, 138, 141, 154,
    158-160, 169, 195, 200, 232,
    239, 241, 245, 247, 249-251,
    254-255, 276
Fort Detroit, 262

Fort Duquesne, 245, 249, 276
Fort Edward
    ambush at Wood Creek and, 118-
        119
    ambush by Caughnawaga warrior
        and, 185
    armaments and, 70
    audacious raid of de La Malgue
        and, 126
    burials and, 130-131
    Captain Stark's rangers and, 51
    Charles Langlade and, 112
    closing off the road to, 167
    Colonel Lyman and, 67
    Colonel Young's reinforcements
        and, 169
    companies of rangers and, 72
    courts-martial and, 86
    daily life in and, 76
    Daniel Webb and, 146, 148-149,
        165, 176, 193-194, 231, 242
    de La Malgue's advance on, 127
    de La Malgue's attack and, 129
    deserters and, 16
    execution of Dominicus Peck and,
        123
    Fort Anne and, 82
    French raids and, 122
    George Monro and, 55, 166, 183,
        192-193
    Halfway Brook and, 117
    Indians feasting on the slaughtered
        bullocks and, 175-176
    Israel Putnam and, 83, 113, 264
    Jabez Fitch and, 68, 88
    James Montresor and, 176, 204,
        232
    John Titcomb and, 128
    John Young and, 149
    Joseph Frye and, 233
    Joseph Marin and, 260
    location of, 6-7, 69
    Lyman calls off pursuit and, 81
    maps and, 85
    massacre and, 221, 225-227
    Montcalm's Indian allies and, 188,
        216
    plans for, 77
    positive atmosphere at, 194

possibility of Indian attacks and,
143
prisoners and, 234-235
provincials encamp at, 276
rapidly growing graveyard and, 144
reinforcements and, 203
Rigaud's raiders and, 39
Robert Rogers and, 16, 246
Rudolphus Faesch and, 71
Schaghticoke and, 64
Samuel Thaxter and, 217
siege of, 238
signal guns and, 48
smallpox and, 73-74
surrender and, 211
trail of Peter Davis and, 87
William Eyre and, 42, 48
work details and, 78-79
Fort Frontenac, 276
Fort George, 152, 273
Fort Hardy, 66
Fort Le Boeuf, 262
Fort Louis, 265
Fort Lydius, 69
Fort Lyman, 70
Fort Massachusetts, 30
Fort Miami, 262
Fort Michilimackinac, 262
Fort Miller, 68
Fort Misery, 68
Fort Mosquito, 111
Fort Necessity, 275
Fort Niagara, xxvii, 95, 120, 139,
250-252, 262, 277
Fort Nicholson, 69
Fort No. 4, 256-257
Fort Ontario, 263
Fort Oswego, xxvii, 6, 12-13, 22-23,
27, 29, 35, 50, 57, 60, 92, 96,
100, 103, 124, 156, 170, 192,
211, 238-239, 258, 276
Fort Ouiatenon, 262
Fort Pitt, 262-263
Fort Presque Isle, 262
Fortrose, 4
Fort Saint Frédéric, xxvii, 37, 256
Fort Saint Jean, 32, 35, 100, 111
Fort Saint Joseph, 262
Fort Sandusky, 262

Fort Ticonderoga, 276
Fort Toronto, 95
Fort Venango, 262
Fort William Henry
Anne-Joseph Malartic and, 36
Artillery Cove and, 179, 186, 199,
201-202, 216, 230, 232
attack at Sabbath Day Point and,
138
audacious raid of de La Malgue
and, 126
Bartman's dispatch and, 184
cease-fire and, 172, 196-197
Charles Langlade and, 103
Daniel Webb and, 124, 149
death of two regulars and, 79
de Bougainville and, 265
defenses of, 145
demolition of, xiii, 235
de Montcalm's proposal to attack
and, 109-110
description of, 44
deserters and, 201
Diamond Point and, 161
digging trenches and, 180-186
drummer boy and, 259
François Le Mercier and, 160
French guns beginning to arrive at,
178
French illustration of the attack on,
181
French planning to attack and, 99
George Monro and, 146
Halfway Brook and, 117
impressment and, 3
improving defenses of, 143
Indians digging up graves and, 231
Israel Putnam and, 148
John Parker and, 133-134
John Winslow and, 9
Kanectagon and, 176
King Louis XVI and, 266
Kisensik and, 104, 152
Luc de La Corne and, 103
map of siege and, 198
maps and, 85
massacre and, 219-227, 256, 269,
271
Montcalm's artillery and, 123

Montcalm's order of battle and, 170

Montcalm's reorganization of troops and, 179

morale at, 132

northernmost point of the British frontier in America, 7

opening bombardment and, 191-194

Ottawa and, 283

possible lines of march to, 122

reconstruction of, 274, 277

reinforcements and, 150

reports of Indian scouts and, 188

Rigaud's attack on, 46-55

Rigaud's burning of sloops and, 37, 133

Rigaud's winter raid on, 29, 39-40, 156, 276

Royal Roussillon Regiment and, 205, 253-254

Saint Patrick's Day celebration and, 43

siege of, xv, 198, 246, 269, 273, 276, 281

surrender of, 210-218

survivors of, 162, 242

sutlers and, 285

Thomas Wilkins and, 268

unfounded rumors and, 195

veterans of, 261, 264, 267

war as a game and, 171

weapons at, 182

William Eyre and, 41, 70

William Johnson and, xxvii

Wolfe's troops and, 250

Fort William Henry Corporation, 274, 277

Fort William Henry Hotel, 273, 277

Forty, Thomas, 85

42nd Highland Regiment of Foot, 2, 5, 8, 275-276

44th Regiment of Foot, 42-43, 50, 54, 256

46th Regiment of Foot, 252

48th Regiment of Foot, 43

Foutenir, Jean, 238

Fox, xvii, 97, 101, 271, 280-282, 285

Fox River, 282

French and Indian War, 73, 120, 261, 263-265, 273-275, 277, 279-282, 284

French Revolution, 267

Freshwater Cove, 247

Frye, Joseph, 57, 59, 64-65, 71, 76, 149-150, 166, 168-169, 191-192, 198, 202-203, 210, 218-222, 225, 227, 233, 238, 240, 245, 264, 267, 276

Furnis, James, 143, 214-215, 219, 221, 227-228, 231, 235

Gabarus Bay, 247

Gage, Thomas, 262

Gallup, Benadam, 66

Ganaouské Bay, 40, 46, 154, 159, 161

Garman, Henry, 84-85

Gifford, Stanley, 273-274

Gilman, John, 60, 221, 233

Glub, Richard, 128, 130-131

Goffe, John, 144

Gore, Charles, 251, 255

Gough, John, 57, 210, 227

Grafton, 4

Grant, James, 245

Graves, George, 79

Graves, Thomas, 266

Great Barrier Reef, 266

Great Lakes, xvii-xviii, 6, 90, 92, 94, 102, 135, 241, 244, 262, 278, 280, 282

Green Mountains, 37

Gridley, Luke, 61-65, 67, 79, 90

Griffin, Jack, 84-85

Griffiths, John, 14

Gulf of Saint Lawrence, 56

Guyenne Battalion, 100-101, 121-122, 158, 160, 253

Hale, Jr., Robert, 65

Half Way Brook, 117, 234-235, 246

Halfway House, 143

Hamilton, William, 230

Henry, Thomas, 60

Hérault, Catherine, 101

Holden, James Austin, 273

Hôtel-Dieu de Paris, 24

Howe, George, 244-245, 253
Howe, William, 253
Hudson, Henry, 11
Hudson River, 16, 62, 70, 73, 77, 89,
    117, 129, 177, 233, 282
Hughes, William, 14, 169, 176
Huron, xvii, xix, xxii, 23, 25-26, 102,
    107, 111, 126, 229, 262, 275,
    278, 281

Île aux Noix, 36, 256, 258
Île d'Orléans, 250
Ince, Charles, 5, 14, 16, 210, 251,
    255, 257
Ingersoll, Joseph, 150, 166
Innis, Alexander, 240
Iowa, 97, 281
Iroquois Confederacy, xvii, xix, xxi, 7,
    32, 97, 100, 275, 278, 281-
    282, 285
Isaac, William, 83-85
Îsle de la Barque, 159

Jeffries, Edward, 14-15
Jeffries, John, 73, 89
Jennings, Dennis, 241
Johnson, William, 42, 48, 63, 70,
    193-194, 203-206, 217, 250-
    252, 262-264, 282
Jones, Jabez, 117, 121

Kanectagon, 116, 157, 166, 168, 176,
    184-185, 194, 196
Kearny, James, 241
Kelly, John, 16-17
Kennedy, John, 117, 121
Kickapoo, 262
King George II, 2-3, 10, 12, 18, 57,
    60-61, 65, 70, 133
King George III, 270, 277
King George's War, xx, 57, 60, 65,
    133, 275
King Louis XV, 27, 50
King Louis XVI, 266
King Philip, 31
King's Highway, 62
King William, 31
King William's War (1689–97), 106,
    275

Kiowa, 271
Kirkwood, Robert, 256
Kisensik, 22, 103-104, 106, 151-152,
    154, 166, 168, 231
Knowles, Samuel, 129, 238

La Boudeuse, 265
Lake Champlain, 23, 29, 33, 36-37,
    42, 69, 79, 122, 141, 151,
    155, 159, 255, 256, 258
Lake Erie, 94, 262
Lake George, 7, 16, 23, 29, 35, 37,
    39, 41-42, 52, 54, 63, 68-69,
    77, 79, 88, 98-99, 112, 122,
    125, 132-137, 148, 150-151,
    154, 157-161, 179, 201, 204,
    218, 234-235, 246, 255, 264,
    267, 273
Lake Huron, 80, 244, 282-283
Lake Memphremagog, 256
Lake Michigan, 80, 244, 282, 285
Lake of Two Mountains, 79, 101-
    102, 276, 279, 283
Lake Ontario, xvii, xxvii, 2, 22, 95,
    276, 278, 281
Lake Oswego, 251
Lake St. Sacrement, 151
Lake Superior, 94-95, 279-280
Lakota, 97
La Licorne, 20, 275
La Montagne Pelée (Bald
    Mountain), 158
Lamson, John, 241
Langlade, Charles, xxiv, 80-81, 103,
    112, 115-118, 134-136, 144,
    157, 235, 264, 267-268
Languedoc Regiment, xxv, 34, 51, 53,
    100, 121-122, 160, 169, 216,
    253
L'Anse au Foulon, 252
La Sarre Regiment, 34, 49, 52, 100,
    121-123, 156, 160, 171, 187,
    201, 232, 234-235, 253
The Last of the Mohicans (Cooper),
    270-271, 277
L'Auguste, 266-267
Lawrence, Charles, 247
Learned, Ebenezer, 65
Le Guerrier, 266

Le Mercier, François, 40, 50-51, 53, 160
Le Prestre, Sébastien, 43, 70
Lewis, Johan, 14-15
Linn, Jock, 60, 221
Littlehales, John, 13
Livingston Forge, 61
Loomis, Nathaniel, 226
Lord Loudoun (John Campbell)
  arrives at New York and, 8-10, 276
  Daniel Webb and, 18, 124-125, 145, 177
  death of, 243
  death of Richard Rogers and, 145
  deserters and, 15
  Indian scalps and, 120
  insolence of a Canadian trader and, 12
  James Belcher and, 14
  letter from Monro and, 242
  letter from Montcalm and, 234
  letter from Webb and, 233
  Louisbourg attack and, 100, 124
  Montcalm's attack and, 239
  on Webb's health and, 124-125
  plans for that summer's campaign and, 56-57
  post–William Henry career and, 243
  praise for the 35th and, 55
  setting sail for colonies and, xxviii
  siege of Oswego and, 124
  treatment of provincials and, 67
  weaknesses of fort and, 44, 46
  William McCloud and, 149
  William Skinner and, 17
Lord Loudoun, 44, 53
Lord Milton, 3
Lorette Huron, 26
Louisbourg, siege of, 247-248, 276
Louis XIV, 34, 75, 104, 151
Louis XV, 28, 200, 212, 265
Lydius, Henry, 10, 69-70
Lyman, Phineas
  Abercrombie's disastrous decision and, 245
  at Havana and, 261
  background of, 62
  Battle of Lake George and, 63, 70

  Connecticut volunteers and, 71, 75, 80
  Fort Lyman and, 70
  Henry Shuntup and, 119
  hunting parties leaving camp and, 66
  Jabez Fitch and, 75, 80-82
  land grants and, 263
  Langlade's Indians and, 80-81
  Marin's raid and, 129-130
  "painted like a Mohog" and, 82
  prostitutes and, 72
  raising the provincials and, 57
  regimental court-martial and, 67
  Robert Niles and, 86
  William Eyre and, xxvi

Mahicans, 31, 60, 121, 282, 284
Malartic, Anne-Joseph, 36, 269
Mamby, William, 5
Manitou, 95
Mante, Thomas, 77
Marquis de Vaudreuil, 10, 12, 22, 27-30, 91-92, 98, 100-101, 111, 140-141, 216, 232, 236-240, 251-252, 259-261, 277
massacre
  1760 woodcut of, 223
  casualty totals and, 227
  de Bougainville and, 222
  de Montcalm and, 224-225
  Indian killing of wounded and, 220
  killing of women and, 222
  reaction of the press and, 238-239
Massé, Genevieve, 69
Maylem, John, 230
McCloud, William, 149, 169, 173, 183, 186, 233
McCrakan, William, 221
McGinnis, Robert, 57, 133, 138
Meir, John, 193
Menominee, 96, 101, 134-135, 244, 278, 282
Mercer, James, 12-13
Meserve, Nathaniel, 57
Meskwaki, 280
Mesquaki, 97
Metacom, 31
Miami, 96-97, 154-155, 262, 282

Michilimackinac, 80, 92, 100, 115-116, 125, 241, 244, 262
Mingo, xxi, 262
Mingo, James, 128
Missisauga, 155
Missisquoi Bay, 256
Missisquois, 31
Mississauga, 23, 95-96, 278, 282
Mississippi River, 263
Mohawk Indians, xvii-xviii, xxv-xxvi, 6-8, 31, 37, 60, 63, 69, 80, 89-90, 102, 107, 111, 120, 122, 133, 193-194, 203-204, 217, 265, 275, 281-282
Mohawk River, 124-125, 204, 251, 281-282
Mohawk Valley, 250
Mohegans, 31, 60, 65, 283
Monro, George
  arrival at Fort William Henry, 276
  bombardment and, 192
  captives and, 238
  cease-fire and, 172-173, 196-197
  Charles Ince and, 5
  complaint to Montcalm and, 230
  Daniel Webb and, 149
  death of, 276
  deserters and, 201
  dispatch to Webb and, 165
  dispatch written to Webb and, 186
  early years of, 1-2
  encirclement of, 167
  final dispatch and, 175
  Fort Edward and, 166
  Fort George and, 273
  giving liquor to enemy and, 239-240
  giving their executioners liquor and, 234
  Henry Fletcher and, 247
  James Furnis and, 228
  La Corne's Indians and, 183
  letter from Webb and, 185, 205-206
  letter to Lord Loudoun and, 242
  letter to Webb and, 177-178, 194, 203
  massacre and, 224
  morale and, 209
  outrageous breach of surrender terms and, 220
  reinforcements and, 149, 168, 193, 197
  setting sail from Plymouth and, 4
  surrender of Fort William Henry and, 206, 210-219, 239, 276
  unfounded rumors and, 195
  war as a game and, 171
Montréal
  captives and, 236-241
  French surrender at, 260
  Indians flocking to, 92
  Menominee and, 96
  Mississauga and, 95
  Montcalm's tour of the missions and, 106
  Murray's army and, 258
  plans for, 93
  Potawatomi and, 94
  presence of undomesticated Indians and, 98
  Sulpician settlement and, 102
Montresor, James, 17-18, 75-76, 79, 122-123, 143, 145-148, 176, 204, 231-232, 267
Morral, Thomas, 15
Mortawamock, William, 60
Murphy, James, 74
Murray, James, 257-259
Muskingum River, 263

Neal, Hugh, 14
New Jersey Blues, 60, 71, 131, 133, 144, 193, 210, 221, 240-241, 255
New York Mercury, victims of the massacre and, 269
Nipissing, xvii, xix, xxii, 22, 79, 102-104, 151-154, 162, 166, 168, 231, 278, 283
Nipmucks, 60, 283

Ogden, Jonathon, 133, 138, 175, 210
Ogilvie, John, 6, 16
Ojibwa, 23, 244, 279
Oka, 102, 151, 153, 276
Oneida, xvii, 100, 107, 281
Onondaga, 281

Ord, Thomas, 143, 145
Ormsby, John, 166-167, 198, 234
Ossipees, 31
Otawanie, 122
Ottawa, xvii, xxiv, 42, 66, 79-80, 92-
    95, 98, 100-101, 111-112,
    116-119, 121, 126-130, 134-
    136, 139-140, 153, 155, 158,
    241, 244, 262, 264, 278, 282-
    284
Oxford University, 14, 88-89

Parker, John, 57, 60, 131, 133-136,
    138, 141, 143-146, 148, 154,
    210
Patagonian Indians, 266
Paul, Caesar Nero, 60, 221
Paul, François-Joseph, 266-267
Payson, Edward, 61
Peck, Dominicus, 123
Pennacooks, 31
Pennahouel, 135, 153
Pequots, 60, 284
Perry, Thomas, 14
Picquet, Abbé François, 101, 108,
    228, 236
Pigwackets, 31
Pine Island, 7
Piquet Yard, 169
Pitt, William, 56, 76, 243-245, 247,
    262
Plains of Abraham, 253, 255, 257,
    277
Plans
  A Plan for Albany (1758), 11
  Fort Edward and, 77
  Fort William Henry and, 45
  Richelieu–Champlain Corridor
    and, 33
Pontiac, 262-263, 269, 277
Poor, Mehitable, 64
Porter, Elijah, 67
Potawatomi, xvii, xix, 23, 94, 101,
    134-135, 154, 262, 278, 282-
    284
Pouchot, Pierre, 95, 120, 139, 250,
    252, 258-259
Pownall, Thomas, 241
Presentation, 153, 228

Prévost, Augustine, 231
Prevost, Jacques, 71, 123
Prideaux, John, 250
Privat, Marc-Antoine, 169, 196
Putnam, Israel
  ambush at East Bay and, 113-114
  ambush at South Bay and, 114-
    115, 276
  ambush at Wood Creek and, 116-
    119
  attack on Fort Edward and, 129-
    130
  Battle of Bunker Hill and, 264
  Battle of Long Island and, 264
  Charles Langlade and, 134-135,
    157
  Colonel Parker's mistake and, 148
  command of ranger companies
    and, 72, 178
  death of, 268
  destruction of Fort William Henry
    and, xiii-xiv
  fighting around Lake George and,
    246
  French raids and, 122
  increase in Indian attacks and, 143
  moonlight ambush and, 126
  Natchez settlement and, 263
  Peter Davis and, 86
  prisoners and, 83, 175
  smoke sightings and, 147, 150
  spies and, 177
  taken prisoner and, 246-247
Putnam, Rufus, 65-66, 176, 245,
    263-264

Queen Anne's War, xx, 32, 69, 106,
    275

Rackliff, William, 241
Rand, Joshua, 241
Rawson, Joshua, 74
Red River War of 1874–75, 271
Reed, Jacob, 80
Richelieu–Champlain Corridor, 33
Richelieu River, 23, 32-33, 36, 258
Rodney, George Brydges, 267
Roeliff Jansen Kill River, 61
Rogers Island, 73-74, 79, 129

Rogers, Richard, 145, 166, 231
Rogers, Robert, 16, 38, 72-73, 246,
    256, 264
Rogers Rock, 39; *see also* Bald
    Mountain
Rogers's Rangers, 120
Ross, John, 14-15
Roubaud, Pierre
    background of, 30-31
    captured livestock and, 169
    digging trenches and, 180
    French Indians and, 191
    greatness of the enemy's loss and,
        232
    Indians as apt pupils and, 188, 196
    massacre and, 223-224, 228-229
    Mahican prisoner and, 174
    Sabbath Day Point and, 138-140
    scene at main camp and, 204
    stench of fear and death, 215
    traveling with the Indians and,
        159-162
    Trois Riviéres and, 256
    wounded soldiers and, 182, 201
Royal Americans, 57, 71, 82, 143,
        147, 149, 202, 210, 221, 227,
        231, 247, 250-251, 253; *see
        also* 3rd Battalion, 60th
        Regiment of Foot
Royal Navy, 241, 243, 249, 261
Royal Proclamation, 263, 270, 277
Royal Roussillon Regiment, 32, 34,
        51, 121-122, 160, 170-171,
        183, 187, 205, 232, 235, 253
Royal Society, 21

Sabbath Day Point
    bloated corpse and, 154
    captives and, 241
    Charles Langlade and, 264
    dates for, 276
    disaster at, 143
    John Parker and, 131
    Montcalm's victory at, 151
    Thomas Shaw and, 240
    troops landing at, 135
    victory at, 159
Saint Anne's church, 244
Saint Charles, 240

Saint Charles River, 24, 25
Saint Dominique, 240
Saint Francis River, 30
Saint Lawrence River, xv, xvii-xviii,
        xxiii-xxiv, 19, 22-24, 26, 32,
        56, 91, 101, 107, 111, 139,
        236, 241, 249-250, 253, 255,
        257-259, 262, 275, 278-280
Saltonstall, Richard, 168-169, 174-
        175, 198, 210
Sandy Cove, 161
Sauk, xvii, 97, 101, 271, 281, 285
Savoy Wharf, 3
Scott, Randolph, 277
Sedgwick's Inn, 61
Seminoles, 271
Seneca, xvii, 97, 111, 262, 281
Seven Years' War, 29, 71, 243, 261,
        275, 277
78th Highlanders, 248
Shawnee, 110, 262, 265
Shaw, Thomas, 240-241
Sheridan, James, 15
Shirley, William, 9, 12
Shoe, Thomas, 14
Shuckburgh, Richard, "Yankee
        Doodle" and, 89
Shuntup, Henry, 60, 117, 119, 121
Sioux, 97, 125
Six Nations, xxi, 7, 153, 275, 281,
        285
60th Regiment of Foot, 103, 123
Skinner, William, 17
Slapp, John, 60
Sloop Island, 47, 49
smallpox
    at Albany and, 18
    epidemic in camps and, 123
    epidemic of late 1757 and, 249
    George Monro and, 1
    hospital and, 73, 79, 273
    Indian settlements of the Great
        Lakes and, 244
    Jonathon Carver and, 270
    Monro's command and, 144
    prisoners and, 240
    quarantined house and, 61-62
    slackened its grip and, 44
Smith, James, 107-108

Sokokis, 31
Spikeman, Thomas, 38, 120
Stark, John, 16, 43-44, 51, 54
Stevens, Ezekiel, 235
Stoughton, John, 67
Strait of Magellan, 265
Success, 240
Sweetland, Elijah, 118-119
Sydenham, 4

Taplin, Jonathon, 198
Thaxter, Samuel, 59, 217
3rd Battalion, 60th Regiment of
    Foot, "Royal Americans," 57,
    71, 123, 143, 247, 250, 253-
    254, 257-258
35th Regiment of Foot
  accidents and, 79
  ailments of, 74
  black month for, 13
  burials and, 131
  civilian labor and, 18
  cold weather and, 18
  Daniel Webb and, 124
  departure from Cork and, 1
  desertions and, 15
  drilling of, 76
  forcibly impressed soldiers and, 58
  George Monro and, 57
  Henry Fletcher and, 3, 71
  inexperience of officers and, 14
  James Abercrombie and, 8
  John Kelly and, 17
  John Parker and, 133
  John Titcomb and, 127
  journey to Albany and, 5
  Loudoun's praise of, 55
  lower ranks in New York and, 5
  Mr. Welch and, 78, 87
  Thomas Forty and, 85
  Thomas Wilkins and, 4, 14, 145,
    221, 254, 268
  William Bell and, 88
  William Isaac and, 83
Thompson, James, 248
Thousand Island Bay, 22
Three Fires, 94-95, 283-284
Titcomb, John, 60-61, 127-130
Townshend, George, 7, 120

Treatise of Military Discipline
    (Bland), 78
Treaty of Paris, 261-262, 277
Trout Brook, 245, 253
Tuscarora, 275, 281
27th Regiment of Foot, 258

Uncas, 271
University of Paris, 21

van Schaick, Sybrant G., 10
Vaudry, Jacques
  de Montcalm's arrival at lines at,
    172
  searching for food and, 174-175
  taken prisoner and, 183-184
Veeder, Harold, 273-274
Victoire, 249
Victor, John, 35-36, 53
Voltaire, 29

Wahcoloosencoochaleva, 69
Waldo, Ralph, 130, 183, 190
Wampanoag, 31
War of Austrian Succession, 1, 65,
    171, 245, 275
War of the League of Augsburg, 275
Warren, William, 241
Washington, George, 113, 245, 264-
    265, 275
Wea, 262
Webb, Daniel
  35th Regiment and, 18
  aftermath of Fort Edward attack
    and, 131
  arguemwnt with Johnson and, 203-
    204
  arrives at New York and, 275
  Augustine Prévost and, 231
  Battle of Lake George and, 144
  British prisoners and, 234
  calling for militia and, 177
  captives and, 238
  death of, 267
  death of Capt. Roger's brother and,
    145
  defending the New York Frontier
    and, 57
  destroying of letter and, 193

dinner with Colonel Montresor
    and, 176
disaster at Sabbath Day Point, 143
final dispatch from Monro and,
    175
garrison of Fort Edward and, 148,
    242
George Monro and, 133, 146, 167,
    177-178, 183, 185-186, 192,
    194, 203, 205-206
health of, 125
Israel Putnam and, 147
letter to Lord Loudoun and, 233
letters to Gabriel Christie and,
    217-218
Lord Loudoun and, 239, 244
orders of, 127
Peck's demise and, 123-124
prearranged signal to, 165
protected from official censure and,
    243
reinforcements and, xiv, 149, 168,
    196-197
scouting around Fort William
    Henry and, 175
"Sort of Council of War" and, 145
troops' morale and, 141
White, Edward, 231
Whitmore, Edward, 247
Whittemore, Nathaniel, 60, 221
Whitworth, Miles, 183, 190, 220,
    237
Wilkins, Thomas, 4, 14, 145, 221,
    254-255, 268
Williams, Ephraim, 89
Williamson, Adam, 50, 132, 145,
    148, 176, 183, 185, 190-191,
    197, 206, 215, 228, 235
Williams, Samuel, 169
Windigowan, 95
Winnebago, 97-98, 101, 285
Winnipessaukees, 31
Winslow, Jedediah, 66
Winslow, John, xxvii, 9-10, 65-66
Wolfe, James, 120, 244, 247-248,
    250-255, 277
Wood Creek, 16, 82, 113-114, 116,
    151
Wounded Knee, 271

Yale University, 62
Young, John, 276
    3rd Battalion of the Royal
        Americans and, 143
    Captain Bartman's letter and, 205
    captured livestock and, 169
    council of war and, 210
    George Monro and, 186, 210
    massacre and, 221, 225, 228, 235-
        236
    regimental commander and, 71
    reinforcements and, 149-150, 178,
        186, 276
    "Sort of Council of War" and, 145
    surrender and, 210-211, 214
    visiting the fort and, 147
    wounding of, 202

ACKNOWLEDGMENTS

Writing this book would not have been possible without the help of numerous archivists and librarians in the United Kingdom, United States, and Canada. In London, I owe a debt of gratitude to the staffs of the National Archives in Kew, the Newspaper Library in Colindale, the National Army Museum in Kensington, and the British Library in Kings Cross. In the United States, the staff of the Huntington Library in California was particularly helpful as were the guides employed at the Fort William Henry Museum, Fort Ticonderoga, and Crown Point State Historic Site. I would also like to thank the employees of the Fort Saint Jean Museum and those at the Musée des Abénakis, Odanak, in Canada.

The encouragement and advice of my publisher, Bruce H. Franklin, was invaluable and I would like to give special thanks to my copyeditor, Laura Pfost, and the author and historian Glenn F. Williams. Shortly before publication, Glenn read a draft of the text and provided a detailed critique. His contribution has improved this book considerably. The responsibility for any errors that may remain is solely my own.

Finally, I would like to acknowledge the contribution of Jane and David Hughes, Jamie Cowper, and Tim Dalrymple who read and commented on various drafts, and to thank Vanessa for her encouragement, patience, and understanding. It is to her and our baby daughter Emily that this book is dedicated.